Lecture Notes in Computer Science 9482

Commenced Publication in 1973
Founding and Former Series Editors:
Gerhard Goos, Juris Hartmanis, and Jan van Leeuwen

More information about this series at http://www.springer.com/series/7410

Joaquin Garcia-Alfaro · Evangelos Kranakis
Guillaume Bonfante (Eds.)

Foundations and Practice of Security

8th International Symposium, FPS 2015
Clermont-Ferrand, France, October 26–28, 2015
Revised Selected Papers

 Springer

Editors
Joaquin Garcia-Alfaro
Télécom SudParis
Evry
France

Evangelos Kranakis
School of Computer Science
Carleton University
Ottawa, ON
Canada

Guillaume Bonfante
École des Mines de Nancy
Université de Lorraine
Nancy Cedex
France

ISSN 0302-9743 ISSN 1611-3349 (electronic)
Lecture Notes in Computer Science
ISBN 978-3-319-30302-4 ISBN 978-3-319-30303-1 (eBook)
DOI 10.1007/978-3-319-30303-1

Library of Congress Control Number: 2016932326

LNCS Sublibrary: SL4 – Security and Cryptology

Printed on acid-free paper

This Springer imprint is published by SpringerNature
The registered company is Springer International Publishing AG Switzerland

Preface

This volume contains the proceedings of the 8th International Symposium on Foundations and Practice of Security, hosted by the University of Auvergne, in Clermont-Ferrand, France, during October 26–28, 2015.

The FPS Symposium was initiated in 2008, following the Canada-France Meeting on Security held at Simon Fraser University, Vancouver, during December 6–8, 2007. Since then, FPS has been held annually, alternating between Canadian and French locations, including Montréal, Grenoble, Toronto, La Rochelle, and Paris.

This year's symposium received 58 submissions, out of which 12 papers were selected as full papers and eight as short papers. All submissions went through a careful anonymous review process (three or more reviews per submission) aided by members of the Technical Program Committee and several external reviewers. The program was completed with two keynote addresses by Evangelos Kranakis (Carleton University, Ottawa, Canada) and David Pointcheval (Ecole Normale Supérieure, Paris, France).

Many people contributed to the success of FPS 2015. First we would like to thank all the authors who submitted their research results. The selection was a challenging task and we sincerely thank all the Program Committee members, as well as the external reviewers, who volunteered to read and discuss the papers. We greatly thank the general chair, Pascal Lafourcade (University of Auvergne), and his organizing team, for their great efforts in organizing and dealing with the logistics during the symposium. We also want to express our gratitude to the publicity chairs, Giovanni Livraga (University of Milan, Italy), Zhiqiang Lin (University of Texas at Dallas, US), and Mizuhito Ogawa (Advanced Institute of Science and Technology, Japan), for their efforts at advertising the symposium. Last but by no means least we want to thank all the sponsors for making the event possible.

We hope the articles in this proceedings volume will be valuable for your professional activities in the area.

December 2015

Joaquin Garcia-Alfaro
Evangelos Kranakis
Guillaume Bonfante

Organization

General Chair

Pascal Lafourcade — University of Auvergne, France

Program Co-chairs

Guillaume Bonfante — Mines de Nancy, France
Joaquin Garcia-Alfaro — Télécom SudParis, France
Evangelos Kranakis — Carleton University, Canada

Publicity Co-chairs

Giovanni Livraga — University of Milan, Italy
Zhiqiang Lin — University of Texas at Dallas, USA
Mizuhito Ogawa — Advanced Institute of Science and Technology, Japan

Program Committee

Samiha Ayed — Télécom Bretagne, France
Michel Barbeau — Carleton University, Canada
Jordi Castella-Roca — Rovira i Virgili University, Spain
Frédéric Cuppens — Télécom Bretagne, France
Nora Cuppens-Boulahia — Télécom Bretagne, France
Mila Dalla Preda — University of Bologna, Italy
Mourad Debbabi — University of Concordia, Canada
Nicola Dragoni — Technical University of Denmark, Denmark
Josep Domingo-Ferrer — Universitat Rovira i Virgili, Spain
Jean-Luc Danger — Telecom ParisTech, France
Sara Foresti — University of Milan, Italy
Marc Frappier — University of Sherbrooke, Canada
Martin Gagne — Wheaton College, USA
Sebastien Gambs — Université de Rennes, France
Flavio D. Garcia — University of Birmingham, UK
Diala Haidar — Dar Al Hekma College, Saudi Arabia
Jordi Herrera-Joancomarti — Autonomous University of Barcelona, Spain
Bruce Kapron — University of Victoria, Canada
Hyoungshick Kim — Sungkyunkwan University, South Korea
Giovanni Livraga — University of Milan, Italy
Luigi Logrippo — Université du Quebec en Outaouais, Canada
Javier Lopez — University of Malaga, Spain

Flaminia Luccio	Ca'Foscari University of Venice, Italy
Joan Melia-Segui	Universitat Oberta de Catalunya, Spain
Ali Miri	Ryerson University, Canada
Guillermo Navarro-Arribas	Autonomous University of Barcelona, Spain
Jordi Nin	Universitat Politecnica de Catalunya, Spain
Melek Önen	Eurecom, France
Andreas Pashalidis	K.U. Leuven, Belgium
Thomas Peters	Ecole Normale Superieure, France
Marie-Laure Potet	Ensimag, France
Silvio Ranise	FBK, Security and Trust Unit, Italy
Claudio Soriente	ETH Zurich, Switzerland
Chamseddine Talhi	ETS Montréal, Canada
Nadia Tawbi	Université Laval, Canada
Emmanuel Thomé	Inria Lorraine, France
Alexandre Viejo	Rovira i Virgili University, Spain
Lena Wiese	Göttingen University, Germany
Nicola Zannone	Eindhoven University of Technology, The Netherlands
Nur Zincir Heywood	Dalhousie University, Canada
Mohammad Zulkernine	Queen's University, Canada

Additional Reviewers

Saed Alrabaee

Carles Anglès-Tafalla

Khodakhast Bibak

Olivier Blazy

Amine Boukhtouta

Marie-Angela Cornelie

Vicenç Creus-Garcia

Guenaelle de Julis

Joeri de Ruiter

Mohammad Hajiabadi

Shahrear Iqbal

Amrit Kumar

Bo Mi

Djedjiga Mouheb

David Nuñez

David Oswald

Cristina Pérez-Solà

Marta Pujol

Jordi Ribes-González

Ruben Rios

Jean-Claude Royer

Julián Salas

Saeed Shafieian

Stefan Thaler

Sam L. Thomas

Tim Waage

Steering Committee

Frédéric Cuppens	Télécom Bretagne, France
Nora Cuppens-Boulahia	Télécom Bretagne, France
Mourad Debbabi	University of Concordia, Canada
Joaquin Garcia-Alfaro	Télécom SudParis, France
Evangelos Kranakis	Carleton University, Canada
Pascal Lafourcade	University of Auvergne, France

Jean-Yves Marion   Lorraine University, France
Ali Miri   Ryerson University, Canada
Rei Safavi-Naini   Calgary University, Canada
Nadia Tawbi   Université Laval, Canada

Contents

Keynote Talks

Optimization Problems in Infrastructure Security

Evangelos Kranakis[1(✉)] and Danny Krizanc[2]

[1] School of Computer Science, Carleton University, Ottawa, ON, Canada
`kranakis@scs.carleton.ca`
[2] Department of Mathematics and Computer Science, Wesleyan University,
Middletown, CT, USA
`dkrizanc@wesleyan.edu`

Abstract. How do we identify and prioritize risks and make smart choices based on fiscal constraints and limited resources? The main goal of *infrastructure security* is to secure, withstand, and rapidly recover from potential threats that may affect critical resources located within a given bounded region. In order to strengthen and maintain secure, functioning, and resilient critical infrastructure, proactive and coordinated efforts are necessary.

Motivated from questions raised by infrastructure security, in this paper we survey several recent optimization problems whose solution has occupied (and continues to occupy) computer science researchers in the last few years. Topics discussed include:

1. Patrolling.
2. Sensor Coverage and Interference.
3. Evacuation.
4. Domain Protection and Blocking.

The central theme in all the problems mentioned above will involve mobility in that the participating agents will be able to move over a specified region with a given speed.

Security in itself is undoubtedly a very broad and complex task which involves all layers of the communication process from physical to network. As such the limited goal of this survey is to outline existing models and ideas and discuss related open problems and future research directions, pertaining to optimization problems in infrastructure security.

Keywords: Blocking · Coverage · Evacuation · Infrastructure security · Interference · Mobile robots · Patrolling

1 Infrastructure Security

Infrastructure security is concerned with securing physical assets so as to withstand, and rapidly recover from potential threats that may affect critical resources located or enclosed within a given bounded region. The apparent diversity of such systems makes potential threats difficult to grasp and the

E. Kranakis—Supported in part by NSERC Discovery grant.

© Springer International Publishing Switzerland 2016
J. Garcia-Alfaro et al. (Eds.): FPS 2015, LNCS 9482, pp. 3–13, 2016.
DOI: 10.1007/978-3-319-30303-1_1

required rigorous security analysis almost impossible to pursue. It turns out that diverse infrastructure sectors such as buildings and roads, border systems, economic structures and materials, energy and water supply systems, internet and telecommunication systems, etc., have surprisingly similar structures that are often amenable to a rigorous risk analysis.

It is generally accepted that before 9/11, infrastructure security was only an afterthought since it was considered unthinkable that anyone would intentionally destroy critical infrastructure such as commercial buildings, power plants, water supplies, voice and data communications. Security was usually sacrificed for economic efficiency and the resulting systems were optimized only for profit, efficient operation, and low cost. In subsequent years researchers motivated by a new security reality attempted to develop critical infrastructure protection as a scientific discipline with formal analysis and design principles.

Research developments focused around a supervisory control and data acquisition (or SCADA for short) system which is a type of large scale computer based industrial control system for monitoring and controlling industrial facility based processes which exist in the physical world and as such may include multiple sites, and large distances. SCADA control systems may include various general buildings, transport systems, heating and ventilation systems, as well as energy production and consumption. Original SCADA architectures were rather primitive in design and conception but evolving systems include distributed and networked control augmented with sensor systems based on the internet of things. Typical designs of SCADA are quite complex and include system concepts and details of system components, control system for human computer interaction by supervisory station(s) employing various types of communication methods as part of the network infrastructure.

The most robust and efficient solutions are networked based and combine security threat assessment with risk analysis. By representing critical resources as nodes in a network with links one can identify critical components by various mathematical techniques involving, for example, counting, location, clustering, etc., and thus provide a measure of the complexity of the security task. Further, by making estimates of the cost and probability of an attack one could provide a "security strategy" which would ultimately reduce security risks in an effective way. Thus, researchers were led to vulnerability analysis and risk assessment which are essentially based on network theory. Standard literature on infrastructure security (see, e.g., book references such as [9, 33, 40] and elsewhere in various network security conferences) describe such techniques and show how to apply quantitative vulnerability analysis to a variety of infrastructure sectors in our society so as to be able to decide in the best way possible how to allocate limited resources that will eventually minimize the overall security risk.

The purpose of this survey is not to repeat methods and techniques which are already described adequately in the infrastructure security literature. The focus is rather on describing how combinatorial optimization techniques can be applied to design new and faster algorithms that will improve the computational complexity required to defend infrastructure in some security problems arising in sensor and robotic research. The four specific tasks selected for study are patrolling, coverage & interference, evacuation, and protection & blocking. Methods proposed have the potential to enhance infrastructure security merely by facilitating the choice of optimal designs. The main characteristic of all the problems discussed is that they rely on mobile agents (robots, sensors) that can move over a given region with specific speeds and in some instances communicate with each other by exchanging messages. For each task we provide a brief literature review, outline its main features as well as solutions and describe some of the models proposed.

2 Patrolling

Patrolling has been defined as the act of surveillance consisting in walking perpetually around an area in order to protect or supervise it. Patrolling occurs in any situation where we are required to monitor a region, such as the perimeter of a building or campus, for activities posing a potential security threat. In the classic surveillance (also known as art gallery) literature, agents are placed at fixed positions to monitor the interior of a polygonal region [37]. This contrasts sharply with our more recent studies on patrolling where the agents move around to cover the region. In such a setting patrolmen are assigned to monitor specified subregions by moving perpetually at regular intervals through areas assigned to them (see Fig. 1). The patrolmen may be looking for any signs of specific problems (including, for example, detecting intrusions or security lapses, responding to service calls, resolving disputes and/or making arrests, reporting crimes, and conducting traffic enforcement) which need to be identified. The duration of patrolling may vary in time depending on the nature of the objective but here we are interested in the perpetual movement of the monitoring agents (human or robotic). The accepted measure of the algorithmic efficiency of patrolling is called *idleness* and it is related to the frequency with which the points of the environment are visited [2]. (This criterion was first introduced in [35].)

Fig. 1. Agents patrol a barrier by moving perpetually at constant speeds. What trajectories should the agents follow so that the time a point on the barrier is left unvisited by a agent is minimized?

We are interested in patrolling a domain represented by a geometric graph in a setting where (1) some of the patrolmen may be unreliable (faulty) in that they fail to report their monitoring activities, and/or (2) parts of the domain are not critical and as such do not need to be patrolled. More specifically, we are interested in the following problem:

Patrolling. We are given a team of patrolmen and a domain to be monitored. Assume that some of the patrolmen may be unreliable. We want to design a strategy constructing perpetual patrolmen trajectories, so that, independently of which subset of them (of a given size) will turn out to be faulty, no critical point of the domain will be ever left unvisited by some reliable agent longer than the allowed *idle time*.

The problem proposed above has been studied in [16] for patrolmen with identical speeds. Patrolling with agents that do not necessarily have identical speeds has been initiated in [15]. As shown in [23, 26] this case offers several surprises both in terms of the difficulty of the problem as well as in terms of the algorithmic results obtained. In particular, no optimal patrolling strategy involving more than three agents has yet been found. Recently, [39] studied the distributed coordination of a set of moving cameras monitoring a line segment to detect moving intruders. Optimal patrolling involving same-speed agents in mixed domains, where the regions to be traversed are fragmented by portions that do not need to be monitored, is studied in [13].

3   Sensor Coverage and Interference

Mobile sensors are being used in many application areas to enable easier access and information retrieval in diverse communication environments, such as habitat monitoring, sensing and diagnostics and critical infrastructure monitoring. Recent reductions in manufacturing costs make deployments of such sensors even more attractive. Since existing sensor deployment scenarios cannot always ensure precise placement of sensors, their initial deployment may be arbitrary. In some cases the sensors were originally randomly scattered over the region according to some (potentially unknown) distribution or they may have drifted to new positions over time. Even initially deterministically placed sensors may create arbitrary patterns of effectiveness due to random failures. Therefore in order to improve the coverage provided by the set of sensors it is necessary to redeploy them by displacing them more evenly throughout a domain (see Fig. 2).

Fig. 2. A set of sensors with respective ranges depicted as closed intervals are initially placed on a barrier. What is the minimum sum of displacements (or maximum displacement) of the sensors required so that every point on the barrier is within the range of a sensor?

By displacing the sensors to new positions one can improve the overall coverage of a given region. Thus, a basic instance of the problem being considered is the following.

Sensor Coverage. What is the cost (expected, if sensor arrangement is random) of moving mobile sensors with a given circular (but bounded) sensing range from their original positions to new positions so as to achieve full coverage of a region, i.e., every point of the region is within the range of at least one sensor.

Given a geometric region in the plane there are two basic formulations of the problem: displace the sensors so as to either ensure (1) full coverage of the region, or (2) coverage of the perimeter of the region. The first problem is referred as *area coverage* and the second as *perimeter or barrier coverage*.

The problem has been investigated in [28] for the uniform random setting. In both instances it is assumed the sensors are deployed initially in the domain uniformly and independently at random. Since such a random deployment does not necessarily guarantee full coverage it is important to displace the sensors so as to ensure all points are covered while at the same time minimizing the transportation cost. The two cost parameters we choose to optimize are the expected sum and maximum of the sensor's displacements, the former being an approximation of the total energy consumed while the latter of the time required to complete the task by the entire system of deployed sensors.

There is also extensive literature on area and barrier or perimeter coverage by a set of sensors (e.g., see [31, 41]). The deterministic sensor movement problem for planar domains with pre-existing anchor (or destination) points was introduced in [8] and for a linear domain (or interval) in [17]. Interestingly enough, the complexity of the problem (i.e., finding an algorithm that optimizes the total or maximum displacement) depends on the types of the sensors, the type of the domain and whether one is minimizing the sum or maximum of the sensor movements. For example, for the unit interval the problem of minimizing the sum is NP-complete if the sensors may have different sensing ranges but is polynomial time in the case where all the ranges are the same [18]. The problem of minimizing the maximum is NP-complete if the region consists of two intervals [17] but is polynomial time for a single interval even when the sensors may have different ranges [11]. Related work on deterministic algorithms for minimizing the total and maximum movement of sensors for barrier coverage of a planar region may be found in [8]. Different metrics for the complexity of barrier coverage are also possible: one is based on robot assisted restoration and is analyzed in [19] and another on the power of the displacement and is analyzed in [25].

A related problem studied in [29] is sensor interference. Assume that for a given parameter $s > 0$ two sensors' signals interfere with each other during communication if their distance is $\leq s$. We are allowed to move the sensors on the line, if needed, so as to avoid interference. We call total movement the sum of displacements that the sensors have to move so that the distance between any two sensors is $> s$.

Sensor Interference. Assume that n sensors are thrown randomly and independently with the Poisson distribution having arrival rate $\lambda = n$ in the interval $[0, +\infty)$. What is the expected minimum total distance that the sensors have to move from their initial position to a new destination so that any two sensors are at a distance more than s apart?

Finally, it is worth mentioning [30] where sensor movement for both coverage and interference at the same time is being studied.

4 Evacuation

The goal of traditional search problems is to find an object which is located
in a specific domain. This subject of research has a long history and there is a
plethora of models investigated in the mathematical and theoretical computer
science literature with emphasis on probabilistic search in [42], game theoretic
applications in [3], cops and robbers in [10], classical pursuit and evasion in [36],
search problems and group testing in [1], plus many more.

We investigate the problem of searching for an *exit* at an unknown location
using k agents, $k \geq 1$. We are interested in minimizing the time it takes until
the *last agent* finds the exit. (Note: the case $k = 1$ is the same as the traditional
search problem.) The agents need to evacuate the region but the location of the
exit is unknown to them; they can cooperate to search for the exit, but it is not
enough for one agent to find the exit, we require all agents to reach the exit as
soon as possible (see Fig. 3). A canonical example of our problem restricts the
domain to be a disk of radius 1:

> $k > 1$ agents are located within a unit disk. At any time the agents can
> move anywhere they choose within the disk with maximum speed 1. The
> agents can communicate with each other either only if they are at the
> same point at the same time (we call this communication model *face-to-
> face communication*) or at any time by wireless communication. Our goal is
> to schedule the trajectories of the agents so as to minimize the *evacuation
> time*, which is the time it takes all agents to reach the exit (for the worst
> case location of the exit). The time is generally reported as the worst case
> ratio of the evacuation time to actual distance to the exit.

The version of the above problem where all agents start at the centre of the
disk was first studied in [14]. The same paper introduced the two communication
models discussed above. Baeza-Yates et al. [4] posed the question of minimizing

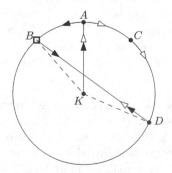

Fig. 3. Evacuation of two agents starting at point K from an unknown exit (at B)
in the face-to-face model. The agents move together towards the perimeter (point A)
and in opposite direction along the perimeter. The first agent to find the exit moves to
meet the second agent (at point D) and bring it to the exit.

the worst-case trajectory of a single agent searching for a target point at an unknown location in the plane. This was generalized to multiple agents in [34], and more recently has been studied in [24,32]. However the agents cannot communicate, and moreover, the objective is only for the first agent to find the target. Two seminal and influential papers (that appeared almost at the same time) on probabilistic search are [5,6] and concern minimizing the *expected time* for the agent to find the target. Useful surveys on search theory can also be found in [7,21]. In addition, the latter citation has an interesting classification of search problems by search objectives, distribution of effort, point target (stationary, large, moving), two-sided search, etc. The evacuation problem considered is related to searching on a line, in that we are searching on the boundary of a disk but with the additional ability to make short-cuts in order to enable the agents to meet sooner and thus evacuate faster. In [12] evacuation algorithms are proposed for agents with different speeds on a line in the face-to-face communication model. Domains other than the disc or line have also been studied. For example, [20] considers evacuation from an equilateral triangle and a square.

5   Domain Protection and Blocking

Consider a set of impenetrable buildings located axis-aligned on a square or rectangular region (see Fig. 4). We are interested in detecting intruders attempting to pass through the region by placing sensors at regularly spaced intervals over the region forming a grid. If an intruder steps within the sensing range of a sensor he or she will be detected. It is desired to prevent potential attacks in either one dimension or two dimensions. A one-dimensional attack succeeds when an intruder enters from the top (North) side and exits out the bottom (South) side of the domain without being detected. Preventing attacks in two dimensions requires that we simultaneously prevent the intruder from either entering North and exiting South or entering East (left side) and exiting West (right side) undetected.

> *Protection & Blocking.* Assume that initially all of the sensors are working properly and the domain is fully protected, i.e., all attacks will be detected, in both dimensions (assuming the grid points are such that neighboring sensors have overlapping sensing ranges and include all four boundaries of the domain). Over time, some of the sensors may fail and we are left with a subset of working sensors. We wish to determine if one- or two-dimensional attack detection still persists and if not, restore protection by adding the least number of sensors required to ensure detection in either one or two dimensions.

Ideally, the set of currently working sensors would provide some amount of fault-tolerance. In particular, it would be advantageous if for a given k, the set of sensors maintains protection (in one or two dimensions) even if up to k of the sensors fail. This leads to the problems of deciding if a subset of the sensors

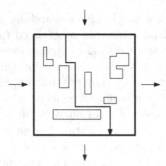

Fig. 4. A geometric region (square) containing impenetrable buildings and structures. An intruder may penetrate the region either from north to south or east to west by following a possibly rectilinear path through the available free space in the region. How should the adversary be blocked using the minimum number of sensors placed on grid points?

provides protection with up to k faults and if not, finding the minimum number of grid points to add sensors to in order to achieve k fault-tolerance. In [27], algorithms are provided for deciding if a set sensors provides k-fault tolerant protection against attacks in both one and two dimensions, for optimally restoring k-fault tolerant protection in one dimension and for restoring protection in two dimensions (optimally for $k = 0$ and approximately otherwise). A closely related work is that of [38] where the authors look at how to best randomly distribute additional sensors in order to maintain barrier coverage under the potential for faults.

In the above version of the problem, sensors are added in order to restore protection. Alternatively, we could consider a version of the problem where we may move the existing sensors rather than add new sensors (assuming the number of existing sensors is sufficient to provide a solution). Can the rectangular grid be protected with the existing and/or the addition of new mobile sensors? If yes, provide an algorithm displacing the sensors so as to provide protection for the grid and which minimizes the sum (or maximum) of distances of the sensors displaced. What is the minimum number of new sensors which in combination with the previously existing sensors could protect the grid? Concerning this version of the problem, in [43] the authors introduce the problem of how to efficiently heal coverage holes in hybrid Wireless Sensor Networks (WSNs) by relocating mobile nodes (this is effectively the *moving sensor* version of the 1D blocking problem introduced above), and propose a hole recovery strategy called Minimal Patching Barrier Healing Strategy (MPBHS).

The paths taken by an intruder in the above model are arbitrary rectilinear paths. In some instances it may only be necessary to protect against attackers traveling along orthogonal straight line paths. Such an attacker has been considered before in the case of barrier coverage [31]. Obviously, it is much easier to defend against the straight line type of adversary, referred to as *weak* protection, and optimal strategies are usually rather straightforward to identify when deciding where to add (immovable) sensors. Interestingly, even this weaker version becomes NP-complete when we consider mobile sensors and the problem of minimizing the maximum movement required [22].

6 Conclusion

In this survey we have discussed several "mobile agent" based optimization problems inspired by infrastructure security. For each of the four problems discussed, the optimization aspect was emphasized and we tried to indicate how efficient algorithms can be used to make security solutions more effective. In all cases considered agent mobility was crucial in obtaining optimal solutions.

However, it is important to take into account the fact that this is only the "tip of the iceberg" since security is a very complex task involving the coordination several layers of the communication process from physical infrastructure to network systems. We hope this presentation will initiate more research on optimization problems arising in infrastructure security in particular and security in general.

References

1. Ahlswede, R., Wegener, I.: Search Problems. Wiley-Interscience, New York (1987)
2. Almeida, A., Ramalho, G.L., Santana, H., Azevedo Tedesco, P., Menezes, T., Corruble, V., Chevaleyre, Y.: Recent advances on multi-agent patrolling. In: Bazzan, A.L.C., Labidi, S. (eds.) SBIA 2004. LNCS (LNAI), vol. 3171, pp. 474–483. Springer, Heidelberg (2004)
3. Alpern, S., Gal, S.: The Theory of Search Games and Rendezvous, vol. 55. Kluwer Academic Publishers, New York (2003)
4. Baeza Yates, R., Culberson, J., Rawlins, G.: Searching in the plane. Inf. Comput. 106(2), 234–252 (1993)
5. Beck, A.: On the linear search problem. Isr. J. Math. 2(4), 221–228 (1964)
6. Bellman, R.: An optimal search. SIAM Rev. 5(3), 274 (1963)
7. Benkoski, S., Monticino, M., Weisinger, J.: A survey of the search theory literature. Naval Res. Logistics (NRL) 38(4), 469–494 (1991)
8. Bhattacharya, B., Burmester, M., Hu, Y., Kranakis, E., Shi, Q., Wiese, A.: Optimal movement of mobile sensors for barrier coverage of a planar region. TCS 410(52), 5515–5528 (2009)
9. Biringer, B., Vugrin, E., Warren, D.: Critical Infrastructure System Security and Resiliency. CRC Press, Boca Raton (2013)
10. Bonato, A., Nowakowski, R.: The Game of Cops and Robbers on Graphs. American Mathematical Society, Providence (2011)
11. Chen, D.Z., Gu, Y., Li, J., Wang, H.: Algorithms on minimizing the maximum sensor movement for barrier coverage of a linear domain. In: Fomin, F.V., Kaski, P. (eds.) SWAT 2012. LNCS, vol. 7357, pp. 177–188. Springer, Heidelberg (2012)
12. Chrobak, M., Gąsieniec, L., Gorry, T., Martin, R.: Group search on the line. In: Italiano, G.F., Margaria-Steffen, T., Pokorný, J., Quisquater, J.-J., Wattenhofer, R. (eds.) SOFSEM 2015. LNCS, vol. 8939, pp. 164–176. Springer, Heidelberg (2015)

13. Collins, A., Czyzowicz, J., Gasieniec, L., Kosowski, A., Kranakis, E., Krizanc, D., Martin, R., Morales Ponce, O.: Optimal patrolling of fragmented boundaries. In: Proceedings of SPAA (2013)
14. Czyzowicz, J., Gąsieniec, L., Gorry, T., Kranakis, E., Martin, R., Pajak, D.: Evacuating robots via unknown exit in a disk. In: Kuhn, F. (ed.) DISC 2014. LNCS, vol. 8784, pp. 122–136. Springer, Heidelberg (2014)
15. Czyzowicz, J., Gąsieniec, L., Kosowski, A., Kranakis, E.: Boundary patrolling by mobile agents with distinct maximal speeds. In: Demetrescu, C., Halldórsson, M.M. (eds.) ESA 2011. LNCS, vol. 6942, pp. 701–712. Springer, Heidelberg (2011)
16. Czyzowicz, J., Gasieniec, L., Kosowski, A., Kranakis, E., Krizanc, D., Taleb, N.: When patrolmen become corrupted: monitoring a graph using faulty mobile robots. In: Elbassioni, K., Makino, K. (eds.) ISAAC 2015. LNCS, vol. 9472, pp. 343–354. Springer, Heidelberg (2015). doi:10.1007/978-3-662-48971-0_30
17. Czyzowicz, J., Kranakis, E., Krizanc, D., Lambadaris, I., Narayanan, L., Opatrny, J., Stacho, L., Urrutia, J., Yazdani, M.: On minimizing the maximum sensor movement for barrier coverage of a line segment. In: Ruiz, P.M., Garcia-Luna-Aceves, J.J. (eds.) ADHOC-NOW 2009. LNCS, vol. 5793, pp. 194–212. Springer, Heidelberg (2009)
18. Czyzowicz, J., Kranakis, E., Krizanc, D., Lambadaris, I., Narayanan, L., Opatrny, J., Stacho, L., Urrutia, J., Yazdani, M.: On minimizing the sum of sensor movements for barrier coverage of a line segment. In: Nikolaidis, I., Wu, K. (eds.) ADHOC-NOW 2010. LNCS, vol. 6288, pp. 29–42. Springer, Heidelberg (2010)
19. Czyzowicz, J., Kranakis, E., Krizanc, D., Narayanan, L., Opatrny, J.: Robot-assisted restoration of barrier coverage. In: Workshop on Approximation and Online Algorithms, pp. 119–131. Springer, Switzerland (2014)
20. Czyzowicz, J., Kranakis, E., Krizanc, D., Narayanan, L., Opatrny, J., Shende, S.: Wireless autonomous robot evacuation from equilateral triangles and squares. In: Papavassiliou, S., Ruehrup, S. (eds.) ADHOC-NOW 2015. LNCS, vol. 9143, pp. 181–194. Springer, Switzerland (2015)
21. Dobbie, J.: A survey of search theory. Oper. Res. **16**(3), 525–537 (1968)
22. Dobrev, S.: Personal communication
23. Dumitrescu, A., Ghosh, A., Tóth, C.D.: On fence patrolling by mobile agents. Electr. J. Comb. **21**(3), 1–15 (2014). P3.4
24. Emek, Y., Langner, T., Uitto, J., Wattenhofer, R.: Solving the ANTS problem with asynchronous finite state machines. In: Esparza, J., Fraigniaud, P., Husfeldt, T., Koutsoupias, E. (eds.) ICALP 2014, Part II. LNCS, vol. 8573, pp. 471–482. Springer, Heidelberg (2014)
25. Kapelko, R., Kranakis, E.: On the displacement for covering a square with randomly placed sensors. In: Papavassiliou, S., Ruehrup, S. (eds.) ADHOC-NOW 2015. LNCS, vol. 9143, pp. 148–162. Springer, Switzerland (2015)
26. Kawamura, A., Kobayashi, Y.: Fence patrolling by mobile agents with distinct speeds. In: Chao, K.-M., Hsu, T., Lee, D.-T. (eds.) ISAAC 2012. LNCS, vol. 7676, pp. 598–608. Springer, Heidelberg (2012)
27. Kranakis, E., Krizanc, D., Luccio, F., Smith, B.: Maintaining intruder detection capability in a rectangular domain with sensors. In: Algosensors 2015, Patras, Greece (2015)
28. Kranakis, E., Krizanc, D., Morales-Ponce, O., Narayanan, L., Opatrny, J., Shende, S.: Expected sum and maximum of displacement of random sensors for coverage of a domain. In: Proceedings of the Twenty-Fifth Annual ACM Symposium on Parallelism in Algorithms and Architectures, pp. 73–82. ACM (2013)

29. Kranakis, E., Shaikhet, G.: Displacing random sensors to avoid interference. In: Cai, Z., Zelikovsky, A., Bourgeois, A. (eds.) COCOON 2014. LNCS, vol. 8591, pp. 501–512. Springer, Heidelberg (2014)
30. Kranakis, E., Shaikhet, G.: Sensor allocation problems on the real line. J. Appl. Probab. (2015, to appear)
31. Kumar, S., Lai, T.H., Arora, A.: Barrier coverage with wireless sensors. In: Proceedings of the 11th Annual International Conference on Mobile Computing and Networking, pp. 284–298. ACM (2005)
32. Lenzen, C., Lynch, N., Newport, C., Radeva, T.: Trade-offs between selection complexity and performance when searching the plane without communication. In: Proceedings of PODC, pp. 252–261 (2014)
33. Lewis, T.G.: Critical Infrastructure Protection in Homeland Security: Defending a Networked Nation. John Wiley & Sons, Hoboken (2014)
34. López-Ortiz, A., Sweet, G.: Parallel searching on a lattice. In: Proceedings of CCCG, pp. 125–128 (2001)
35. Machado, A., Ramalho, G.L., Zucker, J.-D., Drogoul, A.: Multi-agent patrolling: an empirical analysis of alternative architectures. In: Sichman, J.S., Bousquet, F., Davidsson, P. (eds.) MABS 2002. LNCS (LNAI), vol. 2581, pp. 155–170. Springer, Heidelberg (2003)
36. Nahin, P.: Chases and Escapes: The Mathematics of Pursuit and Evasion. Princeton University Press, Princeton (2012)
37. O'Rourke, J.: Art Gallery Theorems and Algorithms, vol. 57. Oxford University Press, Oxford (1987)
38. Park, T., Shi, H.: Extending the lifetime of barrier coverage by adding sensors to a bottleneck region. In: 12th IEEE Consumer Communications and Networking Conference (CCNC). IEEE (2015)
39. Pasqualetti, F., Zanella, F., Peters, J.R., Spindler, M., Carli, R., Bullo, F.: Camera network coordination for intruder detection. IEEE Trans. Contr. Sys. Techn. **22**(5), 1669–1683 (2014)
40. Radvanovsky, R.S., McDougall, A.: Critical Infrastructure: Homeland Security and Emergency Preparedness. CRC Press, Boca Raton (2009)
41. Saipulla, A., Westphal, C., Liu, B., Wang, J.: Barrier coverage of line-based deployed wireless sensor networks. In: INFOCOM, pp. 127–135. IEEE (2009)
42. Stone, L.: Theory of Optimal Search. Academic Press, New York (1975)
43. Xie, H., Li, M., Wang, W., Wang, C., Li, X., Zhang, Y.: Minimal patching barrier healing strategy for barrier coverage in hybrid wsns. In: 2014 IEEE 25th Annual International Symposium on Personal, Indoor, and Mobile Radio Communication (PIMRC), pp. 1558–1563. IEEE (2014)

Secure Distributed Computation
on Private Inputs

Geoffroy Couteau, Thomas Peters, and David Pointcheval[✉]

ENS, CNRS & INRIA, PSL Research University, Paris, France
david.pointcheval@ens.fr

Abstract. The recent notion of encryption switching protocol (ESP) allows two players to obliviously switch between two encryption schemes. Instantiated from multiplicatively homomorphic encryption and additively homomorphic encryption, ESPs provide a generic solution to two-party computation and lead to particularly efficient protocols for arithmetic circuits in terms of interaction and communication.

In this paper, we further investigate their applications and show how ESPs can be used as an alternative to fully-homomorphic encryption (FHE) to outsource computation on sensitive data to cloud providers. Our interactive solution relies on two non-colluding servers which obliviously perform the operations on encrypted data, and eventually send back the outcome in an encrypted form to the appropriate players.

Our solution makes use of a nice combination of the Paillier encryption scheme and the Damgard-Jurik variant with multiple trapdoors, which notably allows cross-user evaluations on encrypted data.

Keywords: Encryption switching protocols · Delegation of computations

1 Introduction

Secure multiparty computation (MPC) targets the following problem: several players, modeled as probabilistic polynomial time Turing machines, wish to jointly compute a public function f of their respective, private inputs. The players want to guarantee the privacy of their inputs: at the end of the protocol, no player should be able to deduce from its view during the execution anything that he could not have deduced from the output and its own input. General solutions for MPC have been proposed, starting with the work of Yao [13] and followed by [7,8].

Delegation of Computations. A particular case of secure MPC is the problem of delegation of computations where a set of clients, with a limited computational power, would like to perform some expensive computation on their data. To do so, they can communicate with a powerful server, but they do not fully trust the server. Typical security requirements for this particular task are both the *privacy*, which says that the server will perform computations on the inputs of the clients

© Springer International Publishing Switzerland 2016
J. Garcia-Alfaro et al. (Eds.): FPS 2015, LNCS 9482, pp. 14–26, 2016.
DOI: 10.1007/978-3-319-30303-1_2

without gaining any knowledge about this input, and the *verifiability*, which says that the clients want to be sure that the correct functions have been evaluated. In this paper, we propose a solution which guarantees both requirements in a specific setting, namely the non-collusion of the two servers.

Encryption Switching Protocols. An encryption switching protocol (ESP) is a protocol which allows two players to obliviously switch from a ciphertext under one encryption scheme to a ciphertext encrypting the same plaintext under the other encryption scheme. We recall the definition of ESP as introduced in [6]: let $(\mathcal{E}, \mathcal{D})$ and $(\overline{\mathcal{E}}, \overline{\mathcal{D}})$ be two encryption schemes, with a common pair of encryption and decryption keys $(\mathsf{pk}, \mathsf{sk})$ —in any case, they can always be the concatenations of the keys of the two schemes—. An ESP between two players, each player holding a share of sk, on input an encryption C of some plaintext m under $\mathcal{E}$, outputs an encryption $\overline{C}$ of the same plaintext m under $\overline{\mathcal{E}}$. Informally, an ESP is *secure* if it satisfies the following requirements:

- **Correctness:** if both players behave honestly, $\overline{\mathcal{D}}(\overline{C}, \mathsf{sk}) = \mathcal{D}(C, \mathsf{sk})$;
- **Soundness:** there is a negligible probability for a malicious player to force an output $\overline{C}$ such that $\overline{\mathcal{D}}(\overline{C}, \mathsf{sk}) \neq \mathcal{D}(C, \mathsf{sk})$ without being detected;
- **Zero-Knowledge:** no information on either m or sk leaks during the protocol execution.

It should be noted that, as the players hold *shares* of the secret key sk, the decryption and encryption switching operations are performed as two-party protocols between the players. They essentially both involve $(2, 2)$-threshold decryption.

Two-Party Computation from ESP. In [6], the authors established that any function on a ring $(\mathcal{R}, +, \times)$ can be evaluated on encrypted data by a two-party protocol relying on two encryption schemes, an additively homomorphic scheme $(\mathcal{E}_{\oplus}, \mathcal{D}_{\oplus})$ and a multiplicatively homomorphic scheme $(\mathcal{E}_{\otimes}, \mathcal{D}_{\otimes})$, operating on the same plaintext space $\mathcal{R}$, with an ESP to obliviously switch between those two schemes. We recall the intuition underlying this result by considering two players, Alice and Bob, who wish to evaluate a N-variate polynomial $P(X_1, \cdots, X_N) = \sum_{j=1}^{M} \prod X_i^{d_{ij}}$ in $\mathcal{R}[X_1, \ldots, X_N]$ on a vector of inputs x shared between the two parties. Let $x_A = (x_A^i)_{i \leq N}$ (resp. $x_B = (x_B^i)_{i \leq N}$) be Alice's share (resp. Bob's share), such that $x = x_A + x_B$, in the ring:

1. Both players start by encrypting their inputs under $\mathcal{E}_{\oplus}$, the additively homomorphic encryption scheme. If we denote $\boxplus$ the homomorphic operator on the ciphertexts for the $+$ operator on the plaintexts, both players can then compute $\mathcal{E}_{\oplus}(x) = \mathcal{E}_{\oplus}(x_A) \boxplus \mathcal{E}_{\oplus}(x_B) = (\mathcal{E}_{\oplus}(x_i))_{i \leq N}$;
2. Both players then perform N ESPs in parallel to get a vector $\mathcal{E}_{\otimes}(x)$ of multiplicatively homomorphic ciphertexts. Let $\boxtimes$ and $\triangle$ be the homomorphic operators for multiplication and exponentiation by a constant on the plaintexts, then both players can compute $(\mathcal{E}_{\otimes}(y_j))_{j \leq M} = (\mathcal{E}_{\otimes}(\prod_i x_i^{d_{ij}}))_{j \leq M} = (\boxtimes_{i \leq N} \mathcal{E}_{\otimes}(x_i) \triangle d_{ij})_{j \leq M}$;

3. Alice and Bob eventually perform M ESPs in parallel to get additively homomorphic encryptions of all the monomials y_j. They compute, from the previous result, an encryption of the sum of all the monomials, which is the target output $P(x_1, \cdots, x_N)$, that they decrypt in a distributed way.

The overall protocol involves two steps of switches (all the other operations are performed locally by each player), with a communication of $O(N + M)$ ciphertexts: this method avoids the dependency in the degree of the polynomial which is inherent to most two-party protocols, and is round-efficient (i.e., independent of the d_{ij}'s, while known protocols for this task typically involve $O(\log(\max_{i,j}(d_{ij})))$ rounds of interaction).

Our Contribution. In this paper, we design a novel application of ESP to delegation of computations in the cloud. Specifically, we consider two non-colluding servers and design a delegation model with the following features:

- Any number of users can generate their own encryption and decryption keys;
- Any player can store its data online, encrypted under its own key;
- Any subset of users can ask for the evaluation of an arbitrary function f over their joint data;
- The communication and interactions between the servers are independent of the depth of the arithmetic circuit to be evaluated, to avoid latency issues;
- If the servers do not collude, then the protocol guarantees the privacy of the data and the correctness of the computation.

For efficiency reasons, we want the computation of the servers to be small, compared to solutions based on fully-homomorphic encryption [5]. But still, our model expects a single round with the cloud providers. It means that the users' encrypted data are sent and stored before any evaluation. At the end of the evaluation, using the stand-alone two-party computation [6] from ESP, all the results are sent to the appropriate users and the protocol is over.

2 Delegation to Non-Colluding Servers

2.1 Delegating Computations to the Cloud

We consider the following scenario: many individuals, with very limited computational resources, would like to securely outsource their data and to be able to delegate computations on these data to the more powerful cloud providers. As the data are possibly sensitive, it should be guaranteed that the privacy of the inputs of each user will be preserved, preferably without restricting the kind of computation that can be outsourced.

A natural solution to this problem is fully-homomorphic encryption (FHE): each user generates his own secret key for an FHE scheme; to outsource its data, the user encrypts his input and sends it to the cloud. When he wants to delegate computations, the user simply sends the target function to the server. Thanks to the homomorphic properties of the scheme, the latter can evaluate any function on the encrypted input and send back the encrypted result to the user, which decrypts it to get his output. Even if secret-key fully-homomorphic encryption is enough in such a context, current schemes remain prohibitively expensive, making this solution impractical for complex functions, which are typically the kind of functions for which a user would like to delegate computations. Moreover, evaluating functions on joint data of several clients, encrypted under different keys, requires the use of a FHE with stronger properties, namely multi-key FHE [10].

An alternative solution to this problem can be obtained by considering two non-colluding servers (or more) instead of a single one. Indeed, it would be natural to see two cloud providers collaborate in order to offer such a service to their customers, but they would arguably not share their own private data to the other provider, as they do not trust each other. In this setting, the two providers could run a two-party protocol on the encrypted data to get an encrypted output, which would be sent back to the user. However, this approach raises two concerns:

1. Multiparty computation protocols to evaluate function on encrypted data typically require the players (here, the cloud providers) to hold shares of the secret key of the encryption scheme, while the scenario under consideration involves many users who wish to outsource data encrypted with their *own* key and to be able to decrypt the result using their own private key;
2. Two-party computation protocols require many interactions (typically, the players exchange messages for each product gate of the circuit to be evaluated), and the scenario we consider involves possibly distant, on-line servers. Therefore, a large number of interactions is highly undesirable because of the latency of the network.

2.2 The Model

In this paper, we propose a solution to address the constraints of the above scenario. In a nutshell, our solution works as follows: we rely on the DJ encryption scheme, introduced by Damgard and Jurik in [3], which improves upon a previous similar scheme of [2]. DJ is an encryption scheme with a particular *double trapdoor* mechanism which ensures that any ciphertext can be decrypted in two ways, either with a *local* secret key specific to a player, or with the *global* master secrey key. A DJ encryption scheme is set up, and the master public key mpk (which is an RSA modulus) is made publicly available. Each player P_i can now generate its own secret key sk_i, and the corresponding public key pk_i. Any message encrypted under the public key pk_i of a player P_i can therefore be decrypted in two ways: either using sk_i, the secret key associated to pk_i generated by P_i, or by using the master secret key msk, which can decrypt ciphertext regardless of the particular key pk_i which was used to encrypt it.

The master secret key is divided into two shares, msk_1 and msk_2, using a secret sharing scheme; hence, each msk_j for $j \in \{1,2\}$ does not reveal (statistically) any information on msk. Each of the two servers receives one share. With these shares, the two servers can now jointly compute functions over data encrypted under *any* particular key pk_i of a player P_i.

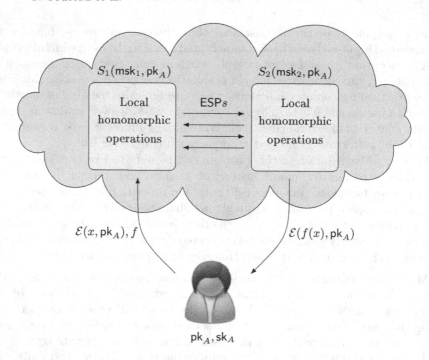

Fig. 1. Delegation of computation to two non-colluding servers

Let S_1 and S_2 be the two non-colluding servers to which the computation will be delegated. All the players encrypt their data under their own key pk_i and outsource the ciphertexts. When a subset S of players $(P_i)_{i \in S}$ asks for the evaluation of some function f on some vector C of data (encrypted under different keys if S contains at least two users), S_1 and S_2 first convert C into a vector C_+ of Paillier ciphertexts using a tailored protocol which takes as input their shares of the master secret key msk. Second, the target function f is divided into *layers*, each layer containing either linear operations, or products and exponentiations. To evaluate a layer of linear operations on the encrypted data, S_1 and S_2 rely on the homomorphic properties of the Paillier encryption scheme, and can thus independently make the evaluation in a deterministic way, to get the same results. To evaluate a layer of products and exponentiations, S_1 and S_2 first interactively convert C_+ into a vector $C_\times$ of *multiplicatively* homomorphic ciphertexts, using an encryption switching protocol; once this is done, S_1 and S_2 can independently evaluate the operations on $C_\times$ using the homomorphic properties of the scheme. They can then interactively switch the result back to additively homomorphic ciphertexts to evaluate linear operations, and so on, until the last layer of operations is performed. The result is then switched back to a vector of DJ ciphertexts, encrypted under the key pk_i of each P_i for $i \in S$, and sent to those players. The model is represented Fig. 1, in the case of a unique player in S.

Since computations are performed on ciphertexts, the privacy of the data is guaranteed. Since both servers do the same homomorphic operations, and the encryption switching protocols are secure against malicious players, if they both output the same result, it is necessarily correct, hence the verifiability, under the non-colluding servers assumption.

3   Formal Construction

We write $a \leftarrow b$ to affect the value of b to the variable a, and $a \xleftarrow{\$} D$ to affect a value sampled uniformly at random from the distribution D to the variable a. To avoid confusions between modular integers and integers, we use brackets to denote integers: $[a \bmod t]$ denotes the value of $a \bmod t$, between 0 and $t - 1$, seen as an integer.

Global Setup. In all the constructions, we assume that the following global setup has been performed: a trusted dealer generates two primes p and q such that $p' = (p-1)/2$ and $q' = (q-1)/2$ are also prime, and sets $n \leftarrow pq$. He sets $\mathsf{mpk} \leftarrow n$ and $\mathsf{sk} \leftarrow (p, q)$. Let $\lambda \leftarrow (p-1)(q-1)/2$ be the maximal order of an element in the multiplicative subgroup $\mathbb{Z}_n^*$.

Jacobi Symbol. The Jacobi symbol is an extension of the Legendre symbol to groups with odd order. It maps invertible elements of the group to $\{-1, +1\}$. The Jacobi symbol of an element of $\mathbb{Z}_n^*$ can be efficiently computed, even when the factorization of the modulus is unknown.

3.1   Assumptions

We review the various assumptions on which the security of the primitives rely.

The Decisional Diffie-Hellman Assumption (DDH). Let $\mathbb{G}$ be some group of order t with generator g. The DDH assumption over $\mathbb{G}$ states that it is computationally infeasible to distinguish the following distributions:

$$\mathcal{D}_0 = \{(A, B, C) \mid (a, b, c) \xleftarrow{\$} \mathbb{Z}_t^3, (A, B, C) \leftarrow (g^a, g^b, g^c)\}$$
$$\mathcal{D}_1 = \{(A, B, C) \mid (a, b) \xleftarrow{\$} \mathbb{Z}_t^2, (A, B, C) \leftarrow (g^a, g^b, g^{ab})\}$$

For any integer t, let us write $\mathsf{QR}(t)$ the group of squares over $\mathbb{Z}_t^*$. The DDH assumption is conjectured to hold in the groups $\mathsf{QR}(n)$ and $\mathsf{QR}(n^2)$, for RSA moduli n, as defined above in the global setup.

The Quadratic Residuosity Assumption (QR). Let $\mathbb{J}_n$ be the group of elements of $\mathbb{Z}_n^*$ with Jacobi symbol +1; it holds that $\mathbb{J}_n = \{x \in \mathbb{Z}_n^* \mid (u,b) \leftarrow \mathbb{Z}_n^* \times \{0,1\}, x \leftarrow (-1)^b u^2\}$. The QR assumption modulo n states that it is computationally infeasible, given some element $x \xleftarrow{\$} \mathbb{J}_n$, to have a non-negligible advantage in guessing whether $x \in \mathsf{QR}(n)$ or $x \in \mathbb{J}_n \setminus \mathsf{QR}(n)$. Note that given the factorization of n, it is easy to break the QR assumption modulo n. Since an element $y \in \mathbb{Z}_{n^2}^*$ can be written as $y = x^n \cdot (1 + rn) \bmod n^2$, with $x \in \mathbb{Z}_n^*$ and $r \in \mathbb{Z}_n$, and $1 + rn$ is always a square in $\mathbb{Z}_{n^2}^*$, $y \in \mathsf{QR}(n^2)$ if and only if $x \in \mathsf{QR}(n)$, or equivalently $x^n = y \bmod n \in \mathsf{QR}(n)$. Hence, the QR assumptions are equivalent modulo n and modulo n^2, and so the unique notation QR.

The Decisional Composite Residuosity Assumption (DCR). Let $D_n = \{x \in \mathbb{Z}_{n^2}^* \mid \exists y \in \mathbb{Z}_n^*, x = y^n \bmod n^2\}$. The DCR assumption states that it is computationally infeasible, given an element x sampled at random from either $\mathbb{Z}_{n^2}^*$ or D_n, to guess whether $x \in D_n$ or not with non-negligible advantage over the random guess.

3.2   Primitives

We recall the descriptions of the primitives which are used in the construction. For convenience, we will slightly abuse the usual notations for encryption, and write $\mathsf{Enc}(m)$ instead of $\mathsf{Enc}(m; r)$ with a random coin r.

Paillier Encryption Scheme. The Paillier encryption scheme was introduced in [11]. The global setup is run; let $\mathsf{msk} := d \leftarrow [\lambda^{-1} \bmod n] \times \lambda \bmod n\lambda$; note that the knowledge of sk implies the knowledge of d.

$\mathsf{Enc}(\mathsf{pk}, m)$: On input $m \in \mathbb{Z}_n$, pick $r \xleftarrow{\$} \mathbb{Z}_{n^2}$ and output $c = \mathcal{E}_{\oplus}(\mathsf{pk}, m; r) = (1 + nm) \cdot r^n \bmod n^2$;

$\mathsf{Dec}(\mathsf{sk}, c)$: on input c, output $m = ([c^d \bmod n^2] - 1)/n$

This scheme is IND-CPA under the DCR assumption over $\mathbb{Z}_{n^2}^*$, and additively homomorphic in $\mathbb{Z}_n$.

Damgard-Jurik Encryption Scheme. The Damgard-Jurik scheme (DJ) was introduced in [3]. It builds upon the Paillier encryption scheme and enhances it with a double trapdoor mechanism: for a fixed ring $\mathbb{Z}_n$, many pairs of public and secret keys can be generated. This property was explicitly identified in [1], in which a similar scheme with comparable properties under weaker assumptions was constructed. A given ciphertext encrypted with a public key pk_i can be decrypted in two ways, either with the associated secret key sk_i in an ElGamal-like fashion, or using the master secret key, i.e., the Paillier's decryption key. We denote $\mathcal{E}_{\oplus}^i$ the DJ scheme for user P_i. Let G be a generator of $\mathbb{J}_n$ added to mpk.

Key(mpk, i) : Pick $a_i \xleftarrow{\$} \mathbb{Z}_{n/2}$ and set $H_i \leftarrow G^{a_i} \bmod n$. Let $\mathsf{pk}_i \leftarrow H_i$ be the
   public key of the player P_i. The secret key is $\mathsf{sk}_i \leftarrow a_i$;

Enc(mpk, pk_i, m) : On input $m \in \mathbb{Z}_n$, pick $r \xleftarrow{\$} \mathbb{Z}_{n/2}$ and output $c = \mathcal{E}_{\oplus}^i(m; r) =$
   $(G^r \bmod n, (1 + mn) \cdot [H_i^r \bmod n]^n \bmod n^2)$;

Dec(sk_i, c) : Parse c as (A, B) and output $m = ([B^2 \cdot [A^{2a_i} \bmod n]^{-n} \bmod n^2] -$
   $1)/n \cdot [2^{-1} \bmod n] \bmod n$.

Alternatively, one can decrypt a ciphertext c with the master secret key
$\mathsf{msk} = d$ simply by dropping the first part A of the ciphertext, and by decrypting
B using the Paillier decryption procedure, since the mask $[H_i^r \bmod n]^n \bmod n^2$
is an n-th power in $\mathbb{Z}_{n^2}^*$.

This scheme is a slight variant of the *proof-friendly* encryption introduced
in [3]. Indeed, in their first scheme, G and H_i are drawn from $\mathsf{QR}(n)$ instead of
$\mathbb{J}_n$. The proof-friendly variant lowers the complexity of zero-knowledge proofs of
validity (or knowledge), at the very moderate cost of adding the QR assumption
to the security: by squaring A and B in the decryption process, we ensure to work
in a group without any small subgroup. This allows to decrypt $2m$ instead of m,
but the factor 2 can be easily removed over $\mathbb{Z}_n$ (as inverses are easy to compute).
In our construction, proofs of knowledge will be required by the servers to prevent
malicious clients from trying to outsource data that they do not own. Hence, we
favor this variant of the scheme in our application to reduce the work of the
client in the model. Note that our construction makes use of another scheme,
the $\mathbb{Z}_n^*$-EG encryption scheme which will be described afterward, whose security
does already rely on the QR assumption. Thereby, adding the QR assumption to
the DJ scheme does not affect the overall security of our construction.

On the IND-CPA security of the DJ scheme. The security of the scheme is proven
in [3]. In a nutshell, it relies on the DDH assumption over $\mathsf{QR}(n^2)$, the QR
assumption, and the DCR assumption. Indeed, $[H_i^r \bmod n]^n \bmod n^2$ is in $X =$
$\{\pm\mu^{2n}, \mu \in \mathbb{Z}_n^*\}$, hence the DDH assumption over X ensures that this value
masks the plaintext. Figure 2 shows why (informally) the DDH assumption holds
over X if it holds over $\mathsf{QR}(n^2)$ and if the DCR and QR assumptions hold.

$\mathbb{Z}_n^*$-EG **Encryption Scheme.** The $\mathbb{Z}_n^*$-EG scheme, denoted $\mathcal{E}_{\otimes}$ in this paper, is
a multiplicatively homomorphic extension of the ElGamal encryption scheme [4]
over $\mathbb{Z}_n^*$. It makes a black-box use of an ElGamal scheme over the group $\mathbb{J}_n$ of
elements with Jacobi symbol $+1$, denoted $\mathbb{J}_n$-EG, with encryption and decryption
algorithms $\mathbb{J}_n$-EG.Enc and $\mathbb{J}_n$-EG.Dec.

   Setup(p, q) : Pick $g_0 \xleftarrow{\$} \mathbb{Z}_n^*$, $s \xleftarrow{\$} \mathbb{Z}_\lambda$, an even $t_p \xleftarrow{\$} \mathbb{Z}_\lambda$, and an odd
   $t_q \xleftarrow{\$} \mathbb{Z}_\lambda$; set $g \leftarrow -g_0^2$ (a generator of $\mathbb{J}_n$, of order λ), $v \leftarrow [p^{-1} \bmod q] \cdot p$
   $\bmod n$ ($v = 0 \bmod p$ and $v = 1 \bmod q$) and $\chi \leftarrow (1 - v) \cdot g^{t_p} + v \cdot g^{t_q} \bmod n$,
   and $g_1 \leftarrow g^s \bmod n$ (for the $\mathbb{J}_n$-EG encryption);

   Enc(pk, m) : On input $m \in \mathbb{Z}_n^*$, compute $(m_1, m_2) \leftarrow (g^a, \chi^{-a}m) \in \mathbb{J}_n^2$
   for $a \xleftarrow{\$} \mathbb{Z}_{n/2}$, so that $J_n(m) = (-1)^a$. Then, choose $r \xleftarrow{\$} \mathbb{Z}_{n/2}$ and compute
   $C \leftarrow \mathbb{J}_n - \mathsf{EG.Enc}(m_2; r) = (c_0 = g^r, c_1 = m_2 g_1^r)$. Return the ciphertext
   $c \leftarrow \mathcal{E}_{\otimes}(m; r) = (C = (c_0, c_1), m_1)$;

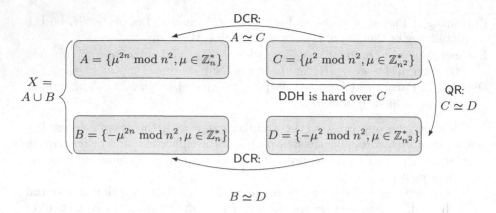

Fig. 2. Hardness of DDH over X

Dec(sk, c) : Parse $c = (C = (c_0, c_1), m_1)$ and check whether $J_n(c_1) = 1$. If not, return $\perp$, otherwise compute $m_2 \leftarrow J_n\text{-EG.Dec}(C) = c_1/c_0^s$ in $\mathbb{Z}_n^*$ and then $m_0 \leftarrow (1-v) \cdot m_1^{t_p} + v \cdot m_1^{t_q}$ mod n. Return $m \leftarrow m_0 m_2$ mod n.

This scheme is IND-CPA under the QR assumption and the DDH assumption over $\mathbb{Z}_p^*$ and $\mathbb{Z}_q^*$.

$\mathbb{Z}_n$-EG Encryption Scheme. The $\mathbb{Z}_n$-EG scheme, denoted $\mathcal{E}_\otimes^0$, is an extension of the $\mathbb{Z}_n^*$-EG scheme to $\mathbb{Z}_n^* \cup \{0\}$. The intuition of the extension is the following: a plaintext $m \in \mathbb{Z}_n^* \cup \{0\}$ is encoded as $(m+b, R^b)$, where b is a bit equal to 1 if and only if $m = 0$, and R is a random square (or in J_n). It is easy to check that this encoding is multiplicatively homomorphic.

Enc(pk, m) : On input $m \in \mathbb{Z}_n^*$, set $b = 1$ if $m = 0$, $b = 0$ else. Picks $(R, R') \xleftarrow{\$} J_n^2$. Return the ciphertext $\mathcal{E}_\otimes^0(m) \leftarrow (\mathcal{E}_\otimes(m + b), J_n - \text{EG.Enc}(R^b), J_n - \text{EG.Enc}(R'^b))$.

Dec(sk, c) : Decrypt the second ciphertext. If it contains any value $R \neq 1$, output 0. If it contains 1, decrypt the first ciphertext and output the result.

The scheme is IND-CPA secure: its IND-CPA security reduces to the IND-CPA security of J_n-EG and $\mathbb{Z}_n^*$-EG. Note that when the decryption of the second part of the ciphertext returns $R \neq 1$, decrypting the first part might compromise the security. This is the reason which the latter should only be decrypted if the former is different from 1. Note also that the third component of the ciphertext is not used in the decryption process; in fact, the scheme would be still secure without this last component. However, this third component is necessary for the encryption switching protocol between this scheme and the Paillier encryption scheme. Since we will do two-party decryption, this will be guaranteed under the non-collusion of the two players.

It is important to note that finding an element outside of the plaintext space $\mathbb{Z}_n^* \cup \{0\}$ of the $\mathbb{Z}_n$-EG scheme is equivalent to factoring; hence, when the secret key is secretly shared between the two players and no single player knows the factorization, with overwhelming probability, no elements outside $\mathbb{Z}_n^* \cup \{0\}$ will ever be exchanged, making the plaintext space of the $\mathbb{Z}_n$-EG scheme equivalent *in practice* to the plaintext space $\mathbb{Z}_n$ of the Paillier scheme: this result implies that ESPs will not compromise the privacy of the plaintexts.

Threshold Schemes. The Paillier scheme and the $\mathbb{Z}_n$-EG scheme admit two-party threshold versions (see [6,9]), in which the secret key is shared between the players and the decryption is performed as a two-party protocol (in fact, the $\mathbb{Z}_n$-EG scheme is secure only in the threshold setting, as the first part of a ciphertext must not be decrypted if the second part does not encrypt 1, which can only be guaranteed when the key is shared). As a consequence, the DJ scheme does also admit a threshold decryption procedure for the alternative decryption procedure, using the master secret key: the players drop the first component of the ciphertext and perform a two-party Paillier decryption procedure on the second component.

Overview of ESP Between Paillier and $\mathbb{Z}_n$-EG (Informal). We outline the intuition underlying the ESP protocol: to switch from a ciphertext C from an encryption scheme E_1 to the other encryption scheme E_2, Alice picks a random mask, uses it to mask C and decrypts the resulting ciphertext with Bob (Bob gets the result). Bob encrypts the outcome under E_2; the mask is then homomorphically removed in the ciphertext space of the second scheme.

3.3   Protocol

A trusted dealer performs the global setup described Sect. 3.2 and generates the secret key $d \in \mathbb{Z}_{n\lambda}$ of the Paillier scheme, the secret key $(v, t_p, t_q, s) \in \mathbb{Z}_n \times \mathbb{Z}_\lambda^3$ of the $\mathbb{Z}_n$-EG scheme; he sets $\mathsf{msk} \leftarrow d$ for the DJ scheme. The dealer secretly shares these keys into two tuples of shares, such that each tuple does individually not reveal anything about the secret key. The dealer sends the first share to the first server S_1 and the second share to the second server S_2. Then, he broadcasts the RSA modulus n.

Outsourcing the Data. To outsource his data, a player P_i performs the Setup algorithm of the DJ scheme on input (n, i) to get $(\mathsf{pk}_i, \mathsf{sk}_i)$. Let $\boldsymbol{x} = (x_1, \cdots, x_N)$ be his data; then

- P_i computes $C \leftarrow \mathcal{E}_\oplus^i(\boldsymbol{x}) = \mathcal{E}_\oplus^i(x_1), \cdots, \mathcal{E}_\oplus^i(x_N)$ and sends it to S_1.
- P_i proves, in zero-knowledge, that he knows plaintexts such that all the cipher-text are encryptions with pk_i of those plaintexts.

On the Zero-Knowledge Proof of Knowledge. The last step ensures that no player will be able to "steal" data from other players by sending a (potentially re-randomized) ciphertext of an other player to the servers as being its own data. Note that the proofs are classical proofs of knowledge of a representation, *à la* Schnorr [12].

One can consider two variants: the player can perform an interactive proof of knowledge with each server, and the servers will let him outsource the data if the proofs succeed. Alternatively, the player can simply append a non-interactive proof to the data he sends, so that the data can be sent to a single server and checked by the two servers when they are asked to perform computation over them. This latter method however requires the random oracle model.

Note that the communication of the zero-knowledge proof can be made independent of the number of inputs by proving the knowledge of the plaintext of the ciphertext $\boxplus_j \lambda_j \mathcal{E}_\oplus^i(x_j)$, where the λ_j's can be derived with either a pseudorandom generator from a seed sent by the verifier or a random oracle on the statement. If the proof succeeds then, with overwhelming probability, all the ciphertexts are valid encryptions with pk_i and P_i knows all the corresponding plaintexts. Note however that this method implies a loss linear in the number of ciphertexts in the security reduction.

Evaluating a Function on Encrypted Data. A subset S of players $(P_i)_{i \in S}$ sends a target function f to the servers S_1 and S_2. For convenience, we assume that f is written in a *layered* form, i.e., as a sequence of layers, each layer containing either linear combinations or monomials computations. First, the servers convert the DJ ciphertexts into Paillier ciphertexts (simply by dropping the first component of each ciphertext). Once this is done, the function is evaluated each layer at a time, by first switching to the encryption scheme with the appropriate homomorphism (using a secure ESP between the Paillier scheme and the $\mathbb{Z}_n$-EG scheme) and evaluating the layer locally and homomorphically. It follows immediately from the Theorem 8 of [6] (which states that two-party computation from ESP is secure) that if at least one of the servers is honest, then:

– The output is a (vector of) Paillier ciphertext(s) which encrypts $f(\boldsymbol{x})$;
– The view of both servers can be simulated without $\boldsymbol{x}$ or the shares of the secret key (hence the privacy of $\boldsymbol{x}$ is guaranteed).

The number of rounds of the protocol is proportional to the number of layers of f (typically, this number is 2 for a multivariate polynomial represented by its canonical form, and will be independent of the degree of f in most practical cases).

Sending the Result Back to P_i for each $i \in S$. For each Paillier ciphertext C obtained as output of the evaluation of f on the encrypted data of the players $(P_i)_{i \in S}$, S_1 and S_2 run the following protocol for each $i \in S$ to convert it into a DJ ciphertext under the key of P_i:

1. S_1 picks $r \xleftarrow{\$} \mathbb{Z}_n$ and sends $C_1 \leftarrow C \boxplus \mathcal{E}_\oplus(r)$ and $C_2 \leftarrow \mathcal{E}^i_\oplus(-r)$ to S_2;
2. S_1 and S_2 jointly decrypt C_1; S_2 gets the result t and sends back $C_i \leftarrow \mathcal{E}^i_\oplus(t) \boxplus C_2$;
3. C_i is sent to P_i, which decrypts it using sk_i.

Note that the protocol has been described in the honest-but-curious setting: malicious servers might deviate from the specifications of the protocol. However, the security can be easily enhanced into full security: the security against malicious adversaries can be ensured by asking S_1 to commit to r and prove the consistency of C_1 and C_2 with the commitment using zero-knowledge proofs. S_2 can also prove, in zero-knowledge, that C' was constructed consistently from C_2 and the plaintext of C_1. Then, both servers send back the result to P_i; if they are not equal, P_i ignores the output. In this setting, it is sufficient that one of the two servers is being honest to ensure that the privacy of P_i's input is guaranteed, and that the output of the protocol is indeed $f(x)$.

Overall, this model ensures the privacy of the data in the stand-alone setting, for a single run of the function evaluation protocol. It would be an interesting future direction of work to extend that to multiple adaptive evaluations on dynamically outsourced data.

Acknowledgments. This work was supported in part by the European Research Council under the European Community's Seventh Framework Programme (FP7/2007–2013 Grant Agreement no. 339563 – CryptoCloud).

References

1. Bresson, E., Catalano, D., Pointcheval, D.: A simple public-key cryptosystem with a double trapdoor decryption mechanism and its applications. In: Laih, C.-S. (ed.) ASIACRYPT 2003. LNCS, vol. 2894, pp. 37–54. Springer, Heidelberg (2003)
2. Cramer, R., Shoup, V.: Universal hash proofs and a paradigm for adaptive chosen ciphertext secure public-key encryption. In: Knudsen, L.R. (ed.) EUROCRYPT 2002. LNCS, vol. 2332, pp. 45–64. Springer, Heidelberg (2002)
3. Damgård, I., Jurik, M.: A length-flexible threshold cryptosystem with applications. In: Safavi-Naini, R., Seberry, J. (eds.) ACISP 2003. LNCS, vol. 2727, pp. 350–364. Springer, Heidelberg (2003)
4. ElGamal, T.: A public key cryptosystem and a signature scheme based on discrete logarithms. IEEE Trans. Inf. Theor. **31**, 469–472 (1985)
5. Gentry, C.: Fully homomorphic encryption using ideal lattices. In: Mitzenmacher, M. (ed.) 41st ACM STOC, pp. 169–178. ACM Press, May/June 2009
6. Couteau, G., Thomas Peters, D.P.: Encryption switching protocols. Cryptology ePrint Archive, Report 2015/990 (2015). http://eprint.iacr.org/
7. Goldreich, O., Micali, S., Wigderson, A.: How to play any mental game or a completeness theorem for protocols with honest majority. In: Aho, A. (ed.) 19th ACM STOC, pp. 218–229. ACM Press, May 1987
8. Goldreich, O., Micali, S., Wigderson, A.: How to prove all NP-statements in zero-knowledge and a methodology of cryptographic protocol design. In: Odlyzko, A.M. (ed.) CRYPTO 1986. LNCS, vol. 263, pp. 171–185. Springer, Heidelberg (1987)

9. Hazay, C., Mikkelsen, G.L., Rabin, T., Toft, T.: Efficient RSA key generation and threshold paillier in the two-party setting. In: Dunkelman, O. (ed.) CT-RSA 2012. LNCS, vol. 7178, pp. 313–331. Springer, Heidelberg (2012)
10. López-Alt, A., Tromer, E., Vaikuntanathan, V.: On-the-fly multiparty computation on the cloud via multikey fully homomorphic encryption. In: Karloff, H.J., Pitassi, T. (eds.) 44th ACM STOC, pp. 1219–1234. ACM Press, May 2012
11. Paillier, P.: Public-key cryptosystems based on composite degree residuosity classes. In: Stern, J. (ed.) EUROCRYPT 1999. LNCS, vol. 1592, pp. 223–238. Springer, Heidelberg (1999)
12. Schnorr, C.-P.: Efficient identification and signatures for smart cards. In: Quisquater, J.-J., Vandewalle, J. (eds.) EUROCRYPT 1989. LNCS, vol. 434, pp. 688–689. Springer, Heidelberg (1990)
13. Yao, A.C.C.: How to generate and exchange secrets (extended abstract). In: 27th FOCS, pp. 162–167. IEEE Computer Society Press, October 1986

RFID, Sensors and Secure Computation

Survey of Distance Bounding
Protocols and Threats

Agnès Brelurut, David Gerault, and Pascal Lafourcade[(✉)]

University Clermont Auvergne, LIMOS, 63000 Clermont-Ferrand, France
{david.gerault,pascal.lafourcade}@udamail.fr

Abstract. NFC and RFID are technologies that are more and more present in our life. These technologies allow a tag to communicate without contact with a reader. In wireless communication an intruder can always listen and forward a signal, so he can mount a so-called *worm hole* attack. In the last decades, several Distance Bounding (DB) protocols have been introduced to avoid such attacks. In this context, there exist several threat models: Terrorist Fraud, Mafia Fraud, Distance Fraud etc. We first show the links between the existing threat models. Then we list more than forty DB protocols and give the bounds of the best known attacks for different threat models. In some cases, we explain how we are able to improve existing attacks. Then, we present some advices to the designers of the DB protocols and to the intruders to mount some attacks.

Keywords: Distance bounding · Threat models · Mafia fraud · Terrorist fraud · Distance fraud · RFID · NFC · Relay attack · Collusion fraud

1 Introduction

Nowadays, Radio Frequency IDentification (RFID) and Near Field Communication (NFC) technologies and more generally the wireless technologies are increasingly developped. They are commonly used in payments, access-control applications and even in many electronic passports [23]. The main purpose of these technologies is to allow a *reader* (or *verifier*) to communicate wirelessly with *tags* (or *provers*) implanted into objects. In this context, an intruder can simply mount relay attacks just by forwarding some signal and then fake the reader by using the signal of a tag that can be far-away. To avoid such attacks, Distance Bounding (DB) protocols were introduced by Brands and Chaum in 1993 [14]. They are a countermeasure against relay attacks since they measure the round-trip delays during a rapid phase of challenge-response. DB protocols check that provers are close to the verifier in the trusted zone. In the literature, there exist several threat models according to the power and the aim of the intruder:

P. Lafourcade—This research was conducted with the support of the "Digital trust" Chair from the University of Auvergne Foundation.

J. Garcia-Alfaro et al. (Eds.): FPS 2015, LNCS 9482, pp. 29–49, 2016.
DOI: 10.1007/978-3-319-30303-1_3

Distance Fraud [14]: a far-away malicious prover tries to convince the verifier that they are close, while the prover is not in the trusted zone. A practical example is house arrest, where a convict wearing an electronic bracelet is forbidden to leave a given area. If he can mount a distance fraud against the electronic surveillance device, then he can pretend he is within allowed area even though he is far away.

Mafia Fraud (MF) [18]: an adversary between a far-away honest prover and a verifier tries to get advantage of his position to authenticate the prover close to the verifier. The adversary can simply relay the message, but he may also modify the messages involved or create new messages (to the prover or to the verifier). To illustrate this attack, imagine a waiting line in which an attacker would relay the signal between the payment card of a custommer who is at the end of the line and the payment terminal. This allows him to make someone else pay for him.

Terrorist Fraud (TF) [18]: a far-away malicious prover, helped by an adversary, tries to convince the verifier that they are close. In fact, the adversary is close to the verifier and the prover gives information to the adversary, but the adversary cannot impersonate the prover during a further protocol execution. An example is someone wanting to let a friend open his locker once, but not willing to allow him to do it later. In other words, he is willing to provide help only if this help can not be used by the friend to authenticate again in the future.

Impersonation Fraud (IF) [5]: an adversary tries to impersonate the prover to the verifier. The aim can be for instance to make someone else blamed of one's bad actions.

Distance Hijacking (DH) [17]: a far-away prover takes advantage of some honest, active provers (to which one is close) to make the verifier grants privileges for the far-away prover. It can be used to forge an alibi.

Contributions: We first explain the relations between the different threats by distinguishing, on one hand, the threats where the prover is dishonest and, on the other hand, the threats where the prover is honest. Then, we present a survey of DB protocols and for each one we give the success probabilities of the best know attacks. For several protocols we were able to improve some attacks. Our list of protocol contains 42 protocols from 1993 up to 2015. We also present more than 24 attack improvements. Finally, we compile the main attack strategies discovered over the years and list some advices to the designer of DB protocols.

Related Work: Distance Bounding was introduced by Brands and Chaum in 1993 [14] to combat relay attacks. They also introduce the attack that we call *distance fraud*: their protocol prevents to the response bits which are sent out too soon. Before the existence of distance bounding protocols, in 1988, Desmedt identifies the *terrorist fraud* and *mafia fraud* [18]. Then, Avoine & Tchamkerten in 2009 [5] study the *impersonation fraud*. In 2012, Cremers *et al.* find an attack that they called *distance hijacking* in [17]. At the same time, some of them lay the groundwork for formally modelling DB protocols [3,19].

Avoine *et al.* proposed a formal framework for cryptanalyzing the DB protocols in [3]. In particular, they defined the adversary strategies for *mafia* and *terrorist fraud* which they called *no-ask*, *pre-ask* and *post-ask* strategy. Two years later, Dürholz *et al.* proposed in [19] the first computational formal framework for providing properties of DB protocols that are based on shared symmetric keys. They give rigorous cryptographic security models for *mafia*, *terrorist,* and *distance fraud.* The BMV model proposed by Boureanu, Mitrokotsa and Vaudenay in [9] generalizes the previous fraud into three group of threats: *distance fraud*, *Man-In-the-Middle* and *collusion fraud.* By their definitions, the *distance fraud* includes *distance hijacking* and the previous *distance fraud*, the *Man-In-the-Middle* contains the *mafia fraud* and the *impersonation fraud,* and, the *collusion fraud* extends the notion of *terrorist fraud.* But they do not establish relations between these three different threat models.

Some papers [10–13,22,26] compare from four to fourteen protocols to their success probabilities for *distance fraud*, *mafia fraud*, *terrorist fraud* and/or *impersonation fraud* attack. Distance Bounding was studied in the context of RFID but also in ad-hoc networks as in the survey proposed by Meghdadi *et al.* [40].

Outline: In Sect. 2, we show the relationship between different threat models. Then in Sect. 3, we list existing DB protocols and the success probability of attacks against them. Finally before concluding, we give some advices for designing DB protocols and also strategies to mount some attacks in Sect. 4.

2 Relations Between Threats for DB Protocols

In [9], Boureanu *et al.* propose a framework, denoted BMV model, that generalizes the definitions of the previously enumerated common frauds into three possible threats: **distance fraud, man-in-the-middle** and **collusion fraud**.

We present the formal definitions given in [9], then we show how these defintions cover usual threats models and prove some relations between some of these notions.

2.1 Threat Models of [9]

The BMV model [9] offers formal definition about DB protocols and their three threats. In the following, provers are denoted by P, verifiers by V, the adversary by $\mathcal{A}$, and P^* denotes dishonest provers. Provers do not have output, and verifiers have one bit output Out_V, where $Out_V = 1$ denotes acceptance and $Out_V = 0$ denotes rejection.

Definition 1 (Distance-Bounding Protocols [9]). *A Distance Bounding (DB) protocol is defined by a tuple $(Gen, P, V, \mathbb{B})$, where:*

1. *Gen is randomised, key-generation algorithm such that $Gen(1^s; r_k) \mapsto (x, y)$, where r_k are random coins of Gen and s is a security parameter;*

2. $P(x; r_P)$ *is a ppt. ITM[1] running the algorithm of the prover with input x and random input r_P;*
3. $V(y; r_V)$ *is a pp. ITM running the algorithm of the verifier with input y, and random input r_V;*
4. $\mathbb{B}$ *is a distance-bound.*

They must be such that the following two properties hold, where we denote by $d(loc_V, loc_P)$ the distance between the localisation of V and P:

- **Termination:** $(\forall s)(\forall \mathbf{R})(\forall r_k, r_V)$ *if $(., y) \to Gen(1^s; r_k)$ and $\mathbf{R} \leftrightarrow V(y; r_V)$ model the execution, it is the case that V halts in $Poly(s)$ computational steps, where $\mathbf{R}$ is any set of (unbounded) algorithms;*
- **p-completeness:** $(\forall s)(\forall loc_V, loc_P$ *such that $d(loc_V, loc_P) \leq \mathbb{B})$ we have:*

$$\Pr_{r_k, r_P, r_V} \left[Out_V = 1 : \begin{matrix} (x, y) \leftarrow Gen(1^s; r_k) \\ P(x, r_P) \leftrightarrow V(y; r_V) \end{matrix} \right] \geq p$$

Throughout, "Pr_r[event: experiment]" denotes the probability that an event takes place after the experiment has happened, taken on the set of random coins r underlying the experiment. The random variable associated to the event is defined via the experiment leading to the description of a random variable

This model implicitly assumes *concurrency* involving participants that do not share the secret inputs amongst them. In the rest of the paper, $\alpha, \beta, \gamma, \gamma' \in [0; 1]$ and the *View* of a participant on an experiment is the collection of all its initial inputs (including coins) and his incoming messages.

Distance Fraud (DF) [9]: it corresponds to the classical notion, but concurrent runs with many participants are additionally considered, *i.e.*, it includes other possible provers (with other secrets) and verifiers. Consequently, this generalized distance fraud also includes distance hijacking.

Definition 2 (α-resistance to DF [9]**).** A protocol is α-resistant to DF if: $\forall s, \forall P^*, \forall loc_V$ such that $d(loc_V, loc_{P^*}) > \mathbb{B}$, and $\forall r_k$, we have:

$$\Pr_{r_V} \left[Out_V = 1 : \begin{matrix} (x, y) \leftarrow Gen(1^s; r_k) \\ P^*(x) \leftrightarrow V(y; r_V) \end{matrix} \right] \leq \alpha$$

where P^* is any (unbounded) dishonest prover. In a concurrent setting, a polynomially bounded number of honest $P(x')$ and $V(y')$ close to $V(y)$ with independent (x', y') are implicitly allowed.

In others words, a protocol is α-resistance to DF if a far-away prover cannot be authenticated by a verifier with probability more than α.

Man-In-the-Middle (MiM) [9]: this formalization considers an adversary that works in two phases. During a *learning phase*, this adversary interacts with

---

[1] ppt. ITM is for polynomial probabilistic time Interactive Turing Machine.

many honest provers and verifiers. Then, the *attack phase* implies a far-away honest prover of given ID and possibly many other honest provers and other verifiers. The goal of the adversary is to make the verifier accept in a session with ID. Clearly, this generalizes the mafia fraud and includes impersonation fraud.

Definition 3 (β-resistance to MiM [9]). *A protocol is β-resistant to MiM attack if: $\forall s, \forall m, l, z$ polynomially bounded, $\forall \mathcal{A}_1, \mathcal{A}_2$ polynomially bounded, for all locations such that $d(loc_{P_j}, loc_V) > \mathbb{B}$, where $j \in \{m+1, ..., l\}$ we have:*

$$Pr\left[Out_V = 1 : \begin{array}{l} (x, y) \leftarrow Gen(1^s) \\ P_1(x), ..., P_m(x) \leftrightarrow \mathcal{A}_1 \leftrightarrow V_1(y), ..., V_z(y) \\ P_{m+1}(x), ..., P_l(x) \leftrightarrow \mathcal{A}_2(View_{\mathcal{A}_1}) \leftrightarrow V(y) \end{array}\right] \leq \beta$$

over all random coins, where $View_{\mathcal{A}_1}$ is the final view of $\mathcal{A}_1$. In a concurrent setting, a polynomially bounded number of $P(x')$, $P^*(x')$ and $V(y')$ with independent (x', y'), is implicitly allowed anywhere.

A protocol is β-resistant to MiM, if the probability that an adversary authenticates a far-away prover to a verifier is at most β even if the adversary has access to information of a first session run between provers close to verifiers.

Definition 3 separates a *learning phase* (with the adversarial behaviour $\mathcal{A}_1$) from an *attack phase* (with the adversarial behaviour $\mathcal{A}_2$). This definition models a practical setting where an attacker would have cloned several tags (provers) and would make them interact with several readers (verifiers) with which they are registered. From such a multi-party communication, the attacker can get potentially more benefits, in a shorter period of time. To increase his gain, the attacker can set up the learning phase as he pleases (otherwise the learning phase is not obligatory). So, the attacker can place prover-tags close to verifier-readers, even if being an active adversary between two neighbouring P and V is technically more challenging than interfering between two far-away parties.

Collusion Fraud (CF) [9]: this fraud considers a far-away prover holding a secret x who helps an adversary to make the verifier accept. This might be in the presence of many other honest participants. However, there should be no man-in-the-middle attack based on this malicious prover, i.e., the adversary should not extract any advantage from this prover to run (later) a man-in-the-middle attack.

Definition 4 $((\gamma, \gamma')$-resistance to CF [9]). *A protocol is (γ, γ')-resistant to CF if: $\forall s, \forall P^*, \forall loc_{V_0}$ such that $d(loc_{V_0}, loc_{P^*}) > \mathbb{B})$ and $\forall \mathcal{A}^{CF}$ppt. such that:*

$$Pr\left[Out_{V_0} = 1 : \begin{array}{l} (x, y) \leftarrow Gen(1^s) \\ P^*(x) \leftrightarrow \mathcal{A}^{CF} \leftrightarrow V_0(y) \end{array}\right] \geq \gamma$$

over all random coins, there exists a (kind of)^2 MiM attack $m, l, \mathcal{A}_1, \mathcal{A}_2$, $P_i, P_j, V_{i'}$ using P and P^* in the learning phase, such that:

---

^{2} Definition 3 defines MiM attack as using a honest $P(x)$. Here, the definition use $P^*(x)$.

$$Pr\left[Out_V = 1 : \begin{array}{c} (x,y) \leftarrow Gen(1^s) \\ P_1^{(*)}(x), ..., P_m^{(*)} \leftrightarrow \mathcal{A}_1 \leftrightarrow V_1(y), ..., V_z(y) \\ P_{m+1}(x), ..., P_l(x) \leftrightarrow \mathcal{A}_2(View_{\mathcal{A}_1}) \leftrightarrow V(y) \end{array}\right] \geq \gamma'$$

where P^* is any (unbounded) dishonest prover and $P^{(*)}$ runs either P or P^*. Following the MiM requirements, $d(loc_{P_j}, loc_V) > \mathbb{B}$, for all $j \in \{m+1, ..., l\}$. In a concurrent setting, a polynomially bounded number of $P(x')$, $P^*(x')$ and $V(y')$ with independent (x', y') is implicitely allowed, but no honest participant close to V_0.

In others words, a protocol is (γ, γ')-resistant to CF, if when an adversary manages to authenticate a far-away prover to a verifier with probability at least γ, then there exists a further MiM attack (See footnote 2), where an adversary manages to authenticate a far-away prover to the verifier with probability at least γ'.

2.2   Relationship Between Different Threat Models

We prove some relations between some of these properties. In the rest of this section, for a given protocol, $X \rightarrow Y$ denotes that if the property X is satisfied then Y is also satisfied, which is equivalent to say that if there exists an attack on the property Y then there exists an attack on the property X. For a given protocol, we also denote by $X \dashrightarrow Y$ the fact that if there exists an attack on the property Y without sending the secret x then there exists an attack on the property X. For classical threat models, we explain how they can be defined using this formal model.

Theorem 1 (DF $\rightarrow$ DH [9]). *If a protocol is α-resistant to DF then it is also α-resistant to DH.*

Proof. Distance Hijacking is included in the definition of resistance of Definition 2. An experiment in which a dishonest far-away prover P^* may use several provers to get authenticated as one, honest P that is close to the verifier is clearly included in the concurrent setting.

$$(x,y) \leftarrow Gen(1^s)$$
$$P^*(x) \leftrightarrow P_1(x'), .., P_n(x') \leftrightarrow V(y) \qquad \square$$

Theorem 2 (MiM$\rightarrow$MF [9] and MiM $\rightarrow$ IF[9]). *If a protocol is β-resistant to MiM, then it is β-resistant to MF and β-resistant to IF.*

Proof. In Definition 3, the classical notion of mafia fraud corresponds to $m = z = 0$ and $l = 1$. The experiment performing this attack can be described as follows:

$$(x,y) \leftarrow Gen(1^s)$$
$$P(x) \leftrightarrow \mathcal{A} \leftrightarrow V(y)$$

In Definition 3, the classical notion of impersonation corresponds to $l = m$, i.e., there is no prover in the attack phase. The experiment corresponding is:

$$(x, y) \leftarrow Gen(1^s)$$
$$P_1(x), ..., P_m(x) \leftrightarrow \mathcal{A}_1 \leftrightarrow V_1(y), ..., V_z(y)$$
$$\mathcal{A}_2(View_{\mathcal{A}_1}) \leftrightarrow V(y) \qquad\qquad \square$$

Theorem 3 (CF $\rightarrow$ TF [9]). *If a protocol is (γ, γ')-resistant to CF, then it is (γ, γ')-resistant to TF.*

Proof. The notion of terrorist fraud is connected with the Definition 4: it is sufficient to take $m = z = 1$, $l = 2$ and $\mathcal{A}_1$ just runs $\mathcal{A}^{CF}$ in the learning phase, i.e., $\mathcal{A}^{CF}$ gets information to directly impersonate the prover. We can model this fraud by:

$$(x, y) \leftarrow Gen(1^s)$$
$$P^*(x) \leftrightarrow \mathcal{A}_1 \leftrightarrow V(y)$$
$$P(x) \leftrightarrow \mathcal{A}_2(View_{\mathcal{A}_1}) \leftrightarrow V(y) \qquad\qquad \square$$

Theorem 4 (TF $\rightarrow$ DF). *If a protocol is not α-resistant to DF, then there exists an attack of kind TF which succeed with probability at least α.*

Proof. We assume that there exists an attack A of type DF such that: $\Pr[A \text{ succeed}] = \alpha \Leftrightarrow \Pr\left[Out_V = 1 : \begin{matrix}(x, y) \leftarrow Gen(1^s; r_k) \\ P^*(x) \leftrightarrow V(y; r_V)\end{matrix}\right] = \alpha$, where α is not negligible. Then we can elaborate an attack of type TF, only if P^* does not transmit his secret in clear, i.e.:

$$\Pr\left[Out_{V_0} = 1 : \begin{matrix}(x, y) \leftarrow Gen(1^s) \\ P^*(x) \leftrightarrow \mathcal{A}^{TF} \leftrightarrow V_0(y)\end{matrix}\right] \geq \alpha$$

with $\mathcal{A}^{TF}$ who simply relays messages and P^* plays the same role as before. But if P^* and $\mathcal{A}^{TF}$ cooperate, it may be that the attack has a better success probability. $\qquad\qquad \square$

In Fig. 1, we summarize all these relations. On the left there are attacks where the prover is far away and dishonnest, and on the right there are the attacks where the prover is close to the verifier. The arrow from TF (or CF) to DH is obtained by transitivity as well as the arrow from CF to DF. Once an attack is discovered against a property, it is easily to extend it to other properties using these results.

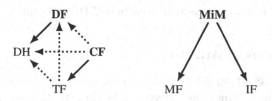

Fig. 1. Relations between different Threats models.

3   Survey

Our aim is to list the utmost number of protocols[3] in order to understand their special features. Table 1 references the success probability of the best known attacks in the literature. The color red highlights the improvements we discovered for some protocols. We do not consider DH threat model in our study since only few papers study this property [17] and mounting such attacks is difficult. We do not recall the description of the protocols for obvious reasons, but for each protocol where we propose one improvement we use the same notations as the ones used in the original paper. However, each DB protocol usually follows this form: one initialization phase where the participant generally share some secret data (often denoted x) or public information often denoted by N_V and N_P respectively for the verifier and the prover. Some encryption, hash function or *Pseudo-Random Function* (PRF) are also often used. Then a fast challenge response phase where usually a sequence of n challenges c_i are sent by the verifier to the prover who answers by some responses denoted r_i. Then the last phase of verification or authentication usually consists in opening a commitment or verifying a common shared data called *transcript*. We present in Fig. 2 the general structure of a DB protocol. In the rest of this section, we explain the new attacks we discovered on some protocols, then the improvements we did for protocols that are using *Pseudo-Random Function* (PRF) in a non appropriated way.

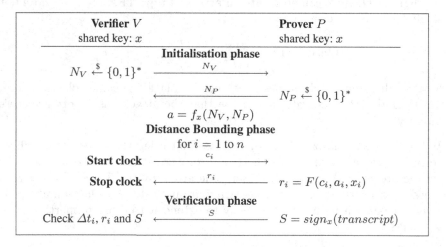

Fig. 2. The general structure of DB protocol.

3.1   Improvements of Attacks

For [5, 7, 20, 31, 34, 38, 41, 49–51, 56], we mount new TF attacks. These attacks all follow the same scheme: the adversary is close to the verifier whereas the

---

[3] Most of the papers are avaible at http://www.avoine.net/rfid/.

prover is far away. During the initialisation phase, the adversary simply relays the messages from the prover to the verifier and the messages from the verifier to the prover. After this phase, the prover computes responses, with the help of his key (the adversary does not have access to this key and the prover does not want him to obtain it). Then the prover sends his responses to his partner (the adversary), so that the adversary can answer to the verifier's challenges in the fast challenge-response phase. The prover sends all the results of these computations because he knows that the adversary cannot recover the shared secret key even if he has access to all results (except for the protocols [28,31] where the adversary receives $n - v$ bits of the secret key). For the last phase, the adversary sends all he receives from the verifier to the prover and so the prover can close the session by sending his signature of the transcript. Using the result about the relation between the threat models we immediately deduce attacks for CF.

We can also see in Table 1 that the column IF is mainly filled with $\left(\frac{1}{2}\right)^s$ (where s is the size of the key). This correspond to the exhaustive research on the key, which is the simplest attack. Most of this column is in red is due to the fact that this threat model is not considered in many papers.

As we can see in Table 2, many of the listed protocols use a PRF [4,5,7, 12,20–22,25,28,29,31,33,34,36–38,41,42,44,45,47,50,51,55,56]. It is possible to mount some attacks if the PRF used follows a certain form. This kind of attacks is first introduced in [8]. By using the idea of [8], we improve some attacks on DF on [7,20–22,34,36,38,42,50,51] and one on MiM on [56]. We detail only one attack on DF and the one on MiM, but for the other protocols we give the PRF construction to mount a successful attack. To succeed during a DF attack, it is necessary for the prover to send his response before receiving the verifier's challenge during the fast challenge-response phase. But, when the PRF's output is split into several parts to precompute responses, using a special PRF the dishonest prover is able to make the response independant of the challenge recieved. We show in Fig. 3 this kind of attack. The PRF f is based on the other PRF g as follows, where z is a special value known by P also called trapdoor:

$$f_x(N_V, N_P) = \begin{cases} a||a & \text{if } N_P = z \\ g_x(N_V, N_P) & \text{otherwise} \end{cases}$$

So this attack succeeds with probability 1.

Munilla and Peinado [42] - DF: let g be a PRF. Let us consider the PRF
$hash$ is constructed as follows: $hash(K, N_a, N_b) = \begin{cases} P||v||v & \text{if } N_b = z \\ g(K, N_a, N_b) & \text{otherwise} \end{cases}$
Consider an instantiation of the Munilla & Peinado protocol where $hash$ is used. In this instance a far-away malicious prover P^* could easily perform a distance fraud attack. By picking N_b equal to z, , he can send the same response r_i regardless of the verifier's challenge c_i . Then, in agreement with this protocol scheme [42] (void challenge-response if $P_i = 1$) if $P_i = 0$ for any challenge c_i the response is the i-th bit of v. If $P_i = 1$, P^* waits a delay

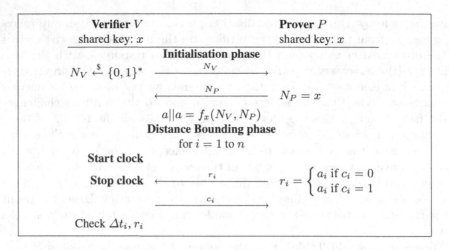

Fig. 3. *Distance fraud* attack against DB protocol using PRF.

before sending the next response r_{i+1}. Thus, if the malicious prover applies this strategy he can defeat the distance-bound.

Kim and Avoine [36] - **DF:** let g be a PRF. The PRF h to perform the DF attack is as follows: $h(K, N_a, N_b) = \begin{cases} T||D||v||v & \text{if } N_b = z \\ g(K, N_a, N_b) & \text{otherwise} \end{cases}$

Benfarah et al. [7] - **DF:** let g be a PRF. We use the PRF f as follows:
$f(k, N_P, N_V) = \begin{cases} S^V||S^P||R||R \text{ if } N_P = z \\ g(k, N_P, N_V) \text{ otherwise} \end{cases}$

Poulidor [50] - **DF:** let g be a PRF. We use the following PRF:
$PRF(x, N_P, N_V) = \begin{cases} 1^{2n}||H^{2n} & \text{if } N_P = z \\ g(x, N_P, N_V) \text{ otherwise} \end{cases}$ where 1^{2n} denotes the number constituted of $2n$ bits equal to 1 and H^{2n} denotes a number of $2n$ random bits.

Kardas et al. [34] - **DF:** we use two PRF f_{K_i} and f_{L_i} based on an other PRF g:

$T = f_{K_i}(r_P, r_V) = \begin{cases} x & \text{if } r_P = z \\ g_{K_i}(r_P, r_V) \text{ otherwise} \end{cases}$ and $f_{L_i}(T) = \begin{cases} v_1||v||v \text{ if } T = x \\ g_{L_i}(T) \text{ otherwise} \end{cases}$

Lee et al. [38] - **DF:** let g be a PRF. The PRF f based on g is as follows:
$f(K, N_V, N_P) = \begin{cases} d||d||v||v & \text{if } N_P = z \\ g(K, N_V, N_P) \text{ otherwise} \end{cases}$

TMA [51] - **DF:** let g be a PRF. We consider the following PRF based on g:
$PRF(x, N_P, N_V) = \begin{cases} 0^n||R||R & \text{if } N_P = z \\ g(x, N_P, N_V) \text{ otherwise} \end{cases}$ where 0^n denotes the number constituted of n bits equal to 0

Baghernejad et al. [22] - **DF:** let g be a PRF. We use the PRF F as follows:
$F(K, N_R, N_T) = \begin{cases} D||a||a & \text{if } N_T = z \\ g(K, N_R, N_T) \text{ otherwise} \end{cases}$

EBT [20] - **DF:** let g be a PRF. We use the PRF h as follows:
$$h(x, N_V, N_P) = \begin{cases} d||d||d||d||d||v||v & \text{if } N_P = z \\ g(x, N_V, N_P) & \text{otherwise} \end{cases}$$

Falahati et al. [21] - **DF:** let g be a PRF. We use the PRF F as follows:
$$F(K, N_U, N_V) = \begin{cases} \text{D a tree with same bit at each level} & \text{if } N_U = z \\ g(K, N_U, N_V) & \text{otherwise} \end{cases}$$

$$F(D, K, C_1, C_2, \ldots, C_i) = \begin{cases} \text{a tree with same bit at} & \text{if D is a tree with} \\ \text{each level} & \text{same bit at each level} \\ g(D, K, C_1, C_2, \ldots, C_i) & \text{otherwise} \end{cases}$$

A MiM attack is successfull when the Man-in-the-Middle adversary recovers the prover's key, or manages to make the verifier accept the authentication of the prover even if the prover is far-away.

Yum et al. [56] - **MiM:** Consider an instantiation of the Yum et al. protocol where $\tau = 1$ and K denotes the shared key. As $\tau = 1$, we have $D = f_\tau(K, N_V, N_P) = 0^n$. So for each round the prover waits a verifier's challenge. Let g be the PRF used to compute $v = g(K, N_V, N_P)$. Let PRF be a PRF and h the PRF based on PRF as follows:
$$Z = h(K, N_V, N_P, C, R) = \begin{cases} K & \text{if } C = 0^{\frac{n}{2}} || v^{\frac{n}{2}} \\ PRF(K, N_V, N_P, C, R) & \text{otherwise} \end{cases}$$

$0^{\frac{n}{2}}$ is the number composed of $\frac{n}{2}$ bits equal to 0 and $v^{\frac{n}{2}}$ — $\mathbf{msb}_{\frac{n}{2}}(f(K, N_V, N_P))$, where $\mathbf{msb}(x)$ denotes the most significant bits of x. The adversary aims to recover the key from the prover, in order to impersonate the prover at any moment. The attacker impersonates the verifier to the prover, he sends an arbitrary N_V to the prover and receives the prover's nonce N_P. The prover computes v. Then the rapid phase of challenge-response begins: for the $\frac{n}{2}$ first rounds, the adversary sends $c_i = 0$, and so he receives the $\frac{n}{2}$ most significant bits (**msb**) of v. For the other half of rounds, the adversary sends one by one the received bits. Then, the prover creates Z and $C = c_1||..||c_n$ such that $C = 0^{\frac{n}{2}} || v^{\frac{n}{2}}$, so in fact by sending Z, the prover sends to the adversary his own secret key K. The attacker is able to impersonate the prover for further executions of the protocol.

3.2 Comparison of DB Protocols

Our survey highlights some points: First, very few protocols are strong against all frauds, only nine protocols insure the security against all kinds of attacks. They are in bold in Tables 1 and 2, and are the following: KZP (2008) [33], Hitomi (2010) [45], NUS (2011) [28], SKI$_{pro}$ (2013) [9], FO (2013) [25], DB1 (2014) [12], DB2 (2014) [12], ProProx (2014) [53] and VSSDB (2014) [26]. The security level for *impersonation fraud* are the same for all these protocols and it is the best security level, *i.e.*, it is equivalent at the security against brute force. Proprox [53] has the best security level against *distance fraud, mafia fraud* and *terrorist fraud* and he is also the most secure against all frauds.

The graph of dependency of protocols, presented in Fig. 4, shows the descendants of some protocols and reveals six families including two large ones (one composed by the descendants of Brands & Chaum and Hancke & Kuhn, the other one by the descendants of Swiss-Knife and SKI$_{pro}$).

Table 1. Summary of the success probability of attacks, where v is such that : for $n - v$ rounds, the adversary knows all responses independently of the challenge's value, and for the v other rounds, for each of them the adversary knows $t - 1$ responses on t values possible for a challenge. For [12], $t \geq 3$. For [48], the last $(n - k)$ bits depend on the first k bits. The number of rounds is always n (expect [39,41,44,46] where there is only one round) and the exponent after the citation is the size of the key. Where $P_1 = \frac{1}{n(|stream_V|-n)(|stream_P|-n)}$, $P_2 = \sum_{t=1}^n \frac{1}{2^t}(\prod_{i=t}^n \max(\Pr(r_1 = c'_i|c_t \neq \tilde{c}_t), ..., \Pr((r_n = c'_i|c_t \neq \tilde{c}_t))) + \frac{1}{2^n}$, $P_3 = \left(\frac{3}{4}\right)^n \times \left(\frac{1}{2}\right)^n + \left(\frac{1}{2}\right)^{n-1} \times \left(1 - \left(\frac{3}{4}\right)^n\right)$, $P_4 = \frac{1}{4}Pr(D_{n-1}) + \frac{1}{2^n} + \frac{1}{8}\sum_{j=1}^{i-1} Pr(D_j)\frac{1}{2^{i-j}}$, $P_5 = \left(\frac{1}{2}\right)^n + Pr(M_n|C_n \neq \widetilde{C_{n-1}})\left(1 - \left(\frac{1}{2}\right)^n\right)$ and $P_6 = \left(\frac{1}{2}\right)^{n-L}\left(\frac{n}{L} + \left(\frac{1}{2}\right)^L\left(1 - \frac{n}{L}\right)\right)$.

Year	Protocol	Success Probability					
		DF	**MiM**	**MF**	**IF**	**CF**	**TF**
1993	$[14]^n$	$\left(\frac{1}{2}\right)^n$ [28]	$\left(\frac{1}{2}\right)^n$ [37]	$\left(\frac{1}{2}\right)^n$ [37]	$\left(\frac{1}{2}\right)^n$	1 [37]	1 [37]
2003	$[16]^n$	$\left(\frac{1}{2}\right)^n$ [28]	$\left(\frac{1}{2}\right)^n$ [10]	$\left(\frac{1}{2}\right)^n$ [37]	$\left(\frac{1}{2}\right)^n$	1 [37]	1 [37]
2004	$[15]^n$	1 [6]	$\left(\frac{1}{2}\right)^n$ [10]	$\left(\frac{1}{2}\right)^n$ [10]	$\left(\frac{1}{2}\right)^n$	1 [6]	1 [6]
2005	$[29]^n$	$\left(\frac{3}{4}\right)^n$ [28] to 1 [8]	$\left(\frac{3}{4}\right)^n$ [37]	$\left(\frac{3}{4}\right)^n$ [37]	$\left(\frac{1}{2}\right)^n$	1 [37]	1 [37]
	$[47]^n$	$\left(\frac{3}{4}\right)^n$ [28] to 1 [8]	$\left(\frac{3}{4}\right)^n$ [37] to 1 [8]	$\left(\frac{3}{4}\right)^n$ [37]	1 [37]	$\left(\frac{3}{4}\right)^v$ [37]	$\left(\frac{3}{4}\right)^v$ [37]
	$[48]^n$	$\left(\frac{1}{2}\right)^k$ [28]	$\left(\frac{1}{2}\right)^n$ [37]	$\left(\frac{1}{2}\right)^n$ [37]	$\left(\frac{1}{2}\right)^n$	1 [37]	1 [37]
2007	$[32]^n$	$\left(\frac{3}{4}\right)^n$ [43]	$\left(\frac{9}{16}\right)^n$ [43] to 1 [37]	$\left(\frac{9}{16}\right)^n$ [43]	1 [37]	$\left(\frac{3}{4}\right)^v$ [43]	$\left(\frac{3}{4}\right)^v$ [43]
	$[39]^s$	$\left(\frac{1}{2}\right)^{|N_V|}$ [39]	$\left(\frac{1}{2}\right)^{|N_V|}$ [39]	$\left(\frac{1}{2}\right)^{|N_V|}$ [39]	$\left(\frac{1}{2}\right)^s$	1 [39]	1 [39]
	$[46]^n$	$\left(\frac{1}{2}\right)^n$ [46]	P_1 [41]	P_1 [41]	$\left(\frac{1}{2}\right)^n$	1 [2]	1 [2]
2008	$[33]^s$	$\left(\frac{3}{4}\right)^n$ [33]	$\left(\frac{1}{2}\right)^n$ [33]	$\left(\frac{1}{2}\right)^n$ [33]	$\left(\frac{1}{2}\right)^s$	$\left(\frac{3}{4}\right)^V$ [33]	$\left(\frac{3}{4}\right)^V$ [33]
	$[42]^n$	$\left(\frac{3}{5}\right)^n$ [28] to 1	$\left(\frac{3}{5}\right)^n$ [42]	$\left(\frac{3}{5}\right)^n$ [42]	$\left(\frac{1}{2}\right)^n$	1 [28]	1 [28]
	$[44]^n$	$1/k$ [44]	$\left(\frac{1}{2}\right)^n$ [44]	$\left(\frac{1}{2}\right)^n$ [44]	$\left(\frac{1}{2}\right)^n$ [44]	1 [37]	1 [37]
	$[5]^n$	$\left(\frac{3}{4}\right)^n$ to 1 [8]	$\left(\frac{1}{2}\right) \times \left(\frac{n}{2} + 1\right)$ [5]	$\left(\frac{1}{2}\right) \times \left(\frac{n}{2} + 1\right)$ [5]	$\left(\frac{1}{2}\right)^n$	1	1
2009	$[37]^n$	$\left(\frac{3}{4}\right)^n$ [37]	$\left(\frac{1}{2}\right)^n$ [37] to 1 [8]	$\left(\frac{1}{2}\right)^n$ [37]	1 [8]	$\left(\frac{3}{4}\right)^v$ [37]	$\left(\frac{3}{4}\right)^v$ [37]
	$[36]^n$	$\left(\frac{7}{8}\right)^n$ [36] to 1	$\left(\frac{1}{2}\right)^n$ [36]	$\left(\frac{1}{2}\right)^n$ [36]	$\left(\frac{1}{2}\right)^n$	1 [28]	1 [28]
	$[49]^s$	$\left(\frac{1}{2}\right)^n$ [49]	$\left(\frac{1}{2}\right)^n$ [49]	$\left(\frac{1}{2}\right)^n$ [49]	$\left(\frac{1}{2}\right)^s$	1	1
	$[7]^s$	$\left(\frac{3}{4}\right)^n$ to 1	$\left(\frac{4x^2-1}{4x^3}\right)^n$ [7]	$\left(\frac{4x^2-1}{4x^3}\right)^n$ [7]	$\left(\frac{1}{2}\right)^s$	1	1
2010	$[7]^s$	$\left(\frac{3}{4}\right)^n$ to 1	$\left(z\left(\frac{5}{2} - 2z\right)\right)^n$ [7]	$\left(z\left(\frac{5}{2} - 2z\right)\right)^n$ [7]	$\left(\frac{1}{2}\right)^s$	1	1
	$[45]^n$	$\left(\frac{1}{2}\right)^n$ [45]	$\left(\frac{1}{2}\right)^n$ [45]	$\left(\frac{1}{2}\right)^n$ [45]	$\left(\frac{1}{2}\right)^n$	$\left(\frac{3}{4}\right)^V$ [45]	$\left(\frac{3}{4}\right)^V$ [45]
	$[50]^n$	$\left(\frac{1}{2}\right)^n$ to 1	P_2 [50]	P_2 [50]	$\left(\frac{1}{2}\right)^n$	1	1
	$[4]^n$	$\left(\frac{3}{4}\right)^n$ [4] to 1 [8]	$\left(\frac{2}{3}\right)^n$ [4] to 1 [8]	$\left(\frac{2}{3}\right)^n$ [4]	1 [8]	$\left(\frac{5}{6}\right)^v$ [4]	$\left(\frac{5}{6}\right)^v$ [4]
2011	$[56]^n$	$\left(\frac{1}{2}\right)^{\tau n}$ [35]	$\left(\frac{1}{2}\right)^n$ [35] to 1	$\left(\frac{1}{2}\right)^n$ [35]	$\left(\frac{1}{2}\right)^n$ to 1	1	1
	$[28]^n$	$\left(\frac{3}{4}\right)^n$ [1]	$\left(\frac{1}{2}\right)^n$ [28]	$\left(\frac{1}{2}\right)^n$ [28]	$\left(\frac{1}{2}\right)^n$ [28]	$\left(\frac{3}{4}\right)^V$	$\left(\frac{3}{4}\right)^V$
	$[34]^{2s}$	$\left(\frac{3}{4}\right)^n$ to 1	$\left(\frac{1}{2}\right)^n$ [34]	$\left(\frac{1}{2}\right)^n$ [34]	$\left(\frac{1}{2}\right)^{2s}$	1	1
	$[55]^n$	$\left(\frac{3}{4}\right)^n$ [55] to 1 [24]	$\left(\frac{3}{4}\right)^n$ [55]	$\left(\frac{3}{4}\right)^n$ [55]	$\left(\frac{1}{2}\right)^n$	1 [24]	1 [24]
2012	$[38]^n$	$\left(\frac{3}{4k}\right)^n$ to 1	$\left(\frac{2k+1}{4k}\right)^n$ [38]	$\left(\frac{2k+1}{4k}\right)^n$ [38]	$\left(\frac{1}{2}\right)^n$	1	1
	$[41]^s$	$\left(\frac{1}{2}\right)^n$ [41]	$\left(\frac{1}{2}\right)^n$ [41]	$\left(\frac{1}{2}\right)^n$ [41]	$\left(\frac{1}{2}\right)^s$	1	1
	$[31]^n$	$\left(\frac{3}{4}\right)^n$ [31]	P_3 [31] to 1 [22]	P_3 [31]	1 [22]	$\left(\frac{3}{4}\right)^v$	$\left(\frac{3}{4}\right)^v$
	$[9]^s$	$\left(\frac{3}{4}\right)^n$ [9]	$\left(\frac{2}{3}\right)^n$ [9]	$\left(\frac{2}{3}\right)^n$ [9]	$\left(\frac{1}{2}\right)^s$	$\left(\frac{5}{6}\right)^v$ [11]	$\left(\frac{5}{6}\right)^v$ [11]
2013	$[25]^{2s}$	$\left(\frac{3}{4}\right)^n$ [52]	$\left(\frac{3}{4}\right)^n$ [52]	$\left(\frac{3}{4}\right)^n$ [52]	$\left(\frac{1}{2}\right)^{2s}$	$\left(\frac{3}{4}\right)^V$ [52]	$\left(\frac{3}{4}\right)^V$ [52]
	$[30]^s$	$\left(\frac{3}{4}\right)^n$ [30]	$\left(\frac{1}{2}\right)^n$ [30]	$\left(\frac{1}{2}\right)^n$ [30]	$\left(\frac{1}{2}\right)^s$ [30]	1 [30]	1 [30]
	$[27]^s$	$\left(\frac{3}{4}\right)^n$ [27]	$\left(\frac{1}{2}\right)^n$ [27]	$\left(\frac{1}{2}\right)^n$ [27]	$\left(\frac{1}{2}\right)^{|G|}$ [27]	1 [27]	1 [27]
	$[12]^s$	$\left(\frac{1}{t}\right)^n$ [12]	$\left(\frac{1}{t}\right)^n$ [12]	$\left(\frac{1}{t}\right)^n$ [12]	$\left(\frac{1}{2}\right)^s$	$\left(\frac{t-1}{t}\right)^v$ [12]	$\left(\frac{t-1}{t}\right)^v$ [12]
	$[12]^s$	$\left(\frac{1}{\sqrt{2}}\right)^n$ [12]	$\left(\frac{1}{2}\right)^n$ [12]	$\left(\frac{1}{2}\right)^n$ [12]	$\left(\frac{1}{2}\right)^s$	$\left(\frac{1}{\sqrt{2}}\right)^v$ [12]	$\left(\frac{1}{\sqrt{2}}\right)^v$ [12]
2014	$[12]^s$	$\left(\frac{1}{t}\right)^n$ [12]	$\left(\frac{1}{t}\right)^n$ [12]	$\left(\frac{1}{t}\right)^n$ [12]	$\left(\frac{1}{2}\right)^n$	1 [12]	1 [12]
	$[53]^s$	$\left(\frac{1}{\sqrt{2}}\right)^{ns}$ [53]	$\left(\frac{1}{2}\right)^{ns}$ [53]	$\left(\frac{1}{2}\right)^{ns}$ [53]	$\left(\frac{1}{2}\right)^s$ [53]	$\left(\frac{1}{\sqrt{2}}\right)^{ns}$ [53]	$\left(\frac{1}{\sqrt{2}}\right)^{ns}$ [53]
	$[51]^s$	P_4 [51]	P_5 [51]	P_5 [51]	$\left(\frac{1}{2}\right)^s$	1	1
	$[26]^s$	$\left(\frac{3}{4}\right)^n$ [26]	$\left(\frac{1}{2}\right)^n$ [26]	$\left(\frac{1}{2}\right)^n$ [26]	$\left(\frac{1}{2}\right)^{2s}$ [26]	$\left(\frac{3}{4}\right)^V$ [26]	$\left(\frac{3}{4}\right)^V$ [26]
	$[20]^s$	$\left(\frac{k+2}{4k}\right)^n$ [20] to 1	$\left(\frac{k+2}{4k}\right)^n$ [20]	$\left(\frac{k+2}{4k}\right)^n$ [20]	$\left(\frac{1}{2}\right)^s$	1	1
	$[21]^n$	$\left(1 + \frac{n}{2}\right)\left(\frac{1}{2}\right)^n$ [21] to 1	$\left(1 + \frac{n}{2}\right)\left(\frac{1}{2}\right)^n$ [21]	$\left(1 + \frac{n}{2}\right)\left(\frac{1}{2}\right)^n$ [21]	$\left(\frac{1}{2}\right)^n$	P_6 [21]	P_6 [21]
	$[22]^n$	$\left(\frac{3}{4}\right)^n$ [22] to 1	P_3 [22]	P_3 [22]	$\left(\frac{1}{2}\right)^s$ [22]	1 [22]	1 [22]
2015	$[54]^s$	$\left(\frac{3}{4}\right)^n$ [54]	$\left(\frac{3}{4}\right)^n$ [54]	$\left(\frac{3}{4}\right)^n$ [54]	$\left(\frac{1}{2}\right)^s$	1 [54]	1 [54]

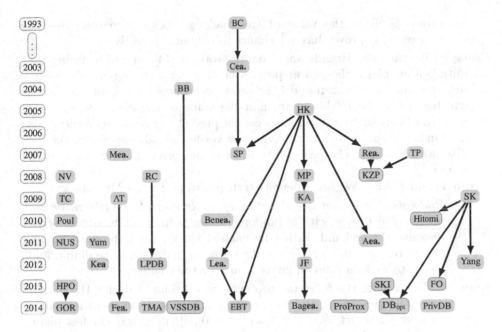

Fig. 4. Graph of dependency of protocols.

4 Tool Box

For each fraud, we describe the different strategies known to increase the chances for a successful attack.

4.1 Attack Strategies

We list all types of attacks that we have found in our survey. For each strategy we also give a simple example.

Distance Fraud (DF): We identified several techniques to mount DF attacks:
- Protocols using two possible responses (one for $c_i = 1$ and the other for $c_i = 0$): the prover computes the two possible responses in advance and examines if they are equal or not. If they are, then the prover responds correctly. Else, he responds randomly.

Example: We consider a protocol which, during the fast phase, uses two independent values: v^0 and v^1. At each round i, the prover responds either v_i^0 if $c_i = 0$ or v_i^1 if $c_i = 1$, v_i^0 and v_i^1 denote respectively the ith bit of v^0 and v^1. So at each round i, the prover has a $\frac{1}{2}$ chance of having $v_i^0 = v_i^1$, and so he responds correctly regardless of the verifier's challenge c_i, or $v_i^0 \neq v_i^1$, and so the prover sends a random response before receiving the challenge c_i to counter the distance bounding. To summmarize, the probability that the prover responds correctly at each round is $\frac{1}{2} \times 1 + \frac{1}{2} \times \frac{1}{2} = \frac{3}{4}$.

- Protocols using the value of the challenge recieved to compute the response: the prover has a $\frac{1}{2}$ chance to respond correctly.

Example: We take the Brands and Chaum protocol [14], in which during the initialisation phase the prover picks a bit-string m. During the challenge-response phase, at each round i the prover computes his response with m_i, which denotes the ith bit of m, and the value of the challenge c_i: $r_i = m_i \oplus c_i$. In this context, the prover cannot predict any response, so he sends his random response before receiving the verifier's challenge to counter the distance bounding. The probability to have the correct answer is $\frac{1}{2}$ at each round.

Mafia Fraud (MF): We list different strategies to perform a MF attack:

- *Protocols that do not use signature of the transcript:* the adversary can pre-ask the prover with a random challenge in order to obtain some responses beforehand. Either he guessed the challenge properly and is able to respond upon recieving the verifier's challenge, or he didn't, and he has to make a random guess to answer the challenge.

Example: We consider the following protocol with 3 rounds: during the initialisation phase, the prover and the verifier compute two values as responses for the next phase, let $v^0 = 1||0||1$ and $v^1 = 0||1||1$ be them. The fast phase runs as follows: the verifier sends a challenge c_i. After receiving the challenge, the prover sends v_i^0 if $c_i = 0$ and v_i^1 if $c_i = 1$ where v_i^0 and v_i^1 denote respectively the ith bit of v^0 and v^1. To authenticate the prover, the verifier checks the response and the round-trip delay time. An adversary between the prover and the verifier, mounts a MF attack as follows. Before the fast phase, he sends to the prover the following challenges: 1, 0, 1. So he receives these responses: 0, 0, 1. Now, he waits for the challenges from the verifier, we suppose they are: 0, 0, 1. For the first round, the adversary does not know the value of v_1^0 so he responds randomly, but for the others challenges he knows the value of the response. Here, the probability of the adversary responds correctly is $\frac{1}{2}$ (the probability to guess correctly the first response), instead of $\left(\frac{1}{2}\right)^3$ (the probability to guess all responses) if he does not ask the prover before.

- *Protocols using signature of the transcript:* The adversary cannot pre-ask the prover in order to have some guaranteed responses, because any wrong guess would change the transcript. Since he is not able to forge a valid signature on a different transcript, he must not alter it.

Example: We consider a protocol in which during the verification phase, the prover sends a signature of R and C, respectively the concatenation of the responses and the challenges transmitted during the fast phase. Because of that, the adversary must not alter the transcript. He can either try to guess the challenge and use a pre ask strategy, or the response by using a post ask strategy. In the latter, he forwards the legitimate challenge to the prover after answering it. We note that both strategies are equivalent in this case, since in both scenarios, the adversary has $\left(\frac{1}{2}\right)^n$ to guess either the challenge or the response for the n successive rounds.

Impersonation Fraud (IF): We enumerate the ways to impersonate the prover:

  – We suppose the prover is close to the verifier. The adversary can play several MiM to recover all key bits.

Example: We consider a protocol where during the first phase, verifier and prover compute two values v and k where v is the result of a function (often a PRF) and k is $k = v \oplus x$. During the challenge response phase, the prover sends v_i if $c_i = 0$ and k_i if $c_i = 1$. An adversary A can impersonate a prover by recovering the secret x during a *man-in-the-middle*. To learn a bit x_i of that key, A can, during the fast bit exchange, toggle the value of challenge bit c_i when it is transmitted from the verifier to prover and leave all other messages unmodified. The attacker then observes the verifier's reaction. As a matter of fact, if the verifier accepts the prover, it means that the prover's answer r_i was nevertheless correct, and thus that $v_i = k_i$. As $k_i = v_i \oplus x_i$, A concludes that $x_i = 0$. Similarly, if the verifier refuses the prover, the adversary concludes that $x_i = 1$.

  – The adversary can always use the exhaustive research to find the key.

Example: For all protocols, the adversary can always make an assumption on the prover's key and try it by running the protocol with the verifier.

Terrorist Fraud (TF): We show two techniques to increase the chance of success of a TF attack:

  – In some protocols, the far-away prover can send his partner A a table that contains all $c_i \mapsto r_i$, without revealing his secret key, so A can respond correctly during the fast phase but he cannot impersonate the prover during an other session.

Example: We consider a protocol which, during the fast phase, uses two independent values: v^0 and v^1. They are obtained from a PRF and do not give any information about the secret key. At each round i, the prover responds either v_i^0 if $c_i = 0$ or v_i^1 if $c_i = 1$, where v_i^0 and v_i^1 denote respectively the ith bit of v^0 and v^1. After computing v^0 and v^1, the far away prover can send all values to his partner, allowing him to successfully run the fast phase with the verifier.

  – In some cases, the far-away prover cannot send his partner the same table as above, because giving both possible answers for all rounds would leak his secret. Then A would be able to impersonate the prover during an other session. To avoid this, and nevertheless be authenticated to the verifier, the prover sends a table where some entries are correctly computed and others are fully random. Like this, his partner performs the rapid phase of challenge-response with the verifier in some cases and he cannot recover all bits of the secret key. This strategy is particularly efficient for protocols that assume a noisy communication channel and allow some errors.

Example: We consider a protocol which during the first phase, verifier and prover compute two values v and k where v is the result of a function and k is $k = v \oplus x$. During the challenge response phase, the prover sends v_i if $c_i = 0$

and k_i if $c_i = 1$. With this protocol, the prover cannot send his partner the complete values of k and v because the partner would recover the key x by computing $x = k \oplus v$. But the prover can send v', which is v where some bits are replaced by random ones. He can similarly generate k' This way, the partner cannot recover all bits of the key but he can respond correctly to a large number of the verifier's challenges, and so increases the chance to the prover to be authenticated by the verifier.

PRF: Protocols using PRF to pre-compute response for the fast phase are often exposed to a DF attack, and protocols using PRF to compute the signature of the *transcript* are often exposed to a MiM attack which permits to the adversary to impersonate the prover.

Example: In Sect. 3.1, we propose such attacks based on PRF construction and show how several protocols using PRF are not protected from DF attack or MiM attack.

4.2　Design

Through our readings, we compile some protocol's features in the Table 2 and we could see that protocol's particularities prevent some attacks described above. We present these features, as guidelines for the construction of secure protocols.

Transcript: We note that the presence of the (signed) *transcript* in the verification phase prevents Mafia Fraud attacks. Indeed, it prevents the adversary from using a pre ask strategy to improve his success probability since the verifier aborts the protocol if the challenges do not correspond to the adversary's challenges. So, all the protocols [12, 14–16, 25–27, 30, 34, 37, 45, 48, 56] that use the signature of the *transcript*, have a success probability to MF at $\left(\frac{1}{t}\right)^n$ where t denotes the number of possible values for a challenge. Except the FO protocol [25], because it uses two modes of execution: one verifies the transcript and the other not.

PRF Output: From the moment where the output of the PRF is cut into several parts like in [4, 5, 7, 20–22, 29, 34, 36, 38, 42, 50, 51, 55], it is possible to mount an attack using PRF construction (see Sect. 3.1) and so an DF attack can be successful. All protocols cited before bear the consequences of this risk. Then it is better to avoid splitting the result of a PRF in order to avoid such kind of attacks like in [12, 25, 28, 33, 37, 44, 45, 47, 56].

Specifics Responses: – Some protocols [14, 56] use two complementary values to respond to the verifier's challenge to prevent DF attack, in other words for a challenge equal to 0 the verifier waits the value $r_i = v_i$ and for the challenge equal to 1 the verifier waits the value $r_i = \bar{v}_i$. Then a dishonest prover cannot predict responses for all rounds.

– Protocols [5, 16, 21, 48, 50, 51] use all challenges received to compute the response r_i. Because of this, an adversary between the verifier and the prover has a lower chance to guess the string of challenges (and so to have correct repsonses).

Table 2. Features of the protocols, where ✓ denotes the presence of the feature and ✗ denotes the absence of the feature. The number next to ✓ represent the number of cutting of the PRF's output during the initialisation phase.

Protocol	PRF	$Sign$(transcript)	based on
Brands and Chaum (1993) [14]	✗	✓	
Capkun et al. (2003) [16]	✗	✓	BC [14]
Bussard and Bagga (2004) [15]	✗	✓	
Hancke and Kuhn (2005) [29]	✓2	✗	
Ried et al. (2007) [47]	✓1	✗	HK [29]
Singele & Preneel (2007) [48]	✗	✓	Cea. [16] and HK [29]
Tu & Piramuthu (2007) [32]	✗	✗	
Meadows et al. (2007) [39]	✗	✗	
RČ (2008) [46]	✗	✗	
KZP (2008) [33]	✓1	✗	Rea. [47] and TP [32]
Munilla & Peinado (2008) [42]	✓3	✗	HK [29]
Nikov & Vauclair (2008) [44]	✓1	✗	
Avoine & Tchamkerten (2009) [5]	✓2	✗	
Swiss-Knife (2009) [37]	✓1	✓	
Kim & Avoine (2009) [36]	✓4	✗	MP [42]
Tippenhauer & Capkun (2009) [49]	✗	✗	
Benfarah et al. A (2010) [7]	✓4	✗	
Benfarah et al. B (2010) [7]	✓4	✗	
Hitomi (2010) [45]	✓1	✓	SK [37]
Poulidor (2010) [50]	✓2	✗	
Avoine et al. (2011) [4]	✓n-1	✗	HK [29]
Yum et al. (2011) [56]	✓1	✓	
NUS (2011) [28]	✓1	✗	
Kardas et al. (2012) [34]	✓3	✓	
Yang et al. (2012) [55]	✓3	✗	SK [37]
Lee et al. (2012) [38]	✓4	✗	HK [29]
LPDB (2012) [41]	✓2	✗	RČ [46]
Jannati & Falahati (2012) [31]	✓2	✗	KA [36]
SKI$_{pro}$ (2013) [9]	✓1	✗	
Fischlin & Onete (2013) [25]	✓1	✓	SK [37]
HPO (2013) [30]	✗	✓	
GOR (2014) [27]	✗	✓	HPO [30]
DB1 (2014) [12]	✓1	✓	SKI [9] and SK [37]
DB2 (2014) [12]	✓1	✓	SKI [9] and SK [37]
DB3 (2014) [12]	✓1	✓	SKI [9] and SK [37]
ProProx (2014) [53]	✗	✗	
TMA (2014) [51]	✓3	✗	
VSSDB (2014) [26]	✗	✓	BB [15]
EBT (2014) [20]	✓6	✗	HK [29] and Lea. [38]
Falahati et al. (2014) [21]	✓1	✗	AT [5]
Baghernejad et al. (2014) [22]	✓3	✗	JF [31]
PrivDB (2015) [54]	✗	✗	

5   Conclusion

We first used the model proposed in [9] to review how classical threat models are covered by this general framework. Then we explicited some relations between these notions. Our main contribution is the list of existing attacks for 42 DB protocols of the literature. For 17 of them we were able to improve the best known attacks. Finally from this experience we could extract the common features to the most secure protocols, and compile them into a tool box that can be used to design safe protocols.

In the future, we would like to improve the classification of all these protocols and possibly extract the best features of each to build new, more robust ones. Another extension is to study DH property for all these protocols, which is a recent threat model and for which it is not always obvious to mount some attacks. In the same vein, the anonimity and privacy properties are more and more studied in new protocols, hence it would be interesting to include them in future work.

References

1. Abyaneh, M.R.S.: Security analysis of two distance-bounding protocols (2011). CoRR abs/1107.3047
2. Aumasson, J.-P., Mitrokotsa, A., Peris-Lopez, P.: A note on a privacy-preserving distance-bounding protocol. In: Qing, S., Susilo, W., Wang, G., Liu, D. (eds.) ICICS 2011. LNCS, vol. 7043, pp. 78–92. Springer, Heidelberg (2011)
3. Avoine, G., Bingöl, M.A., Kardas, S., Lauradoux, C., Martin, B.: A formal framework for cryptanalyzing RFID distance bounding protocols. IACR Crypt. ePrint Arch. **2009**, 543 (2009)
4. Avoine, G., Lauradoux, C., Martin, B.: How secret-sharing can defeat terrorist fraud. In: Wisec 2011, pp. 145–156. ACM (2011)
5. Avoine, G., Tchamkerten, A.: An efficient distance bounding RFID authentication protocol: balancing false-acceptance rate and memory requirement. In: Samarati, P., Yung, M., Martinelli, F., Ardagna, C.A. (eds.) ISC 2009. LNCS, vol. 5735, pp. 250–261. Springer, Heidelberg (2009)
6. Bay, A., Boureanu, I., Mitrokotsa, A., Spulber, I., Vaudenay, S.: The bussard-bagga and other distance bounding protocols under man-in-the-middle attacks. In: Inscrypt (2012)
7. Benfarah, A., Miscopein, B., Gorce, J., Lauradoux, C., Roux, B.: Distance bounding protocols on TH-UWB radios. In: GLOBECOM, pp. 1–6 (2010)
8. Boureanu, I., Mitrokotsa, A., Vaudenay, S.: On the pseudorandom function assumption in (secure) distance-bounding protocols. In: Hevia, A., Neven, G. (eds.) LatinCrypt 2012. LNCS, vol. 7533, pp. 100–120. Springer, Heidelberg (2012)
9. Boureanu, I., Mitrokotsa, A., Vaudenay, S.: Practical and provably secure distance-bounding. IACR Crypt. ePrint Arch. **2013**, 465 (2013)
10. Boureanu, I., Mitrokotsa, A., Vaudenay, S.: Secure and lightweight distance-bounding. In: Avoine, G., Kara, O. (eds.) LightSec 2013. LNCS, vol. 8162, pp. 97–113. Springer, Heidelberg (2013)
11. Boureanu, I., Mitrokotsa, A., Vaudenay, S.: Towards secure distance bounding. In: Moriai, S. (ed.) FSE 2013. LNCS, vol. 8424, pp. 55–68. Springer, Heidelberg (2014)

12. Boureanu, I., Vaudenay, S.: Optimal proximity proofs. In: Lin, D., Yung, M., Zhou, J. (eds.) Inscrypt 2014. LNCS, vol. 8957, pp. 170–190. Springer, Heidelberg (2015)
13. Boureanu, I., Vaudenay, S.: Challenges in distance bounding. IEEE Secur. Priv. **13**(1), 41–48 (2015)
14. Brands, S., Chaum, D.: Distance bounding protocols. In: Helleseth, T. (ed.) EURO-CRYPT 1993. LNCS, vol. 765, pp. 344–359. Springer, Heidelberg (1994)
15. Bussard, L., Bagga, W.: Distance-bounding proof of knowledge to avoid real-time attacks. In: IFIP SEC 2005 (2005)
16. Capkun, S., Buttyn, L., Hubaux, J.-P.: Sector: secure tracking of node encounters in multi-hop wireless networks. In: ACM Workshop on Security of Ad Hoc and Sensor Networks (SASN), pp. 21–32 (2003)
17. Cremers, C., Rasmussen, K.B., Schmidt, B., Capkun, S.: Distance hijacking attacks on distance bounding protocols. In: IEEE S & P (2012)
18. Desmedt, Y.: Major security problems with the "unforgeable" (feige-)fiat-shamir proofs of identity and how to overcome them. In: Securicom 1988, pp. 147–159 (1988)
19. Dürholz, U., Fischlin, M., Kasper, M., Onete, C.: A formal approach to distance-bounding RFID protocols. In: Lai, X., Zhou, J., Li, H. (eds.) ISC 2011. LNCS, vol. 7001, pp. 47–62. Springer, Heidelberg (2011)
20. Entezari, R., Bahramgiri, H., Tajamolian, M.: A mafia and distance fraud high-resistance RFID distance bounding protocol. In: ISCISC, pp. 67–72 (2014)
21. Falahati, A., Jannati, H.: All-or-nothing approach to protect a distance bounding protocol against terrorist fraud attack for low-cost devices. Electron. Commer. Res. **15**(1), 75–95 (2015)
22. Fatemeh Baghernejad, M.S., Bagheri, N.: Security analysis of the distance bounding protocol proposed by Jannati, Falahati. Electr. Comput. Eng. **2**(2), 85–92 (2014)
23. Finkenzeller, K.: RFID Handbook: Fundamentals and Applications in Contactless Smart Cards and Identification, 2nd edn. Wiley, New York (2003)
24. Fischlin, M., Onete, C.: Provably secure distance-bounding: an analysis of prominent protocols. IACR Crypt. ePrint Arch. **2012**, 128 (2012)
25. Fischlin, M., Onete, C.: Terrorism in distance bounding: modeling terrorist-fraud resistance. In: Jacobson, M., Locasto, M., Mohassel, P., Safavi-Naini, R. (eds.) ACNS 2013. LNCS, vol. 7954, pp. 414–431. Springer, Heidelberg (2013)
26. Gambs, S., Killijian, M.-O., Lauradoux, C., Onete, C., Roy, M., Traoré, M.: VSSDB: A verifiable secret-sharing and distance-bounding protocol. In: Balkan-CryptSec 2014 (2014)
27. Gambs, S., Onete, C., Robert, J.: Prover anonymous and deniable distance-bounding authentication. IACR Crypt. ePrint Arch. **2014**, 114 (2014)
28. Özhan Gürel, A., Arslan, A., Akgün, M.: Non-uniform stepping approach to RFID distance bounding problem. In: Garcia-Alfaro, J., Navarro-Arribas, G., Cavalli, A., Leneutre, J. (eds.) DPM 2010 and SETOP 2010. LNCS, vol. 6514, pp. 64–78. Springer, Heidelberg (2011)
29. Hancke, G.P., Kuhn, M.G.: An RFID distance bounding protocol. In: SECURECOMM 2005, pp. 67–73. IEEE Computer Society, Washington, DC (2005)
30. Hermans, J., Peeters, R., Onete, C.: Efficient, secure, private distance bounding without key updates. In: WISEC 2013, pp. 207–218 (2013)
31. Hoda Jannati, A.F.: Mutual implementation of predefined and random challenges over RFID distance bounding protocol. In: ISCISC, pp. 43–47 (2012)

32. ju Tu, Y., Piramuthu, S.: RFID distance bounding protocols. In: First International EURASIP Workshop on RFID Technology (2007)
33. Kapoor, G., Zhou, W., Piramuthu, S.: Distance bounding protocol for multiple RFID tag authentication. In: IEEE/IPIP EUC 2008, pp. 115–120 (2008)
34. Kardaş, S., Kiraz, M.S., Bingöl, M.A., Demirci, H.: A novel RFID distance bounding protocol based on physically unclonable functions. In: Juels, A., Paar, C. (eds.) RFIDSec 2011. LNCS, vol. 7055, pp. 78–93. Springer, Heidelberg (2012)
35. Kim, C.H.: Security analysis of YKHL distance bounding protocol with adjustable false acceptance rate. IEEE Commun. Lett. **15**(10), 1078–1080 (2011)
36. Kim, C.H., Avoine, G.: RFID distance bounding protocol with mixed challenges to prevent relay attacks. In: Garay, J.A., Miyaji, A., Otsuka, A. (eds.) CANS 2009. LNCS, vol. 5888, pp. 119–133. Springer, Heidelberg (2009)
37. Kim, C.H., Avoine, G., Koeune, F., Standaert, F.-X., Pereira, O.: The swiss-knife RFID distance bounding protocol. In: Lee, P.J., Cheon, J.H. (eds.) ICISC 2008. LNCS, vol. 5461, pp. 98–115. Springer, Heidelberg (2009)
38. Lee, S., Kim, J.S., Hong, S.J., Kim, J.: Distance bounding with delayed responses. IEEE Commun. Lett. **16**(9), 1478–1481 (2012)
39. Meadows, C., Poovendran, R., Pavlovic, D., Chang, L., Syverson, P.F.: Distance bounding protocols: authentication logic analysis and collusion attacks. In: Secure Localization and Time Synchronization for Wireless Sensor and Ad Hoc Networks, pp. 279–298 (2007)
40. Meghdadi, M., Ozdemir, S., Gler, I.: A survey of wormhole-based attacks and their countermeasures in wireless sensor networks. IETE Tech. Rev. **28**(2), 89–102 (2011)
41. Mitrokotsa, A., Onete, C., Vaudenay, S.: Mafia fraud attack against the RČ distance-bounding protocol. RFID-TA **2012**, 74–79 (2012)
42. Munilla, J., Peinado, A.: Distance bounding protocols for RFID enhanced by using void-challenges and analysis in noisy channels. Wirel. Commun. Mob. Comput. **8**(9), 1227–1232 (2008)
43. Munilla, J., Peinado, A.: Security analysis of tu and piramuthu's protocol. NTMS **2008**, 1–5 (2008)
44. Nikov, V., Vauclair, M.: Yet another secure distance-bounding protocol. SECRYPT **2008**, 218–221 (2008)
45. Peris-Lopez, P., Castro, J.C.H., Estévez-Tapiador, J.M., van der Lubbe, J.C.A.: Shedding some light on RFID distance bounding protocols and terrorist attacks (2009). CoRR abs/0906.4618
46. Rasmussen, K.B., Capkun, S.: Location privacy of distance bounding protocols. CCS **2008**, 149–160 (2008)
47. Reid, J., Nieto, J.M.G., Tang, T., Senadji, B.: Detecting relay attacks with timing-based protocols. In: ASIACCS 2007, pp. 204–213. ACM (2007)
48. Singelée, D., Preneel, B.: Distance bounding in noisy environments. In: Stajano, F., Meadows, C., Capkun, S., Moore, T. (eds.) ESAS 2007. LNCS, vol. 4572, pp. 101–115. Springer, Heidelberg (2007)
49. Tippenhauer, N.O., Čapkun, S.: ID-based secure distance bounding and localization. In: Backes, M., Ning, P. (eds.) ESORICS 2009. LNCS, vol. 5789, pp. 621–636. Springer, Heidelberg (2009)
50. Trujillo-Rasua, R., Martin, B., Avoine, G.: The poulidor distance-bounding protocol. In: Ors Yalcin, S.B. (ed.) RFIDSec 2010. LNCS, vol. 6370, pp. 239–257. Springer, Heidelberg (2010)
51. Trujillo-Rasua, R., Martin, B., Avoine, G.: Distance-bounding facing both mafia, distance frauds: technical report (2014). CoRR abs/1405.5704

52. Vaudenay, S.: On modeling terrorist frauds. In: Susilo, W., Reyhanitabar, R. (eds.) ProvSec 2013. LNCS, vol. 8209, pp. 1–20. Springer, Heidelberg (2013)
53. Vaudenay, S.: Proof of proximity of knowledge. IACR ePrint Arch. **2014**, 695 (2014)
54. Vaudenay, S.: Private and secure public-key distance bounding. In: Böhme, R., Okamoto, T. (eds.) FC 2015. LNCS, vol. 8975, pp. 207–216. Springer, Heidelberg (2015)
55. Yang, A., Zhuang, Y., Wong, D.S.: An efficient single-slow-phase mutually authenticated RFID distance bounding protocol with tag privacy. In: Chim, T.W., Yuen, T.H. (eds.) ICICS 2012. LNCS, vol. 7618, pp. 285–292. Springer, Heidelberg (2012)
56. Yum, D.H., Kim, J.S., Hong, S.J., Lee, P.J.: Distance bounding protocol with adjustable false acceptance rate. IEEE Commun. Lett. **15**(4), 434–436 (2011)

Inferring Touch from Motion in Real World Data

Pascal Bissig[✉], Philipp Brandes, Jonas Passerini, and Roger Wattenhofer

ETH Zurich, Zürich, Switzerland
{pascal.bissig,philipp.brandes,jonas.passerini,roger.wattenhofer}@ethz.ch
http://www.disco.ethz.ch/

Abstract. Most modern smartphones are equipped with motion sensors to measure the movement and orientation of the device. On Android and iOS, accessing the motion sensors does not require any special permissions. On the other hand, touch input is only available to the application currently in the foreground because it may reveal sensitive information such as passwords. In this paper, we present a side channel attack on touch input by analyzing motion sensor readings. Our data set contains more than a million gestures from 1'493 users with 615 distinct device models. To infer touch from motion inputs, we use a classifier based on the Dynamic Time Warping algorithm. The evaluation shows that our method performs significantly better than random guessing in real world usage scenarios.

Keywords: Motion sensing · Side-channel attack · Touch input

1 Introduction

Smartphones have become an integral part of our daily lives. Motion sensors measure the movement and orientation of such devices which are useful to, e.g., adjust the screen orientation or to control games. These sensors are not considered to reveal sensitive information. Therefore, they can be accessed by any application installed on the device, even by applications running in the background. This holds for Android as well as iOS devices, together making up more than 90 % of the market share in mobile operating systems in 2014. For security reasons, the same does not apply for touch screen input. Only foreground apps are granted access to touch input data since it reveals, among other things, characters being typed on the on-screen keyboard which may include passwords or private information in text messages. However, when touching the screen of a phone, the phone will also move. Depending on the usage scenario this motion might be very small and hard to track, for example when the phone is lying on a table. Interaction with handheld mobile devices usually causes the device to move so much that the built in accelerometer and gyroscope sensors are able to track this motion. In addition to that, it has been shown that this motion varies, as different areas of the screen are being touched. This tight relation between touch and motion raises the question: how well one can infer touch from motion input? Being able to do so presents a security threat for most of today's smartphones.

© Springer International Publishing Switzerland 2016
J. Garcia-Alfaro et al. (Eds.): FPS 2015, LNCS 9482, pp. 50–65, 2016.
DOI: 10.1007/978-3-319-30303-1_4

Mobile devices are by design used in a large variety of environments that directly influence the motion sensor readings. This drastically complicates the task of inferring touch from motion and therefore has to be taken into account when evaluating any inference mechanism. To build a data set that reflects variable real world environments, we collect data through an Android game. Players are not instructed to hold or interact with the device in a specific way. Therefore, we do not know or take into account if a player is sitting in a train or walking while playing.

The player's task is to memorize and imitate patterns that mimic the lock-screen patterns found on most current mobile operating systems.

We describe how an attacker could collect both touch and motion data to train a classifier, that can be used to derive touch input in any application being used on the device under attack. We use the Dynamic Time Warping (DTW) algorithm to compare and classify gestures and evaluate classification accuracy for touch inputs. By performing this side channel attack, an attacker can steal passwords or at least reduce the number of guesses required to do so. Our results are based on a large scale user study that covers arbitrary and unknown usage scenarios, 1'493 users and 615 of different Android device models. We show that varying environmental influences impact performance heavily.

2   Related Work

Touch-Motion Side Channel Attacks. Motion sensors have previously been used for side channel attacks. In most cases data was recorded in controlled environments, thereby reducing the impact of real world effects such as varying user activities. An attacker cannot be sure that motion data was recorded when the user was sitting still, instead the user might be walking or riding a train.

Examples of such results include the paper by Cai and Chen [3], who showed that side channel attacks on touch input using motion sensors are feasible in a lab environment. Aviv et al. [2] collected data from 26 participants while sitting or walking. Although this study helps understanding the effects of added disturbances, the environment is still controlled and known. The study with the largest data set has been performed by Cai et al. [4]. They collected 47'814 keystrokes from 21 test persons, with 4 devices in a lab setting. Miluzzo et al. [11] performed a study comparing multiple classification algorithms with data from 10 test persons while sitting or standing. Although their results identify how to best infer touch from motion input, their data set also limits the applicability of their results in the real world. The work of Xu et al. [15] focuses on tap gestures and describes a game which collects training gestures when running in the foreground and test gestures when running in the background. However, their data set spans only three users and was recorded in a controlled environment. Owusu et al. [13] focus on random forests to detect passwords on smartphones by analyzing the accelerometer readings of 4 test persons. Other studies [7,16] show that smartphone users can be distinguished based on their touch and motion input behavior. Hinckley et al. [6] show that the combination of touch and motion data can be used to create novel ways to interact with our mobile devices.

In contrast to the papers described above, we focus on collecting data in uncontrolled environments. Namely, our data set originates from users that were primarily concerned with playing a game on their smartphone and were not instructed about how and where to do so. The environments may range from office spaces to airplanes or trains. Since our data acquisition process can be replicated by an attacker, our data set allows us to assess how realistic a side channel attack on touch input really is. We collected data from 1'493 test users, which generated more than a million gestures on 615 distinct device models. This is roughly 50 to 200 times more participants and up to 20 times more gestures than in previous studies. To our knowledge, there is no similar work with the same magnitude of collected data in similarly unconstrained environments.

Smartphone Side Channel Attacks. Touch input was not the only target of side channel attacks using motion sensor data. Liu et al. [8] tried to infer three-dimensional, free-hand movements using accelerometer readings. They collected 4'480 gestures from 8 test persons over several weeks. With (sp)iPhone, Marquardt et al. [9] developed a mechanism to infer input on a physical keyboard by analyzing the motion sensor readings of a phone laying next to the keyboard. The proof of concept Android application Gyrophone [10] demonstrates that it is possible to recognize speech using a gyroscope sensor. Niu et al. [12] used Dynamic Time Warping to measure the similarity of gestures to authenticate users. Recognizing ten distinct gestures, Chong et al. [5] used the motion sensors to unlock the phone by performing a user defined series of gestures. Since the gesture detection is performed independently of the user and the raw information is not used in the authentication process, this is very similar to a password composed of ten letters that are entered through performing gestures instead of pressing keys.

3   Data Collection

To simulate a realistic attack scenario, we decided not to invite test persons into a test laboratory with a predefined and controlled environment. Instead, we developed an Android game, which we distributed on the Google Play store[1] to collect data. The same method can be used by an attacker and might already be exploited. In the game, the player's task is to memorize and reproduce patterns on the screen as shown in Fig. 1. The patterns are displayed in the bottom half of the screen, where one usually finds the keyboard or pin input field. As the levels get harder, the grid resolution is increased from 3×3 to 4×4 touch elements, which we call cells. The game not only asks the user to press specific cells in this area, which we call tap gesture, but also to connect cells using swipe gestures. In contrast to an attacker, we informed users upon installation and first launch of the game that motion data is collected for research purposes and only

---

[1] Game on Google Play. https://play.google.com/store/apps/details?id=ch.ethz. pajonas.ba.imitationgame.android (2015-03-13).

when the game is running in the foreground. Touch input is measured in terms of x, y coordinates or a series of them for swipe gestures. In addition to touch input, the game also records the x, y, z coordinates of both accelerometer and gyroscope sensors built into the device. All recorded data is linked to a randomly generated unique id that is generated when the game is first installed. Since different users might play the game on the device, this unique id is device (and not user) specific. In addition to this, we collect basic device information such as the device manufacturer and type. When connected to a WLAN, the compressed log files are sent to a central database. When analyzing users with bad classification performance, we observed that their motion sensor measurements contain random readings close to zero. This indicates, that the device might not be moving enough, possibly being placed on a table or otherwise fixed. We excluded such users from our experiments. The number of users evaluated for each experiment are mentioned in the respective sections.

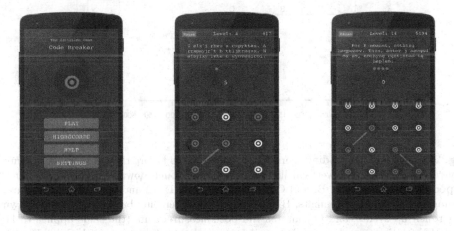

Fig. 1. Screens of the game showing the main menu, and both the 3×3 as well as the 4×4 grid the player interacts with during the game.

4   Preprocessing

The motion data is first segmented using the touch input as ground truth. To account for device motion that occurs before and after the screen is touched, we leave a variable amount of sensor readings before the touch gesture starts and after it ends. The time window is at most 100 ms. Figure 2 illustrates the segmentation process in more detail. This segmentation can also be performed in an attack scenario, at least for the training data collection phase, using the same technique. For the classification task, we can use device events to segment motion data. For example, power on and unlock events provided by the operating system can be used to segment pattern or pin inputs performed to unlock the device.

To remove the effects of gravity and gyroscope drift, we remove the mean values for each individual sensor axis. We thereby implicitly assume that the device orientation and velocity is the same at the beginning and at the end of each gesture.

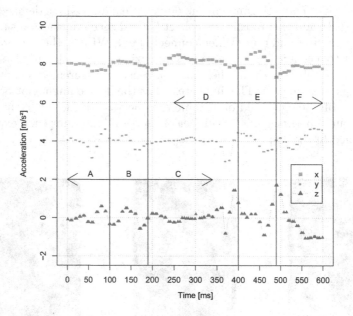

Fig. 2. Accelerometer readings containing two gestures before they get segmented into separated gestures. The vertical lines represent the touch down and touch up events respectively. Segments A, B, and C describe the first, D, E, and F the second gesture. A marks the pre-measurements, B encloses all measurements between the touch down and touch up events, and C contains the post measurements (the same applies to D, E, and F for the second gesture). C and D may overlap, but not C with E nor D with B. The length of the segments A and C (D and F respectively) may vary and are set to 150 ms in this example.

5   Classification

We do not attempt to guess the exact pixel the user touched, but rather predict the cell, which was pressed or swiped by the user. We build a classifier for each separate unique id and assume an id to relate to one single player although multiple users might play the game on the same device. To quantify the similarity of two gestures, we use the DTW algorithm [1] with varying cost functions to compare individual time samples as described in Sect. 5.1. The user model M consists of 10 motion sensor recordings for each cell i on the grid M_i. In order to classify a test gesture t, our algorithm computes the DTW distance to all samples in M and selects the cell with the minimal DTW distance (see Eq. 1). We also evaluated different metrics, such as the average and median DTW distance (Eq. 2).

$$\text{class}(t) = \arg\min_x \min_{i \in M_x} \text{dtw}(t, i) \tag{1}$$

$$\text{class}(t) = \arg\min_x \left(\frac{1}{|M_x|} \sum_{i \in M_x} \text{dtw}(t, i) \right) \tag{2}$$

However, the average DTW distance is not robust against outliers in the training set, and therefore was expected to produce worse results than the min and median distances. Alternative classification techniques used in similar work are Hidden Markov Models [2] or feature based approaches, Support Vector Machines [14].

5.1 Dynamic Time Warping Cost Functions

To perform the time series analysis using the DTW algorithm, we need to select features, which we can use to describe the distance or matching cost between two sensor events from two different gestures. Each motion sensor event consists of 3 accelerometer and 3 gyroscope measurements, one for each spatial dimension. These 6 coordinates form a feature vector $A = \{\text{acc}_x,\ \text{acc}_y,\ \text{acc}_z,\ \text{gyro}_x,\ \text{gyro}_y, \text{gyro}_z\}$, representing the values of the $x, y,$ and z accelerometer and gyroscope coordinates of a single sensor event in a touch or swipe gesture. One possible metric to calculate the distance between two sensor events is the Euclidean distance, as Niu et al. suggest in their work [12]. Cai et al. [4] propose a different feature, calculating the two-argument arctangent (atan2) using the x and y axis of the accelerometer readings, arguing that motion data on the z axis is not a good feature to infer keystrokes (see Eq. 3). We designed a new metric which pairwise calculates atan2 for all accelerometer and gyroscope axes combinations and then sums up their absolute differences (Eq. 4). The equations below show how those three metrics are used to compare two sensor events i, and j in two different gestures A and B. Variations of the metrics above and others like the Manhattan distance or the L_∞-norm are also included in our experiments. The Manhattan distance is the sum of the accelerometer and gyroscope differences between two measurements.

$$c_{acc}^{xy}(A_i, B_j) = \left| \text{atan2}(A_{acc}^{i,x}, A_{acc}^{i,y}) - \text{atan2}(B_{acc}^{j,x}, B_{acc}^{j,y}) \right| \tag{3}$$

$$c_{acc}(A_i, B_j) = c_{acc}^{xy}(A_i, B) + c_{acc}^{xz}(A_i, B_j) + c_{acc}^{yz}(A_i, B_j)$$

$$c_{sum}(A_i, B_j) = c_{acc}(A_i, B_j) + c_{gyro}(A_i, B_j) \tag{4}$$

5.2 Dynamic Time Warping Penalty

In order to penalize sequences whose time axis needs to be stretched a lot, we employ different penalization factors p. See Eq. 5 for the recursive definition of an entry in the DTW matrix $d(i, j)$. In the penalization experiment, we use the c_{sum} distance metric to compare two measurements A_i and B_j at times i and j respectively. By increasing p, the cost of advancing time i and j unevenly is penalized. This leads to a higher DTW matching cost for sequences of uneven length or speed.

$$d(i, j) = \min\{ \; d(i-1, j-1) + c_{sum}(A_i, B_j) \\ d(i, j-1) \quad + c_{sum}(A_i, B_j) \cdot p \\ d(i-1, j) \quad + c_{sum}(A_i, B_j) \cdot p \; \} \tag{5}$$

6   Data Set

At the end of the 4 month data collecting phase, the game reached 2'049 installations. Most of the users are from India, USA, Italy, or Switzerland. The Android application received 70 ratings in the Google Play Store, with an average rating of 4.01 stars out of 5. The most used device to play the game is the Google Nexus 5. Figure 3 shows that most players' phones are produced by Samsung, and the most popular Android version is 4.4. Data has been collected from 615 device models with over 38 different screen sizes. The server application received data from 1'493 users, who played a total of 87'962 levels. With an average of 15 gestures per level, this corresponds to more than a million collected gestures. Since the data has not been collected in a laboratory, it contains unknown external influences on the motion data, devices with malfunctioning motion sensors, and users with very few gestures.

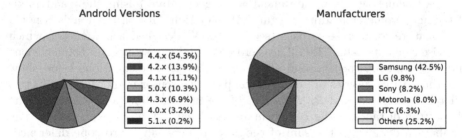

Fig. 3. Variety of the devices and Android versions on which we collected our data set. Data has been collected from 615 distinct device models from 25 manufacturers with over 38 different screen sizes.

7   Evaluation Setup

A training gesture is a gesture for which we know the motion sensor readings as well as the ground truth touch data, which we collected with our Android application. A test gesture on the other hand, is a gesture for which the touch input is ignored and the task is to infer the correct touch gesture using only the motion sensor readings. Only users with working accelerometer and gyroscope sensors are included in the experiments. Not all players generated enough data to generate a model for each cell. In these cases, we only classify cells with at least 10 recorded training gestures. Hence, a user might have fewer than 9 or 16 cells with enough training data. The random guessing probability is adapted to compensate for the reduced solution space of the classification problem. To generate enough training data for every single cell, a user is required to interact with the Android application for about 30 min. Depending on the experiment, between 10 and 500 players were used to evaluate performance changes.

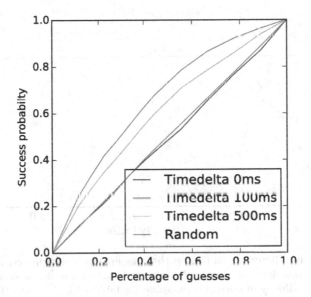

Fig. 4. Comparison of different segmentation time windows. A larger window means that there are more pre- and post- measurements. In this plot, tap gestures on the 3 × 3 board from 14 users have been evaluated

7.1 Segmentation Time Window

The segmentation time window controls the number of pre- and post-measurements of each gesture. This window can be varied to optimize the classification performance since the device moves already before touch input is registered. For this experiment, we use our sum of atan2 cost function as described in Eq. 4. The DTW penalty is set to 240 % and we use the min classification method as described in Eq. 1. Figure 4 shows different time windows of the length 0 ms, 100 ms, and 500 ms. Including no measurements that are recorded before the touch gesture starts produced bad results. This leads to the conclusion that the motion of the device before the touch event actually starts is the most discriminant. The time window of 500 ms also performs significantly worse than 100 ms, which is why we chose 100 ms for all the other experiments. In our work, we do not focus on the segmentation of the test gestures. To detect the unlock pattern, it seems to be sufficient to trigger the measurements using the unlock events of the smartphone. To infer PIN entries or multiple gestures, one would need to segment the test gestures. According to previous results [4, 15], there exist promising segmentation methods to achieve this.

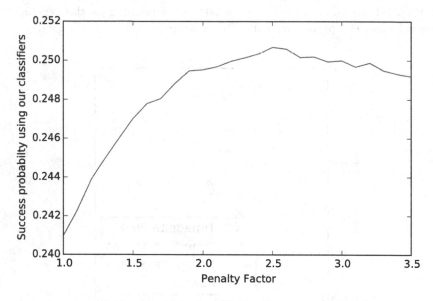

Fig. 5. Influence of different penalties on the classification performance. In this experiment, all users have been evaluated for tap gestures on the 3 × 3 board. We have evaluated the probability of correctly guessing the label with the first attempt.

7.2   *DTW* Penalty

To evaluate the effect of varying DTW time penalties, we analyzed the classification results from all players on the 3 × 3 grid utilizing the sum of atan2 metric as described in Eq. 4 and the min classification method as described in Eq. 1. We evaluate the penalty in the range of $p = 100\,\%$ to $p = 350\,\%$ in 10 % increments. Figure 5 shows the effect of a varying DTW penalty. As expected, penalties that are very small or large result in worse performance. For very small penalties, sequences can be stretched beyond what is to expect due to the natural variance each user causes. In case of very high penalties, the DTW algorithm mostly matches sequences without stretching either time axis, resulting in a score that is very close to the sum of all corresponding sample costs. The best classification results can be achieved with p at 240 % but as one can see, the performance differences are marginal for non extreme choices of p.

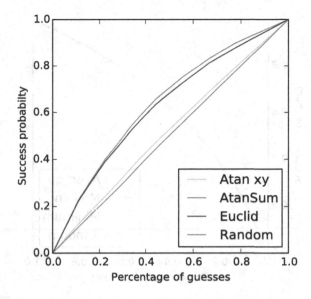

Fig. 6. Comparison of the distance metrics used in the DTW algorithm (described in Sect. 5.1). The sum over all atan2 features performs best and is used as the distance metric for the other experiments. In this plot, all users have been evaluated for tap gestures on the 3×3 board.

7.3 DTW Cost Functions

Figure 6 shows the comparison of the four presented distance metrics in the DTW algorithm. For this experiment, all users were evaluated using a DTW penalty of 240 %. Our proposed sum over all atan2 features metric performs slightly better than the atan2 function and is therefore chosen as the distance metric in all other experiments. The euclidean distance function performs worse than both of the other distance metrics, but still much better than other metrics we tested (Manhattan, L_∞) which we omit on this plot.

7.4 Classification Methods

The performance comparison for the presented classification distance metrics for all users on the 3×3 grid is shown in Fig. 7. The DTW penalty was set to 240 %. Interestingly, performance variations are insignificant for all three methods. Since our training sets may include outliers, we expected the average method to perform significantly worse than the min and median method, respectively. If the user e.g., bumped into someone or walked up steps while performing the tap gesture, then this outlier will skew the results and make the classification task more difficult. The minimum distance method performed best in this experiment and is therefore used in the other evaluation tasks.

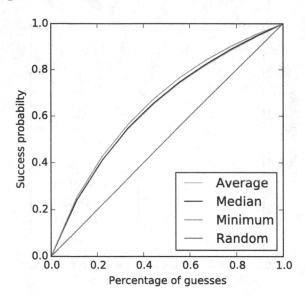

Fig. 7. Comparison of the classification methods min, mean and median as described in Sect. 5. The min metric performs best and is used for the other experiments. In this plot, all users have been evaluated on the 3×3 board.

7.5   External Influences

To evaluate the impact of changing environments, we compare the performance of heavy- and light-users while using a fixed training set of 10, a DTW penalty of 240 %, the min classification method (Eq. 1), and the sum of atan2 features. Heavy users played more levels and hence, produced more data. We expect their data set not only to be bigger, but also to contain more varied environments. Since we limit the training set size to 10 for both user groups, we expect the performance for heavy users to be bad since the small training set cannot capture all environments the game was played in. Figure 8a shows the 20 users with the most collected gestures (heavy) in blue and the 20 users with the least gestures in red (light) out of more than 200 users in total. Guessing the correct cell in the first try for the bottom 20 users is with 29 % roughly 10 % higher than for the top 20 users (19 %).

7.6   Training Set Size

The results in the previous section beg to evaluate the same two user groups while using larger training sets for the heavy users. Performance for heavy users should increase as the training set captures more environments. To evaluate the effect of varying training set size, we lifted the restriction to only use 10 and instead trained our model with as all available samples for each user. This means that only the test gesture is excluded from the training set. Thereby we remove the advantage of light users being able to capture a larger fraction of

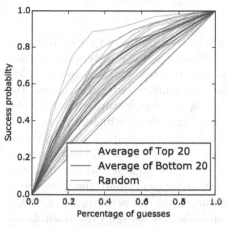 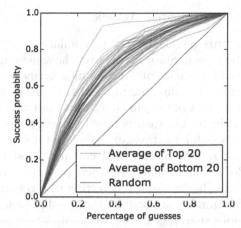

(a) Performance comparison between heavy- and light users with fixed training set size. The environments in which heavy users played the game cannot be captured by a small training set size. Therefore, small training sets are sufficient, as long as the environmental effects are similar in both the training and testing phase.

(b) Impact of varying training set sizes on the classification performance. In this experiment, all training samples were used for each user on the 3×3 grid. Users with the most training data (in blue) show similar performance as compared to the users with the least training data (in red).

Fig. 8. Classification performance heavily depends on the range of environments in which the motion data is recorded (Color figure online).

the environmental effects in the training set when compared to the heavy users. In our data set this means that the training set can be up to two orders of magnitude larger. Classification was performed using the min metric (Eq. 1). Figure 8b shows the 20 users with the most collected gestures in blue and the 20 users with the least gestures in red (out of more than 200 users in total). The classification rate of the top 20 users differs insignificantly (1.5 % on the first guess) from the bottom 20.

Since both heavy- and light-users are tested using training sets that capture all environments the game was played in, performance is consistent for both user groups. For an attacker, this means that small training set sizes are sufficient, as long as the environment under which touch input inference should be performed is similar to the one predominant during training data set collection.

Both the experiment on the training set size, as well as the one on the environmental effects were performed using the exact same two user groups. As long as the training set captured the external influences affecting the classification phase, performance is insensitive to the size of the training set. Collecting a large training set therefore helps capturing more environmental influences but does not allow the classification accuracy to improve significantly once an environment has been captured.

7.7 Repeated Attack

In this section we try to emulate an attack on the user's pin code to unlock the screen. Since users enter the same pin code over and over again, an attacker could use multiple motion measurements to improve the guessing accuracy. We know that after turning on the screen, the first number entered is always the first digit of the pin code. Thus, instead of using one test gesture, we use several of them. The task is now to classify these gestures, about which we know that they belong to the same label, but not to which one. The simplest approach is to cast a vote for each test gesture's most likely label according to the previously described method and then pick the label with the highest number of votes. Note that we limit our setting to k gestures in order to evaluate the influence of the number of votes on the classification accuracy we can achieve. If a user has more than k gestures, we limit it to k artificially and we keep the training set size fixed to 10.

The results are shown in Fig. 9. As one can seen in Fig. 9a, the chance to correctly guess the label in the first attempt increases with k. The chance dramatically increases for very small values of k. Performance stagnates around 40 % when using more than 20 test gestures at once and starts deteriorating when using more than 35 test gestures. We believe that this is because of the limited training set size for users as discussed in Sect. 7.6. If we only consider users with more than 30 gestures per label, then these users need to have a lot

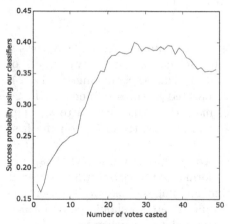

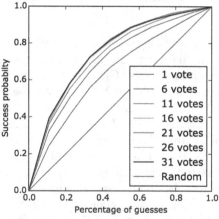

(a) The probability of guessing the correct label for a given set of test gestures improves from less than 20% to more than 40% when increasing k from 1 to 27 test gestures

(b) Not only the first guess accuracy improves, but all consecutive guesses are more accurate as well. More than 50% of gestures are classified correctly in two guesses.

Fig. 9. Credentials are often entered repeatedly. By collecting the data repeatedly the same input, we can reduce the influence of noise in the measurements. The accuracy of the attack increases as the number test gestures available to guess one label grows.

of gestures and thus have played the game in varying environments. Hence, the more we increase k, the noisier the data gets. Thus, the advantage of having more votes to cancel out noise is balanced out by more noise introduced by later samples. As show in Fig. 9b the performance not only increases for the first guess, but helps predicting the correct gesture with higher accuracy also for the following guesses. In our case, the peak performance of 40 % of first guesses being correct was reached when using 27 test gestures. This means that an attacker can more easily guess pins or passwords that are repeatedly entered.

In addition to that, the attacker needs to solve the problem of recognizing repeated inputs. In case of device unlock pins or patterns, this is easily achieved through events triggered by the operating system.

8   Additional Observations

We observed a heavy preference in which direction a gesture is performed. Most people have a preference on how they imitate a certain pattern. A pattern with a straight horizontal line can either be drawn with a swipe gesture from left to right or a swipe gesture from right to left. The same applies for vertical or diagonal lines. We analyzed the behavior of 452 users. The results are shown in Fig. 10. One can see that most of the people prefer to perform the vertical gestures downwards and the horizontal gestures from left to right. When it comes to the diagonal gestures, there is an overall preference for the "Down - Right" gesture instead of the opposite direction, but for the "Up - Right" respectively "Down - Left" gestures, there is less of a general preference.

The profiles created in the previous subsection may reveal further information about the user. For single test persons, we observed that the gesture preference

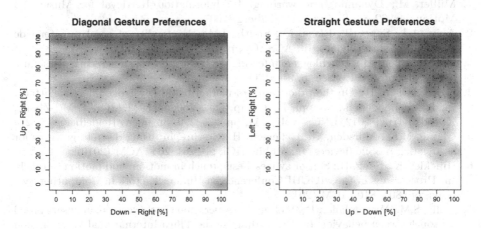

Fig. 10. Gesture preferences of 452 analyzed users. "Down - Right" indicates a downward diagonal line from left to right, "Up - Right" an upward diagonal line from left to right. "Up - Down" is a downward, vertical line, "Left - Right" a horizontal line from left to right.

may be related to the handedness of the user. We could not confirm this claim, since we did not collect the corresponding ground truth data with the Android application. In future work, one could collect this data from test users to answer this question.

9   Conclusion

In this paper, we discussed a side channel attack on touch input by analyzing motion sensor readings. Firstly, we collected data by distributing an Android application. Secondly, we trained a DTW based classifier using the collected data to infer touch gestures. In contrast to similar work, we collected real world data in a way an attacker could also do. The evaluation has shown that the side channel attack presents a realistic threat. Especially for touch input which is repeated often, such as unlock patterns or pin codes, motion sensor data can help an attacker to guess the correct touch input.

As opposed to software vulnerabilities, the side channel attack we analyzed in this paper is not caused and cannot be fixed by app developers. Background access to motion sensors needs to be limited on the operating system level because otherwise no application can protect itself against these attacks. Since we expect motion sensors to become more accurate in the future, the risk of a successful side channel attack grows even further. With mobile payment solutions becoming more and more popular, the incentive to spy on touch input on mobile devices increases.

References

1. Müller, M.: Dynamic time warping. In: Information Retrieval for Music and Motion, pp. 69–84. Springer, Heidelberg (2007)
2. Aviv, A.J., Sapp, B., Blaze, M., Smith, J.M.: Practicality of accelerometer side channels on smartphones. In: ACSAC, pp. 41–50. ACM (2012)
3. Cai, L., Chen, H.: Touchlogger: inferring keystrokes on touch screen from smartphone motion. In: HotSec, p. 9 (2011)
4. Cai, L., Chen, H.: On the practicality of motion based keystroke inference attack. In: Katzenbeisser, S., Weippl, E., Camp, L.J., Volkamer, M., Reiter, M., Zhang, X. (eds.) Trust 2012. LNCS, vol. 7344, pp. 273–290. Springer, Heidelberg (2012)
5. Chong, M.K., Marsden, G., Gellersen, H.: Gesturepin: using discrete gestures for associating mobile devices. In: Mobile HCI, pp. 261–264. ACM (2010)
6. Hinckley, K., Song, H.: Sensor synaesthesia: touch in motion, and motion in touch. In: Proceedings of the SIGCHI Conference on Human Factors in Computing Systems, pp. 801–810. ACM (2011)
7. Kolly, S.M., Wattenhofer, R., Welten, S.: A personal touch: recognizing users based on touch screen behavior. In: Proceedings of the Third International Workshop on Sensing Applications on Mobile Phones, p. 1. ACM (2012)
8. Liu, J., Wang, Z., Zhong, L., Wickramasuriya, J., Vasudevan, V.: uwave: accelerometer-based personalized gesture recognition and its applications. In: PerCom, pp. 1–9. IEEE Computer Society (2009)

9. Marquardt, P., Verma, A., Carter, H., Traynor, P.: (sp)iphone: decoding vibrations from nearby keyboards using mobile phone accelerometers. In: ACM CCS, pp. 551–562. ACM (2011)
10. Michalevsky, Y., Boneh, D., Nakibly, G.: Gyrophone: recognizing speech from gyroscope signals. In: 23rd USENIX Security Symposium, pp. 1053–1067. USENIX Association, San Diego, August 2014
11. Miluzzo, E., Varshavsky, A., Balakrishnan, S., Choudhury, R.R.: Tapprints: your finger taps have fingerprints. In: MobiSys, pp. 323–336. ACM (2012)
12. Niu, Y., Chen, H.: Gesture authentication with touch input for mobile devices. In: Prasad, R., Farkas, K., Schmidt, A.U., Lioy, A., Russello, G., Luccio, F.L. (eds.) MobiSec 2011. LNICST, vol. 94, pp. 13–24. Springer, Heidelberg (2012)
13. Owusu, E., Han, J., Das, S., Perrig, A., Zhang, J.: Accessory: password inference using accelerometers on smartphones. In: Proceedings of the Twelfth Workshop on Mobile Computing Systems and Applications, HotMobile 2012, pp. 9: 1–9: 6. ACM, New York (2012)
14. Wu, J., Pan, G., Zhang, D., Qi, G., Li, S.: Gesture recognition with a 3-D accelerometer. In: Zhang, D., Portmann, M., Tan, A.-H., Indulska, J. (eds.) UIC 2009. LNCS, vol. 5585, pp. 25–38. Springer, Heidelberg (2009)
15. Zhi, X., Bai, K., Zhu, S.: Taplogger: inferring user inputs on smartphone touchscreens using on-board motion sensors. In: WISEC, pp. 113–124. ACM (2012)
16. Zheng, N., Bai, K., Huang, H., Wang, H.: You are how you touch: user verification on smartphones via tapping behaviors. In: IEEE 22nd International Conference on Network Protocols (ICNP), pp. 221–232. IEEE (2014)

Point-Counting Method for Embarrassingly Parallel Evaluation in Secure Computation

Toomas Krips[2,3]($\boxtimes$) and Jan Willemson[1,3]

[1] Cybernetica, Ülikooli 2, Tartu, Estonia
[2] Institute of Computer Science, University of Tartu, Liivi 2, Tartu, Estonia
[3] STACC, Ülikooli 2, Tartu, Estonia
toomaskrips@gmail.com

Abstract. In this paper we propose an embarrassingly parallel method for use in secure computation. The method can be used for a special class of functions over real numbers - namely, for functions f for which there exist functions g and h such that $g(f(x), x) = h(x)$ and $g(\cdot, x)$ is monotonous. These functions include $f(x) = \frac{1}{x}$ and $f(x) = \sqrt{x}$, but also the logarithm function or any function that can be represented as finding a root of a polynomial with secret coefficients and a sufficiently low rank. The method relies on counting techniques rather than evaluation of series, allowing the result to be obtained using less rounds of computations with the price of more communication in one round. Since the complexity of oblivious computing methods (like secret-shared multi-party computations (SMC)) is largely determined by the round complexity, this approach has a potential to give better performance/precision ratio compared to series-based approaches. We have implemented the method for several functions and benchmarked them using Sharemind SMC engine.

1 Introduction

The problem setting for privacy-preserving data mining (PPDM) is inherently self-contradictory. On one hand we collect data with a certain purpose, e.g. make policy decisions based on its analysis. On the other hand, due to increasing ease of data misuse, privacy regulations have become more strict in time. This in turn sets tighter limits to data collection, storage and utilisation.

In order to still make use of the data analysis, various PPDM techniques have been proposed. In this paper we will concentrate on secure multi-party computations (SMC), as this approach currently seems to offer good trade-off between performance loss (which is inevitable taking privacy restrictions into account) and provided security guarantees.

SMC applications work by sharing data between several computing nodes, whereas the privacy guarantees hold when not too many of them collude. Computations on such a set-up assume communication between these nodes. As the

This research was supported by the European Regional Development Fund through Centre of Excellence in Computer Science (EXCS) and the Estonian Research Council under Institutional Research Grant IUT27-1 and Estonian Doctoral School in Information and Communication Technologies.

J. Garcia-Alfaro et al. (Eds.): FPS 2015, LNCS 9482, pp. 66–82, 2016.
DOI: 10.1007/978-3-319-30303-1_5

computing nodes should ideally be placed in physically and/or organisation-ally independent environments to provide the privacy guarantees, communication complexity of the computing protocols becomes a major bottleneck. Hence, development of the protocols having smaller communication complexity is essential to increase the performance of SMC applications.

This paper proposes a new approach for evaluating certain special-form functions in SMC setting. We will make use of the observation that communication complexity in SMC case is mostly determined by the number of communication rounds, whereas the amount of data sent within one round may be rather large without significantly decreasing the overall computation speed [3,13]. So far this property was mostly useful while computing with large datasets, as many instances of the same protocols could run in parallel, giving a good aggregated speed. The methods described in this paper can fully use this property for small datasets, but are also flexible enough to be also well usable for large datasets.

One class of methods for function evaluation using many parallel independent attempts is know as Monte-Carlo methods. We can "throw" points into the plane to compute integrals, or onto the line to evaluate single-variable functions, and then count the points satisfying a certain relation. The key observation is that both "throwing" and counting can be implemented in parallel, allowing us to save considerably on communication rounds. In this paper we will not actually select the points randomly, hence the resulting method can be viewed as only inspired by Monte-Carlo approach.

The paper is organised as follows. We first describe the notation and the primitives that we can use in Sect. 3. Then Sect. 4 presents an important technical tool for the implementation of our method. In Sect. 5 we introduce the central algorithm, present its details and give the corresponding proofs for its correctness. In Sect. 6 we give examples of function to which the algorithm can be applied and also present how the algorithm can be used to compute logarithms or the roots of polynomials with secret coefficients. Finally, we give the benchmarking results in Sect. 7 and draw some conclusions in Sect. 8.

2   Previous Work

SMC has traditionally been done over integer values, however, in the recent years, there have been also solutions that use number types that represent real numbers, such as fixed-point numbers or floating-point numbers. Such data types allow for applications that are not possible when using only integer type such as the satellite collision problem [10], privacy-preserving statistical analysis [9], QR-decomposition of matrices [14], secure linear programming with applications in secure supply chain management [5,11], and other problems.

Catrina and Saxena developed secure multiparty arithmetic on fixed-point numbers in [6], and their framework was extended with various computational primitives (like inversion and square root) in [6,14].

However, since the precision of fixed-point is inherently limited, secure floating-point arithmetic has been developed independently by various groups of researchers, see Aliasgari et al. [1], Liu et al. [15], and Kamm and Willemson [10].

In [12], we designed protocols that use fixed-point arithmetic inside of floating-point protocols for better performance.

However, since the fixed-point protocols we used in that paper used polynomial approximation to calculate different functions, the resulting accuracy was limited. This is because better approximation polynomials require computing greater powers of x and also have larger coefficients. These in turn increase the cumulative rounding errors resulting from the fixed-point format and thus, past some point, increasing the accuracy of the polynomial does not increase the accuracy of the method since the rounding error will dominate past that point. This also means that the method was not really flexible concerning the performance-precision trade-off. Also, the value of the polynomial might go outside a certain range and thus correction protocols must be applied to the fixed-point result.

3   Preliminaries

Our methods aim at working with fixed-point real numbers. The amount of bits after the radix point is globally fixed and is usually denoted by m. We will not introduce special notation for distinguishing between different types of numbers, as the type of a number will generally be clear from the context.

We differentiate between secret (private) and public values in this work. To denote that the value of some variable x is secret, we denote it with $[\![x]\!]$. A concrete instantiation of the value protection method depends on the implementation of the computation system. The reader may think of the value $[\![x]\!]$ as being secret shared [16], protected by fully homomorphic encryption [7,8] or some other method allowing to compute with the protected values.

Given a set X and a function f we denote with $f(X)$ the set $\{f(x)|x \in X\}$. Given a number x, and a positive integer k we will define by $\beta_k(x)$ the number formed by the $n - k$ least significant bits of x where n is the total number of bits of our data type. We also define $\alpha_k(x) := x - \beta_k(x)$. In this paper, $\log x$ refers to the binary logarithm $\log_2(x)$. When we give a bit-decomposition of a value x by $x_0, x_1, \ldots, x_{n-1}$, we presume that x_{n-1} is the most significant bit.

3.1   Security Setting

We assume that we use a system that has some specific computational primitives and the universal composability property - that is, if two protocols are secure then their composition is also secure. More precisely, we will assume availability of the following computational primitives working on private fixed-point values.

- Addition.
- Multiplication of public fixed-point numbers and private integers.
- Comparison. We assume access to an operator $\mathsf{LTEProtocol}([\![a]\!], [\![b]\!])$ that takes the value $[\![1]\!]$ if $a \le b$, and $[\![0]\!]$ otherwise. We will also use notation $c = a \overset{?}{\le} b$ to express this comparison operator.

– For functions f specified in the Sect. 5, we must have some easily computable functions g and h so that $g(f(x), x) \equiv h(x)$ on private inputs. These g and h depend on which function f we want to compute, but to achieve efficient implementation they must be fast to evaluate on private fixed-point values. For example, for inverse and square root functions that we implemented, we only needed a small number of fixed-point multiplications to implement them.

All these universally composable primitives are available on several privacy-preserving computation frameworks, e.g. the framework by Catrina and Saxena [6] or Sharemind [2, 12].

4 Simple Example of the Main Idea

We start by presenting a simple method for evaluating functions where we know that the input belongs to some small range and where the function is suitably well-behaved. This method is similar in essence to the main method of the paper. We present this method here to help build intuition about the general strategy and thus make the main method easier to understand. Like the main method, this method uses many comparison operations in parallel to bring the round complexity to a minimum at the cost of increased number of computations in one round.

Often when we need to evaluate some function, we have some kind of information about it letting us know that it belongs to some small range $[a, b)$. If the function is twice derivable and its first two derivatives are not too large, we can use the following method. For a secret input $[\![x]\!]$ and a range $[a, b)$, we choose a large number of equidistributed points a_i where $a_i := a + i \cdot h$ for some small h. We then compute $[\![c_i]\!] := a_i \stackrel{?}{\leq} [\![x]\!]$. Then let $[\![d_0]\!] := 1 - [\![c_0]\!]$ and $[\![d_i]\!] := [\![c_{i-1}]\!] - [\![c_i]\!]$ for all $i \geq 1$. Note that only one of the variables $[\![d_i]\!]$ is equal to one, the rest are equal to zero. The j for which $[\![d_j]\!] = 1$ is the greatest j for which a_j is smaller than or equal to $[\![x]\!]$. Thus a_j is either the closest or second closest a_i to x and $f(a_j)$ can be considered as an approximation for $f([\![x]\!])$.

Thus we compute the scalar product $\sum_i f(a_i) \cdot [\![d_i]\!]$.

We noted that $\sum_i f(a_i) \cdot [\![d_i]\!] = f(a_j)$ where $a_j \leq [\![x]\!] < a_{j+1}$. We note that $|x - a_j| \leq h$. We assumed that f has first and second derivatives in $[a, b)$. Let $c_1 := \max_{y \in [a,b)} |f'(y)|$ and $c_2 := \max_{y \in [a,b)} |f''(y)|$. Then, according to Taylor's theorem, $|f(x) - f(a_j)| \leq c_1 h + \frac{c_2 h^2}{6}$. We can also add the error resulting from the inaccuracy of the fixed-point representation, but the error will be dominated by $c_1 h$.

Note that the method might also be usable for functions that do not have first and second derivatives, but in that case, a different error estimation is needed.

5 Functions with Simply Computable Monotone Inverses in Bounded Areas

There are functions that, in terms of elementary operations such as addition and multiplication, can be relatively complicated to compute but for which the

---

Data: $[\![x]\!], h, \ell, \{b_i\}_{i=0}^{\ell-1}, a, b$
Result: Given a secret number $[\![x]\!]$ such that $[\![x]\!] \in [a,b)$, and numbers
$\quad\quad\quad b_i \approx f(a + i \cdot h)$, computes a number $[\![z]\!]$ that is approximately
$\quad\quad\quad$ equal to $f(x)$.
$\{a_i\}_{i=0}^{\ell-1} \leftarrow a + i \cdot h$
$\{[\![c_i]\!]\}_{i=0}^{\ell-1} \leftarrow \mathsf{LTEProtocol}(\{a_i\}_{i=0}^{\ell-1}, \{[\![x]\!]\}_{i=0}^{\ell-1})$
$[\![d_0]\!] \leftarrow 1 - [\![c_0]\!]$
for $i = 1, i < \ell, i{+}{+}$ **do**
$\quad | \quad [\![d_i]\!] \leftarrow [\![c_{i-1}]\!] - [\![c_i]\!]$
end
$[\![z]\!] = \sum_{i=0}^{\ell-1} [\![d_i]\!] \cdot [\![b_i]\!]$
return $[\![z]\!]$

Algorithm 1. Simple example of the main idea.

inverse functions require much less computational power. For example, for computing $\sqrt[k]{x}$ requires computing an approximation series and it is only accurate in a small interval, but computing x^k requires only approximately $\log k$ multiplications and is accurate for all x for which x^k is a representable real number. Thus it would be useful if we could use computing x^k to compute $\sqrt[k]{x}$. Since round complexity is the important factor here, it is sufficient if we can compute $\sqrt[k]{x}$ by computing many instances of x^k in parallel.

We shall now describe a method that follows a similar idea. The main idea is the following. We want to compute a function $f(x)$ where the input x is secret, but of which we know that $f(x)$ belongs to the interval $[a, a + 2^k)$ where a can be private or public and where there are are easily computable functions g and h where $g(f(x), x) \equiv h(x)$ where $g(\cdot, x)$ is also monotonous in the area $[a, a + 2^k)$. For example, if $f(x) = \frac{1}{\sqrt{x}}$, then $g(x, y) = x^2 \cdot y$ and $h(x) = 1$.

Suppose that we know that the output $f(x)$ will be in some $[a, a + 2^k)$ and that we want to achieve precision 2^{k-s}. We then consider values $a_i := a + i \cdot 2^{k-s}$ for every $i \in \{1, \ldots, 2^s - 1\}$, compute $g(a_i, x)$, do secret comparisons by setting $c_i := g(a_i, x) \overset{?}{\leq} h(x)$ if g is increasing and $c_i := g(a_i, x) \overset{?}{\geq} h(x)$ if g is decreasing and finally set the result to be $a + 2^{k-s} \cdot (\sum c_i)$.

Intuitively, this gives a correct answer because for one $j \in \{0, \ldots, 2^s\}$, a_j is approximately equal to $f(x)$. If g is increasing, we can measure the position of this j in $\{0, \ldots, 2^s\}$ by testing whether $g(a_i, x) \overset{?}{\leq} h(x)$ for all i — due to monotonicity, for all i smaller than j, $g(a_i, x) \leq h(x)$ but for all i greater than j, $g(a_i, x) > h(x)$. Thus the number of i that"pass the test" is proportional to the position of j in $\{0, \ldots, 2^s\}$. A similar argument holds when g is decreasing. The following theorem shows why the approach works.

Theorem 1. *Let f be a function. Let g, g_x and h be such functions that $g(f(x), x) \equiv h(x)$, $g_x(y) := g(y, x)$ and g_x is strictly monotonous in $[a, a + 2^k)$. Let $x \in X$ be such that $f(x) \in [a, a + 2^k)$. Let $y_0, y_1, \ldots, y_{2^s}$ be such that $y_i := a + i \cdot 2^{k-s}$. Let $Y := \{y_1, \ldots, y_{2^s-1}\}$. Let $Z := g_x(Y)$.*

Let $j := |\{y_i \in Y | g_x(y_i) \leq h(x)\}|$ *and* $j' := |\{y_i \in Y | g(y_i, x) \geq h(x)\}|$. *Then* $f(x) \in [y_j, y_{j+1})$ *if* g *is monotonously increasing and* $f(x) \in [y_{j'}, y_{j'+1})$ *if it is monotonously decreasing.*

Proof. We will give a proof for a monotonously increasing g_x. The proof for monotonously decreasing g_x is the same, *mutatis mutandis*. First note that $g_x(y_1) < g_x(y_2) < \cdots < g_x(y_{2^s-1})$, because g_x is monotonously increasing. We know that $f(x) \in [y_r, y_{r+1})$ for some r. Since g_x is monotone, this is equivalent to $g_x(f(x)) \in [g_x(y_r), g_x(y_{r+1}))$. Rewriting this gives us $h(x) \in [g_x(y_r), g_x(y_{r+1}))$. Because $g_x(y_1) < g_x(y_2) < \cdots < g_x(y_{2^s-1})$, this is equivalent to $h(x) \geq g_x(y_1), \ldots, g_x(y_r)$ and $h(x) < g_x(y_{r+1}), \ldots, g_x(y_{2^s-1})$, which is equivalent to $|\{g(y_i) \in Z | h(x) \geq g(y_i)\}| = r$. This in turn gives us $|\{y_i \in Y | h(x) \geq g_x(y_i)\}| = r$, which gives us $r = j$ which is what we wanted to show.   □

We shall use this theorem for Algorithm 2. Namely, to compute $f(\llbracket x \rrbracket)$, we first create values $\llbracket y_1 \rrbracket, \llbracket y_2 \rrbracket, \ldots, \llbracket y_{2^s-1} \rrbracket$ be such that $\llbracket y_i \rrbracket := \llbracket a \rrbracket + i \cdot 2^{k-s}$. We compute, $g(\llbracket y_i \rrbracket)$, for every i, in parallel. Then, using the LTEProtocol in parallel, we set c_i to be $g(y_i) \overset{?}{\leq} h(x)$ for every i. We compute $r = \sum c_i$. By the theorem, $r = j$ and thus we set the answer to be $\llbracket a \rrbracket + r \cdot 2^{k-s}$.

We shall now give two remarks about how the theorem still applies for some slightly weaker assumptions. We did not use these assumptions in the theorem due to the sake of clarity.

Remark 1. Note that even if $h(x)$ is not easily computable but there exists an easily computable function $\tilde{h}(x)$ such that $h(x) \in [g_x(y_r), g_x(y_{r+1})) \Leftrightarrow \tilde{h}(x) \in [g_x(y_r), g_x(y_{r+1}))$ then we can replace $h(x)$ with $\tilde{h}(x)$ in the algorithm and the output is the same.

Remark 2. We also note that it is not strictly necessary for g_x to be monotonous in $[a, a + 2^k)$. It suffices for it to be monotonous in $[a, a + 2^k - 2^{k-s}]$.

When we refer to functions g, g_x, h or $\tilde{h}$ later in this paper, we assume that they have the meanings described in this section. Also, when the function $g(y, x)$ does not depend on x, we shall just write $g(y)$. Also, in that case, $g_x(y) \equiv g(y)$ and thus we will write $g(y)$ instead of $g_x(y)$.

5.1   Iteration

Note that when the range of input is large and we want good accuracy, we have to perform a large number of tests in parallel — i.e. s will be rather large. However, due to network saturation, there is an upper bound to how many operations does it make sense to perform in parallel. Let this number be 2^σ. Up to $2^{\sigma-1}$, doubling the number of tests should increase the overall computation time by a factor that is strictly smaller than 2. Past that point, however, doubling the number of tests will double the performance time. This is not a very serious loss, but we can also propose a method that can ideally achieve much greater accuracy gain while only doubling the performance time.

Data: $[\![x]\!], [\![a]\!], k, n, s, \mathsf{sign}$

Result: Computes one round of function f of $[\![x]\!]$ where we already know
  that $f(x) \in [[\![a]\!], [\![a]\!] + 2^k)$. Here g and h are functions so that
  $g(f(x), x) \equiv h(x)$. The public flag sign is 1 if the function is
  increasing and 0 if it is decreasing. We use $2^s - 1$ test
  points and we work on n-bit data types.

$[\![w]\!] \leftarrow h([\![x]\!])$

$\{[\![a_i]\!]\}_{i=1}^{2^s-1} \leftarrow \{[\![a]\!] + i \cdot 2^{k-s}\}_{i=1}^{2^s-1}$

$\{[\![b_i]\!]\}_{i=1}^{2^s-1} \leftarrow \{[\![g(a_i, x)]\!]\}_{i=1}^{2^s-1}$

if sign $== 1$ **then**

  $\quad \{[\![c_i]\!]\}_{i=1}^{2^s-1} \leftarrow \mathsf{LTEProtocol}(\{[\![b_i]\!]\}_{i=1}^{2^s-1}, \{[\![w]\!]\}_{i=1}^{2^s-1})$

else

  $\quad \{[\![c_i]\!]\}_{i=1}^{2^s-1} \leftarrow \mathsf{LTEProtocol}(\{[\![w]\!]\}_{i=1}^{2^s-1}, \{[\![b_i]\!]\}_{i=1}^{2^s-1})$

end

$[\![c]\!] = \sum_{i=1}^{2^s-1} 2^{k-s}[\![c_i]\!]$

return $[\![a]\!] + [\![c]\!]$

Algorithm 2. Computing a function with an easily computable inverse.

The idea is, in essence, 2^σ-ary search. We note that in the beginning of
Algorithm 3 we start with the knowledge that $f([\![x]\!]) \in [[\![a]\!], [\![a]\!] + 2^k)$ and in the
end we know that $f([\![x]\!]) \in [[\![a']\!], [\![a']\!] + 2^{k'})$ where k' is smaller than k. Thus it is
rather natural to run Algorithm 3 again assuming that $f([\![x]\!]) \in [[\![a']\!], [\![a']\!] + 2^{k'})$
with a suitable number of test points in that interval. This can be done several
times in a row, until the precision we want has been achieved.

More precisely, suppose that we want to compute v instances of some function f in parallel with accuracy of t bits and so that we beforehand know that
$[\![f(x_i)]\!] \in [a_i, a_i + 2^k)$ for every $i \in \{1, \ldots, v\}$. Suppose also that our system
can perform at most approximately 2^σ comparison operations or operations g in
parallel and we want to achieve precision 2^t.

Then we have to perform approximately $\frac{(k-t)\log v}{\sigma}$ rounds where in every
round the total number of operations performed is no greater than 2^σ.

However, if the number of operations we wish to do in parallel is too great,
then we must perform more than 2^σ operations in one round. In this case, we
shall compute only one extra bit each round because that is the smallest possible
amount.

The resulting procedure is presented as Algorithm 3, where the Ro subroutine
refers to Algorithm 2.

6 Applications of the Method

The class of functions f described in Theorem 1 (for which there exist easily
computable functions g and h such that $g(f(x), x) \equiv h(x)$ and $g(\cdot, x)$ is also
monotonous) is rather abstract and not easy to interpret. This Section studies
this class more closely.

Data: $v, \{[\![x_i]\!]\}_{i=0}^{v-1}, \{[\![a_i]\!]\}_{i=0}^{v-1}, k, \sigma, n, t, \{\text{sign}_i\}_{i=0}^{v-1}$

Result: Computes function f of values $\{[\![x_i]\!]\}_{i=0}^{v-1}$. We know that
$[\![f(x_i)]\!] \in [a_i, a_i + 2^k)$ for all $i \in \{0, \ldots, v-1\}$. We can perform at
most 2^σ comparison or g operations in parallel. We work on
n-bit data types and we wish to achieve precision 2^t

$s \leftarrow \max\{\lfloor \sigma - \log v \rfloor, 1\}$
$r \leftarrow \lfloor \frac{k-t}{s} \rfloor$
$s' \leftarrow k - t - s \cdot r$
if $s' == 0$ **then**
$\quad \mid \quad s' \leftarrow s$
$\quad \mid \quad r \leftarrow r - 1$
end
$\{[\![y_{0,i}]\!]\}_{i=0}^{v-1} \leftarrow Ro(\{[\![x_i]\!]\}_{i=0}^{v-1}, \{[\![a_i]\!]\}_{i=0}^{v-1}, k, n, s', \{\text{sign}_i\}_{i=0}^{v-1})$
for $j = 1; j \leq r; j++$ **do**
$\quad \mid \quad \{[\![y_{j,i}]\!]\}_{i=0}^{v-1} \leftarrow Ro(\{[\![x_i]\!]\}_{i=0}^{v-1}, \{[\![y_{j-1,i}]\!]\}_{i=0}^{v-1}, k - s' - (j-1) \cdot s, n, s, \{\text{sign}_i\}_{i=0}^{v-1})$
end
return $[\![y_r]\!]$

Algorithm 3. Computing f using iteration.

The functions described by Theorem 1 are perhaps best understood when considering the possible options for the easily computable functions g, h and $\tilde{h}$. Which functions exactly are easy to compute depends on the underlying implementation of secure computation engine. Typically such functions would include constants, additions, subtractions, multiplications and their compositions. However, depending on the system, other operations such as bit decompositions, shifts or other functions might be cheap and thus different functions might belong into that class in that case.

The compositions of constants, additions, subtractions, multiplications are polynomials. Thus, one subset of the functions computable using this method are equivalent to finding the root of a polynomial with secret coefficients in a range where the polynomial is injective.

For example:

- computing $\frac{1}{[\![a]\!]}$ is equivalent to finding a root of $[\![a]\!]x - 1 = 0$;
- computing $\sqrt{[\![a]\!]}$ is equivalent to finding a root of $x^2 - [\![a]\!] = 0$;
- computing $\frac{1}{\sqrt{[\![a]\!]}}$ is equivalent to finding a root of $[\![a]\!]x^2 - 1 = 0$;
- computing $\frac{[\![a]\!]}{[\![b]\!]}$ is equivalent to finding a root of $[\![b]\!]x - [\![a]\!] = 0$.

This class of problems can also be extended to finding the roots of polynomials with secret coefficients in general, whether they are injective in an area or not, and this is done in Sect. 6.1. Later, in Sect. 6.2, we will present the computation routine for binary logarithm.

6.1 Finding Roots of Polynomials

We saw that finding the roots of injective polynomials is a large subclass of problems that can be solved using the point-counting method described above.

We will now present a method for making point-counting applicable also for polynomials that are not injective in the given interval. Denoting the rank of the polynomial by k, the extended method will possibly be up to k^2 times slower, hence it should be used only for polynomials with a suitably small rank.

The key observation for the extended method is the fact that if we can divide $[a, b)$ into intervals $[a, c_1), [c_1, c_2), .., [c_k, b)$ so that the polynomial $p(x)$ is monotone in all those intervals then we can still use the point-counting method — we can separately use the point-counting method in all those intervals.

The polynomial is monotone in an interval if the derivative of the polynomial does not change signs there. Since the derivative of a polynomial is a continuous function, it changes signs only when it is equal to zero. Thus we can find the points $c_1, \ldots, c_k$ by computing the roots of $p'(x)$. Now we again must find the roots of a polynomial — but that polynomial has a smaller rank than the original one. This, rather naturally, gives us a recursive algorithm. If $p'(x)$ is an injective function, we can directly use the point-counting algorithm. If it is not, we can compute its roots recursively.

If the rank of the polynomial $p(x)$ is k, then its $(k-1)$st derivative is a linear function and thus injective, which means that the recursion has no more than $k - 1$ steps.

We presume that we have access to the following functions.

First, we naturally assume that we have access to the function that evaluates the polynomial. We denote with $\mathsf{p}(\llbracket a_0 \rrbracket, \ldots, \llbracket a_n \rrbracket, \llbracket x_0 \rrbracket)$ the function that evaluates the polynomial $\sum_{i=0}^{n} \llbracket a_i \rrbracket x^i$ at $\llbracket x_0 \rrbracket$.

Second, we assume access to the function $\mathsf{Der}(\llbracket a_0 \rrbracket, \ldots, \llbracket a_n \rrbracket)$ that takes in the coefficients of a polynomial and returns the coefficients of its derivative.

Third, we presume that we have access to a version of Algorithm 3 that, in an interval where a polynomial is injective, returns a root of the polynomial if it has one or an endpoint of the interval if it does not. However, we need to modify the function Ro that it calls, i.e. Algorithm 2. We shall replace it with the Algorithm 4 which differs from Algorithm 2 in two ways.

First, unlike in Algorithm 2, we do not know the length of the interval where our result may be. It might even happen that the interval has length zero. We solve this problem in the following way. Suppose that we know that our solution is in $[\llbracket a \rrbracket, \llbracket b \rrbracket]$.

We then compute the values of g_x as usual in the interval $[\llbracket a \rrbracket, \llbracket a + 2^k \rrbracket)$ where 2^k is such a number such that $\llbracket b \rrbracket \leq \llbracket a \rrbracket + 2^k$. However, now we also compare every point $\llbracket a_i \rrbracket = \llbracket a \rrbracket + i \cdot h$ with $\llbracket b \rrbracket$. After computing the comparison vector $\{\llbracket c_i \rrbracket\}$, we compute $\llbracket c_i' \rrbracket := \llbracket a_i \rrbracket \overset{?}{\leq} \llbracket b \rrbracket$ and compute $\llbracket \overline{c_i} \rrbracket = \llbracket c_i \rrbracket \cdot \llbracket c_i' \rrbracket$. We then proceed as usual, using $\llbracket \overline{c_i} \rrbracket$ instead of $\llbracket c_i \rrbracket$. After this procedure we can be certain that the result is in $[\llbracket a \rrbracket, \llbracket b \rrbracket]$. This is because if $f(x) \leq b$, then if $c_i = 1$ then also $c_i' = 1$ and thus $c_i \cdot c_i' = c_i$ and hence $\overline{c_i} = c_i$ for every i - in this case multiplying with c_i' does not have any effect. However, if $f(x) > b$, then $\overline{c_i} = 1$ if and only if $c_i <= b$ and thus $a + 2^{k-s} \sum \overline{c_i}$ is equal to the largest a_i that is not greater than b.

Note that although we use intervals in the format $[a, b]$ instead of $[a, a + 2^t)$, we can still use the Theorem 1 due to Remark 2.

The second way Algorithm 4 differs from Algorithm 2 is the fact that we do not know whether the polynomial $p(x) = \sum_{i=0}^{n} a_i x^i$ is increasing or decreasing in the interval $[\![a]\!], [\![b]\!]]$ where it is injective. We solve this problem by executing the algorithm in both cases and then computing $p(a) \overset{?}{\leq} p(b)$ to perform oblivious choice between the two options.

Because p is injective in the interval, the only case when it can happen that $p([\![a]\!]) = p([\![b]\!])$ is when $[\![a]\!] = [\![b]\!]$, but then the output of the function is always $[\![a]\!]$ and does not depend on whether we use the increasing or decreasing version of the algorithm. In other cases comparing $p([\![a]\!])$ and $p([\![b]\!])$ will give us whether the function is increasing or decreasing in that interval and thus the correct output. Thus we obtain Algorithm 4.

Data: $[\![x]\!], [\![a]\!], [\![b]\!], k, n, s$

Result: Computes one round of function f of $[\![x]\!]$ where we already know
that $f(x) \in [[\![a]\!], [\![b]\!]]$. Here g and h are functions so that
$g(f(x), x) \equiv h(x)$. We use $2^s - 1$ test points and we work on
n-bit data types. We know that the function is monotone but
not whether it is increasing or decreasing.

$[\![w]\!] \leftarrow h([\![x]\!])$

$\{[\![a_i]\!]\}_{i=1}^{2^s-1} \leftarrow \{[\![a]\!] + i \cdot 2^{k-s}\}_{i=1}^{2^s-1}$

$\{[\![b_i]\!]\}_{i=1}^{2^s-1} \leftarrow \{[\![g(a_i, x)]\!]\}_{i=1}^{2^s-1}$

$\{[\![c_{i,0}]\!]\}_{i=1}^{2^s-1} \leftarrow \mathsf{LTEProtocol}(\{[\![b_i]\!]\}_{i=1}^{2^s-1}, \{[\![w]\!]\}_{i=1}^{2^s-1})$

$\{[\![c_{i,1}]\!]\}_{i=1}^{2^s-1} \leftarrow \mathsf{LTEProtocol}(\{[\![w]\!]\}_{i=1}^{2^s-1}, \{[\![b_i]\!]\}_{i=1}^{2^s-1})$

$\{[\![c_i']\!]\}_{i=1}^{2^s-1} \leftarrow \mathsf{LTEProtocol}(\{[\![a_i]\!]\}_{i=1}^{2^s-1}, \{[\![b]\!]\}_{i=1}^{2^s-1})$

$\{[\![\overline{c_{i,0}}]\!]\}_{i=1}^{2^s-1} \leftarrow \{[\![c_{i,0}]\!]\}_{i=1}^{2^s-1} \cdot \{[\![c_i']\!]\}_{i=1}^{2^s-1}$

$[\![c_0]\!] = 2^{k-s} \cdot \sum_{i=1}^{2^s-1} [\![\overline{c_{i,0}}]\!]$

$\{[\![\overline{c_{i,1}}]\!]\}_{i=1}^{2^s-1} \leftarrow \{[\![c_{i,1}]\!]\}_{i=1}^{2^s-1} \cdot \{[\![c_i']\!]\}_{i=1}^{2^s-1}$

$[\![c_1]\!] = 2^{k-s} \cdot \sum_{i=1}^{2^s-1} [\![\overline{c_{i,1}}]\!]$

$[\![z_a]\!] \leftarrow \mathsf{p}([\![a_0]\!], \ldots, [\![a_n]\!], [\![a]\!])$

$[\![z_b]\!] \leftarrow \mathsf{p}([\![a_0]\!], \ldots, [\![a_n]\!], [\![b]\!])$

$[\![z]\!] \leftarrow \mathsf{LTEProtocol}(z_a, z_b)$

$[\![c]\!] \leftarrow [\![z]\!] \cdot [\![c_0]\!] + (1 - [\![z]\!]) \cdot [\![c_1]\!]$

return $[\![a]\!] + [\![c]\!]$

Algorithm 4. Computing a function with an easily computable inverse in a secret interval. Function may be either increasing or decreasing.

If we thus replace the call to Algorithm 2 with a call to Algorithm 4 in Algorithm 3, we shall obtain a function that we call $\mathsf{injecRoot}([\![a_0]\!], \ldots, [\![a_n]\!], [\![a]\!], [\![b]\!])$ that takes in a secret interval $[[\![a]\!], [\![b]\!]]$ and the secret coefficients $[\![a_0]\!], \ldots, [\![a_n]\!]$ of a polynomial such that the polynomial has at most one root in $[[\![a]\!], [\![b]\!]]$. The function outputs the root of the polynomial in $[[\![a]\!], [\![b]\!]]$ if it exists. If it does not exist, the function outputs the point $[\![a]\!]$ if the function has only positive values and is increasing in the interval or has only negative values and is decreasing in the interval. In other cases, it outputs the largest representable value in $[[a], [b]]$.

We shall now present Algorithm 5. Algorithm 5 is used to compute the recursive function $\mathsf{polyRoot}([a_0], \ldots, [a_n], [a], [b], t)$ that returns n values, in increasing order, among which are all the real roots of the polynomial.

First it finds the polynomial that is the derivative of the polynomial $\sum_{i=0}^{n} [a_i] x^i$. If that is a linear function, it applies the function $\mathsf{injecRoot}$ to it to obtain its root if it has one. If the derivative has a higher order, it recursively calls $\mathsf{polyRoot}$ to obtain $n-1$ values $c_1, \ldots, c_{n-1}$, in increasing order, among which are all the real roots of the derivative.

We then set $[c_0] = [a]$ and $[c_n] = [b]$. We then apply the function $\mathsf{injecRoot}$ to the original polynomial in the intervals $[[c_i] + 2^t, [c_{i+1}]]$ where 2^t is the precision of the function $\mathsf{injecRoot}$. We return the outputs of $\mathsf{injecRoot}$, ordered.

Data: $[a_0], \ldots, [a_n], [a], [b], t$
Result: Gets as input the polynomial with coefficients $[a_0], \ldots, [a_n]$
　　　　 and an interval $[[a], [b]]$. Returns n values, in an increasing
　　　　 order, among which are all the real roots of the polynomial.
　　　　 Has precision 2^t.
if $n > 1$ **then**
　　$[b_0], \ldots, [b_{n-1}] \leftarrow \mathsf{Der}([a_0], \ldots, [a_n])$
　　$[c_1], \ldots, [c_{n-1}] \leftarrow \mathsf{polyRoot}([b_0], \ldots, [b_{n-1}], [a], [b], t)$
　　$[c_0] \leftarrow [a]$
　　$[c_n] \leftarrow [b]$
　　for $i = 0, i < n, i + +$ **do**
　　　　$[d_i] \leftarrow \mathsf{injecRoot}([a_0], \ldots, [a_n], [c_i + 2^t], [c_{i+1}])$
　　end
　　return $[d_0], \ldots, [d_{n-1}]$
else
　　return $\mathsf{injecRoot}([a_0], \ldots, [a_1], [a], [b])$
end

Algorithm 5. Computing roots of a polynomial.

Based on Theorem 1, we note that each step gives correct answers provided that the function under question is injective in the intervals where it is called. Based on properties of the derivative of a polynomial we conclude the correctness of the algorithm.

The reason why we chose the specific intervals for $\mathsf{injecRoot}$ as $[[c_i]+2^t, [c_{i+1}]]$ is the following. We know that the derivative of the function may be zero in $[[c_i], [c_i] + 2^t)$ and $[[c_{i+1}], [c_{i+1}] + 2^t)$, but not between those intervals. Thus the function is injective in $[[c_i] + 2^t, [c_{i+1}]]$ and the algorithm gives the desired output. Also, this does not exclude any points, given the precision level t.

6.2 Logarithm

In this Section we show how the point-counting method can be applied to computing binary logarithms.

As noted by Aliasgari et al. [1], an approximation of the exponential function can be computed using the bits of the input to obliviously choose between 2^{2^i} and 1 and then computing the product over all bits, as illustrated by the following formula.

$$2^y = 2^{y_0 y_1 \cdots y_m \cdot y_{m+1} \cdots y_n} = \prod_{i=0}^{n} 2^{y_i 2^{i-m}} = \prod_{i=0}^{n} (y_i 2^{2^{i-m}} + (1 - y_i)) \qquad (1)$$

Here $y_0 y_1 \ldots y_m$ is the fractional part of y and $y_{m+1} \ldots y_n$ is the integer part of y. We can thus use 2^x for the function g. At first, it may seem that this requires us to perform bit-decomposition and many multiplications for computing the function g. However, we will later see that it can be done in a manner where we only need a multiplication of a private and a public value to compute g.

To avoid technical details arising from the need to handle negative numbers, we only present here the point-counting method for logarithms that only works on inputs greater than one. We refer to the discussion in Sect. 7 how to overcome this limitation.

Let us have input $[\![x]\!]$ and suppose that we want to compute $[\![\log x]\!]$. We assume that $[\![\log x]\!] \in [[\![a]\!] 2^b, ([\![a]\!] + 1) 2^b)$ for some $[\![a]\!]$ and b. Let us have n-bit numbers as input. Let us also have computed the value $[\![2^{2^b a}]\!]$. We let $f(x) = \log x$ and $g(y) = \overline{g_{a,b,s}}(y_0, \ldots, y_{n-1})$, where $y_0, \ldots y_{n-1}$ are the bits of y and $\overline{g_{a,b,s}}(y_0, \ldots, y_{n-1})$ is the function defined in the following way.

$$\overline{g_{a,b,s}}(y_0, \ldots, y_{n-1}) = 2^{2^b a} \prod_{i=n-b}^{s} (y_i \cdot 2^{2^i} + (1 - y_i) \cdot 1). \qquad (2)$$

Note that this performs oblivious choice between 2^{2^i} and 1 every step using the bit y_i, and essentially computes an approximation of the exponent that uses only the first s bits of y. In fact, $g(y) \equiv 2^{\alpha_s(y)}$. Let us have 2^{s-b} test points a_r in such a way that $a_i = i \cdot 2^{n-s}$. Thus $h(x) = \overline{g_{a,b,s}}(\log x) = 2^{\alpha_s(\log x)}$.

This gives us $h(x) = 2^{\alpha_s(\log x)}$. However, this is difficult to compute.

We now use Remark 1 and set $\tilde{h}(x) = x$.

We need to confirm that $h(x) \in [g(a_r), g(a_{r+1})) \Leftrightarrow \tilde{h}(x) \in [g(a_r), g(a_{r+1}))$. Indeed,

$$h(x) \in [g(a_r), g(a_{r+1})) \Leftrightarrow 2^{\alpha_s(\log x)} \in [2^{\alpha_s(a_r)}, 2^{\alpha_s(a_{r+1})}) \Leftrightarrow$$
$$\alpha_s(\log x) \in [\alpha_s(a_r), \alpha_s(a_{r+1})) \Leftrightarrow \alpha_s(\log x) = \alpha_s(a_r) \Leftrightarrow$$
$$x = 2^{\alpha_s(a_r)} \cdot 2^{\beta_s(x)} \Leftrightarrow x \in [2^{\alpha_s(a_r)}, 2^{\alpha_s(a_{r+1})}) \Leftrightarrow \tilde{h}(c) \in [g(a_r), g(a_{r+1})).$$
$$(3)$$

The equivalence $\alpha_s(\log x) \in [\alpha_s(a_r), \alpha_s(a_{r+1})) \Leftrightarrow \alpha_s(\log x) = \alpha_s(a_r)$ holds because the only point in $[\alpha_s(a_r), \alpha_s(a_{r+1}))$ to which $\alpha_s(\cdot)$ maps is $\alpha_s(a_r)$.

We now note that if we know $[\![2^{2^b a}]\!]$, then computing $g(x)$ can be done at the cost of multiplying a public value with a private value. Namely, we note that given the bit representation of a_i as $a_{i_{n-1}} a_{i_{n-2}} \cdots a_{i_0}$, the product $\Pi^s_{j=n-b}(a_{i_j} \cdot 2^{2^j} + (1 - a_{i_j}) \cdot 1)$ is public since the individual bits $a_{i_{n-b}}, \ldots, a_{i_s}$ are public as they only depend on i. Thus we only need to compute the product of $[\![2^{2^b a}]\!]$ and $\Pi^s_{j=n-b}(a_{i_j} \cdot 2^{2^j} + (1 - a_{i_j}) \cdot 1)$ to compute $g(a_i)$.

We also note that the constraint that we should have the value $[\![2^{2^b a}]\!]$ before computation is not too restricting. If we have performed no rounds before, then it can be set to 1. However, if it is not the first round, then we can compute it based on the values we obtained from the previous round using the method described in Sect. 4. Note that we have computed values $[\![c_i]\!] = [\![g(x)]\!] \overset{?}{\leq} [\![x]\!]$. We then compute $[\![d_0]\!] := 1 - [\![c_0]\!]$ and $[\![d_i]\!] := [\![c_{i-1}]\!] - [\![c_i]\!]$ for all $i \in \{1, \ldots, 2^s - 1\}$. We now note that there is only one $[\![j]\!]$ for which $[\![d_j]\!] = 1$, namely, the one for which $g(a_{[\![j]\!]}) \leq [\![x]\!] < g(a_{[\![j+1]\!]})$. Now we compute $\sum_{i=0}^{2^s-1} d_i [\![g(a_i)]\!]$ which is equal to the $g(a_{[\![j]\!]})$ for which it holds that $g(a_{[\![j]\!]}) \leq [\![x]\!] < g(a_{[\![j+1]\!]})$. Note that this means $2^{\alpha_s(a_{[\![j]\!]})} \leq [\![x]\!] < 2^{\alpha_s(a_{[\![j]\!]}) + 2^{n-s}}$. We note that by taking $b = n - s$ and $a = \frac{\alpha_s(a_j)}{2^{n-s}}$ this is equivalent to $[\![a]\!] 2^b \leq x < ([\![a]\!] + 1) 2^b$ and thus we can take $[\![g(a_j)]\!] = \sum_{i=0}^{2^s-1} d_i [\![g(a_i)]\!]$ for the new $[\![a]\!] 2^b$.

7 Results

7.1 Security Settings of the Benchmarking Process

For implementation and benchmarking we used the Sharemind 3 SMC platform[1]. Sharemind 3 is based on secret sharing and is information-theoretically secure in the passive security model and contains the necessary universally composable primitives for fixed-point numbers, as described in Sect. 3.1.

7.2 Benchmarks

We implemented four functions – inverse, square root and logarithm using the point-counting technique, and the Gaussian error function using the method described in Sect. 4. All three computing nodes for the Sharemind platform that we used contained two Intel X5670 2.93 GHz CPUs with 6 cores and had 48 GB of RAM. Although we optimised the methods concerning round-efficiency, total communication cost became the deciding factor for efficiency. Since these methods were designed to fully use the communication capacity of channels, communication cost is proportional to time. We performed tests for 32-bit numbers and 64-bit numbers as the basic integer data type, and with different precision levels. To see how vector size affects the performance, we ran tests for different

---

[1] http://sharemind.cyber.ee/.

vector sizes. We performed 20 tests for every value given here for the inverse, square root and the Gaussian error function and 10 tests for every value for the logarithm and averaged the result.

For clearer comparison, we used the floating-point methods for the inverse function and the square root function presented in [12], but replaced the fixed-point subroutines with the methods proposed in this paper. We also did not need as much correction algorithms, since our new algorithms allow for much higher accuracy without significant loss in performance. The results of the tests are presented in Tables 1, 2 and 4, respectively.

We chose the precision parameters for square root and inverse for the following reasons. We wished to have a near-maximal precision for both 32-bit and 64-bit numbers but for practical reasons, we implemented the method for 30 or 62 bits of precision. This precision is much higher than the previous results of [10,12] for the respective data types while taking about 2 to 6 times more time than the results of [12]. We also ran tests for 16 bits of precision for 32-bit numbers and 32 bits of precision for 64-bit numbers. These precisions are approximately half of the near-maximal precision but also close to the precisions of the protocols of [12] (Table 3).

Comparing these benchmarks with the near-maximal precision we can see how doubling the number of bits for precision also approximately doubles the execution time. Based on the nature of the protocol, we can also assume that this pattern also holds more generally — when a protocol with n bits precision would take time t, then the same protocol would take time $2t$ for $2n$ bits of precision. Consequently, this protocol can be used with reasonable efficiency for applications needing very high precision. Verifying this conclusion assumes implementation of our algorithms on a platform providing 128-bit primitive types, so this remains the subject for future research.

We can also see that for 64-bit numbers, the performance for vector size 10000 is poorer than for vector size 1000. This happens because for 64-bit numbers,

Table 1. Operations per second for different implementation of the inverse function for different input sizes.

	1	10	100	1000	10000
Catrina, Dragulin, AppDiv2m 128 bits, [4]	3.39				
Catrina, Dragulin, Div2m, 128 bits [4]	1.26				
Kamm and Willemson, 32 bits, accuracy 2^{-18} [10]	0.17	1.7	15.3	55.2	66.4
Kamm and Willemson, 64 bits, accuracy 2^{-18} [10]	0.16	1.5	11.1	29.5	47.2
Krips and Willemson, 32 bits, accuracy 2^{-13} [12]	0.99	8.22	89.73	400.51	400.51
Krips and Willemson, 64 bits, accuracy 2^{-26} [12]	0.82	8.08	62.17	130.35	130.35
Current paper, 32 bits, accuracy 2^{-30}	0.34	3.60	21.97	98.13	106.15
Current paper 64 bits, accuracy 2^{-62}	0.24	2.21	10.8	48.1	37.1
Current paper, 32 bits, accuracy 2^{-16}	0.61	8.25	40.8	190.9	212.01
Current paper 64 bits, accuracy 2^{-32}	0.45	4.11	23.31	100.0	67.13

Table 2. Operations per second for different implementation of the square root function for different input sizes.

	1	10	100	1000	10000
Liedel, 110 bits, accuracy 2^{-78} [14]	0.204				
Kamm and Willemson, 32 bits [10]	0.09	0.85	7	24	32
Kamm and Willemson, 64 bits [10]	0.08	0.76	4.6	9.7	10.4
Krips and Willemson, 32 bits, accuracy 2^{-17} [12]	0.77	7.55	70.7	439.17	580.81
Krips and Willemson, 64 bits, accuracy 2^{-34} [12]	0.65	6.32	41.75	78.25	119.99
Current paper, 32 bits, accuracy 2^{-30}	0.30	2.98	19.97	94.13	101.8
Current paper 64 bits, accuracy 2^{-62}	0.21	1.93	9.23	44.79	37.13
Current paper, 32 bits, accuracy 2^{-16}	0.49	5.98	35.2	152.0	202.3
Current paper 64 bits, accuracy 2^{-32}	0.38	3.59	21.2	86.0	79.5

Table 3. Operations per second for different implementation of the gaussian error function for different input sizes.

	1	10	100
Kamm and Willemson, 32 bits [10]	0.1	0.97	8.4
Kamm and Willemson, 64 bits [10]	0.09	0.89	5.8
Krips and Willemson, 32-bit, accuracy 2^{-13} [12]	0.5	4.41	30.65
Krips and Willemson, 64-bit, accuracy 2^{-13} [12]	0.46	4.13	21.97
Current paper, 32-bit, accuracy 2^{-12}	0.9	5.85	13.26
Current paper, 64-bit, accuracy 2^{-12}	0.81	3.94	6.13
Current paper, 32-bit, accuracy 2^{-13}	0.86	4.88	8.61
Current paper, 64-bit, accuracy 2^{-13}	0.75	2.59	3.75
Current paper, 32-bit, accuracy 2^{-14}	0.8	3.4	5.34
Current paper, 64-bit, accuracy 2^{-14}	0.57	1.19	1.54

$2^{\sigma} < 10000$ and thus we have to perform more operations in a round than can be computed in parallel.

Since precision is an important aspect of our methods, we included precision of other methods to those methods where the precision could be found or computed. For the error function, we can see that for small vector sizes, our implemented method outperforms previous methods for several different precisions, being able to be both faster and more precise than our previous result [12]. However, if the vector size is larger, then the performance quickly decreases as precision grows. Thus it is preferable to use this method only for small vector sizes.

As for the logarithm, we implemented a logarithm function for 32-bit and 64-bit fixed-point numbers. In the implementation presented in this paper we assumed that the result of the logarithm operator would be positive. However, it is straightforward to also implement the absolute value of the negative case using

Table 4. Operations per second for different implementation of the logarithm function for different input sizes.

	1	10	100	1000	10000	100000
Aliasgari, accuracy 2^{-256} [1]		12.36	12.5	13.3	13.3	13.5
Current paper, 32-bit, accuracy 2^{-15}	2.39	15.43	119.2	549.9	1023.6	1288.9
Current paper, 64-bit, accuracy 2^{-31}	0.90	6.8	37.9	152.5	244.3	275.6

the same method and then execute one oblivious choice. This would increase the computation time by approximately two times.

Our implemented methods had precisions of 2^{-15} and 2^{-31}, respectively, due to the respective radix-point used — for the radix-point used, higher precision was not possible. We can see that while the method proposed by Aliasgari *et al.* can achieve very high precision due to the nature of the floating-point data type, our method is faster, and for larger vector sizes, faster by several orders of magnitude.

8   Conclusions

This paper presented a method for oblivious evaluation of special-format single-variable functions, including, but not limited to functions that can be represented as finding roots of polynomials with secret coefficients. Several important functions belong to this class (e.g. various power functions and binary logarithm). Our method is easy to implement and rather flexible as it can be used for various vector sizes and precisions, is designed to fully use the communication capacities of channels, and it offers good performance/precision ratio and can effectively be used for both small and large datasets and give maximal precision for fixed-point data types.

References

1. Aliasgari, M., Blanton, M., Zhang, Y., Steele, A.: Secure computation on floating point numbers. In: NDSS (2013)
2. Bogdanov, D., Laur, S., Willemson, J.: Sharemind: a framework for fast privacy-preserving computations. In: Jajodia, S., Lopez, J. (eds.) ESORICS 2008. LNCS, vol. 5283, pp. 192–206. Springer, Heidelberg (2008)
3. Bogdanov, D., Niitsoo, M., Toft, T., Willemson, J.: High-performance secure multi-party computation for data mining applications. Int. J. Inf. Secur. 11(6), 403–418 (2012)
4. Catrina, O., Dragulin, C.: Multiparty computation of fixed-point multiplication and reciprocal. In: 20th International Workshop on Database and Expert Systems Application, DEXA 2009, pp. 107–111 (2009)
5. Catrina, O., de Hoogh, S.: Secure multiparty linear programming using fixed-point arithmetic. In: Gritzalis, D., Preneel, B., Theoharidou, M. (eds.) ESORICS 2010. LNCS, vol. 6345, pp. 134–150. Springer, Heidelberg (2010)

6. Catrina, O., Saxena, A.: Secure computation with fixed-point numbers. In: Sion, R. (ed.) FC 2010. LNCS, vol. 6052, pp. 35–50. Springer, Heidelberg (2010)
7. Gentry, C.: Fully homomorphic encryption using ideal lattices. In: STOC 2009, pp. 169–178 (2009)
8. Gentry, C., Halevi, S.: Implementing gentry's fully-homomorphic encryption scheme. In: Paterson, K.G. (ed.) EUROCRYPT 2011. LNCS, vol. 6632, pp. 129–148. Springer, Heidelberg (2011)
9. Kamm, L.: Privacy-preserving statistical analysis using secure multi-party computation. Ph.D. thesis, University of Tartu (2015)
10. Kamm, L., Willemson, J.: Secure floating-point arithmetic and private satellite collision analysis. Cryptology ePrint Archive, Report 2013/850 (2013). http://eprint. iacr.org/
11. Kerschbaum, F., Schroepfer, A., Zilli, A., Pibernik, R., Catrina, O., de Hoogh, S., Schoenmakers, B., Cimato, S., Damiani, E.: Secure collaborative supply-chain management. Computer **44**(9), 38–43 (2011)
12. Krips, T., Willemson, J.: Hybrid model of fixed and floating point numbers in secure multiparty computations. In: Chow, S.S.M., Camenisch, J., Hui, L.C.K., Yiu, S.M. (eds.) ISC 2014. LNCS, vol. 8783, pp. 179–197. Springer, Heidelberg (2014)
13. Laur, S., Willemson, J., Zhang, B.: Round-efficient oblivious database manipulation. In: Lai, X., Zhou, J., Li, H. (eds.) ISC 2011. LNCS, vol. 7001, pp. 262–277. Springer, Heidelberg (2011)
14. Liedel, M.: Secure distributed computation of the square root and applications. In: Ryan, M.D., Smyth, B., Wang, G. (eds.) ISPEC 2012. LNCS, vol. 7232, pp. 277–288. Springer, Heidelberg (2012)
15. Liu, Y.-C., Chiang, Y.-T., Hsu, T.S., Liau, C.-J., Wang, D.-W.: Floating point arithmetic protocols for constructing secure data analysis application. Procedia Comput. Sci. **22**, 152–161 (2013)
16. Shamir, A.: How to share a secret. Commun. ACM **22**(11), 612–613 (1979)

Security Policies and Biometrics

Security Mechanisms Planning to Enforce Security Policies

Anis Bkakria[1(⊠)], Frédéric Cuppens[1], Nora Cuppens-Boulahia[1],
and David Gross-Amblard[2]

[1] Télécom Bretagne, Rennes, France
{anis.bkakria,frederic.cuppens,nora.cuppens}@telecom-bretagne.eu
[2] IRISA, Université de Rennes 1, Rennes, France
david.gross_amblard@irisa.fr

Abstract. This paper presents an approach allowing for a given security and utility requirements, the selection of a combination of mechanisms and the way it will be applied to enforce them. To achieve this goal, we firstly use an expressive formal language to specify the security and utility properties required by data owners and the security mechanisms that can be used to enforce them. Second, we extend and use a Graphplan-based approach to build a planning graph representing all possible transformations of the system resulting from the application of security mechanisms. Finally, we define a method to search the best security mechanisms execution plan to transform the used system from its initial state to a state in which the security requirements are enforced.

1   Introduction

In recent years, the concept of data outsourcing has become quite popular since it offers many features, including reduced costs from saving in storage, increasing availability as well as minimizing management effort. Many security-related research issues associated with data outsourcing have been studied focusing on data confidentiality [2,12], data authentication and integrity [15,16], Copyright protection [11], privacy and anonymity [21], because outsourced data often contains highly sensitive information which will be stored and managed by third parties. To tackle those traditional security issues, data protection mechanisms have recently been the focus of huge interest, especially cryptographic and information hiding techniques such as encryption, anonymization, watermarking, fragmentation, etc. These mechanisms are known to be efficient when used independently. However, in many situations they have to be combined to ensure security requirements.

To illustrate, let us take an example in which a company wants to outsource its stored and collected data. Let us suppose that the company considers that a first part of the data (Data I) to be outsourced are sensitive and must be protected, a second part of the data (Data II) is not sensitive but it could be stolen and used by competitors, so the company wants to be able to prove its ownership for the outsourced data. A third part of the data (Data III) could disclose the identities of the customers of the company, and that it should be able to perform mathematical and

© Springer International Publishing Switzerland 2016
J. Garcia-Alfaro et al. (Eds.): FPS 2015, LNCS 9482, pp. 85–101, 2016.
DOI: 10.1007/978-3-319-30303-1_6

statistical operations such as data mining over this part of data. In order to preserve confidentiality of Data I, the company may use encryption. It can also use a watermarking mechanism to embed some robust proof of ownership over Data II, and to anonymize Data III in order to preserve its privacy. As you know, many encryption, watermarking and anonymization mechanisms have been proposed recently. The problem then is to define a reasoning method allowing the company to choose the best mechanisms to enforce its security requirements. Moreover, if we suppose that Data I, Data II, and Data III are intersecting, then there will be a piece of data over which encryption, watermarking, and anonymization will be applied. Therefore, these mechanisms must be combined in an appropriate way to provide the security functionalities without one harming the other.

In this paper, we strive to design an approach allowing for given security requirements, selection of the combination of mechanisms and the way it will be applied (e.g., the order of application of the mechanisms) to enforce security requirements. To meet this goal, we present in Sect. 3 an expressive language [3] to formally express the security requirements to be enforced and the security mechanisms that can be used to enforce the corresponding policy. Section 4 presents the problem we want to address in this paper. In Sect. 5,we extend and use the Graphplan approach [5] to build a planning graph representing all possible states of the system resulting from the application of security mechanisms. Section 6 presents our reasoning method to search the best security mechanisms execution plan that can transform the target system from its initial state to a state in which the security requirements are enforced. Section 7 presents the implementation and experimental testing results of our approach. Finally, Sect. 8 reports our conclusions.

2   Related Work

Few research efforts have investigated how to combine security mechanisms to enforce security policies over outsourced data. One of the firsts attempt is proposed in [8], it consists of combining data fragmentation together with encryption to protect outsourced data confidentiality and can only be applied over one-relation databases[1]. Recently, authors of [1,2] have improved the approach presented in [8] in such a way that it can deal with multi-relation databases. They have also proposed a secure and effective technique for querying data distributed in several service providers and improve the security of their querying technique in order to protect data confidentiality under a collaborative Cloud storage service providers model. Popa et al. [19] and Bkakria et al. [4] have proposed approaches based on adjustable encryption, they combine different encryption schemes to get the best trade-off between data confidentiality and data utility for outsourced relational databases. Boho et al. [6] have proposed interesting approach combining watermarking and encryption to protect both the confidentiality and traceability of outsourced multimedia files. All previously cited approaches have three main limitations: First, they are defined in such a way that only two pre-selected security mechanisms can be combined together. Second, they cannot deal with all security properties that

---

[1] Databases composed of only one table.

can be required by data owners as each approach can provide at most two security properties. Finally, they cannot deal with all data structures that can be used to store outsourced data. In our first attempt to overcome these limitations, we define in [3] an expressive formal language based on epistemic linear temporal logic (Epistemic LTL). This formal language allows as to: (1) formally model the system (e.g., data owner, cloud server, etc.) and the data structure on which the security policy should be enforced, (2) formally express the security policy, and (3) formally specify existing security mechanisms that can be used to protect outsourced data. Then, we have defined a reasoning method for our formal model allowing as to pick up the set of security mechanisms that can enforce each security property requirement by the data owner. However, the reasoning method we proposed in [3], does not take into consideration conflicts that may occur between security mechanisms which makes finding a combination of security mechanisms that satisfy many security requirements hard to fulfill.

3   System Specification[3]

We define and use the language $\mathcal{L}$ to formalize our system. In particular, we define formulas describing the basic knowledge of each agent, the formalization of the security and utility requirements to be enforced, and the formalization of the security mechanisms that can be used to enforce the policy. The first-order temporal epistemic language $\mathcal{L}$ is made up of a set of predicates $\mathcal{P}$, propositional connectives $\vee$, $\wedge$, $\neg$, $\rightarrow$ and $\leftrightarrow$, the quantifiers $\forall$, $\exists$. We take the future connectives $\bigcirc$ (next), $\Diamond$ (eventually), $\square$ (always) [10]. For knowledge we assume a set of agents $A_g = \{1, \cdots, m\}$ and use a set of unary modal connectives K_j, for $j \in A_g$, in which a formula $K_j\psi$ is to be read as "agent j knows ψ".

Definition 1. *Let φ and ψ be propositions and P_i be a predicate of arity n in $\mathcal{P}$. The set of well-formed formulas of $\mathcal{L}$ is defined as follows:*
$\phi := P_i(t_1, \cdots, t_n) \mid K_i\psi \mid \neg\varphi \mid \varphi \vee \psi \mid \varphi \wedge \psi \mid \bigcirc \varphi \mid \Diamond\varphi \mid \square\varphi \mid \rightarrow \psi \mid \varphi \leftrightarrow \psi \mid \exists x\psi \mid \forall x\psi$

Definition 2. *An interpretation of the language $\mathcal{L}$ is the triple $\mathcal{K} = (\mathcal{W}, \mathcal{I}, \Phi)$ consisting of a sequence of states $\mathcal{W} = \{w_0, w_1, \cdots\}$, a set of classical first-order structures $\mathcal{I}$ that assigns for each states $w_i \in \mathcal{W}$ a predicate $I_{w_i}(P) : |I_{w_i}|^n \rightarrow \{True, False\}$ for each n-places predicate $P \in \mathcal{P}$ and Φ a transition function which defines transitions between states due to the application of mechanisms (actions). $\Phi(w_i, m_k) = w_j$ if the mechanism m_k transits our system from states w_i to state w_j.*

Definition 3. *Let $\mathcal{W}$ be a sequence of states, w_i $(i \geq 0)$ denote a state of $\mathcal{W}$, and let v be an assignment. The satisfaction relation $\vDash$ for a formula ψ of $\mathcal{L}$ is defined as follows:*

- $(w_i, \mathcal{W}) \vDash P(t_1, \cdots, t_n) \iff I_{w_i}(P)(v(t_1), \cdots, v(t_n)) = True$
- $(w_i, \mathcal{W}) \vDash \neg \psi \iff (w_i, \mathcal{W}) \nvDash \psi$
- $(w_i, \mathcal{W}) \vDash \psi \rightarrow \varphi \iff (w_i, \mathcal{W}) \nvDash \psi$ or $(w_i, \mathcal{W}) \vDash \varphi$
- $(w_i, \mathcal{W}) \vDash \psi \leftrightarrow \varphi \iff (w_i, \mathcal{W}) \vDash (\psi \rightarrow \varphi) \wedge (\varphi \rightarrow \psi)$
- $(w_i, \mathcal{W}) \vDash \forall x \psi \iff (w_i, \mathcal{W}) \vDash \psi[x/c]$ for all $c \in |I_{w_i}|$
- $(w_i, \mathcal{W}) \vDash \psi \wedge \varphi \iff (w_i, \mathcal{W}) \vDash \psi$ and $(w_i, \mathcal{W}) \vDash \varphi$
- $(w_i, \mathcal{W}) \vDash \psi \vee \varphi \iff (w_i, \mathcal{W}) \vDash \psi$ or $(w_i, \mathcal{W}) \vDash \varphi$
- $(w_i, \mathcal{W}) \vDash \bigcirc \psi \iff (w_{i+1}, \mathcal{W}) \vDash \psi$
- $(w_i, \mathcal{W}) \vDash \Diamond \psi \iff (w_k, \mathcal{W}) \vDash \psi$ for some $k \geq i$
- $(w_i, \mathcal{W}) \vDash \Box \psi \iff (w_k, \mathcal{W}) \vDash \psi$ for all $k \geq i$

3.1 Security Policy Specification

The security policy to be enforced over the target system are specified through a set of security constraints and a set of utility goals.

Security Constraints: Using security constraints, the data owner specifies the security requirements that should be met by the target system. We define five types of security constraints.

- **Confidentiality Constraint:** It requires the protection of the confidentiality of an object in the target system.

$$\Box \; [\forall o, \forall e. \; object(o) \wedge sensitive(o) \wedge untrusted(e) \rightarrow \neg K_e \, o]. \tag{1}$$

Formula 1 specifies that in any state of the target system, an untrusted entity e should not knows any sensitive object o.
- **Privacy Constraint:** The data owner requires the prevention of identity disclosure.

$$\Box \; [\forall o, \forall e. \; object(o) \wedge identifier(o) \wedge untrusted(e) \rightarrow \neg K_e \, o]. \tag{2}$$

Formula 2 specifies that an object o that can be exploited to identify an identity should not be known by any untrusted entity e in any state of the used system.
- **Traceability Constraint (Traitor Detection):** In the applications where a database contents are publicly available over a network, the content owner would like to discourage unauthorized duplication and distribution. For this the owner wants to give to a set of entities E' the ability to check that the content has been released to an authorized user.

$$\Box \; [\forall o, \forall e. \; object(o) \wedge sensitive(o) \wedge untrusted(e) \wedge K_e o$$
$$\rightarrow \bigwedge_{e_1 \in E'} K_{e_1}(\exists E_r. \bigwedge_{e_r \in E_r} (trusted(e_r) \wedge responsible(e_r, o)))]. \tag{3}$$

Formula 3 means that in any state of the system, if an untrusted entity knows a sensitive object o, the set of entities E' should be able to know the set of entities E_r responsible of the disclosure of the sensitive object o.

- **Ownership Constraint:** The data owner wants to give a set of entities E the ability to verify the ownership of the object o_2.

$$\square \,[\forall o_1.\forall o_2, e \; object(o_1) \wedge object(o_2) \wedge copy\_of(o_1, o_2) \wedge$$

$$\bigwedge_{e_r \in E} K_{e_r} owner(e, o_1) \rightarrow \bigwedge_{e_r \in E} K_{e_r} owner(e, o_2)]. \tag{4}$$

Formula 4 specifies that in any state of the system, if there are two objects o_1 and o_2 such that o_2 is a copy of o_1 and a set of entities E which know that the owner of o_1 is e, therefore E should be able to know that o_2 belongs to e.
- **Integrity Assessment Constraint:** Verifying the accuracy and consistency of an object o over its entire life-cycle. This means that data cannot be modified in an undetected manner. In the target system, we should be able to check if o has been modified or not. A data owner may want to give a set of entities E' the ability to check the integrity of an object o.

$$\square \,[\, object(o) \rightarrow \bigwedge_{e_1 \in E'} K_{e_1}(is\_modified(o) \vee is\_unmodified(o))]. \tag{5}$$

Utility Goals: Using utility goals, the data owner can require that some functionalities should be provided. An utility goals is specified using the formula 6 meaning that the utility requirement req is to be provided over the o.

$$utility\_requirement(req) \wedge provides(req, o) \tag{6}$$

3.2 Mechanisms Specification

The security mechanisms to be used in the system are specified using preconditions formulas and effects formulas.

Preconditions. For each mechanism, preconditions are represented by a set of formulas which are necessary conditions required for the application of the security mechanism. We define the two-places predicate $is\_applicable$. The formula $is\_applicable(m, o)$ is to be read "the mechanism m can be applied over the object o". Preconditions of a security mechanism m are specified using a formula of the following form:

$$\square \,(is\_applicable(m, o) \rightarrow \Delta_m) \tag{7}$$

where Δ_m represents necessary conditions for the applicability of the mechanism m. A formula of the form (7) is to be read "At any state of the system, m can be applied if the preconditions Δ_m hold". **Effects.** Modifications resulting from the application of a mechanism m that transits the system from a state w_i to a state w_j. We use the two-places predicate $apply(m, o)$ to say that the mechanism m is applied over the object o. For a mechanism m, effects are represented by a set of formulas Σ_m such that:

$$\Phi(w_i,\ apply(m,o)) = w_j \ \rightarrow \ (w_j \vDash \Sigma_m) \tag{8}$$

Axiom 8 states that if the application of the mechanism m over the object o transits the system from a state w_i to a state w_j, therefore the set of effects Σ_m of the application of the mechanism m is satisfied on the state w_j.

4   Problem Statement

We strive to plan a sequence of mechanisms allowing to transform the system from its initial state to a state in which the goals are reached while respecting a set of defined constraints. Planning efficiency can be improved by allowing parallel application of mechanisms, which leads to minimize the number of parallel plan steps. In order to be able to apply mechanisms parallelly, we should figure out which mechanisms are compatible by finding different kind of conflicts between mechanisms.

Definition 4 *Conflicting Mechanisms: Two mechanisms M_1 and M_2 represented respectively by $(\Delta_{M_1}, \Sigma_{M_1})$ and $(\Delta_{M_2}, \Sigma_{M_2})$ where Δ_{M_i} and Σ_{M_i} represents respectively the specifications of preconditions and the effects of M_i, are effectively incompatible if and only if one of the following deductions hold:*

(i) $\Sigma_{M_1} \cup \Sigma_{M_2} \vdash \bot$
(ii) $\Sigma_{M_i} \cup \Delta_{M_j} \vdash \bot$ *with* $1 \le i, j \le 2$ *and* $i \neq j$
(ii) $\Delta_{M_1} \cup \Delta_{M_2} \vdash \bot$

Item (i) means that the effects of M_1 and M_2 are inconsistent. Item (ii) means that the effects of the application of M_i dissatisfy the preconditions of M_j. Item (iii) states that M_1 and M_2 have a competing preconditions such that they cannot be true in the same state.

Definition 5 *Parallel Plan: Consider a set of available mechanisms $\mathcal{M}$. A parallel plan is a finite sequence of sets of mechanisms $\mathcal{P} = \{p_1, \cdots, p_n\}$ such that any $p_i \in \mathcal{P}, p_i \subseteq \mathcal{M}$.*

Definition 6 *Correctness: Given a system $\mathcal{S}$, its current state w_1, a finite set of mechanisms $\mathcal{M}$, a parallel plan $\mathcal{P} = \{p_1, \cdots, p_n\}$ is correct regarding $\mathcal{S}$ and w_1 if and only if the following conditions hold:*

(i) $\exists w_2, \cdots, w_n$ *such that* $: \forall M \in p_i, w_i \vDash \Delta_M, 1 \le i \le n$.
(ii) $\forall p_i \in \mathcal{P}, \forall M_1, M_2 \in p_i :\ M_1$ *and* M_2 *are not conflicting.*

Parallel Planning Problem: Consider a system $\mathcal{S}$, its current state w_1, a set of mechanisms $\mathcal{M}$ that can be applied over the system, a set of goals $\mathcal{G}$ that should be achieved, and a set of constraints $\mathcal{C}$ that should be respected. The Parallel Planning Problem consists on finding a sequence of sets of mechanisms $\mathcal{P} = \{p_1, \cdots, p_n\}$ such that the following conditions hold:

(i) $\mathcal{P}$ is correct regarding $\mathcal{S}$ and w_1.

(ii) $\forall w_i = \Phi(w_{i-1}, p_{i-1})$, $\forall c \in \mathcal{C} : w_i \vDash c, 2 \leq i \leq n$.

In next part, we briefly introduce the Graphplan's basic operations as defined in [5]. Graphplan uses action schemata in the STRIPS format in witch each action is represented as preconditions and effects which is suitable with the representation of our mechanisms parallel planning problem.

4.1   Graphplan Description

Graphplan is a directed, leveled graph composed of two kinds of nodes and tree kinds of edges. Graphplan levels alternate between *fact levels* containing *fact nodes* (each node is labeled with a predicate), and *action levels* composed of *action nodes* (each labeled with some security mechanism). Relations between actions and predicates in a Graphplan are explicitly represented through edges. *Preconditions-edges* are used to connect action nodes of an action level i to their preconditions in the fact level i. *Effects-edges* connect action nodes belonging to the action level i to their effects in the fact level $i + 1$. *Mutual-exclusion edges* are relations connecting action nodes belonging to the same Graphplan level. They represent conflicts between action nodes identified according to Definition 4.

   Graphplan is based on two main phases: The first is called Graphplan construction phase consisting of growing a planning graph. The second phase allows to extract possible solutions (plans) from the graphplan by performing a backward searching phase starting with the goals. In the graph construction phase, we start with a planning graph having only a single fact level which contains the initial specification of the used system. GraphPlan construction method runs in stages, in each stage i, it extends the planning graph resulting from the stage $i - 1$ by adding one time step which contains the next action level and the following fact level. After each stage, Graphplan check if all predicates representing the goals are presented in the last fact level in the planning graph, if it is the case, search a valid plan that transform the system from its initial state to a state in which all the goals are achieved.

4.2   Graphplan Modeling of the Problem

The STRIPS system [9] used by Graphplan is represented by four lists, a finite set $\mathcal{C}_s$ of ground atomic formulas called conditions, a finite set of operators $\mathcal{O}_s$ where each operator is composed of two formulas (satisfiable conjunction of conditions) representing its preconditions and effects, a finite set of predicates $\mathcal{I}_s$ that denotes the initial state, and a finite set of predicates $\mathcal{G}_s$ that denotes goal state. As we have seen in the previous section, our planning problem is composed of a system $\mathcal{S}$, a set of security mechanisms $\mathcal{M}$, a set of constraints $\mathcal{C}$, and a set of goals $\mathcal{G}$. Obviously, $\mathcal{S}$, $\mathcal{M}$, and $\mathcal{G}$ can be easily modeled as a STRIPS planning problem by expressing $\mathcal{S}$ as $\mathcal{C}_s$ and $\mathcal{I}_s$, $\mathcal{M}$ as $\mathcal{O}_s$, and $\mathcal{G}$ as $\mathcal{G}_s$. According to the Sect. 3.1, $\mathcal{C}$ will be composed of security constraints and utility goals. Utility goals specify the functionalities that should be provided for $\mathcal{S}$ (e.g. the ability to compare the equality of objects). A plan P satisfies a set of utility goals C_u if at its end none of the utility goals in C_u is violated. Consequently, utility constraints will be expressed as goals in the STRIPS planning problem. Security constraints specify the requirements that should be respected during the transformation of $\mathcal{S}$, they can be considered as safety constraint meaning that those requirements are to be satisfied in all states of $\mathcal{S}$. However, the STRIPS language as it is defined in [9] cannot express this kind of constraints. To overcome this limitation, we extend the STRIPS system language by adding the operator *Constraint* allowing to express the set of security constraints. For instance, a confidentiality constraint (rule 1) is to be expressed as follows:

Constraint (confidentiality_constraint$_1$(o, e):
  Formula: $object(o) \wedge sensitive(o) \wedge untrusted(e) \wedge K_e o$)

In the previous expression, *confidentiality_constraint*$_1$ *(o,e)* is used to denote the name of the constraint and the variables (bounded variables of the rule 1) to be instantiated. The *Formula* field represents the conjunction of predicates indicating the condition under which the constraint is violated (the negation of CNF representation of the constraint).

5   Extending Graphplan

5.1   Graph Construction Phase Extension

We extend Graphplan's construction method of the planning graph in two ways. The first extension allows to build a planning graph of a planning problem which contains *Domain Axioms* (axioms that formally specify relations between different objects of the system). Second, we improve the Graphplan's construction method of the planning graph to avoid the violation of security constraints while building the planning graph.

The Need of Axioms. In Graphplan approach, the lack of axioms disrupts the ability to represent real-word domains containing normally quite complex conditions and rules. Without the use of axioms, mechanisms preconditions and effects can become quickly too complex and unreadable. In our approach, we believe that the use of axiom will provide a natural way of deriving supervenient properties, representing logical consequences of the effects of applied mechanisms.

Updating Knowledge Using an Inference Graph

In this part, we present how we define axioms in our approach and the way they will be used in the planning process. We define an axiom as an expression in the following form:

$$\bigwedge_{i=1}^{n} p_i \rightarrow \bigwedge_{j=1}^{m} q_j \tag{9}$$

Where each p_i and q_j are predicates of our defined language.

According to a state w of the used system, we want to be able to infer all possible new facts based on a set of axioms that represents relationships between different predicates in our language. To meet this goal, we utilize the same construction method used in Graphplan in order to build an inference graph. In this construction method, we consider each axiom in our system as an action, then the left part of the representation of the axiom (9) will be the preconditions of the action and the right part is its effects. The idea consists on applying in each layer of the graph the set of applicable actions (axioms) until we infer all possible new facts. Algorithm 1 describes how the inference graph is constructed. Once it is built, it allows to extract the set of facts that are derived using the set of defined axioms. In fact, the set of inferred facts is $\mathcal{IG}_l \setminus \mathcal{IG}_0$ were $\mathcal{IG}_0$ and $\mathcal{IG}_l$ represent respectively the set of predicate-nodes in the first fact level and the set of predicate-nodes in the last fact level of the inference graph.

```
input  :
         G    /* planning graph (Graphplan) */
         last_fl_G = {f_1, ··· , f_n} /* set of facts in the last fact level of G */
         A_x = {Ax_1, ··· , Ax_m}    /* the set of domain axioms */
output:
         inferred_facts   /* the set of derived new facts */
1  Main
2  IG = ∅   /* inference graph initialization */
3  add_fact_level(IG, last_fl)   /* add the last fact level of G to the inference graph IG */
4  for i = 0 to m do
5      new_fact_level = ∅   /* new empty fact level */
6      new_fact_level = last_level(IG)   /* copy the last fact level of IG to new_fact_level */
7      foreach axiom in A_x do
8          instances = instantiate(axiom)   /* get all instances of the axiom */
9          foreach inst in instances do
10             /* axioms can be divided into left and right parts (rule 9) */
11             if (last_level(IG) ⊨ left_part(inst)) then
12                 new_fact_level = new_fact_level ∪ right_part(inst)
13             end
14         endfch
15     endfch
16     if (new_fact_level == last_level(IG)) then
17         inferred_facts = new_fact_level \ last_fl_G
18         break
19     else
20         add_fact_level(IG, new_fact_level)
21     end
22 end
```

Algorithm 1. Building inference graph and getting new derived facts

Theorem 1. *Given the set of formulas Σ_w representing the system S in the state w, and a set of n consistent axioms $\mathcal{A} = \{ax_1, \cdots, ax_n\}$, the height of the graph representing the graph inference of S using $\mathcal{A}$ will be at most n.*

Theorem 2. *Consider a system S composed of n objects and represented by p predicates in a state w_i, and m axioms each having a constant number of bounded variables. Let q be the largest number of predicates in the right-side of each axiom (formula 9). Then, the size of a k-level inference graph and the time required to build it, are polynomial n, m, q, p and k.*

Building Planning Graph Under Security Constraints

The specification of security constraints requires that some properties should be respected during all the states of the target system. Since each fact level of the planning graph is built using the construction method of Graphplan, it can be considered as a possible state of the system, our idea consists of verifying the satisfiability of security constraints on each new created fact level of the planning graph during its construction.

Definition 7 *Violated Security Constraint: Consider a planning graph G composed of n fact levels $fl_1, \cdots, fl_n$, each fact level fl_i is composed of a set of facts w_i. A security constraint C specified in our formal language using the set of formulas Σ_C and specified in the STRIPS system language by $\overline{\Sigma_C}$ (the negation of CNF of Σ_C) is violated in a fact level fl_i if and only if $w_i \vDash \overline{\Sigma_C}$.*

Graphplan uses directed edges to connect each action instance node belonging to the ith action level of the graph to the set of fact nodes belonging to the ith fact level representing its preconditions, and to the set of fact nodes belonging to the $(i + 1)$th fact level representing its effects. Thanks to this property, we are able to find the combinations of actions belonging to the ith action level of the graph and leading to security constraints violation in the $(i + 1)$th fact level.

Algorithm 2 describes the used method to get the combinations of actions leading to violate a security constraint. The correctness and the complexity of the Algorithm 2 are proved by the following theorems.

Theorem 3 *(Correctness): Given a violated security constraint C and a set of fact nodes cause_nodes that causes the violation of C, the Algorithm 2 terminates and computes all the combinations of actions that lead to violate C.*

Theorem 4 *(Complexity): Given a violated security constraint C, a set of cause nodes $CN = \{n_1, \cdots, n_n\}$ representing the set of fact nodes that causes the violation of C, the complexity of the algorithm 2 is $O(\prod_{i=1}^{n} l_i)$ in time, where l_i is the number of different actions providing the fact node n_i.*

```
   input  :
           C   /* the violated security constraint */
           cause_nodes   /* the set of fact_nodes that causes the violation of C */
   output:
           action_combinations   /* the set of combinations of actions that violate the
           constraint C */
 1 Main
 2   combination = ∅
 3   all_combinations(causes_nodes, action_combination)
 4 End Main
 5
 6 Recursive Procedure all_combination(nodes, combination)
 7 if (Card(nodes) == 0) then
 8   |    add(combination, action_combination) /* add combination to action_combination */
 9 end
10 first_node = nodes.first   /* get the first node in the set nodes */
11 remove(nodes, first_nodes)   /* remove the first_node from the set nodes */
12 foreach action_node in first_nodes.in_edges do
13   |    copy_combination = combination
14   |    if (action_node ∉ copy_combination) then
15   |    |    add(action_node, copy_combination)
16   |    end
17   |    all_combinations(causes_nodes, copy_combination)
18 endfch
```

Algorithm 2. Getting all combinations of actions that violate a constraint

Once we know the combination of actions $\mathbb{C}_c$ that leads to the violation of the security constraint C. The trivial way to solve this violation problem would be to remove $\mathbb{C}_c$ and its corresponding effects from the planning graph. However, this solution can be useless in many cases as it can prevent some actions in $\mathbb{C}_c$ (a subset of $\mathbb{C}_c$) that do not violate C to be used.

Avoiding Security Constraints Violation. In Graphplan, mutual exclusions are basically used to specify that no valid plan could possibly contain conflictual actions in the same plan step. Since, a security constraint C is violated if all actions in a combination $\mathbb{C}_c$ that violates C are applied in the same action level of the planning graph, our solution to prevent this violation is to use mutual exclusion relations as following:

(i) If $|\mathbb{C}_c| \geq 2$: $\forall$ $node_a \in \mathbb{C}_c$, create a mutual-exclusion between $node_a$ and $\mathbb{C}_c \setminus \{node_a\}$.

(ii) If $|\mathbb{C}_c| = 1$, remove the action-node in $\mathbb{C}_c$ and its corresponding effects from the planning graph.

where $|\mathbb{C}_c|$ represents the number of action-nodes in $\mathbb{C}_c$. (i) ensures that if the number of action-nodes in $\mathbb{C}_c$ is more that one, therefore we will create a mutual-exclusion between each action-node $node_a$ in $\mathbb{C}_c$ and the set of other action-nodes in $\mathbb{C}_c$. This allows in one side to ensure that no correct plan could possibly contain $node_a$ and $\mathbb{C}_c \setminus \{node_a\}$ together which allows to avoid the violation of the security constraint C, and on the other side allows the largest subsets of action-nodes ($\mathbb{C}_c \setminus \{node_a\}$) in $\mathbb{C}_c$ that do not violate C to be used together in the same plan. (ii) states that if $\mathbb{C}_c$ is composed of only one action-node, therefore, the unique solution to avoid the violation of C is to remove the action-node in $\mathbb{C}_c$ as well as its corresponding effects from the planning graph.

6 Searching the Best Plan

Given a planning graph $\mathcal{G}$ constructed using our previously explained extension of GraphPlan, our goal is to find the best mechanisms execution plan (parallel plan) that enforces the chosen security and utility requirements. For this end, and to be able to compare different mechanisms execution plans, as a first step, we assign a weight for each action-node in $\mathcal{G}$ representing a security mechanism using the metric described in Definition 8. As a second step, we define a second metric to measure a score for each mechanisms execution plan that can satisfy the defined policy as described in Definition 9.

Definition 8. *Consider an action-node an_M in $\mathcal{G}$ representing the application of the security mechanism M over the object ob. Suppose that M provides n security properties $sp_1, \cdots, sp_n$ and m utility properties $up_1, \cdots, up_m$. The weight ω which will be assigned to an_M is measured as following:*

$$\omega = \alpha_{ob} \sum_{i=1}^{n} \tau_i + \beta_{ob} \sum_{i=1}^{m} \nu_i - \delta_{ob}\, \varepsilon_M$$

where $\tau_i \in [0,1]$ represents the robustness level of the provided security property sp_i, $\nu_i \in [0,1]$ represents the satisfiability level of the provided utility property up_i, $\varepsilon_M \in [0,1]$ is the deployment efficiency level of the mechanism M, and $\alpha_{ob} \in [0,1]$, $\beta_{ob} \in [0,1]$, and $\delta_{ob} \in [0,1]$ represents respectively the security, utility, and deployment efficiency factors of ob such that α_{ob}, β_{ob}, and δ_{ob} are complementary.

The intuitions behind the use of the robustness level τ (1), the satisfiability level ν (2), the deployment efficiency level ε (3), and the security, utility and deployment efficiency factors (4) to measure the weight of an action-node is that: (1) Some security mechanisms are not as robust as they should be to fully ensure their provided security properties under well known attacks. For example, encryption-based mechanisms are supposed to ensure the confidentiality of the objects over which they are applied. However an Order-preserving encryption based mechanisms such as Boldyreva [7] preserves the order of the plaintexts, which may enable many attacks. It was concluded that order-preserving encryption leaks at least half of the plaintexts bits [22]. Hence, the confidentiality robustness level $\tau_{confidentiality}$ will be less that 0.5 for Boldyreva. (2) Some security mechanisms cannot fully provide some utility requirements. In these cases, the satisfiability level factor ν is used to specify the level of providability of an utility requirement. For illustrative purpose, let us take the example of homomorphic-based encryption mechanisms which are supposed to provide computation (addition + multiplication) over encrypted objects. However, Paillier cryptosystem [17] is homomorphic-based encryption mechanisms allowing to perform only addition over encrypted data. Therefore, satisfiability level factor of computation for Paillier cryptosystem will be $\nu_{computation} = 0.5$. (3) Some security mechanisms are expensive in terms of deployment time compared to other security mechanisms, we take this fact into consideration by using the deployment efficiency level ε_M, as much as the mechanism M can be efficiently deployed, ε_M will be closer to 1. (4) The weight of an_M representing the application of M over ob should also take into account the security, utility and deployment efficiency factors represented respectively by ϵ_{ob}, ρ_{ob}, and δ_{ob}, which are specified by the data owner for ob. For illustrative purpose, let us take a file f_1 storing information about the payment parameters used by the costumers of a company. The company attributes the value 0.8 to ϵ_{f_1}, 0.1 to ρ_{f_1}, and 0.1 to δ_{ob} as it considers that the utility of f_1 as well as deployment efficiency of the policy over f_1 are not important compared to its security. That is why the action-node in $\mathcal{G}$ representing a security mechanism applied over f_1 which ensures the highest level of robustness for security properties will have the highest weight compared to others having high providability of utility requirements, high deployment efficiency and weakly robustness for security properties.

Definition 9. *Consider a parallel plan* $\mathcal{P} = \{p_1, \cdots, p_n\}$. *Suppose that each* $p_i \in \mathcal{P}$ *is composed of* m_i *action-nodes* $an_1^i, \cdots, an_{m_i}^i$. *The score* Sc *of* $\mathcal{P}$ *is:*

$$Sc = \sum_{i=1}^{n} \sum_{j=1}^{m_i} \omega_j^i$$

where ω_j^i *is the weight of the action-node* an_j^i *measured according to the Definition 8.*

Definition 10. *Consider a security policy* $\mathcal{SP}$ *and a set of parallel plans* $\mathcal{P}_1, \cdots, \mathcal{P}_n$ *in* $\mathcal{G}$ *each satisfying* $\mathcal{SP}$ *and all having respectively the scores* $Sc_1, \cdots, Sc_n$. *A parallel plan* $\mathcal{P}$ *having the score* Sc *is the best parallel plan in* $\{\mathcal{P}_1, \cdots, \mathcal{P}_n\}$ *if the following condition holds:*

$$\forall i \in 1 \cdots n, \ Sc \geq Sc_i$$

Obliviously, finding the best parallel plan in a planning graph $\mathcal{G}$ that enforces a security policy $\mathcal{SP}$ requires finding all parallel plans in $\mathcal{G}$ that satisfy $\mathcal{SP}$.

Theorem 5. *Computing all parallel plans in a planning graph that enforce a security policy* $\mathcal{SP}$ *is NP-hard.*

Heuristic Search Based Planning

Our goal is to find the parallel plan having both the maximum score regarding our metric (defined in Definitions 8, 9, and 10), and the minimum number of steps. To this end, we use the cost-optimal planner CO-PLAN [20] which proceeds in four stages:

- Planning graph conversion to CNF wff: Convert the planning graph into a CNF notation by constructing proposition formula as described in [13].
- Wff solving: CO-PLAN uses a modified version of RSAT [18] called CORSAT to process the CNF formulae which allows to figure out: (1) If a solution exists for the given decision problem, and (2) if a solution exists, it is identified with minimal plan costs.

- Bounded forward-search: CO-PLAN uses the speed and efficiency of SAT-based planners allowing to obtain a good admissible initial bound on the cost of an optimal plan. In the second phase, CO-PLAN performs then a bounded forward-search in the problem state space.
- Plan extraction: If a model of the wff is found, then the model is converted to the corresponding plan; otherwise, the length of planing graph is incremented and the process repeats.

In fact, CO-PLAN identify the solution having the minimal parallel plan costs. To be able to use it, we transform our parallel plan score maximization problem to a minimization plan cost problem by considering that $Cost_\mathcal{P} = -Sc_\mathcal{P}$, where $Cost_\mathcal{P}$ and $Sc_\mathcal{P}$ represent respectively the cost of the parallel plan $\mathcal{P}$ and the score of $\mathcal{P}$ measured according to Definition 9.

7   Implementation and Evaluations

In the experimental part of this work, we measure the computational performance of our approach.

7.1   Implementation

We develop a prototype implementing our approach to find a near-optimal security mechanisms plan allowing to enforce security policies for outsourced data using available open source C++ libraries. For GraphPlan construction, we used the SATPLAN'06 library [14] allowing to create a planning graph up to some length k. We extend SATPLAN'06 library (as described in Sect. 5) to support: (1) the use of domain axioms allowing to deduce new facts about objects of the system to be used, and (2) we improve the Graphplans construction method of the planning graph to avoid the violation of security constraints while building the planning graph. For analyzing the planning graph and searching the best mechanisms plan, we used CO-PLAN library [20].

7.2   Experimental Setup

The domain that we have used in evaluating our prototype is composed of:

- A data owner;
- A finite set of users:
  - Trusted users: which can access and use the outsourced data
  - Untrusted users: which are not supposed to be able to violate the policy. In all experiments, we suppose that we have two untrusted users, a cloud server and an external adversary.
- A finite set of objects that represents the data to be outsourced, we consider that the data owner wants to outsource a file system. So the objects are the set of files and directories in the file system to be outsourced.

- A finite set of security and utility requirements representing the policy to be enforced. We suppose that the data owner will specify some security constraints and utility goals over some objects in the file system to be outsourced. Only the objects over which the data owner has specified the policy will be considered in the planning problem.
- A finite set of security mechanisms that can be used to enforce the security policy. We specified 20 security mechanisms, including 8 encryption-based mechanisms, 4 anonymization-based mechanisms, 6 watermarking-based mechanisms, and 2 information transfer protocols HTTPS and SSH that can be used to send the objects to be outsourced to the cloud server.

We ran the all experiments on a server with Intel core i7 2.50 GHz, 16 GB of RAM, and running Debian 7.

7.3   Experimental Results

We conducted a set of experiments to evaluate the performance of our prototype. Table 1 shows the parameters used in each experiment, the number of nodes in the planning graph built to resolve the problem, and the time needed to find a near-optimal solution using the method we presented in Sect. 6. Due to lack of space, we will not be able to include the specifications of the constraints and the security mechanisms that are used in each experiment.

Table 1. Our prototype performance with respect to: the number of objects that will be outsourced (objects), the number of constraints defined over the object to be outsourced (constraints), the number of users involved in the used system (users), the number of security mechanisms that can be used to enforce the policy (mechanisms). Column "number of nodes" indicates the number of nodes in the planning graph.

Parameters				Number of nodes	Time(s)
Objects	Constraints	Users	Mecanisms		
5	5	5	15	75952	1.9
10	10	5	15	121385	9.7
20	15	5	15	721385	97.65
100	50	5	20	1951423	721.5

8   Conclusion

In this paper, we have presented a new framework allowing: first, a data owner to formally specify different security and utility requirements that should be enforced over the data to be outsource. Second, to specify existing security mechanisms that can be used to enforce the policy defined by the data owner. Finally, to choose the near-optimal security mechanisms execution plan that enforces the policy while offering the best tradeoff between security, utility and complexity.

References

1. Bkakria, A., Cuppens, F., Cuppens-Boulahia, N., Fernandez, J.M., et al.: Confidentiality-preserving query execution of fragmented outsourced data. In: Mustofa, K., Neuhold, E.J., Tjoa, T.J., Weippl, E., You, I. (eds.) ICT-EurAsia 2013. LNCS, vol. 7804, pp. 426–440. Springer, Heidelberg (2013)
2. Bkakria, A., Cuppens, F., Cuppens-Boulahia, N., Fernandez, J.M., Gross-Amblard, D.: Preserving multi-relational outsourced databases confidentiality using fragmentation and encryption. JoWUA 4(2), 39–62 (2013)
3. Bkakria, A., Cuppens, F., Cuppens-Boulahia, N., Gross-Amblard, D.: Specification and deployment of integrated security policies for outsourced data. In: Atluri, V., Pernul, G. (eds.) DBSec 2014. LNCS, vol. 8566, pp. 17–32. Springer, Heidelberg (2014)
4. Bkakria, A., Schaad, A., Kerschbaum, F., Cuppens, F., Cuppens-Boulahia, N., Gross-Amblard, D.: Optimized and controlled provisioning of encrypted outsourced data. In: 19th ACM Symposium on Access Control Models and Technologies, SACMAT 2014, London, ON, Canada, 25–27 June 2014, pp. 141–152 (2014)
5. Blum, A., Furst, M.L.: Fast planning through planning graph analysis. In: Proceedings of the Fourteenth International Joint Conference on Artificial Intelligence, IJCAI 1995, Montréal Québec, Canada, 20–25 August 1995, vol. 2, pp. 1636–1642 (1995)
6. Boho, A., Van Wallendael, G., Dooms, A., De Cock, J., Braeckman, G., Schelkens, P., Preneel, B., Van de Walle, R.: End-to-end security for video distribution: the combination of encryption, watermarking, and video adaptation. IEEE Sig. Process. Mag. 30(2), 97–107 (2013)
7. Boldyreva, A., Chenette, N., Lee, Y., O'Neill, A., et al.: Order-preserving symmetric encryption. In: Joux, A. (ed.) EUROCRYPT 2009. LNCS, vol. 5479, pp. 224–241. Springer, Heidelberg (2009)
8. Ciriani, V., De Capitani di Vimercati, S., Foresti, S., Jajodia, S., Paraboschi, S., Samarati, P.: Fragmentation and encryption to enforce privacy in data storage. In: Biskup, J., López, J. (eds.) ESORICS 2007. LNCS, vol. 4734, pp. 171–186. Springer, Heidelberg (2007)
9. Fikes, R., Nilsson, N.J.: STRIPS: a new approach to the application of theorem proving to problem solving. Artif. Intell. 2(3/4), 189–208 (1971)
10. Gabbay, D., Pnueli, A., Shelah, S., Stavi, J.: On the temporal analysis of fairness. In: Proceedings of the 7th ACM SIGPLAN-SIGACT Symposium on Principles of Programming Languages, POPL 1980, pp. 163–173. ACM, New York (1980)
11. Gross-Amblard, D.: Query-preserving watermarking of relational databases and xml documents. ACM Trans. Database Syst. 36(1), 3 (2011)
12. Hacigümüs, H., Iyer, B.R., Li, C., Mehrotra, S.: Executing SQL over encrypted data in the database-service-provider model. In: Proceedings of the ACM SIGMOD International Conference on Management of Data, Madison, Wisconsin, 3–6 June 2002, pp. 216–227 (2002)
13. Kautz, H.A., Selman, B.: Pushing the envelope: planning, propositional logic and stochastic search. In: Proceedings of the Thirteenth National Conference on Artificial Intelligence and Eighth Innovative Applications of Artificial Intelligence Conference, AAAI 1996, IAAI 1996, Portland, Oregon, 4–8 August 1996, vol. 2, pp. 1194–1201 (1996)
14. Kautz, H.A., Selman, B., Hoffmann, J.: SatPlan: planning as satisfiability. In: Abstracts of the 5th International Planning Competition (2006)
15. Mykletun, E., Narasimha, M., Tsudik, G.: Authentication and integrity in outsourced databases. In: Proceedings of the Network and Distributed System Security Symposium, NDSS, San Diego, California (2004)

16. Narasimha, M., Tsudik, G.: DSAC: an approach to ensure integrity of outsourced databases using signature aggregation and chaining. IACR Cryptology ePrint Arch. **2005**, 297 (2005)
17. Paillier, P.: Public-key cryptosystems based on composite degree residuosity classes. In: Stern, J. (ed.) EUROCRYPT 1999. LNCS, vol. 1592, pp. 223–238. Springer, Heidelberg (1999)
18. Pipatsrisawat, K., Darwiche, A.: Rsat 2.0: Sat solver description. Technical report (2007)
19. Popa, R.A., Redfield, Catherine M. S Zeldovich, N., Balakrishnan, H.: Cryptdb: protecting confidentiality with encrypted query processing. In: Proceedings of the 23rd ACM Symposium on Operating Systems Principles, SOSP 2011, Cascais, Portugal, 23–26 October 2011, pp. 85–100 (2011)
20. Robinson, N., Gretton, C., Pham, D.-N.: Co-plan: combining sat-based planning with forward-search. In: Proceedings of IPC-6 (2008)
21. Sweeney, L.: k-anonymity: a model for protecting privacy. Int. J. Uncertainty, Fuzziness Knowl.Based Syst. **10**(5), 557–570 (2002)
22. Xiao, L., Yen, I.-L.: Security analysis for order preserving encryption schemes. In: 46th Annual Conference on Information Sciences and Systems, CISS , Princeton, 21–23 March 2012, pp. 1–6 (2012)

Runtime Enforcement with Partial Control

Raphaël Khoury[(✉)] and Sylvain Hallé

Laboratoire d'informatique formelle, Département d'informatique et de
mathématique, Université du Québec à Chicoutimi, Chicoutimi, Canada
`raphael.khoury@uqac.ca, shalle@acm.org`

Abstract. This study carries forward the line of enquiry that seeks to
characterize precisely which security policies are enforceable by runtime
monitors. In this regard, Basin et al. recently refined the structure that
helps distinguish between those actions that the monitor can potentially
suppress or insert in the execution, from those that the monitor can
only observe. In this paper, we generalize this model by organizing the
universe of possible actions in a lattice that naturally corresponds to the
levels of monitor control. We then delineate the set of properties that
are enforceable under this paradigm and relate our results to previous
work in the field. Finally, we explore the set of security policies that are
enforceable if the monitor is given greater latitude to alter the execution
of its target, which allows us to reflect on the capabilities of different
types of monitors.

1   Introduction

Runtime monitoring is an approach to enforcing security policies that seeks to
allow untrusted code to run safely by observing its execution and reacting as
needed to prevent a violation of a user-supplied security policy. This method of
ensuring the security of code is rapidly gaining acceptance in practice and several
implementations exist [18]. One question seems to recur frequently in multiple
studies: exactly which set of properties are *monitorable*, in the sense that they
are enforceable by monitors. Previous research has identified several factors that
can affect the set of security policies enforceable by monitors. These include the
means at the disposal of monitors to react to a potential violation of the security
policy [3], the availability of statically gathered data about the target program's
possible executions [3,9], memory and computability constraints [13,14] etc.

One specific aspect that can have a considerable impact on the monitor's
expressiveness is its ability to either suppress certain actions performed by the
target program from occurring during the execution (while allowing the remainder of the execution to continue unaffected) or to insert additional events in an
ongoing execution. These abilities, when available, extend the monitor's enforcement power considerably. Indeed, a lower bound on the enforcement power of

S. Hallé—The authors gratefully acknowledge the financial support of the Natural
Sciences and Engineering Research Council of Canada (NSERC).

J. Garcia-Alfaro et al. (Eds.): FPS 2015, LNCS 9482, pp. 102–116, 2016.
DOI: 10.1007/978-3-319-30303-1_7

monitors is given by Schneider [26] who shows that the set of properties enforceable by a monitor whose only possible reaction to a potential violation of the desired security policy is to abort the execution coincides with the set of safety properties. Conversely, Ligatti et al. [23] consider the case of a monitor with an unlimited ability to delay any event performed by the target program until it has ascertained that its occurrence in the execution would not violate the security policy. In effect, the monitor is simulating the execution of the program until it is certain that the behaviour it has so far witnessed is correct. When behaving in this manner, the monitor can enforce a vast range of security properties, termed the set of infinite renewal properties, which includes all safety policies, some liveness policies and some policies that are neither safety nor liveness.

Yet, it may not be realistic to assume that the monitor has an unlimited ability to simulate the execution of the target program. To this end, Basin et al. propose a middle ground [2]. They partition the set of possible program actions in two disjoint subsets: a set of controllable actions, which the monitor may freely suppress from the execution, and a set of observable actions, whose occurrence the monitor can only observe. This allows for a more precise characterization to the set of monitorable properties. Section 2 will discuss these concepts in more detail.

In Sect. 3, we further generalize this analysis by organizing the set of possible actions along a lattice that distinguishes between four types of atomic actions, namely *controllable* actions (which a monitor can insert or block from an execution), *insertable* actions (which a monitor can add to the execution but not suppress), *suppressible* actions (the converse) and *observable* actions (which the monitor can only observe). We then delineate the set of properties that are enforceable under this paradigm and relate our results to previous work in the field.

Finally, we explore in Sect. 4 the set of security policies that are enforceable if the monitor is given greater latitude to alter the execution of its target, rather than be bounded to return a syntactically identical execution sequence if the original execution is valid. In particular, we consider a monitor which can *add* any action into the execution, but cannot prevent any action from occurring if the target program requests it. We also consider a monitor can *remove* potentially malicious actions performed by the target program but cannot add any action to the execution. We show how both can be handled by our model by simply considering a different equivalence relation between traces.

2 Preliminaries

2.1 Executions

Executions are modelled as sequences of atomic actions taken from a finite or countably infinite set of actions Σ. The empty sequence is noted ϵ, the set of all finite length sequences is noted Σ^*, that of all infinite length sequences is noted Σ^ω, and the set of all possible sequences is noted $\Sigma^\infty = \Sigma^\omega \cup \Sigma^*$. Let $\tau \in \Sigma^*$ and $\sigma \in \Sigma^\infty$ be two sequences of actions. We write $\tau; \sigma$ for the concatenation of τ and σ. We say that τ is a prefix of σ noted $\tau \preceq \sigma$, or equivalently $\sigma \succeq \tau$ *iff* there exists a sequence σ' such that $\tau; \sigma' = \sigma$. Let $\tau, \sigma \in \Sigma^\infty$ be a sequence, we write acts (σ) for the set of actions present in σ. We write $res_{\hat{P}}(\sigma)$ for the residual of $\hat{P}$ with regard to σ, i.e. the set of sequence $S \subseteq \Sigma^\infty$ s.t. $\forall \tau \in S : \sigma; \tau \in \hat{P}$. Finally, let $\tau, \sigma \in \Sigma^\infty$, τ is said to be a suffix of σ iff there exists a $\sigma' \in \Sigma^*$ such that $\sigma = \sigma'; \tau$.

Following [23], if σ has already been quantified, we freely write $\forall \tau \preceq \sigma$ (resp. $\exists \tau \preceq \sigma$) as an abbreviation to $\forall \tau \in \Sigma^* : \tau \preceq \sigma$ (resp. $\exists \tau \in \Sigma^* : \tau \preceq \sigma$). Likewise, if τ has already been quantified, $\forall \sigma \in \Sigma^\infty : \sigma \succeq \tau$ (resp. $\exists \sigma \in \Sigma^\infty : \sigma \succeq \tau$) can be abbreviated as $\forall \sigma \succeq \tau$ (resp. $\exists \sigma \succeq \tau$).

Let τ be a sequence and a be an action, we write $\tau \backslash a$ for the left cancellation of a from τ, which is defined as the removal from τ of the first occurrence of a. Formally:

$$a; \tau \backslash a' = \begin{cases} \tau & \text{if } a = a'; \\ a; (\tau \backslash a') & \text{otherwise} \end{cases}$$

Observe that $\epsilon \backslash a = \epsilon$. Abusing the notation, we write $\tau \backslash \tau'$ to denote the sequence obtained by left cancellation of each action of τ' from τ. Formally, $\tau \backslash a; \tau' = (\tau \backslash a) \backslash \tau'$. For example, $abcada \backslash daa = bca$.

A finite word $\tau \in \Sigma^*$ is said to be a subword of a word ω, noted $\tau \triangleleft_\Sigma \sigma$, iff $\tau = a_0 a_1 a_2 a_3 ... a_k$ and $\omega = \sigma_0 a_0 \sigma_1 a_1 \sigma_2 a_2 \sigma_3 a_3 ... \sigma_k a_k v$ with $\sigma_0, \sigma_1, \sigma_2 ... \in \Sigma^*$ and $v \in \Sigma^\infty$. Let τ, σ be sequences form Σ^*. We write $cs_\tau(\sigma)$ to denote the longest subword of τ which is also a subword of σ. For any $\tau \neq \epsilon$, $\tau.last$ denotes the last action of sequence τ.

2.2   Security Policies and Security Properties

A security policy P is a property iff it can be characterized as a set of sequences for which there exists a decidable predicate $\hat{P}$ over the executions of $\Sigma^\infty : \hat{P}(\sigma)$ iff σ is in the policy [26]. In other words, a property is a policy for which the membership of any sequence can be determined by examining only the sequence itself[1]. Such a sequence is said to be *valid* or to *respect* the property. Since, by definition, all policies enforceable by monitors are properties, P and $\hat{P}$ are used interchangeably in our context. Additionally, since the properties of interest represent subsets of Σ^∞, we follow the common usage in the literature and freely use $\hat{P}$ to refer to these sets.

A number of classes of properties have been defined in the literature and are of special interest in the study of monitoring. First are *safety* properties [21], which proscribe the occurrence of a certain "bad thing" during the execution. Formally, let Σ be a set of actions and $\hat{P}$ be a property. $\hat{P}$ is a *safety* property iff

$$\forall \sigma \in \Sigma^\infty : \neg \hat{P}(\sigma) \Rightarrow \exists \sigma' \preceq \sigma : \forall \tau \succeq \sigma' : \neg \hat{P}(\tau) \qquad \text{(safety)}$$

---

[1] Security policies whose enforcement necessitates the examination of multiples execution sequences, such as noninterference policies, are not generally enforceable by monitors.

Informally, this states that any sequence does not respect the security property if there exists a prefix of that sequence from which any possible extension does not respect the security policy. This implies that a violation of a safety property is irremediable: once a violation occurs, nothing can be done to correct the situation.

Alternatively, a *liveness* property [1] is a property prescribing that a certain "good thing" must occur in any valid execution. Formally, for an action set Σ and a property $\hat{P}$, $\hat{P}$ is a liveness property iff

$$\forall \sigma \in \Sigma^* : \exists \tau \in \Sigma^\infty : \tau \succeq \sigma \wedge \hat{P}(\tau) \qquad \text{(liveness)}$$

Informally, the definition states that a property is a liveness property if any finite sequence can be extended into a valid sequence.

Another class of security properties that are of interest is that of *renewal* properties [23]. A property is in renewal if every infinite valid sequence has infinitely many valid prefixes, while every infinite invalid sequence has only finitely many such prefixes. Observe that every property over finite sequences is in infinite renewal. The set of renewal properties is equivalent to the set of response properties in the safety-progress classification [10].

$$\forall \hat{P} \subseteq \Sigma^\omega : \hat{P}(\sigma) \Leftrightarrow \exists \sigma' \preceq \sigma : \exists \tau \preceq \omega : \tau \succeq \sigma' \wedge \hat{P}(\tau). \qquad \text{(renewal)}$$

It is often useful to restrict our analysis to properties for which the empty sequence ϵ is valid. Such properties are said to be *reasonable* [23]. Formally,

$$\forall \hat{P} \subseteq \Sigma^\infty : \hat{P}(\epsilon) \Leftrightarrow \hat{P} \text{ is reasonable} \qquad \text{(reasonable)}$$

In the remainder of this paper, we will only consider reasonable properties. Furthermore, in order to avoid having the main topic of this paper be sidestepped by decidability issues, will consider that $\hat{P}(\sigma)$ is decidable for all properties and all execution sequences. Likewise, we also consider that other predicates or functions over sequences are decidable.

2.3 Security Property Enforcement

Finally, we need to provide a definition of what it means to "enforce" a security property $\hat{P}$. A number of possible definitions have been suggested. The most widely used is effective$_\cong$ enforcement [3]. Under this definition, a property is effectively$_\cong$ enforced iff the following two criterion are respected.

1. Soundness: All observable behaviours of the target program respect the desired property, i.e. every output sequence is present in the set of executions defined by $\hat{P}$.
2. Transparency: The semantics of valid executions is preserved, i.e. if the execution of the unmonitored program already respects the security property, the monitor must output an equivalent sequence, with respect to an equivalence relation $\cong \subseteq \Sigma^\infty \times \Sigma^\infty$.

Syntactic equality is the most straightforward equivalence relation, and the one that has been the most studied in the literature. It models the behaviour of a monitor that enforces the desired property by suppressing (or simulating) part of the execution, only allowing it to be output when it has ascertained that the execution up to that point is valid. In Sect. 4, we consider two alternative notions of equivalences, which can be used to characterize alternative behaviours on the part of the enforcement mechanism.

2.4   Related Work

Initial work on the question of delineating which security policies are or are not enforceable by monitor was performed by Schneider [26]. He considered the capabilities of a monitor that observes the execution of its target, with no knowledge of its possible future behaviour and no means to affect the target except by aborting the execution. Each time the target program attempts to perform an action, the monitor has to either accept it immediately, or abort the execution. Under these constraints, the set of properties enforceable by monitors coincides with the set of *safety* properties.

Ligatti et al. [22] extend Schneider's modelling of monitors along three axes:

1. According to the means at the disposal of the monitor to react to a potential violation of the security policy. These include truncating the execution, inserting new actions into the execution, suppressing some part of the executions or both inserting and suppressing actions
2. According to the availability of statically gathered data describing the target program possible execution paths
3. According to how much latitude the monitor is given to alter executions that already respect the security policy.

By combining these three criteria, they build a rich taxonomy of enforceable properties, and contrast the enforcement power of different types of monitors.

Basin et al. [2] generalize Schneider's model by distinguishing between observable actions, whose occurrence the monitor cannot prevent, and controllable actions, which the monitor can prevent from occurring by aborting the execution.

The enforcement power of monitor operating with memory constraints is studied in [4,13,27–29].

The computability constraints that can further restrict a monitor's enforcement power are discussed in [14,20]; that of monitors relying upon an *a priori* model of the program's possible behaviour is discussed in [9,22].

Falcone et al. [11,12] show that the set of infinite renewal properties coincides with the union of four of the 6 classes of the safety-progress classification of security properties [10]. Khoury and Tawbi [16,17] and Bielova et al. [5–7] further refine the notion of enforcement by suggesting alternative definitions of enforcement. In [24] Ligatti and Reddy introduced an alternative model, the mandatory-result automaton. This model distinguishes between the action set of the target and that of the system with which it interacts. This distinction makes it easier to study the interaction between the target program, the monitor and the system. A thorough survey of the question of enforceable properties by monitors is provided in [18].

3   Monitoring with Partial Control

The previous works each consider monitors where actions belong to particular sets. For example, Schneider's model assumes that all actions can be suppressed by the monitor; conversely, Ligatti et al. assume that all actions can be indefinitely delayed. Basin et al. propose a middle ground where every action can either be freely suppressed, or can only be observed. In this section, we define a generalized model of actions where each of these works becomes a particular case. We then study what properties are enforceable in this generalized model.

3.1   A Lattice of Actions

We organize the set of possible actions along a lattice that distinguishes between four types of atomic actions: namely controllable actions ($\mathcal{C}$), insertable actions ($\mathcal{I}$), suppressible actions ($\mathcal{D}$ —for delete) and observable actions ($\mathcal{O}$), as is shown in Fig. 1.

- Controllable actions ($\mathcal{C}$) are the basic actions such as opening a file or sending data on the network, which the monitor can either insert into the execution or prevent from occurring if they violate the security policy. In Ligatti's model, all actions are controllable.
  Insertable actions ($\mathcal{I}$) can be added into the execution but not suppressed if they are present. An example of an insertable action is an additional delay before processing a request to bring it unto compliance with a resource usage policy. The monitor may add such actions to the execution sequence but cannot remove them if the target program executes them.
- Suppressible actions ($\mathcal{D}$ —for delete) are those actions that the monitor can prevent from occurring, but cannot insert in the execution if the target program does not request them. Sending an email, decrypting a file or receiving a user input are all examples of suppressible actions. In Schneider's model, all actions are suppressible.
- Observable actions $\mathcal{O}$ can only be observed by the monitor, which can neither insert them in the execution when they are not present nor suppress them if they occur. In Basin et al.'s model, all actions are either suppressible or observable.

As the examples above illustrate, we believe that the lattice model we propose is a more realistic description of the reality encountered by the monitor, and will thus allow a more precise characterization of the set of enforceable properties. Observe than the monitor may only abort the execution if the next action is in $\mathcal{C} \cup \mathcal{D}$. Moreover, the sets $\mathcal{C}, \mathcal{I}, \mathcal{D}, \mathcal{O}$ are disjoint and that the universe of possible program actions is $\Sigma = \mathcal{C} \cup \mathcal{I} \cup \mathcal{D} \cup \mathcal{O}$.

Fig. 1. The lattice of possible actions

The following notation is useful for comparing different enforcement mechanisms. Let Σ be a universe of actions and let $\mathcal{L}$ be a lattice over the set Σ as described in Sect. 2. Let $\mathcal{S} \subseteq \Sigma^\infty$ stand for a subset of possible execution sequences and let $\cong \subseteq \Sigma^\infty \times \Sigma^\infty$ be an equivalence relation. We write $\mathcal{L}^\mathcal{S}$-enforceable$_\cong$ to denote the set of proprieties that are enforceable$_\cong$ by a monitor when the set of possible sequences is $\mathcal{S}$ and the set of possible actions is organized alongside lattice $\mathcal{L}$.

Let $\mathcal{L}$ be a lattice as described above. We write $\mathcal{L}_\mathcal{O}$ (resp. $\mathcal{L}_\mathcal{I}$, $\mathcal{L}_\mathcal{D}$, $\mathcal{L}_\mathcal{C}$) for the set $\mathcal{O}$ (resp. $\mathcal{I}$, $\mathcal{D}$, $\mathcal{C}$) in $\mathcal{L}$. We write $\mathcal{L} = \langle \Sigma_1, \Sigma_2, \Sigma_3, \Sigma_4 \rangle$ for the lattice where $\mathcal{L}_\mathcal{O} = \Sigma_1$, $\mathcal{L}_\mathcal{I} = \Sigma_2$, $\mathcal{L}_\mathcal{D} = \Sigma_3$ and $\mathcal{L}_\mathcal{C} = \Sigma_4$. Let $A, B \in \{\mathcal{O}, \mathcal{I}, \mathcal{D}, \mathcal{C}\}$ and let $a \in \Sigma$, we write $\mathcal{L}_{A \xrightarrow{a} B}$ to indicate the lattice $\mathcal{L}'$ defined such that $\mathcal{L}'_A = \mathcal{L}_A \backslash \{a\}, \mathcal{L}'_B = \mathcal{L}_B \cup \{a\}$ and $\forall C \in \{\mathcal{O}, \mathcal{I}, \mathcal{D}, \mathcal{C}\} : C \notin \{A, B\} \Rightarrow \mathcal{L}'_C = \mathcal{L}_C$. In other words, $\mathcal{L}_{A \xrightarrow{a} B}$ is the lattice built by moving only element a from set A to another B, leaving all other sets unchanged.

3.2 Enforceable Properties

We begin by reflecting on the set of properties that are $\mathcal{L}^{\Sigma^\infty}$-enforceable$_=$, i.e. properties that are enforceable if the monitor is bounded to output any valid sequence exactly as it occurs (with syntactic equality as the equivalence relation between valid inputs and the monitor's output). This is the enforcement paradigm that has been the most studied in the literature. A monitor that seeks to enforce a property in this manner may take any one of three strategies, depending on the desired property and the ongoing execution, and the set of $\mathcal{L}^{\Sigma^\infty}$-enforceable$_=$ properties can be derived by combining the three.

First, using a model in which every action is controllable, Ligatti et al. argued that a monitor can enforce any reasonable renewal property by suppressing the execution until a valid prefix is reached at which point the monitor can output the suffix of the execution it has previously suppressed. We generalized the definition of renewal as follows:

$$\forall \sigma \in \Sigma^\infty : \hat{P}(\sigma) \Leftrightarrow \forall \sigma' \preceq \sigma : (\exists \tau \preceq \sigma : \sigma' \preceq \tau \wedge \hat{P}(\tau) \wedge$$
$$\forall \tau' \preceq \tau : \tau' \succeq \sigma' \Rightarrow \tau'.last \in \mathcal{C}). \quad (\mathcal{L}\text{-Renewal})$$

Observe that the definition now applies to all sequences in Σ^∞, rather than just to infinite sequences. The second half of the equation always evaluates to true if all the actions are controllable (Ligatti's model) and always evaluates to false if all the actions are suppressible or observable (Schneider or Basin's models).

Second, Ligatti et al. observe that a property is enforceable if there exists a prefix beyond which there is only one valid extension. In that case, the monitor can abort the execution and output that sequence. This allows some nonsafety properties to be monitored. Ligatti et al. refer to this case as the "corner case" of effective enforcement. We generalize this case as follows:

$$\forall \sigma \in \Sigma^\infty : \hat{P}(\sigma) \vee \exists \sigma' \preceq \sigma : \forall \sigma'; \tau \succeq \sigma' : \hat{P}(\sigma'; \tau) \Rightarrow \sigma'; \tau = \sigma \wedge$$
$$\sigma'.last \in \mathcal{D} \cup \mathcal{C} \wedge acts(\tau) \subseteq \mathcal{I} \cup \mathcal{C}. \quad (\mathcal{L}\text{-Corner case})$$

Once again, observe that the equation restricts all sequences, rather than only infinite ones. This equation always evaluates to false in the Schneider-Basin model and the second conjunct always evaluates to true in Ligatti's model.

Finally, the monitor can simply abort the execution if it is irremediably invalid. This is a generalization of the set of safety properties to our framework.

$$\forall \sigma \in \Sigma^\infty : \neg \hat{P}(\sigma) \Rightarrow \exists \tau; a \preceq \sigma : \hat{P}(\tau) \wedge a \in \mathcal{D} \cup \mathcal{C}$$
$$\wedge \neg \exists \tau' \succeq \tau : \dot{P}(\tau'). \quad (\mathcal{L}\text{-Safety})$$

The set of $\mathcal{L}^{\Sigma^\infty}$-enforceable$_=$ properties can now be stated. The definition is not simply the conjunction of the tree preceding set as it must take into account the possibility that enforcement might begin by suppressing and reinserting part of the execution, and then abort the execution using of one of the other methods.

Theorem 1

$$\hat{P} \in \mathcal{L}^{\Sigma^\infty} - enforceable_= \Leftrightarrow \forall \sigma \in \Sigma^\infty :$$

$$(\hat{P}(\sigma) \Leftrightarrow \forall \sigma' \preceq \sigma : \exists \tau \preceq \sigma : \sigma' \preceq \tau \wedge \hat{P}(\tau) \wedge (\forall \tau' \preceq \tau : \neg \dot{P}(\tau') \Rightarrow \tau'.last \in \mathcal{C}) \vee$$

$$(\exists \tau; a \preceq \sigma : a \in \mathcal{D} \cup \mathcal{C} \wedge \forall \tau' \preceq \tau; a : \neg \hat{P}(\tau') \Rightarrow \tau'.last \in \mathcal{C} \wedge (\forall \tau' \succeq \tau; a : \hat{P}(\tau') \Rightarrow$$

$$\tau' = \sigma \vee (\hat{P}(\tau) \wedge \neg \exists \tau' \succeq \tau : \dot{P}(\tau') \wedge acts(\sigma \backslash \tau'; a) \in \mathcal{C} \cup \mathcal{I}))))$$

Proof. Proofs of the theorems and corollaries in this work are contained in our companion Technical Report [15]. We omit them here due to space constraints.

This definition narrows the set of monitorable properties somewhat, compared with previous work. For example, bounded availability is given in [23] as an example of a monitorable policy. In fact, it is monitorable only if every action that occurs between the acquisition and release of a protected resource is controllable. Likewise, the *"no send after read"* property described in [26] is only enforceable if every action which might violate the property is deletable or controllable.

While the set-theoretic characterization of enforceable property is somewhat involved, an LTL property can characterize such properties.

Theorem 2. *Let valid be a predicate identifying a valid sequence:*

$$valid(\sigma) \Leftrightarrow \hat{P}(\sigma)$$

Let cc be a predicate that identifies a sequence in the $\mathcal{L}$-corner case:

$$cc(\sigma) \Leftrightarrow \hat{P}(\sigma) \wedge \exists \sigma' \preceq \sigma : \forall \sigma'; \tau \succeq \sigma' : \hat{P}(\sigma'; \tau) \Rightarrow$$
$$\sigma'; \tau = \sigma \wedge \sigma'.last \in \mathcal{D} \cup \mathcal{C} \wedge acts(\tau) \subseteq \mathcal{I} \cup \mathcal{C}$$

Let C be a predicate identifying a sequence ending on a controllable action, and D a predicate that identifies a sequence ending on a deletable action:

$$C(\sigma) \Leftrightarrow \sigma.last \in \mathcal{C}$$
$$D(\sigma) \Leftrightarrow \sigma.last \in \mathcal{D}$$

Then we have:

$$\hat{P} \in \mathcal{L}^{\Sigma^{\infty}}\text{-}enforceable_= \Leftrightarrow \forall \sigma \in \Sigma^{\infty} :$$
$$\mathbf{G}\,(C\,\mathbf{W}\,valid) \vee (C\,\mathbf{W}\,valid \vee \mathbf{X}\,((D \vee C) \wedge (\mathbf{G}\,\neg valid \vee cc)))$$

In this theorem, we assume that any execution sequence from Σ^{∞} is possible. In other words, at each step of the execution, the monitor must assume that any action from Σ is a possible next action, or that the execution of the target program could stop. This is called the uniform enforcement context. The monitor often operates in a context where it knows that certain executions are impossible (the nonuniform context). This situation occurs when the monitor benefits from a static analysis of its target, that provides it with a model of the target's possible behaviour. We can adapt the above theorem to take into account the fact that the monitor could operate in a nonuniform context.

Theorem 3

$$\hat{P} \in \mathcal{L}^{S}\text{-}enforceable_= \Leftrightarrow \forall \sigma \in S :$$
$$(\hat{P}(\sigma) \Leftrightarrow \forall \sigma' \preceq \sigma : \exists \tau \preceq \sigma : \sigma' \preceq \tau \wedge \hat{P}(\tau) \wedge (\forall \tau' \preceq \tau : \neg\hat{P}(\tau') \Rightarrow$$
$$(\tau'.last \in \mathcal{C} \wedge \tau \in S)) \vee$$
$$(\exists \tau; a \preceq \sigma : a \in \mathcal{D} \cup \mathcal{C} \wedge \forall \tau' \preceq \tau; a : (\neg\hat{P}(\tau') \wedge \tau' \in S) \Rightarrow \tau'.last \in \mathcal{C} \wedge$$
$$(\forall \tau' \succeq \tau; a : \hat{P}(\tau') \Rightarrow \tau' = \sigma \vee (\hat{P}(\tau) \wedge \neg\exists \tau' \succeq \tau :$$
$$\hat{P}(\tau') \wedge \tau' \in S \wedge acts(\sigma\backslash\tau'; a) \in \mathcal{C} \cup \mathcal{I}))))$$

We can now restate the results of previous research in our new formalism.

Theorem 4 *(from [26]). If $\mathcal{L} = \langle \emptyset, \emptyset, \Sigma, \emptyset \rangle$ then $\mathcal{L}^{\Sigma^{\infty}}$ enforceable$_=$ is Safety.*

Theorem 5 *(from [23]). If $\mathcal{L} = \langle \emptyset, \emptyset, \emptyset, \Sigma \rangle$ then $\mathcal{L}^{\Sigma^{\infty}}$ enforceable$_=$ is the union of Infinite Renewal and the corner case.*

3.3   Additional Results

Corollary 1. *Let $\mathcal{L}$ be a lattice over a set of actions Σ as described above and let $\Sigma_1, \Sigma_2 \in \{\mathcal{O}, \mathcal{D}, \mathcal{I}, \mathcal{C}\}$ and $\Sigma_1 \sqsubset \Sigma_2$. $\forall a \in \Sigma : \mathcal{L}_{\Sigma_1}$-enforceable$_= \subset \mathcal{L}_{\Sigma_1 \xrightarrow{a} \Sigma_2}$- enforceable.*

Corollary 1 indicates that the set of enforceable properties increases monotonically with the capabilities of the monitor. Thus, any effort made to improve the capabilities of the monitor to control its target is rewarded by a augmented set of enforceable security properties. Conversely, if every action from the set Σ is in $\mathcal{O}$, only the inviolable property is enforceable.

Corollary 2. *Let $\mathcal{L} = \langle \Sigma, \emptyset, \emptyset, \emptyset \rangle$, $\hat{P} \in \mathcal{L}_{\Sigma}$-enforceable $\Leftrightarrow \hat{P} = \Sigma^\infty$.*

Corollary 2 follows immediately from Theorem 1.

4   Alternative Equivalence Relations

The above results apply only to the case of effective$_=$ enforcement. This corresponds to the enforcement power of a monitor that sometimes delays the occurrence of actions in its target, or abort its execution, but does not add additional actions or permanently suppress part of the execution sequence, allowing the remainder of the execution to continue. Syntactic equality (and subclasses of that relation) is the only equivalence relation that has been extensively studied in the literature. This naturally does not exhaust the enforcement capabilities of monitors. In this section, we explore alternative equivalence relations (that characterize alternative enforcement mechanisms) and determine the set of enforceable properties for each.

4.1   Subword Equivalence and Insertion Enforcement

The first alternative equivalence relation that we examine is subword equivalence, noted $\cong_\lhd$. This corresponds to the enforcement power of a monitor which can *add* any action into the execution, but cannot prevent any action from occurring if the target program requests it. For example, the monitor can enforce a property stating that any opened file is eventually closed by adding the missing close file action before the end of the program's execution. This model is interesting to understand the capabilities of certain types of inline monitors, that are injected into the program in the form of guards or run in parallel with their target, such as those based upon the aspect-oriented programming paradigm [8,19,25].

Let $\sigma, \sigma', \tau \in \Sigma^*$, we write $\sigma_\tau \cong_\lhd \sigma' \Leftrightarrow (\sigma \lhd_\Sigma \tau \wedge \sigma' \lhd_\Sigma \tau)$, and designate by enforceable$_{\cong_\lhd}$ the set of properties that are enforceable when $_\tau \cong_\lhd \sigma'$ is the equivalence relation and τ is the original input. This is a very permissive equivalence relation, which in effect allows the monitor to insert any action or actions into the execution, and consider the transformed execution equivalent to the original execution (τ) if all actions performed by the target program are still present. While this equivalence relation may be too permissive to be realistic, it does allow us to deduce an upper bound to the set of policies enforceable under this paradigm.

We begin by considering the cases that occur when the monitor has only limited control over the action set. When the monitor can only suppress actions or abort the execution, the set of enforceable$_{\cong_\triangleleft}$ properties coincides with that of safety properties, since the monitor is unable to take advantage of the permissiveness of the equivalence relation.

Theorem 6. *Let* $\mathcal{L} = \langle \emptyset, \emptyset, \Sigma, \emptyset \rangle$. $\mathcal{L}^{\Sigma^\infty}$*-enforceable$_{\cong_\triangleleft}$ is the set of safety properties.*

Another interesting case occurs when the monitor cannot delay the occurrence of the actions present in the execution sequence, but can only react to them by inserting additional actions afterwards. In other words, any action output by the target program must be immediately accepted, but can be followed by other actions inserted by the monitor. An intuitive lower bound to the set of enforceable properties in this context is the intersection of renewal properties and liveness properties. That is, properties for which any invalid sequence can be corrected into a valid sequence with a finite number of corrective steps. Additionally, some safety properties and some persistence properties are also enforceable. For example, the property $\hat{P}_{\neg aa}$ imposing that no two 'a' actions occur consecutively is a safety property since an invalid sequence cannot be corrected by the insertion of any subsequent actions. However, the policy is $\mathcal{L}^{\Sigma^\infty}$-enforceable$_{\cong_\triangleleft}$ since the monitor can insert any action other than 'a' after the occurrence of each 'a' action to ensure the respect of the security property. What characterizes properties outside the intersection of renewal and liveness that are nonetheless $\mathcal{L}^{\Sigma^\infty}$-enforceable$_{\cong_\triangleleft}$ is that there exists a property $\hat{P}'$ in renewal $\cap$ liveness such that the property of interest includes $\hat{P}'$. In the case of the example above, the property "any a action is immediately followed by some action different from a (or the end of sequence token)" is a renewal property included in $\hat{P}_{\neg aa}$. The monitor can enforce the property $\hat{P}_{\neg aa}$ by enforcing $\hat{P}'$.

Theorem 7. *Let* $\hat{P} \subseteq \mathcal{P}(\Sigma^\infty)$ *and let* $\mathcal{L} = \langle \emptyset, \Sigma, \emptyset, \emptyset \rangle$. *If the monitor cannot delay the occurrence of actions performed by the target program, then* $\hat{P} \in \mathcal{L}^{\Sigma^\infty}$*-enforceable$_{\cong_\triangleleft}$* $\Leftrightarrow \exists \hat{P}' : \hat{P}' \subseteq \hat{P}$ *and* $\hat{P}'$ *is infinite renewal* $\cap$ *liveness.*

Allowing the monitor to insert a finite number of actions before or after an action taken by the target program increases the set of enforceable properties further. Consider for example the property $\hat{P}_{os}$ stating that a *write* action only be performed on a previously opened file. The property is a safety property, and falls outside the set of $\hat{P} \in \mathcal{L}^{\Sigma^\infty}$-enforceable$_{\cong_\triangleleft}$ properties defined in Theorem 7 if the number of files is infinite. The property can be $\mathcal{L}^{\Sigma^\infty}$-enforced$_{\cong_\triangleleft}$ by a monitor that inserts the corresponding *open* file action anytime the target program attempts to write to a file that has not yet been opened. More generally, if all actions are in the set $\mathcal{C}$, then a property $\hat{P}$ is enforceable iff there exists a property $\hat{P}' \subseteq \hat{P}$, s.t. $\hat{P}'$ is in the intersection of Renewal and Liveness or if it is a safety property and for any action $a \in \Sigma$, and for any sequence σ in $\hat{P}'$, there is a sequence τ in the residual of $\hat{P}'$ with regard to σ s.t. $a \in acts(\sigma)$. In other words, if for any sequence in the subproperty $\hat{P}'$ and for any possible action a, there is a continuation τ s.t. τ contains a. The monitor can $\mathcal{L}^{\Sigma^{\infty}}$-enforces$_{\cong_{\triangleleft}}$ such a property by appending a sequence from the residual containing any action requested by the target program.

Theorem 8. Let $\mathcal{L} = \langle \emptyset, \Sigma, \emptyset, \emptyset \rangle$. $\mathcal{L}^{\Sigma^{\infty}}$-enforceable$_{\cong_{\triangleleft}}$ iff there exists a property $\hat{P}' \subseteq \hat{P} \subseteq Liveness \cap Renewal \cup Safety : \forall \sigma \in \hat{P}' : \bigcup\limits_{\sigma' \in res_{\hat{P}'}(\sigma)} acts(\sigma') = \Sigma.$

The upper bound naturally occurs when all actions are controllable. We found it harder to give a specific upper bound to the set of enforceable$_{\cong_{\triangleleft}}$ properties. Indeed, this set seems to include almost every properties, with the exception of a number of hard to define special cases. Observe that because the subword relation is reflexive, a monitor that enforces$_=$ the property also enforces$_{\cong_{\triangleleft}}$ it. This equivalence relation is so permissive that only a few very particular cases seem unenforceable.

Observe that while this result indicates that the security properties that are $\mathcal{L}^{\Sigma^{\infty}}$-enforceable$_{\cong_{\triangleleft}}$ are largely the same as those that are $\mathcal{L}^{\Sigma^{\infty}}$-enforceable$_=$, the manner of enforcement is quite different. $\mathcal{L}^{\Sigma^{\infty}}$-enforcement$_=$ guarantees that any valid sequence is output *as is*, without any modification by the monitor. For invalid sequences, $\mathcal{L}^{\Sigma^{\infty}}$-enforceable$_=$ ensures that the longest valid prefix is always output [5]. $\mathcal{L}^{\Sigma^{\infty}}$-enforcement$_{\cong_{\triangleleft}}$ does not provide these guarantees. Instead, as seen above, for non-safety properties $\mathcal{L}^{\Sigma^{\infty}}$-enforcement$_{\cong_{\triangleleft}}$ can ensure that any action present in the original program is eventually output, whether the execution sequence is valid or not. $\mathcal{L}^{\Sigma^{\infty}}$-enforcement$_{\cong_{\triangleleft}}$ also evidently has a much reduced memory overhead, since this enforcement paradigm does not impose on the monitor that it keep in memory an indefinitely long segment of the execution trace, as $\mathcal{L}^{\Sigma^{\infty}}$-enforcement$_=$ does. Since memory constraints were showed in [13] to significantly affect the set of enforceable properties it is certain that once such constraints are taken into account, some properties will be found to be $\mathcal{L}^{\Sigma^{\infty}}$-enforceable$_{\cong_{\triangleleft}}$ but not $\mathcal{L}^{\Sigma^{\infty}}$-enforceable$_=$.

4.2 Suppression Enforcement

Another interesting enforcement paradigm is suppression enforcement [3], which occurs when the monitor can remove potentially malicious actions performed by the target program but cannot add any action to the execution. In that case, the monitor's enforcement is bounded by the reverse subword equivalence, meaning that the monitor's output is a subword of the original sequence. This enforcement paradigm is similar to the one described in [24], where the monitor is interposed between the target program and the system. Any action requested by the target program is intercepted by the monitor which must accept or reject it, and allows us to pose an upper bound to this enforcement paradigm.

Let $\sigma, \sigma', \tau \in \Sigma^*$, we write $\sigma_{\tau} \cong_{\triangleright} \sigma' \Leftrightarrow (\tau \triangleleft_{\Sigma} \sigma \wedge \tau \triangleleft_{\Sigma} \sigma')$. As was the case in Sect. 4.1, this is a very permissive equivalence relation, which characterizes the behaviour of a monitor that can potentially *suppress* any action or actions from the execution. We write $\cong_\triangleright$ for this equivalence relation where τ is the original input.

We begin by determining an upper bound to the set, which occurs when every action is suppressible. In that case, every reasonable property is enforceable, simply by always outputting the empty sequence (or possibly the longest valid prefix). While this may not be a particularly useful enforcement, it does however serve as a useful upper bound to begin reflecting about the capabilities of different types of monitors. It also argues for a stronger notion of transparency, as discussed in [17], which allows us to reason about the capabilities of monitor in a context that is more similar to that of a real-life monitor. Such monitors would normally be bounded with respect to the alterations that they are allowed to performed on valid and invalid executions alike.

Theorem 9. *If* $\mathcal{L} = \langle \emptyset, \emptyset, \Sigma, \emptyset \rangle$ *then* $\mathcal{L}^{\Sigma^\infty}$*-enforceable$_{\cong_\triangleright}$ $= \mathcal{P}(\Sigma^\infty)$.*

Corollary 3. *Let* $\mathcal{L} = \langle \emptyset, \emptyset, \Sigma, \emptyset \rangle$. $\forall a \in \mathcal{L}_\mathcal{D} : \mathcal{L}^{\Sigma^\infty}$*-enforceable$_{\cong_\triangleright}$ $= \mathcal{L}^{\Sigma^\infty}_{\mathcal{D} \xrightarrow{a} \mathcal{C}}$-enforceable$_{\cong_\triangleright}$.*

Corollary 4. *Let* $\mathcal{L} = \langle \emptyset, \emptyset, \Sigma, \emptyset \rangle$. $\forall S \subseteq \Sigma^\infty : \mathcal{L}^{\Sigma^\infty}$*-enforceable$_{\cong_\triangleright}$ $= \mathcal{L}^S$-enforceable$_{\cong_\triangleright}$.*

A more interesting characterization occurs when we consider that some subset of Σ is unsuppressible. These may be actions that the monitor lacks the ability to suppress (such as internal system computations) or actions that cannot be deleted without affecting the functionality of the target program. When that is the case, a property is enforceable iff every invalid sequence has a valid prefix ending on an action in $\mathcal{D}$. In that case, the property of interest includes a safety property that can be enforced by truncation.

Theorem 10. *If* $\mathcal{L} = \langle \mathcal{O}, \emptyset, \mathcal{D}, \emptyset \rangle$ *then* $\forall \sigma \in \Sigma^\infty : \hat{P}(\sigma) \in \mathcal{L}^{\Sigma^\infty}$*-enforceable$_{\cong_\triangleright}$ $\Leftrightarrow$ $\exists \hat{P}' \subseteq \hat{P} : \hat{P}' \in \mathcal{L}$-safety.*

5   Conclusion

In this paper, we reexamined the delimitation of enforceable properties by monitors, and proposed a finer characterization that distinguishes between actions that are only observable, actions which the monitor can delete but not insert into the execution, actions which the monitor can insert in the execution but not suppress if they are already present and completely controllable actions. Our study is a generalization of previous work on the same topic, and provides a finer characterization of the set of security properties that are enforceable by monitors in different contexts.

Additionally, we explored the set of properties that are enforceable by the monitor is given broader latitude to transform valid sequences, rather than be bounded to return a syntactically identical execution sequence if the original execution is valid. We argue that our results point to the need for an alternative definition of enforcement.

Part of the reason the sets of $\mathcal{L}^{\Sigma^\infty}$−enforceable$_{\cong_\triangleright}$ and $\mathcal{L}^{\Sigma^\infty}$−enforceable$_{\cong_\triangleleft}$ properties are so large is that, in the definition of effective$_\cong$ enforcement, the transparency requirement is so weak. This leads to monitors with unusually broad licence to alter invalid sequences in order to correct them. For monitors with broad capabilities to add and remove actions from the execution sequence, the desired behaviour of real-life security policy enforcement mechanism would be more accurately characterized by a more constraining definition of *enforcement*. For example, a practical suppression monitor should be bounded to remove from an invalid execution sequence only those actions that violate the security policy. Any valid behaviour present in an otherwise invalid sequence should be preserved.

In the future, we would like to consider that the cost of inserting or deleting an action may not be the same for all actions. This would allow us to contrast different enforcement strategies for the same security property. A lattice-based framework is well-suited to model such a restriction.

References

1. Alpern, B., Schneider, F.: Defining liveness. Inf. Process. Lett. **21**(4), 181–185 (1985)
2. Basin, D., Jugé, V., Klaedtke, F., Zalinescu, E.: Enforceable security policies revisited. ACM Trans. Inf. Syst. Secur. **16**(1), 3 (2013)
3. Bauer, L., Ligatti, J., Walker, D.: More enforceable security policies. In: Foundations of Computer Security, Copenhagen, Denmark (2002)
4. Beauquier, D., Pin, J.-E.: Languages and scanners. Theoret. Comput. Sci. **84**(1), 3–21 (1991)
5. Bielova, N., Massacci, F.: Do you really mean what you actually enforced? - edit automata revisited. Int. J. Inf. Secur. **10**(4), 239–254 (2011)
6. Bielova, N., Massacci, F.: Predictability of enforcement. In: Erlingsson, U., Wieringa, R., Zannone, N. (eds.) ESSoS 2011. LNCS, vol. 6542, pp. 73–86. Springer, Heidelberg (2011)
7. Bielova, N., Massacci, F., Micheletti, A.: Towards practical enforcement theories. In: Jøsang, A., Maseng, T., Knapskog, S.J. (eds.) NordSec 2009. LNCS, vol. 5838, pp. 239–254. Springer, Heidelberg (2009)
8. Bodden, E., Lam, P., Hendren, L.J.: Partially evaluating finite-state runtime monitors ahead of time. ACM Trans. Program. Lang. Syst. **34**(2), 7 (2012)
9. Chabot, H., Khoury, R., Tawbi, N.: Extending the enforcement power of truncation monitors using static analysis. Comput. & Secur. **30**(4), 194–207 (2011)
10. Chang, E., Manna, Z., Pnueli, A.: The safety-progress classification. In: Bauer, F., Brauer, W., Schwichtenberg, H. (eds.) Logic and Algebra of Specifications. NATO ASI Series, vol. 94, pp. 143–202. Springer, Heidelberg (1991)
11. Falcone, Y., Fernandez, J.-C., Mounier, L.: Synthesizing enforcement monitors wrt. the safety-progress classification of properties. In: Sekar, R., Pujari, A.K. (eds.) ICISS 2008. LNCS, vol. 5352, pp. 41–55. Springer, Heidelberg (2008)
12. Falcone, Y., Fernandez, J.-C., Mounier, L.: Runtime verification of safety-progress properties. In: Bensalem, S., Peled, D.A. (eds.) RV 2009. LNCS, vol. 5779, pp. 40–59. Springer, Heidelberg (2009)

13. Fong, P.: Access control by tracking shallow execution history. In: Proceedings of the 2004 IEEE Symposium on Security and Privacy, California, USA, May, Oakland (2004)
14. Hamlen, K.W., Morrisett, G., Schneider, F.B.: Computability classes for enforcement mechanisms. ACM Trans. Program. Lang. Syst. **28**, 175–205 (2006)
15. Khoury, R., Hallé, S.: Runtime enforcement with partial control. Technical report, Université du Québec à Chicoutimi (2015)
16. Khoury, R., Tawbi, N.: Using equivalence relations for corrective enforcement of security policies. In: Kotenko, I., Skormin, V. (eds.) MMM-ACNS 2010. LNCS, vol. 6258, pp. 139–154. Springer, Heidelberg (2010)
17. Khoury, R., Tawbi, N.: Corrective enforcement: A new paradigm of security policy enforcement by monitors. ACM Trans. Inf. Syst. Secur. **15**(2), 10:1–10:27 (2012)
18. Khoury, R., Tawbi, N.: Which security policies are enforceable by runtime monitors? a survey. Comput. Sci. Rev. **6**(1), 27–45 (2012)
19. Kiczales, G., Hilsdale, E.: Aspect-oriented programming. SIGSOFT Softw. Eng. Notes **26**(5), 313 (2001)
20. Kim, M., Kannan, S., Lee, I., Sokolsky, O., Viswanathan, M.: Computational analysis of run-time monitoring - fundamentals of java-mac. Electr. Notes Theor. Comput. Sci. **70**(4), 80–94 (2002)
21. Lamport, L.: Proving the correctness of multiprocess programs. IEEE Trans. Softw. Eng. **3**(2), 125–143 (1977)
22. Ligatti, J., Bauer, L., Walker, D.: Edit automata: Enforcement mechanisms for run-time security policies. Int. J. Inf. Secur. **4**(1–2), 2–16 (2004)
23. Ligatti, J., Bauer, L., Walker, D.: Run-time enforcement of nonsafety policies. ACM Trans. Inf. Syst. Secur. **12**(3), 1–41 (2009)
24. Ligatti, J., Reddy, S.: A theory of runtime enforcement, with results. In: Gritzalis, D., Preneel, B., Theoharidou, M. (eds.) ESORICS 2010. LNCS, vol. 6345, pp. 87–100. Springer, Heidelberg (2010)
25. Meredith, P., Roşu, G.: Runtime verification with the RV system. In: Barringer, H., et al. (eds.) RV 2010. LNCS, vol. 6418, pp. 136–152. Springer, Heidelberg (2010)
26. Schneider, F.: Enforceable security policies. Inf. Syst. Secur. **3**(1), 30–50 (2000)
27. Talhi, C., Tawbi, N., Debbabi, M.: Execution monitoring enforcement for limited-memory systems. In: Proceedings of the PST 2006 Conference (Privacy, Security, Trust), October 2006
28. Talhi, C., Tawbi, N., Debbabi, M.: Execution monitoring enforcement under memory-limitation constraints. In: Proceedings of FCS-ARSPA 2006 (Joint Workshop on Foundations of Computer Security and Automated Reasoning for Security Protocol Analysis) associated with FLOC 2006 (Federated Logic Conference), August 2006
29. Talhi, C., Tawbi, N., Debbabi, M.: Execution monitoring enforcement under memory-limitations constraints. Inf. Comput. **206**(1), 158–184 (2008)

Privacy-Preserving Fuzzy Commitment for Biometrics via Layered Error-Correcting Codes

Masaya Yasuda[1](✉), Takeshi Shimoyama[2], Narishige Abe[2],
Shigefumi Yamada[2], Takashi Shinzaki[2], and Takeshi Koshiba[3]

[1] Institute of Mathematics for Industry, Kyushu University, 744 Motooka Nishi-ku,
Fukuoka 819-0395, Japan
yasuda@imi.kyushu-u.ac.jp
[2] Fujitsu Laboratories Ltd., 1-1, Kamikodanaka 4-chome, Nakahara-ku,
Kawasaki 211-8588, Japan
[3] Division of Mathematics, Electronics and Informatics,
Graduate School of Science and Engineering, Saitama University,
255 Shimo-Okubo, Sakura, Saitama 338-8570, Japan

Abstract. With the widespread development of biometrics, concerns about security and privacy are increasing. In biometrics, template protection technology aims to protect the confidentiality of biometric templates (i.e., enrolled biometric data) by certain conversion. The fuzzy commitment scheme gives a practical way to protect biometric templates using a conventional error-correcting code. The scheme has both concealing and binding of templates, but it has some privacy problems. Specifically, in case of successful matching, stored biometric templates can be revealed. To address such problems, we improve the scheme. Our improvement is to coat with two error-correcting codes. In particular, our scheme can conceal stored biometric templates even in successful matching. Our improved scheme requires just conventional error-correcting codes as in the original scheme, and hence it gives a practical solution for both template security and privacy of biometric templates.

Keywords: Fuzzy commitment · Biometric template protection · Error-correcting codes

1 Introduction

Biometric authentication (or biometrics) is one of the user authentication techniques by using their physical (e.g., fingerprint, iris, face and vein) or behavioral characteristics (e.g., signature, keystroke dynamics and gait). Compared to the commonly used ID/password authentication, biometrics does not require users to remember their long and complex passwords, and hence the use of biometrics is now expanding in various applications ranging from international border control

---

A part of this research was done when the first author belonged to Fujitsu Laboratories Ltd.

© Springer International Publishing Switzerland 2016
J. Garcia-Alfaro et al. (Eds.): FPS 2015, LNCS 9482, pp. 117–133, 2016.
DOI: 10.1007/978-3-319-30303-1_8

systems to securing information in databases (e.g., see [25] for US-VISIT). On the other hand, concerns about security and privacy regarding stored templates are rapidly increasing at the same time.

1.1   Template Protection and Its Approaches

In biometrics, the most important issue is to protect templates, since once leaked templates can be neither revoked nor replaced. During rapid expansion of biometrics, template protection technology has been intensively investigated (e.g., see [1,12]), and its basic method is to store biometric features transformed by certain conversion, instead of storing raw ones. According to [12, Section 3], an ideal biometric template protection scheme should satisfy the following four requirements (see also [15]);

(R-1) Diversity: secure templates (i.e., transformed templates) must not allow cross-matching across databases.
(R-2) Revocability: it should be straightforward to revoke a compromised template and reissue a new secure template based on the same biometric data.
(R-3) Security: it must be computationally hard to obtain the original biometric template from a secure template.
(R-4) Performance: the scheme should not degrade the recognition performance (e.g., FAR = False Acceptance Rate and FRR = False Rejection Rate).

According to [12, Section 3], there are four main approaches for template protection (sometimes homomorphic encryption approach is considered as yet another approach for template protection[1]); salting (e.g., biohashing [24]), non-invertible transform (e.g., robust hashing [23]), key-binding (e.g., fuzzy vault [13] and fuzzy commitment [14]), and finally key-generation (e.g., secure sketch-fuzzy extractor [5]). Each approach has both advantages and limitations, and none of them can achieve an ideal scheme. In particular, the key-binding approach tries to protect templates by monolithically binding it with a user's specific key using cryptographic tools, and it enables various authentication ways.

1.2   Fuzzy Commitment and Privacy Issues

In this paper, we focus on the fuzzy commitment scheme proposed by Juels and Wattenberg [14], which is one of the most popular schemes in the key-binding approach. A number of implementations of the scheme for biometric systems have been proposed so far (e.g., see [8,22] for iris-based authentication, [26] for face recognition, and [9] for recent work about gait authentication on mobile phone). The fuzzy commitment scheme makes use of an error-correcting code C, and biometric data are treated as a corrupted codeword. The scheme works as follows: During the enrollment phase, a user binds his or her biometric data x

---

[1] Homomorphic encryption is encryption with additional property that it can support operations on encrypted data (without decryption). In other words, this encryption enables certain meaningful operations while preserving the confidentiality of data.

with a codeword $c \in C$ to generate a secure template $(x+c, H(c))$ (called a *helper data* in the key-binding approach), where H is a cryptographically-secure hash function (the codeword c is often generated from the user's specific key). During the authentication phase, a new biometric data y is presented by the user to claim his or her identity. Then an authentication server computes $(x+c)-y = c+\delta$ with $\delta = x - y$, and the hash value $H(c')$ of the codeword $c' = D(c + \delta) \in C$, where D is a decoding function of C. If y is close to x (in the sense of the Hamming distance), then the codeword c' equals to c (note that D outputs the nearest codeword of C). Namely, the condition $H(c') = H(c)$ indicates successful verification of users. However, in case of successful verification, the correct codeword c is recovered and hence the user's template x can also be recovered from the secure template $(x + c, H(c))$ in the authentication server, which raises a privacy issue (information leakage in the fuzzy commitment scheme is also discussed and analyzed in [10,11]). Then the scheme always requires a trusted authentication server, and it cannot be applied to various application scenarios such as remote biometrics authentication over public networks (e.g., over clouds).

1.3   Our Contribution

To solve the above problem, we have improved the fuzzy commitment scheme so that biometric templates cannot be revealed even in case of successful verification. Our new technique is to coat with two error-correcting codes for protecting both security and privacy of biometric templates.

Sketch of Our Scheme. Here we give a sketch of our improved scheme. Let C_1 and C_2 denote two error-correcting codes, and assume that C_1 is a linear code. Let w be a codeword of C_2 (generated from user's specific key), and let E_1 denote an encoding function of C_1. In our scheme, given a biometric template x, a secure template is given by

$$h = (x + E_1(w + s), H(w)),$$

where s is a randomly chosen binary vector of light Hamming weight. During authentication, given a biometric data y for query, the user sends $-y + E_1(s')$ instead of plain y to an authentication server, where s' is also a randomly chosen binary vector of light Hamming weight. As in the original scheme, we now consider

$$T = (x + E_1(w + s)) + (-y + E_1(s')).$$

By the linearity of C_1, we have $E_1(w + s) + E_1(s') = E_1(w + s + s')$. Then a decoding function of C_1 for T can output $w+s+s'$ if x is close to y. Furthermore, since $s + s'$ has light Hamming weight by construction, a decoding function of C_2 can output the codeword w of C_2 and hence the verification result can be checked by comparing hash values as in the original scheme. In our scheme, the authentication server can know $w + s + s'$ and w. Then the server can obtain the sum $s+s'$, but cannot know each of s and s'. Therefore the biometric template

x cannot be revealed from the secure template h, and the hardness depends on the Hamming weight of s and s', which also depends on the correction capability of the code C_2.

Organization. In Sect. 2, we briefly review error-correcting codes and present the basic construction of the fuzzy commitment scheme. In Sect. 3, we show some problems of the original fuzzy commitment scheme and give our improvement. In Sect. 4, we choose suitable parameters of Reed-Solomon and BCH codes for our improved scheme, and show our implementation results. In Sect. 5, we compare our scheme with related protocols for biometrics. Finally, in Sect. 6, we conclude this work and give our future work.

2   Preliminaries

In this section, we begin to review error-correcting codes, and mainly present the basic construction of the fuzzy commitment scheme of [14].

2.1   Error-Correcting Code

Let Σ be a finite alphabet. An error-correcting code C of length n over Σ is a subset of Σ^n. The elements of C are called the *codewords* in C. We say that C is a *q-ary code* if $\#\Sigma = q$. In particular, when $q = 2$, we say that C is a *binary code*. To use an error-correcting code, we require an encoding function E and a decoding function D. For the dimension k of message space, the encoding function $E : \Sigma^k \to C$ represents a one-to-one mapping of message transmission. The inverse image function E^{-1} is sometimes used to retrieve the original message from a codeword. On the other hand, the decoding function $D : \Sigma^n \to C \cup \{\phi\}$ is used to map arbitrary elements of Σ^n to codewords. In successful case, the function D maps a string $x \in \Sigma^n$ of length n to the nearest codeword in C. Otherwise, the function D fails to map x to a codeword in C, and outputs ϕ (error-correcting codes may work somewhat differently, and D may yield a set of candidate codewords, rather than a single correct one).

Given two strings $x = (x_i)_{i=1}^n$ and $y = (y_i)_{i=1}^n$, the Hamming distance $\Delta(x, y)$ between x and y is defined as the number of positions at which the two strings differ, namely, $\Delta(x, y) = \#\{i \mid x_i \neq y_i\}$. The robustness of a code C depends on the minimum distance between two codewords, where the minimum distance is defined as $\Delta(C) = \min_{c_1, c_2 \in C, c_1 \neq c_2} \Delta(c_1, c_2)$. More precisely, for any codeword $c \in C$ and any error $\delta \in \Sigma^n$ with $\mathrm{wt}(\delta) \leq t$, we have $D(c + \delta) = c$, where $\mathrm{wt}(\delta)$ is the Hamming weight of δ (i.e., the number of non-zero symbols in the string δ). Furthermore, we say that a code C has a *correction threshold of size t* if there exists a decoding function D for C that has correction threshold t. In this case, we note that the distance between any two codewords in C must be at least $2t + 1$. In the below, we give the definition of linear codes:

Definition 1 (Linear Codes). *A q-ary code C is said to be a linear code if Σ is the finite field $\mathbb{F}_q$ with q elements and C is a subspace of Σ^n.*

Remark 1. Note that a q-ary linear code C of length n and dimension k is referred to as an $[n, k]_q$ code. When the alphabet size q is clear from the context or irrelevant for discussion, we omit the subscript.

2.2 Framework of Key-Binding Approach

Before presenting the construction of the fuzzy commitment scheme, we give the framework of the key-binding approach. The approach involves two parties, a user and an authentication server. The specific flow is as follows:

- (Enrollment Phase) Given user's template x and specific key z, an association (called a *helper data h*) is generated from the pair (x, z) using certain cryptographic tools, and then the association is stored in a database of the server as the secure template (i.e., the converted template).
  (Authentication Phase) The correct key z can be extracted from the helper data h only when user's queried biometric feature y is close to the original template x. Then a validity check is performed using the extracted key to output the decision for authentication.

One of the main advantages of this approach is that instead of providing the "match/non-match" decision, the system can authenticate a user using the extracted key z in various ways such as digital signature, document encryption/decryption and an authentication system without ID. The template security (R-3) in the key-binding framework relies on the computational hardness of the following problem:

($\bigstar$) "Given only the helper data h, can we recover either the key z or the original template x without any knowledge of user's biometric data?"

2.3 Construction of Fuzzy Commitment Scheme

The fuzzy commitment scheme was first proposed by Juels and Wattenberg [14]. At present, it is known as a typical scheme to achieve the key-binding approach (the fuzzy vault scheme [13] gives another one in the approach). The construction of the scheme requires an error-correcting code C with length n and a hash function H. Here we assume that any biometric data can be represented as binary vectors of length n and the Hamming distance is used as a measure to compute the similarity of two biometric feature vectors.

Enrollment. Let c be the codeword of C generated from user's key z (i.e., $c = E(z)$ where E is an encoding function of C). Given user's biometric template $x \in \{0, 1\}^n$, a user binds it by using the codeword c as the witness. Then the helper data h of the scheme consists of a pair

$$h = F(c, x) := (x + c, H(c)),$$

which is stored in a database of the authentication server.

Authentication. During authentication, the user presents a biometric feature vector $y \in \{0,1\}^n$. The authentication server subtracts $x + c$ stored in the database from y to obtain $c' = c + \delta$ with $\delta = x - y$. If y is close to x (in the sense of the Hamming distance), the vector c' is close to c since $x - y = c' - c$. Therefore the vector c' can be decoded to c, the nearest codeword of c', provided that the Hamming distance $\Delta(c, c')$ is less that the error-correcting capacity of the code C. Reconstruction of c indicates a successful verification by checking $H(c) = H(c')$ (in this scheme, it is not necessary to recover the user's key z from the codeword c).

2.4   Security of Fuzzy Commitment Scheme

For simplicity, as in [14], we here assume that any biometric feature vectors x are uniformly sampled from $\{0,1\}^n$. According to [14, Section 5.1], the security of the fuzzy commitment scheme consists of two properties, namely, template security (see also ($\bigstar$) of Section 2.2), and strongly binding. On the template security, the following result is shown in [14, Theorem 1]:

Proposition 1 ([14]). *Suppose that for $c \in_R C$ and $x \in_R \{0,1\}^n$, an attacker is able to determine c from $F(c, x)$ in time T with probability $p(T)$. Then it is possible for the attacker to invert $H(c')$ on a random input $c' \in_R C$ in time T with probability $p(T)$.*

The result of Proposition 1 indicates that template security level is given by the number of the codewords in C, as long as the hash function H has sufficient preimage resistance. More precisely, given a security parameter λ, it requires $\#C \geq 2^\lambda$ if the security level of H against preimage attacks is higher than 2^λ.

We say that F is *strongly binding* if it is infeasible for any polynomially bounded attacker to produce a *witness collision* on F. A witness collision is a commitment $F(c, x)$ and a pair of witnesses (x_1, x_2) both of which yield valid commitments, but x_1 and x_2 are not "close" in the sense of the error-correcting code C (see [14, Section 5.1] for details). As discussed in [14], this notion is very useful for the security of biometric systems. In particular, the property of strongly binding ensures the security against a repudiation attack, where a user of biometric system resisters two different keys and then claims his or her data has been compromised by a party possessing a different key. The following result on the strongly binding for the fuzzy commitment scheme is also shown in [14, Claim1 in Section 5.1]:

Proposition 2 ([14]). *F is strongly binding if H is collision resistant. In particular, suppose that an attacker is capable of finding a witness collision. Then the attacker can find a collision on H.*

By Propositions 1 and 2, the fuzzy commitment scheme has both template security and strongly binding if the used hash function H is cryptographically secure (in particular, it has preimage and collision resistance).

3 Our Improvement

In this section, we first address some problems of the original fuzzy commitment scheme, and then give our improvement and the construction of our improved scheme in more details.

3.1 Problems of Original Fuzzy Commitment

As discussed in Sect. 2.4, the fuzzy commitment scheme has advantage on security (i.e., template security and strongly binding). However, the scheme has some problems on privacy for biometric authentication. Specifically, it has the following two problems (see also [10,11] for privacy issues of fuzzy commitment):

- During the authentication phase, every biometric feature vector y queried by a user is exposed to an authentication server (even if communication between the user and the authentication server is protected by encryption). While a template vector x is concealed as a helper data $h = F(c, x)$ in the authentication server, the server can obtain a biometric feature vector y similar to x in case of successful verification.
- The codeword c of user's key z is also recovered in case of successful verification, and hence the template x can be obtained from $F(c, x)$ in the authentication server.

In order to solve the above problems, we shall present a privacy-preserving fuzzy commitment scheme using two layered error-correcting codes in the next subsection. Specifically, our scheme will prevent the authentication server from getting biometric feature vectors y queried by a user and templates x (in successful verification, the codeword of user's specific key will be revealed for authentication, but the associated template will not be recovered in our scheme).

Remark 2. Instead of sending y, a user receives $x + c$ from the authentication server, computes $c' = c + \delta$ and correct c and then sends only $H(c)$ back to the server. In this case, the server can authenticate the user without learning any information about biometric data x and y. However, this protocol requires users to compute most of the matching processing and it also increases communication costs. Therefore this protocol is not suitable for remote authentication, which we aim to achieve. Then we do not consider the protocol in this paper.

3.2 Privacy-Preserving Fuzzy Commitment

Our improvement requires two error-correction codes and a hash function for construction:

C_1: $[n_1, k_1]_q$ code with encoding function E_1 and decoding function D_1. We assume that D_1 has correction threshold of size t_1.

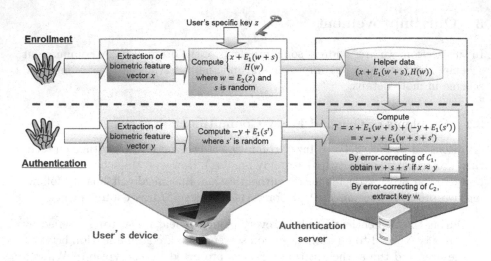

Fig. 1. An overview of our privacy-preserving fuzzy commitment scheme

C_2: $[n_2, k_2]_q$ code with encoding function E_2 and decoding function D_2. We assume that D_2 has correction threshold of size t_2 (note that the linearity of C_2 is not necessary for construction).

H: hash function (we assume that H is cryptographically-secure)

As in the fuzzy commitment scheme, we here assume that any biometric feature vectors are represented as binary vectors of length n (e.g., $n = 2048$), and the Hamming distance gives a measure to compute the similarity between two biometric feature vectors. We assume $n \leq n_1$ to embed a biometric feature vector $x \in \{0,1\}^n$ into an element of $\mathbb{F}_q^{n_1}$. Let $\mathcal{M}_1$ (resp., $\mathcal{M}_2$) denote the message space of the code C_1 (resp., C_2). We also assume

$$w + s \in \mathcal{M}_1 = \mathbb{F}_q^{k_1} \text{ for any } w \in \text{Image}(E_2) \text{ and } s \in \{0,1\}^{k_1}, \qquad (1)$$

and each user's specific key is chosen from $\mathcal{M}_2 = \mathbb{F}_q^{k_2}$. The specific flow of our scheme is as follows (see also Fig. 1 for an overview of our scheme):

Enrollment. Given user's specific key $z \in \mathcal{M}_2$, a user generates his codeword $w = E_2(z) \in \text{Image}(E_2)$ of the second code C_2. The user binds his or her biometric template $x \in \{0,1\}^n$ with the codeword $E_1(w + s)$ of $w + s \in \mathcal{M}_1$ (by the assumption (1)), where let $s \in \{0,1\}^{k_1}$ denote a random binary vector with $\text{wt}(s) \leq t_2$ chosen by the user. A helper data h of our improved scheme consists of a pair

$$h := (x + E_1(w + s), H(w)), \qquad (2)$$

which is stored in a database of an authentication server.

Authentication. Given user's biometric feature vector $y \in \{0,1\}^n$, the user generates

$$- y + E_1(s'), \qquad (3)$$

where $s' \in \{0,1\}^{k_1}$ is a randomly chosen vector with $\mathrm{wt}(s') \leq t_2$. For authentication, the user sends $-y + E_1(s')$ to the authentication server, instead of the plain biometric feature vector y. Next the authentication server computes

$$T = (x + E_1(w + s)) + (-y + E_1(s')).$$

The linearity of C_1 implies that the difference T is equal to $x - y + E_1(w + s + s')$. As in the original scheme, if y is sufficiently close to x (more precisely, if the Hamming distance $\Delta(x,y) \leq t_1$), then the decoding function D_1 of C_1 enables to output the codeword $E_1(w + s + s')$ of C_1 and hence recover $w + s + s'$ by using the inverse image function E_1^{-1}. Furthermore, since $\mathrm{wt}(s + s') \leq t_2$ by construction (we here assume that $s + s'$ is XOR-operation over a predefined subset of $\{0,1\}^{k_1}$), the decoding function D_2 of C_2 for $w + s + s'$ can output the codeword $w = E_2(z)$ of C_2. Then the authentication server can output the decision for authentication by checking whether $H(w) = H(w')$ as in the fuzzy commitment scheme, where we compute

$$w' = D_2 \circ E_1^{-1} \circ D_1(T). \qquad (4)$$

3.3   Security and Privacy of Our Improved Scheme

Here we shall discuss security and privacy of our improved scheme. As in the original scheme, we assume that any biometric feature vectors (resp., any user's specific keys) are uniformly sampled from $\{0,1\}^n$ (resp., $\mathcal{M}_2$)^2.

Template Security. The template security problem in our scheme (see ($\bigstar$) in Sect. 2.2) is to find the template x or user's specific key z from a helper data $h = (x + E_1(w + s), H(w))$. Set $c = E_1(w + s)$, and then h has almost the same form $(x + c, H(w))$ as in the original scheme. Then, by a similar argument for Proposition 1 (see the proof of [14, Theorem 1]), the computational hardness of the problem depends only on the number of candidates $w + s$ as long as the hash function H is cryptographically-secure. More precisely, give a security parameter λ, it requires

$$\#\mathcal{M}_2 \cdot 2^{t_2} \geq 2^\lambda \qquad (5)$$

for template security since $w \in \mathcal{M}_2$ and $s \in \{0,1\}^{k_1}$ satisfying $\mathrm{wt}(s) \leq t_2$. In particular, for λ-bit security, the size of s should be chosen with $\lambda \leq \mathrm{wt}(s) \leq t_2$.

---

^{2} The original fuzzy commitment is vulnerable against statistical attack (e.g., see [21] for iris-biometric case) since biometric feature vectors are non-uniform in general. Then we need to consider the security of our scheme in case that biometric feature vectors are non-uniform. But we do not discuss this here due to space restriction.

Remark 3. In our improved scheme, the codeword $w = E_2(z)$ of user's key z is revealed in successful matching. This z is typically chosen from user's passwords, and it should be protected if possible, which is our future work. But this z can be changed for each biometric system.

Strongly Binding. By Proposition 1, our improved scheme also has strongly binding (see the proof of [14, Claim1 in Section 5.1] for details). Apart from the property of strongly binding, given a helper data $h = (x + E_1(w + s), H(w))$, an attacker may repeatedly generate $y \in \{0,1\}^n$ and try to input y close to x (i.e., $\Delta(x, y) \leq d_1$) for illegally logging into a biometric system. Such impersonation attack gives a threat in practice, and the hardness of the attack for our scheme depends on the threshold t_1. But, as in the original scheme, the threshold t_1 is determined by the balance between FAR and FRR (i.e., the matching accuracy of a biometric system), and we here do not care it for our scheme. However, in Sect. 4 below, we assume that biometric feature vectors are represented as binary vectors of 2048-bit, and we take the threshold t_1 as 25 % ($t_1 = 512$) and 35 % ($t_1 = 716$) of 2048-bit. In the setting, the cost of the impersonation attack is estimated as $2^{2048}/N$ with $N = \sum_{k=0}^{t_1} \binom{2048}{k}$, which is the number of binary vectors of Hamming weight less than t_1. Hence we estimate that the attack takes 2^{392} (resp., 2^{141}) in case of $t_1 = 512$ (resp., $t_1 = 716$). Therefore such thresholds can give enough security against the impersonation attack.

Privacy on Biometric Feature Vectors. During authentication, the authentication server can know the four values

$$h = (x + E_1(w + s), H(w)), \quad -y + E_1(s'), \quad w + s + s' \text{ and } w$$

in successful verification. Given $w + s + s'$ and w, the server can know the error $s + s' \in \{0,1\}^{k_1}$. However, the server can know neither s nor s' (as long as s and s' are randomly chosen), and hence the plain vector y cannot be revealed from $-y + E_1(s')$ in the authentication server. As well as y, the template x cannot be recovered from the helper data h even in successful verification. A typical method for finding each s or s' from $s + s'$ is brute-force attack. The cost of the brute-force attack is at least 2^{t_2} since both s and s' satisfy $\text{wt}(s)$ and $\text{wt}(s') \leq t_2$. Then our scheme requires

$$t_2 \geq \lambda \tag{6}$$

in order to prevent the authentication server from getting biometric feature vectors x and y.

In summary, by (5) and (6), our scheme requires $t_2 \geq \lambda$ for both security and privacy of biometric templates. Furthermore, our improvement does not change the property of strongly binding of the original scheme.

4   Experimental Evaluation

There are a number of algorithms to extract a biometric feature vector from a biometric image. For example, from a scanned iris image, the algorithm of [3,4] can generate a binary vector of 2048-bit, called an iris vector. In 2013, it is announced in [7] that it has developed a new extraction algorithm for matching feature vectors of 2048-bit from palm vein images. In [3,4,7], the Hamming distance is used as a measure of the similarity between two extracted vectors.

In this section, we give implementation results of our improved scheme. For our experiments, we assume that any biometric data are commonly represented as binary vectors of 2048-bit as above. According to [3, Figure11], the range of suitable thresholds for both FAR and FRR of iris codes is 25 % ~ 35 %. Then we here consider two cases of 25 % and 35 % thresholds. More precisely, we take $\theta = 2048 \times 25\% = 512$ and $2048 \times 35\% \approx 716$ as two thresholds of the Hamming distance for authentication.

4.1   Choice of Codes and Suitable Parameters

For implementation, we use two types of error-correcting codes, Reed-Solomon and binary BCH codes (e.g., see [2,17] for details), which are conventional and applicable for our improved fuzzy commitment scheme. Here we present the construction of the two codes and give suitable parameters of each code for two thresholds $\theta = 512$ and 716.

Reed-Solomon Code. Here we consider the case of Reed-Solomon code. Let us begin with the construction of the code.

Construction. Given a positive integer m, let $n = 2^m - 1$ be the length and $\mathbb{F} := \mathbb{F}_{2^m}$ denote the alphabet of the Reed-Solomon code. We take k with $1 \leq k < n$ as the dimension, and fix a primitive element α in the multiplicative group $\mathbb{F}^\times = \mathbb{F} \setminus \{0\}$. Then the Reed-Solomon code $\mathrm{RS}[n, k]$ is defined by

$$\left\{ (p(1), p(\alpha), \ldots, p(\alpha^{n-1})) \in \mathbb{F}^n \mid p(X) \in \mathbb{F}[X] \text{ has degree} \leq k - 1 \right\}. \quad (7)$$

To encode a message $M = (m_0, \ldots, m_{k-1}) \in \mathbb{F}^k$, we represent the message as

$$p(X) = m_0 + m_1 X + \cdots + m_{k-1} X^{k-1},$$

and then the codeword of M is given by $(p(1), p(\alpha), \ldots, p(\alpha^{n-1})) \in \mathbb{F}^n$. We easily see from (7) that $\mathrm{RS}[n, k]$ is a linear code. Furthermore, it is known that $\mathrm{RS}[n, k]$ has minimal Hamming distance $d_{\min} = r + 1$ and hence correction threshold of size $t = \lfloor \frac{r}{2} \rfloor$, where we let $r = n - k$.

Suitable Parameters. Let $C_1 = \mathrm{RS}[n_1, k_1]$ and $C_2 = \mathrm{RS}[n_2, k_2]$ be two Reed-Solomon codes used for our improved scheme. In the following, we shall describe how to choose suitable parameters (n_1, k_1) and (n_2, k_2) for each threshold of $\theta = 512$ and 716.

Case $\theta = 512$: Let t_1 (resp., t_2) be the size of correction threshold of the code C_1 (resp., C_2). For this θ, we set $t_1 = \theta = 512$ in order to accept the robust of biometric feature vectors. We also take $n_1 = 2^{11} - 1 = 2047$ for handling biometric feature vectors of 2048-bit (in this setting, we only use 2047-bit vectors, but we here ignore the last bit of a biometric feature vector for efficiency). Then we have $k_1 = n_1 - 2t_1 = 1023$. On the other hand, for both security and privacy of biometric templates, our scheme requires $t_2 \geq \lambda$ as discussed in Sect. 3.3, where λ denote the security parameter. We here consider $\lambda = 80$, and hence we set $t_2 = 80$. Furthermore, we need to set n_2 so that the code $\mathrm{RS}[n_2, k_2]$ is included in the message space of C_1 in order to overlay two codes C_1 and C_2 in our scheme. It requires $n_2 \leq k_1 = 1023$, and we here take $n_2 = 2^9 - 1 = 511$, which setting satisfies the condition (1). Then we also have $k_2 = n_2 - 2t_2 = 351$. In summary, for $\theta = 512$, we set

$$(n_1, k_1) = (2047, 1023) \ and \ (n_2, k_2) = (511, 351). \tag{8}$$

Case $\theta = 716$: We need to set $t_1 = \theta = 716$ in this case. From a similar argument as in the above case, we set

$$(n_1, k_1) = (2047, 615) and (n_2, k_2) = (511, 351). \tag{9}$$

Binary BCH Code. Here we consider the case of binary BCH code. As in the above, we begin with the construction of the code.

Construction. Let m be a positive integer. For a length $n = 2^m - 1$, a distance d, and a primitive element $\alpha \in \mathbb{F}_{2^m}^{\times}$, the binary BCH code $\mathrm{BCH}[n, k]$ with dimension k is defined by (note that the alphabet of the code is given by $\mathbb{F}_2$)

$$\left\{ (c_0, \ldots, c_{n-1}) \in \mathbb{F}_2^n \mid c(X) = \sum_{i=0}^{n-1} c_i X^i \text{ with } c(\alpha) = \cdots c(\alpha^{d-1}) = 0 \right\}. \tag{10}$$

As in the Reed-Solomon code, the binary BCH code is linear. Furthermore, it is known that the dimension k is determined by $n - tm$, where let t denote the size of correction threshold given by $\lfloor \frac{d-1}{2} \rfloor$.

Suitable Parameters. Let $C_1 = \mathrm{BCH}[n_1, k_1]$ and $C_2 = \mathrm{BCH}[n_2, k_2]$ be two binary BCH codes. In the following, we shall describe how to choose suitable parameters (n_1, k_1) and (n_2, k_2) for each threshold of $\theta = 512$ and 716.

Case $\theta = 512$: As in the case of Reed-Solomon code, let t_1 (resp., t_2) be the size of correction threshold of the code C_1 (resp., C_2). Then we set $t_1 = 512$ in this case. For security and privacy of biometric templates, we also set $t_2 = 80$ for $\lambda = 80$-bit security level. In order to make the code C_1 have $t_1 = 512$ correction capability, we need $n_1 \geq 2^{13} - 1 = 8191$ and here we set $n_1 = 8191$, which is sufficient for handling biometric feature vectors of 2048-bit. Then we have $k_1 = n_1 - 13t_1 = 1535$. Furthermore, we need to set n_2 so that the code $C_2 = \text{BCH}[n_2, k_2]$ is included in the message space of C_1 in order to overlay two codes C_1 and C_2 in our scheme. Then we set $n_2 = 1023 \leq k_1$, and then we have $k_2 = n_2 - 10t_2 = 223$ (note $n_2 = 2^{10} - 1$). This setting satisfies the condition (1). In summary, for $\theta = 512$, we fix

$$(n_1, k_1) = (8191, 1535) \quad and \quad (n_2, k_2) = (1023, 223). \tag{11}$$

Case $\theta = 716$: In this case, we need to set $t_1 = \theta = 716$. From a similar argument as above, we here fix

$$(n_1, k_1) = (16383, 6359) \text{ and } (n_2, k_2) = (1023, 223). \tag{12}$$

4.2   Implementation and Performance

For our chosen parameters of Reed-Solomon and binary BCH codes (see Sect. 4.1 for details), we implemented our improved scheme in C programs. Our experiments ran on an Intel Xeon X3480 at 3.07 GHz with 16 GByte memory. Our implementation for a decoding algorithm of both Reed-Solomon and binary BCH codes is based on the Chien search and the Berlekamp-Massey algorithms (e.g., see [2,17] for decoding algorithms of Reed-Solomon and binary BCH codes). In Table 1, we show our implementation results on performance. Note that the results of Table 1 does not include the cost of a hash function H since it is not dominant compared to performance of error-correcting codes.

Performance. In case $\theta = 512$, for Reed-Solomon codes with parameters (8) (resp., binary BCH codes with parameters (11)), it takes 4.65 milliseconds (ms) (resp., 0.09 ms) to generate a secure template (2), 1.70 ms (resp., 0.02 ms) to generate a secure query (3), and finally 8.42 ms (resp., 19.39 ms) for secure matching computation (4), which mainly requires a decoding procedure of C_1 and C_2. For generating secure template and query, binary BCH codes give much faster performance than Reed-Solomon codes. However, Reed-Solomon codes are faster than binary BCH codes for secure matching computation (i.e., decoding algorithms). Furthermore, Reed-Solomon codes are about 1.3 times faster than binary BCH codes in total (RS: 14.80 ms vs BCH: 19.54 ms). In case $\theta = 716$, according to Table 1, Reed-Solomon codes give about 3.6 times faster performance than binary BCH codes in total (RS: 15.66 ms vs BCH: 55.61 ms).

Size of Secure Template. A secure template (2) in our scheme has form $(x + c, H(w))$ with $c \in C_1$ and $w \in C_2$. The size of the hash value $H(w)$ is not so large when we use a conventional function (e.g., SHA-1 outputs a value of 160-bit). Here we only consider the size of $x + c$, which is determined by the size of $c \in C_1$. The bit-size of $c \in C_1$ is given by $m_1 n_1$ (resp., n_1) if we use $C_1 = \text{RS}[n_1, k_1]$ (resp., $C_1 = \text{BCH}[n_1, k_1]$), where m_1 is given by $n_1 = 2^{m_1} - 1$. Then, in case $\theta = 512$, the bit-size of $c \in C_1$ is given by $m_1 n_1 = 11 \cdot 2047$ (resp., $n_1 = 8191$) for Reed-Solomon codes with parameters (8) (resp., binary

Table 1. Performance of our improved fuzzy commitment scheme using Reed-Solomon (RS) and binary BCH codes for biometric feature vectors of 2048-bit (it does not include the cost of a hash function H, which is not dominant at all in our scheme)

Thresholds	Codes and parameters	Secure template (2)	Secure query (3)	Secure matching (4)	Total
$\theta = 512$	RS codes (8)	4.65 ms	1.70 ms	8.42 ms	14.80 ms
(25 %)	BCH codes (11)	0.09 ms	0.02 ms	19.39 ms	19.54 ms
$\theta = 716$	RS codes (9)	4.16 ms	1.18 ms	10.27 ms	15.66 ms
(35 %)	BCH codes (12)	0.17 ms	0.04 ms	55.37 ms	55.61 ms

BCH codes with parameters (11)), and hence binary BCH codes give about 2.7 times smaller sizes than Reed-Solomon codes. In case $\theta = 716$, the bit-size of $c \in C_1$ is given by $m_1 n_1 = 11 \cdot 2047$ (resp., $n_1 = 16383$) for Reed-Solomon codes with parameters (9) (resp., binary BCH codes with parameters (12)), and hence binary BCH codes give about 1.4 times smaller sizes than Reed-Solomon codes.

Summary. According to the above discussion, Reed-Solomon codes give faster performance in total, but larger sizes than binary BCH codes.

5   Related Work and Comparison

In 2005, Pandey, Ojha and Sharma [20] combined the fuzzy commitment scheme of [14] with McEliece encryption scheme [16] for enhancing the security. The aim of the work is not for securing a biometric system, but for giving a candidate for post-quantum cryptography (hence the aim is quite different from ours). In 2007, Nandakumar, Nagar and Jain [18] modified the fuzzy vault scheme using a password for authentication in order to provide (R-1) and (R-2) (see Sect. 1.1 for requirements of template protection). Their method can be easily applied to both the original fuzzy commitment and our improved schemes, and hence our scheme using a password can be an ideal template protection scheme. However, we note that the security of such password-based scheme is same as that of the original scheme if the password is compromised.

    In 2010, Failla, Sutcu and Barni [6] proposed a privacy-preserving fuzzy commitment scheme. Their encrypted-sketch scheme, called *e-sketch*, prevents the information leakage mentioned in [10], and provides an efficient solution to the user privacy along with template security. Their e-sketch protocol is based on multi-party computation relying on additively homomorphic encryption such as the Paillier scheme [19]. The security of their protocol relies on cryptographic tools and it is cryptographically-secure, but their protocol is less efficient than ours, since their protocol requires more communication costs (see [6, Figure 3] for their matching computation) and its performance is estimated to be slower due to the use of the Paillier scheme. Unfortunately, no implementation result for the e-sketch protocol is reported in [6]. But their protocol require to encrypt a biometric feature vector bit-by-bit, and it requires 2048 times encryption in our case. Furthermore, it requires at least 2048 homomorphic additions for secure Hamming distance computation. If we assume that it takes 0.1 ms for one homomorphic addition (it requires fast implementation for the Paillier scheme), then it takes at least $0.1 \times 2048 \approx 200$ ms for secure matching, which is at least 4 times slower than our implementation results. Therefore, compared to [6], our scheme gives a more practical solution for biometric template protection. Note that although the e-sketch protocol can provide (R-2) for template protection, our scheme cannot provide it due to the same reason as in the original fuzzy commitment scheme[3]

6 Conclusion and Future Work

In this paper, we proposed an improvement of the fuzzy commitment scheme for both security and privacy of biometric templates. Our improved scheme makes use of two layered error-correcting codes, and it can give practical performance for biometric authentication (see Table 1 for our implementation results). Since our improved scheme cannot reveal any biometric information even in successful matching, our scheme is suitable for remote authentication over public networks, and hence it enables secure matching over a non-trusted server (e.g., the cloud).

While for simple discussion we assumed that any biometric feature vectors are uniformly sampled, our future work is to analyze security and privacy of our improved scheme for practical biometric feature vectors (those vectors are non-uniform in general). We also need to analyze information leakage of our improved scheme as in [10,11]. On the other hand, we need to propose various protocols based on our improvement (e.g., challenge-response protocol against replay attacks) in order to address a number of requirements for security and privacy in real biometrics. We also may need to carefully choose error-correcting codes (e.g., concatenated codes) for efficiency of our scheme.

References

1. Belguechi, R., Alimi, V., Cherrier, E., Lacharme, P., Rosenberger, C.: An overview on privacy preserving biometrics. In: Yang, J. (ed.) Recent Application in Biometrics. InTech, Croatia (2011)
2. Blahut, R.E.: Algebraic Codes on Lines, Planes, and Curves: An Engineering Approach. Cambridge University Press, Cambridge (2008)
3. Daugman, J.: High confidence visual recognition of persons by a test of statistical independence. IEEE Trans. Pattern Anal. Mach. Intell. **15**(11), 1148–1161 (1993)

---

[3] In the e-sketch protocol, templates can be revoked by changing keys for encryption and decryption. On the other hand, both the original fuzzy commitment scheme and ours require no keys for authentication. Therefore it is possible for an attacker to recover biometric data by generating biometric data similar to stored templates permanently.

4. Daugman, J.: The importance of being random: statistical principles of iris recognition. Pattern Recogn. **36**(2), 279–291 (2003)
5. Dodis, Y., Reyzin, L., Smith, A.: Fuzzy extractors: how to generate strong keys from biometrics and other noisy data. In: Cachin, C., Camenisch, J.L. (eds.) EUROCRYPT 2004. LNCS, vol. 3027, pp. 523–540. Springer, Heidelberg (2004). Full version in SIAM Journal on Computing, 38 (1), 97–139 (2008)
6. Failla, P., Sutcu, Y., Barni, M.: Esketch: a privacy-preserving fuzzy commitment scheme for authentication using encrypted biometrics. In: Proceedings of the 12th ACM Workshop on Multimedia and Security, pp. 241–246. ACM (2010)
7. Fujitsu Laboratories Ltd.: Press release: Fujitsu develops world's first authentication technology to extract and match 2,048-bit feature codes from palm vein images (2013), http://www.fujitsu.com/global/news/pr/archives/month/2013/20130805-01.html
8. Hao, F., Anderson, R., Daugman, J.: Combining crypto with biometrics effectively. IEEE Trans. Comput. **55**(9), 1081–1088 (2006)
9. Hoang, T., Choi, D., Nguyen, T.: Gait authentication on mobile phone using biometric cryptosystem and fuzzy commitment scheme. Int. J. Inf. Secur. **14**(6), 1–12 (2015)
10. Ignatenko, T., Willems, F.M.: On privacy in secure biometric authentication systems. In: IEEE International Conference on Acoustics, Speech and Signal Processing–ICASSP, vol. 2, pp. 121–124 (2007)
11. Ignatenko, T., Willems, F.M.: Information leakage in fuzzy commitment schemes. IEEE Trans. Inf. Forensics Secur. **5**(2), 337–348 (2010)
12. Jain, A.K., Nandakumar, K., Nagar, A.: Biometric template security. EURASIP J. Adv. Signal Process. **2008**, 113:1–113:17 (2008). http://dx.doi.org/10.1155/2008/579416
13. Juels, A., Sudan, M.: A fuzzy vault scheme. Des. Codes Crypt. **38**(2), 237–257 (2006)
14. Juels, A., Wattenberg, M.: A fuzzy commitment scheme. In: Proceedings of the 6th ACM Conference on Computer and Communications Security, pp. 28–36. ACM (1999)
15. Maltoni, D., Maio, D., Jain, A.K., Prabhakar, S.: Handbook of fingerprint recognition, 2nd edn. Springer, Heidelberg (2009)
16. McEliece, R.J.: A public-key cryptosystem based on algebraic coding theory. DSN Prog. Rep. **42**(44), 114–116 (1978)
17. Moon, T.K.: Error correction coding. Mathematical Methods and Algorithms. Wiley, Hoboken (2005)
18. Nandakumar, K., Nagar, A., Jain, A.K.: Hardening fingerprint fuzzy vault using password. In: Lee, S.-W., Li, S.Z. (eds.) ICB 2007. LNCS, vol. 4642, pp. 927–937. Springer, Heidelberg (2007)
19. Paillier, P.: Public-key cryptosystems based on composite degree residuosity classes. In: Stern, J. (ed.) EUROCRYPT 1999. LNCS, vol. 1592, pp. 223–238. Springer, Heidelberg (1999)
20. Pandey, J., Ojha, D., Sharma, A.: Enhance fuzzy commitment scheme: an approach for post quantum cryptosystem. J. Appl. Theor. Inf. Technol. **9**, 16–19 (2005)
21. Rathgeb, C., Uhl, A.: Statistical attack against iris-biometric fuzzy commitment schemes. In: IEEE Computer Society Conference on Computer Vision and Pattern Recognition Workshops–CVPRW, pp. 23–30 (2011)
22. Rathgeb, C., Uhl, A., Wild, P.: Iris-biometric fuzzy commitment schemes under image compression. In: Ruiz-Shulcloper, J., Sanniti di Baja, G. (eds.) CIARP 2013, Part II. LNCS, vol. 8259, pp. 374–381. Springer, Heidelberg (2013)

23. Sutcu, Y., Sencar, H.T., Memon, N.: A secure biometric authentication scheme based on robust hashing. In: Proceedings of the 7th Workshop on Multimedia and Security, pp. 111–116. ACM (2005)
24. Teoh, A.B., Goh, A., Ngo, D.C.: Random multispace quantization as an analytic mechanism for biohashing of biometric and random identity inputs. IEEE Trans. Pattern Anal. Mach. Intell. **28**(12), 1892–1901 (2006)
25. U.S. Department of Homeland Security: Privacy impact assessment for the biometric storage system (28 March 2007)
26. Zhou, X., Kevenaar, T.A., Kelkboom, E., Busch, C., Veen, M., Nouak, A.: Privacy enhancing technology for a 3D-face recognition system. BIOSIG **108**(2), 3–14 (2007)

Evaluation of Protocols and Obfuscation Security

Performance Evaluations of Cryptographic Protocols Verification Tools Dealing with Algebraic Properties

Pascal Lafourcade[1,3] and Maxime Puys[2,3(✉)]

[1] University Clermont Auvergne, LIMOS, 63000 Clermont-Ferrand, France
[2] Université Grenoble Alpes, VERIMAG, 38000 Grenoble, France
Maxime.Puys@imag.fr
[3] CNRS, VERIMAG, 38000 Grenoble, France

Abstract. There exist several automatic verification tools of cryptographic protocols, but only few of them are able to check protocols in presence of algebraic properties. Most of these tools are dealing either with Exclusive-Or (XOR) and exponentiation properties, so-called Diffie-Hellman (DH). In the last few years, the number of these tools increased and some existing tools have been updated. Our aim is to compare their performances by analysing a selection of cryptographic protocols using XOR and DH. We compare execution time and memory consumption for different versions of the following tools OFMC, CL-Atse, Scyther, Tamarin, TA4SP, and extensions of ProVerif (XOR-ProVerif and DH-ProVerif). Our evaluation shows that in most of the cases the new versions of the tools are faster but consume more memory. We also show how the new tools: Tamarin, Scyther and TA4SP, can be compared to previous ones. We also discover and understand for the protocol IKEv2-DS a difference of modelling by the authors of different tools, which leads to different security results. Finally, for Exclusive-Or and Diffie-Hellman properties, we construct two families of protocols $Pxor_i$ and Pdh_i that allow us to clearly see for the first time the impact of the number of operators and variables in the tools' performances.

Keywords: Verification tools for cryptographic protocols · Algebraic properties · Benchmarking · Performances' evaluations

1 Introduction

Nowadays cryptographic protocols are commonly used to secure communication. They are more and more complex and analysing them clearly outpaces humans capacities. Hence automatic formal verification is required in order to

P. Lafourcade—This research was conducted with the support of the "Digital trust" Chair from the University of Auvergne Foundation.
M. Puys—This work has been partially supported by the LabEx PERSYVAL-Lab (ANR-11-LABX-0025).

© Springer International Publishing Switzerland 2016
J. Garcia-Alfaro et al. (Eds.): FPS 2015, LNCS 9482, pp. 137–155, 2016.
DOI: 10.1007/978-3-319-30303-1_9

design secure cryptographic protocols and to detect flaws. For this goal, several automatic verification tools for analysing cryptographic protocols have been developed, like Avispa [2] (OFMC [8], TA4SP [12], CL-Atse [59], Sat-MC [4]), Tamarin [47], Scyther [24], Hermes [16], ProVerif [10], NRL [46], Murphi [48], Casper/FDR [42,53], Athena [57], Maude-NPA [32], STA [14], the tool S^3A [30] and [22]. All these tools can verify one or several security properties and rely on different theoretical approaches, *e.g.*, rewriting, solving constraints system, SAT-solvers, resolution of Horn clauses, or tree automata *etc.* All these tools work in the symbolic world, where all messages are represented by an algebra of terms. Moreover, they also consider the well-known Dolev-Yao intruder model [29], where a powerful intruder is considered [19]. This intruder controls the network, listens, stops, forges, replays or modifies some messages according to its capabilities and can play several sessions of a protocol. The perfect encryption hypothesis is often assumed, meaning that without the secret key associated to an encrypted message it is not possible to decrypt the cipher-text. In such model most of the tools are able to verify two security properties: secrecy and authentication. The first property ensures that an intruder cannot learn a secret message. The authentication property means that one participant of the protocol is sure to communicate with another one.

Historically, formal methods have been developed for analysing cryptographic protocols after the flaw discovered by Lowe [41] 17 years after the publication of Needham-Schoreder protocol [49]. The security of this protocol has been proven for one session using the BAN logic in [15,18]. The flaw discovered by Lowe [41] works because the intruder plays one session with Alice and in the same time a second one with Bob. In this second session, Bob believes that he is talking to Alice. Then the intruder learns the shared secret key that Bob thinks that he shares with Alice. This example clearly shows that even for a protocol of three messages the number of possible combinations outpaces the humans' capabilities.

In presence of algebraic properties, the number of possible combinations to construct traces blows up. The situation is even worse because some attacks can be missed. Let consider the following 3-pass Shamir protocol composed of three messages, where $\{m\}_{KA}$ denotes the encryption of m with the secret key KA:

1. $A \rightarrow B : \{m\}_{KA}$
2. $B \rightarrow A : \{\{m\}_{KA}\}_{KB}$
3. $A \rightarrow B : \{m\}_{KB}$

This protocol works only if the encryption has the following algebraic property: $\{\{m\}_{KA}\}_{KB} = \{\{m\}_{KB}\}_{KA}$. In order to implement this protocol one can use the One Time Pad (OTP) encryption, also known as Vernam encryption because it is generally credited to Gilbert S. Vernam and Joseph O. Mauborgne, but indeed it was invented 35 years early by Franck Miller [9]. The encryption of the message m with the key k is $m \oplus k$. This encryption is perfectly secure according to Shanon information theory, meaning that without knowing the key no information about the message is leaked [6,60]. Moreover the OTP encryption is key commutative since: $\{\{m\}_{KA}\}_{KB} = (m \oplus KA) \oplus KB = (m \oplus KB) \oplus KA = \{\{m\}_{KB}\}_{KA}$. Unfortunately combining the OTP encryption and the 3-pass Shamir leads to an attack against a passive intruder that only listens to all communications between Alice and Bob. Hence the intruder collects the following three messages: $m \oplus KA$; $(m \oplus KA) \oplus KB$; $m \oplus KB$. Then he can learn m just by performing the Exclusive-Or of these three messages, since $m = m \oplus KA \oplus (m \oplus KA) \oplus KB \oplus m \oplus KB$. This attack relies on the algebraic property of the encryption and cannot be detected if the modelling of the encryption is not precise enough. It is why considering algebraic operators is important. In [23] the authors proposed a survey of exiting protocols dealing with algebraic properties. In order to fill this gap, some tools have been designed to consider some algebraic properties [8, 10, 32, 38, 39, 55, 59]. Indeed doing automatic verification in presence of an algebraic property is more challenging, it is why there exist less tools that are able to deal with algebraic properties. More precisely, the algebraic properties for Diffie-Hellman are only the commutativity of the exponentiation: $(g^a)^b = (g^b)^a$. For Exclusive-Or the following four properties are considered: $(A \oplus B) \oplus C = A \oplus (B \oplus C)$ (Associativity), $A \oplus B = B \oplus A$ (Commutativity), $A \oplus 0 = A$ (Unit element), and $A \oplus A = 0$ (Nilpotency).

Contributions: We compare performances of cryptographic verification tools that are able to deal with two kinds of algebraic properties: Exclusive-Or and Diffie-Hellman. In order to perform this evaluation, we analyse execution time and also memory consumption for 21 protocols that use algebraic operators from the survey [23] or directly from the libraries proposed by each tool. Modelling all these protocols in all the considered tools is a complex task, since it requires to really understand each tool and to be able to write for each protocol the corresponding input file in each specific language. We discover that the modelling of one protocol differs in the library of Avispa and in the library of Scyther. Our investigations show that Avispa finds a flaw and Scyther does not. By building exactly the same models for the two tools, both are able to prove the security of one version and to find an attack in the second one. It clearly demonstrates that the modelling phases is crucial and often fancy even for experts. Finally for tools that can deal with Exclusive-Or and Diffie-Hellman, we construct two families of protocols $Pxor_i$ and Pdh_i, in order to evaluate the impact of the number of operators and variables used in a protocol. We discover that it provokes an exponential blowup of the complexity. Having this in mind, the results of our experimentations become clearer.

We would like to thank the designers of the tools that helped us to face some modelling tricks we had for some protocols.

State-of-the-Art: Comparing to the number of papers for describing and developing tools and the numbers of works that are using such tools to find flaws or prove the security of one protocol, there are only few works that compare the performances of cryptographic protocols verification tools. This comes from the fact that it requires to know how all the tools work. Moreover it is a time consuming task since the protocols need to be coded in the different specific input languages of each tool.

In 1996, Meadows [45] proposed a first comparison work that analyses the approach G. Lowe used in FDR [52] on the Needham-Schroeder protocol [49] with the one used in NRL [46]. It happened that both tools were complementary as FDR is faster but requires outside assistance, while NRL was slower but automatic. In 2002, the AVISS tool [3] was used to analyse a large set of protocols and timing results are given. As this tool is composed of three back-end tools, the aim was to compare these tools. In 2006, Avispa [2][1] was created as the successor of AVISS and composed of the same three back-end tools plus one new. These back-ends have been compared by Vigano in [61]. Still in 2006, Hussain and Seret [35] qualitatively compared Avispa and Hermes [16], studying their complexity and ease to use. Hermes has been declared more suited for simple protocols while Avispa is better when scalability is needed. In 2007, Cheminod et al. [20] provided a comparison of S^3A (Spi calculus Specifications Symbolic Analyzer) a prototype of the work [30], OFMC [8], STA [14] and Casper/FDR [42]. The purpose was to check for each tool if it was able to deal with specific types of flaw. In 2009, Cremers et al. proposed in [26] a fair comparison of Casper/FDR, ProVerif, Scyther and Avispa. Timings were given as well as a modelling of state spaces for each tool. For the first time, the authors were able to show the difference of performances between the Avispa tools. In 2010, Dalal et al. [27] compared the specifications of ProVerif and Scyther on six various protocols. No timing was given since the objective was to show the differences of the tools in term of features. Still in 2010, Patel et al. [50] provided a detailed list of cryptographic protocols verification tools split into different categories depending of their inner working. They compared the features of Scyther and ProVerif.

All these works only compare selected tools on protocols that do not require algebraic properties except [50] that consider Diffie-Hellman using ProVerif. In [40], P. Lafourcade et al. analysed some protocols dealing with algebraic properties. The results of this analysis clearly show that there is no clear winner in term of efficiency. This work also conjectures that the tools are influenced by the number of occurrences of the operator in the protocols. Moreover, none of them consider memory consumption.

Our aim is to revise the work of [40], because new versions of compared tools are now available and we also want to include new tools and protocols in the comparison. Moreover we propose two families of protocols to give a first answer to the conjecture given in [40] and to understand which parameters influence the performances of the tools dealing with Exclusive-Or and Diffie-Hellman.

Outline: In Sect. 2, we present the different tools that we compare. In Sect. 3, we explain the results of our benchmark. We also detail our experimentations on the impact of the number of variables involved in Exclusive-Or and Diffie-Hellman operations on the tools. Finally we conclude in Sect. 4.

---

[1] http://www.avispa-project.org/.

2   Tools

We present the six tools used for our comparison and give the different tool versions used in our analysis. To the best of our knowledge, those are the main free available tools dealing with two common algebraic properties used in cryptographic protocols: Exclusive-Or or Diffie-Hellman.

CL-Atse [59] (Version 2.2-5 (2006) and 2.3-4 (2009)) *Constraint-Logic-based Attack Searcher*[2], developed by M. Turuani, runs a protocol in all possible ways over a finite set of sessions, translating traces into constraints. Constraints are simplified thanks to heuristics and redundancy elimination techniques allowing to decide whether some security properties have been violated or not.

OFMC [7] (Version 2006-02-13 and 2014) The *Open-source Fixed-point Model-Checker*[3], developed by S. Mödersheim, applies symbolic analysis to perform protocol falsification and bounded analysis also over a finite set of sessions. The state space is explored in a demand-driven way.

TA4SP [13] (Version 2014) *Tree Automata based on Automatic Approximations for the Analysis of Security Protocols*[4], developed by Y. Boichut, approximates the intruder knowledge by using regular tree languages and rewriting. For secrecy properties, it can either use over-approximation or under-approximation to show that the protocol is flawed or safe for any number of session. However, no attack trace is provided by the tool and only the secrecy is considered in presence of algebraic properties.

CL-Atse, OFMC and TA4SP are backend tools used within Avispa (*Automated Validation of Internet Security Protocols and Applications*). All these tools take as input a common language called HLPSL (*High Level Protocol Specification Language*).

ProVerif[5] [10,11] (Version: 1.16 (2008) and 1.90 (2015)) developed by B. Blanchet analyses an unbounded number of sessions. Inputs can be written either in Horn clauses format or using a subset of the Pi-calculus. It uses over-approximation techniques such as an abstraction of fresh nonce generation to prove that a protocol satisfies user-given properties. If a property cannot be proven, it reconstructs an attack's trace.

In [38] (2008) and [39] (2009) R. Küster and T. Truderung proposed two translators named XOR-ProVerif and DH-ProVerif. These tools respectively transform a protocol using Exclusive-Or and Diffie-Hellman properties, written as Prolog file into a protocol in Horn clauses which is compatible with ProVerif. Both of these tools require the version 5.6.14 of SWI/Prolog to work. Since these works, ProVerif has been enhanced to support Diffie-Hellman on its own, by adding a specific equational theory in each protocol specification.

Scyther[6] [24] (Version 1.1.3 (2014)) developed by C. Cremers, verifies bounded and unbounded number of runs with guaranteed termination, using

---

[2] http://webloria.loria.fr/equipes/cassis/softwares/AtSe/.
[3] http://www.imm.dtu.dk/~samo/.
[4] http://www.univ-orleans.fr/lifo/membres/Yohan.Boichut/ta4sp.html.
[5] http://prosecco.gforge.inria.fr/personal/bblanche/proverif/.
[6] https://www.cs.ox.ac.uk/people/cas.cremers/scyther/.

a symbolic backwards search based on patterns. Scyther does not support Exclusive-Or or Diffie-Hellman off the shelf but under-approximates Diffie-Hellman by giving the adversary the capability of rewriting such exponentiations at fixed subterm positions, which are derived from the protocol specification. This trick has been first introduced by Cremer in [25] on the protocols of IKEv1 and IKEv2 suite. Those modelizations are presented in the protocols' library of the tool.

Tamarin[7] [47,55] (Version 0.9.0 (2013)) is a security protocol prover able to handle an unbounded number of sessions. Protocols are specified as multiset rewriting systems with respect to (temporal) first-order properties. It relies on Maude [31] tool[8] and only supports Diffie-Hellman equational theory.

3   Experimentations and Discussion

We present the results on the modellings of the analysed protocols with OFMC, CL-Atse, TA4SP, Tamarin, Scyther and extensions of ProVerif. We analyse the same protocols as in the paper [40] in order to see how the tools have been updated. This list of the protocols in [40] contains: Bull's Authentication Protocol [17,54], e-Auction [34], Gong's Mutual Authentication Protocol [33], Salary Sum [56], TMN [43,58], Wired Equivalent Privacy Protocol [1], Diffie-Hellman [28] and IKA [5]. We also add some protocols that are given in the benchmarks of the new considered tools (*Secure Shell (SSH) Transport Layer Protocol* [62], *Internet Key Exchange Protocol version 2 (IKEv2)* [36,37]), NSPKxor [44] and 3-Pass Shamir described in the introduction. We selected these protocols as they were either proposed by the tool's authors or listed in the survey [23].

Our experiments were run on an Intel(R) Core(TM) i5-4310U 2.00GHz CPU with 16 GB of RAM. Memory usage per process is not limited (ulimit -m unlimited). Timings and memory consumption were determined using the GNU *time*[9] command computing the *Real time* and the *Maximum Resident Set Size* for each run of each tool. All testcases were run with a timeout of 24 h using the GNU *timeout*[10] command. All our codes of each protocol modeling for each tool are availaible in [51].

For accuracy reasons, we launched each run 50 times if it takes less than 1 h for the tool to analyse the protocol. Then we computed the mean of all timings and memory usages. When it takes more than 1h, we restrict to 10 iterations. We denote a protocol by -*fix* for its corrected version if any and *v2* for its simplified versions if needed.

Table 1 summarizes the secrecy results of tools dealing with Exclusive-Or (OFMC, CL-Atse, TA4SP and ProVerif) on some protocols. Table 2 compiles results we obtain on secrecy with all the tools on Diffie-Hellman based protocols. Finally, Table 3 recaps results obtained by all the tools (but TA4SP which only

---

[7] http://www.infsec.ethz.ch/research/software/tamarin.html.
[8] http://maude.cs.uiuc.edu/download/.
[9] http://linux.die.net/man/1/time.
[10] http://linux.die.net/man/1/timeout.

deals with secret) on protocols with authentication properties. Numbers in paren-
thesis denotes the number of property specified for each modelization. Notice
that TA4SP is able to run either in over-approximation or under-approximation.
However, due to the time taken by the tool, we were not able to check any protocol (except NSPKxor) using under-approximation within our timeout. Thus
all results from TA4SP only use over-approximation.

Obviously, the transformation algorithm proposed by Küster and Truderung
in [38] and [39] adds an overhead in terms of computation time and memory
usage. However, we found out that this overhead was often less than 1 s and
3000 Kb of memory consumption. It appears to be different only for *BAPv2* and
BAPv2-fix protocols for which it was respectively 1.78 s and 6.05s (memory was
not blowing up). Except for these two protocols, the overhead induced by the
transformation was negligible and constant so it is not shown in our results.

It is important to notice that all tools do not have the same objectives.
CL-Atse and OFMC are designed to find attacks and stop once they found
one. TA4SP, Tamarin and Scyther are provers and try to find attacks on each
property specified even if they already violated one. ProVerif is also designed
to prove all the properties that are specified but the pretreatments added by
R. Kuesters et al. can make him stop once an attack is found or not depending
on the modelization (in particular the presence of *begin* and *end* statements).
To be completely fair, we need to check unsafe protocols one property after one
other to make sure all are tested. Obviously this is not needed for safe protocols
since all the properties must be verified for such verdict.

3.1 Comparing Old and New Versions of the Tools

In [40], the authors compared the performances of CL-Atse, OFMC and ProVerif.
Since then, they have been updated. We use the most recent version of each tool
in this comparison. Nevertheless, we also run all of our experimentations using
the same version than in [40] to compare how the tools have evolved. For all
testcases, we computed the *speedup* indicator as the result of $S = \frac{T_{old}}{T_{new}}$ where S
is the resultant speedup and T_{old} (resp. T_{new}) is the timing obtained with the
old (new) version of the tool. We choose to not compute it for values less than
1 s as they are hardly representative. The exact same computation have been
done with memory usages. For each tool tested in [40] we compare the results
obtained with the new version and the former one, all theses results can also be
found in Tables 1, 2 and 3.

CL-Atse: We compare the version 2.2-5, released in 2006 with the version 2.3-4,
released in 2009. By looking at the speedup indicator, the tool seems slightly
slower in its newer version (0.97 times on average). The old version has a minimum memory usage of about 1570 Kb (reached in 53 % of the protocols). This
minimum has increased to about 5024 Kb (reached in 90 % of the protocols).
Thus, we can notice that memory usages are pretty stable in particular with the
new version.

Table 1. Comparison of all the tools on 13 protocols using XOR on secrecy properties (memory consumptions in Kb).

Protocol studied	CL-Atse v2.3-4 [59]	(Kb)	OFMC 2014 [7]	(Kb)	TA4SP 2014 [13]	(Kb)	XOR-ProVerif 1.90 [10,11]	(Kb)	Speedup CL-Atse	Speedup OFMC	Speedup ProVerif
BAP [17,54] UNSAFE	0.12s / +0.12s / =0.24s	5024 / 5024 / 5024	0.09s / +0.15s / =0.24s	9317 / 20581 / 20581	No result / TA4SP error / Out of memory		XOR-ProVerif / Does not end (>24h) / 71Go output		= / = / =	0.51 / 0.53 / 0.52	= / = / =
BAPv2 [17,54] UNSAFE	0.12s / +0.12s / =0.24s	5024 / 5024 / 5024	0.08s / +0.14s / =0.22s	10077 / 20581 / 20581	No result / TA4SP error / Out of memory		2.20s / +2.20s / =4.40s	153060 / 153048 / 153060	0.33 / 0.37 / 0.35	0.48 / 0.53 / 0.51	0.92 / 0.92 / 0.92 / 0.92 / 0.93 / 0.92
BAF-fix [17,54] SAFE	33m55s	5979	Does not end (>24h)		No result / TA4SP error / Out of memory		Does not end (>24h) / 71Go output	153060	0.94 / 2.43	=	=
BAPv2-fix [17,54] SAFE	1m30s	5156	33m8s	376669	No result / TA4SP error / Out of memory		1m6s	798236	0.97 / 0.96 / 0.97	0.80 / 0.81 / 0.81	1.4 / 1.4 / 1.4 / 0.61 / 0.61 / 0.61 / 0.82 / 0.82 / 0.82
E-auction [34] SAFE	0.85s	85223	0.13s	11373	TA4SP error / Out of memory		0.01s	4767	0.51	0.42	0.86
Gong [33] SAFE	40.76s	5024	7.77s	604267	No result / TA4SP error / Out of memory		Killed by kernel / Because of memory / exhausted		1.06 / 0.38 / 1.18	=	=
Salary Sum [55] UNSAFE	0.08s / +0.08s / +0.08s / +0.08s / =0.32s	5025 / 5024 / 5024 / 5024 / 5025	0.07s / +0.06s / +0.06s / +0.06s / =0.25s	7741 / 6623 / 6818 / 6822 / 7741	No result / TA4SP error / Out of memory		23h37m / 23h38m / 23h37m / 23h38m	927024 / 926975 / 927015 / 927024 (ProVerif error)	0.31 / 0.31 / 0.31 / 0.31 / 0.31	0.42 / 0.41 / 0.42 / 0.41 / 0.42	=
Salary Sum v2 [55] UNSAFE	0.08s / +0.08s / +0.08s / +0.08s / =0.32s	5025 / 5024 / 5024 / 5024 / 5025	0.07s / +0.06s / +0.06s / +0.06s / =0.25s	7663 / 6553 / 6561 / 6558 / 7663	No result / TA4SP error / Out of memory		10.17s / +9.98s / +10.11s / +10.06s / =40.32s	29760 / 29760 / 29760 / 29761 / 29761	0.31 / 0.31 / 0.31 / 0.31 / 0.31	0.42 / 0.42 / 0.42 / 0.42 / 0.42	1.67 / 1.80 / 1.63 / 1.61 / 1.68 / 0.42 / 0.42 / 0.42 / 0.42 / 0.42
TMN [43,58] UNSAFE	0.04s / +0.04s / =0.08s	5024 / 5025 / 5025	0.05s / +0.07s / =0.12s	7505 / 10824 / 10824	8m53s / +8m42s / =17m35s	83860 / 83940 / 83940	0.01s / +0.01 / =0.02s	5493 / 5493 / 5493	0.31 / 0.31 / 0.31	0.51 / 0.51 / 0.51	0.88 / 0.88 / 0.88
WEP [1] UNSAFE	0.04s	5024	0.04s	5341	4.05s	50908	0.01s	4510	0.31	0.40	=
WEP-fix [1] SAFE	0.04s	5024	0.04s	5369	4.02s / INCONCL.	50908	0.01s	4523	0.31	0.43	0.86
NSP-xor [44] UNSAFE	0.04s / +0.04s / =0.08s	5024 / 5024 / 5024	0.04s / +0.04s / =0.08s	5365 / 5405 / 5405	21.6s / +22.24s / =43.9s	50968 / 50696 / 50968	0.08s / +0.08s / =0.16s	6954 / 6942 / 6954	0.31 / 0.31 / 0.31	2.42 / 0.58 / 1.50	0.68 / 0.98 / 0.83
3-Pass Shamir UNSAFE	0.04s	5024	0.04s	5469	TA4SP error		0.01s	3091	0.31	0.44	0.92

Table 2. Comparaison of all the tools on 8 protocols using DH on secrecy properties (memory consumptions in Kb).

Protocol studied	CL-Atse v2.3-4 [5?]		OFMC 2014 [7]		TA4SP 2014 [13]		DH-ProVerif 1.90 [10,11]		Tamarin 0.9.0 [55,47]		Scyther 1.1.3 [24]		Speedup CL-Atse	Speedup OFMC	Speedup ProVerif
DH [28]	0.02s	5060	0.04s	5408	0.36s	51736	0.01s	4616	5.23s	23944	0.01s	610	= 0.31	= 0.46	= 0.86
	+ 0.03s	5064	+ 0.04s	5364	+ 1.36s	51684	+ 0.01s	4616	+ 5.32s	25046	+ 0.01s	608	= 0.31	= 0.43	= 0.86
UNSAFE	= 0.05s	5064	= 0.08s	5408	= 1.72s	51736	= 0.02s	4616	= 10.54s	25046	= 0.02s	610	= 0.31	= 0.45	= 0.86
IKA [5]	0.05s	5024	0.05s	5885	No result		0.01s	4934	Does not end (>24h)		0.18s	631	= 0.31	= 0.46	= 0.87
	+ 0.05s	5024	+ 0.05s	6509	TA4SP error		+ 0.01s	4302			+ 0.01s	606	= 0.31	= 0.47	= 0.86
UNSAFE	+ 0.05s	5024	+ 0.04s	5801	Stack overflow		+ 0.01s	4378			+ 0.01s	606	= 0.31	= 0.45	= 0.86
	= 0.15s	5024	= 0.14s	6509			= 0.03s	4934			= 0.20s	631	= 0.31	= 0.46	= 0.86
SSH [62] SAFE	0.58s	5024	8.76s	717841	Does not end (>24h)		0.02s	5902	40.07s	89790	0.16s	736	= 0.36	1.27 = 0.45	= 0.88
IKEv2-DS [36,37] SAFE	0.20s	5024	1.12s	101486	0.55s	50864	0.06s	7441	1.91s	38251	38.46s	5932	= 0.36	1.27 = 0.42	= 0.94
IKEv2-DS-fix [36,37] SAFE	0.21s	5024	5.58s	535196	1.40s	34494	0.03s	6373	3.14s	54729	42.81s	5952	= 0.36	1.29 = 0.37	= 0.90
IKEv2-DSv2-fix [36,37] SAFE	0.15s	5024	1.09s	98878	0.55s	34646	0.06s	7425	1.91s	37669	36.04s	6007	= 0.31	1.26 = 0.42	= 0.91
IKEv2-CHILD [36,37] SAFE	0.05s	5023	0.20s	16493	0.56s	34467	0.02s	5747	19.44s	52857	2.24s	1496	= 0.31	= 0.41	= 0.92
IKEv2-MAC [36,37] SAFE	0.05s	5024	1.06s	96365	0.52s	50889	0.01s	5395	31.50s	70715	4m9s	29176	= 0.31	1.27 = 0.42	= 0.87

Table 3. Comparison of all the tools on authentication properties for 10 XOR and DH protocols (memory consumptions in Kb).

Protocol studied	CL-Atse v2.3-4 [59]		OFMC 2014 [7]		(XOR/DH)-ProVerif 1.90 [10,11]		Tamarin 0.9.0 [55,47]		Scyther 1.1.3 [24]		Speedup CL-Atse	Speedup OFMC	Speedup ProVerif
E-auction [34] SAFE	0.62s	5024	0.13s	11377	0.01s	4768	Not supported		Not supported		= 0.39	= 0.42	= 0.85
NSPKxor [44]	0.04s	5060	0.05s	6440	0.03s	5788	Not supported		Not supported		= 0.31	= 0.42	= 0.89
	+ 0.18s	5060	+ 0.06s	6532	+ 0.03s	5784					= 0.31	= 0.42	= 0.89
UNSAFE	= 0.22s	5060	= 0.11s	6532	= 0.06s	5788					= 0.31	= 0.42	= 0.89
DH [28]	0.04s	5064	0.04s	5376	0.01s	4616	5.35s	22540	0.01s	581	= 0.31	= 0.43	= 0.86
	+ 0.04s	5060	+ 0.04s	5572	+ 0.01s	4620	+ 5.64s	21740	+ 0.01s	621	= 0.31	= 0.45	= 0.86
UNSAFE	= 0.08s	5064	= 0.08s	5572	= 0.02s	4620	= 10.99s	22540	= 0.02s	621	= 0.31	= 0.44	= 0.86
IKA [5]	0.05s	5060	0.06s	7532	0.01s	5052	Does not end		0.01s	588	= 0.31	= 5.94	= 0.86
	+ 0.06s	5060	+ 0.05s	6392	+ 0.01s	5064	19.65s	406888	0.01s	584	= 0.31	= 0.41	= 0.86
	+ 0.07s	5056	+ 0.04s	5928	+ 0.01s	5056	19.70s	384480	+ 0.01s	584	= 0.31	= 0.44	= 0.86
	+ 0.06s	5056	+ 0.05s	6480	+ 0.01s	5044	19.67s	361748	+ 0.01s	584	= 0.31	= 6.90	= 0.86
	+ 0.06s	5060	+ 0.06s	7516	+ 0.01s	5048	Does not end		+ 0.01s	584	= 0.31	= 5.95	= 0.86
UNSAFE	= 0.30s	5060	= 0.26s	7532	= 0.05s	5064	-		= 0.05s	588	= 0.31	= 3.93	= 0.86
SSH [62] SAFE	0.30s	5024	6.49s	656602	0.02s	5902	57.94s	106956	0.03s	699	= 0.36	= 0.44	= 0.88
IKEv2-DS [36,37]	0.14s	5060	1.06s	95344	0.07s	7416	1.87s	34784	0.01s	660	= 0.31	1.23 0.42	= 0.90
	+ 0.06s	5060	+ 0.08s	9556	+ 0.07s	7428	+ 1.74s	36816	+ 0.03s	724	= 0.31	= 0.50	= 0.90
UNSAFE	= 0.20s	5060	= 1.14s	95344	= 0.14s	7428	= 3.61s	36816	= 0.04s	724	= 0.31	1.23 0.46	= 0.90
IKEv2-DS-fix [36,37] SAFE	3.05s	5024	5.34s	516206	0.02s	6062	4.06s	58614	41.08s	5660	0.94 0.37	1.34 0.43	= 0.89
IKEv2-DSv2-fix [36,37] SAFE	0.12s	5025	1.11s	93665	0.06s	7415	1.74s	43059	31.70s	5304	= 0.31	1.35 0.43	= 0.91
IKEv2-CHILD [36,37] SAFE	0.06s	5024	0.20s	15205	0.02s	5772	20.37s	55102	1.50s	1276	= 0.31	= 0.45	= 0.91
IKEv2-MAC [36,37] SAFE	0.05s	5024	1.07s	92269	0.01s	5395	31.14s	73231	3m46s	27237	= 0.31	1.37 0.42	= 0.87

OFMC: We compare the version 2006 of the tool with the version 2014. Here we can notice a more clear trend on the reduction of timings (around 1.29 times faster), contrasted by a clear trend on the augmentation of memory usages (0.45, meaning more than doubling). However, unlike we previously said on CL-Atse, memory usage of OFMC can vary a lot (from 5341 Kb to more than 717 Mb). This can be explained by the fact that OFMC is looking for some fix points and this research can require a large memory.

ProVerif: We compare the version 1.16, released in 2008 with the version 1.90 released in early 2015. Looking at the representative timings, we are not able to notice any clear variation (*BAPv2* and *BAPv2-fix* are slower but *Salary Sum v2* is faster). However, ProVerif also has increased his memory usage with a variation of 0.90. The principal aim of ProVerif is to analyse some cryptographic protocols without equational theory. In our comparison, we use two tools developed by R. Kuesters to analyse our protocols and they have not been updated.

3.2   Observation on the Results of the New Tools

Here we summarize and explain the individual results of the tools we added since [40].

TA4SP seems to have hard time when dealing with the complexity of Exclusive-Or properties as only 33 % of our protocols produce a result. Moreover, the performances of TA4SP are far behind CL-Atse, OFMC and ProVerif. However, when dealing with Diffie-Hellman properties, TA4SP is pretty competitive as its timings are close to the ones of CL-Atse, OFMC and ProVerif. Its memory usages are also always higher than CL-Atse and ProVerif but lower then OFMC in 75 % of our protocols.

Tamarin seems really slower than CL-Atse and ProVerif either on secrecy or authentication. It is only faster than OFMC when checking *IKEv2-DS-fix*. The reason may be that the granularity of the modelling is too thin and complexifies the analysis. However, Tamarin is the only tool being able to deal with temporal properties and it would be interesting to try to analyse some protocols using Diffie-Hellman and satisfying such properties.

Scyther does not have Diffie-Hellman properties built in its algorithm. We use a trick that consists to introduce an extra role in the protocol to perform the commutation of the exponentiation, This role is a kind of oracle that is called by the tool when a protocol is analysed. Then Scyther is able to compete with other tools. In selected protocols, the Diffie-Hellman oracle is only called on small messages, then Scyther is pretty efficient (for example in *SSH*). However, protocols such as *IKEv2-CHILD* or *IKEv2-MAC* are still to complex for this hack and would need Diffie-Hellman properties to be built in the tool to be able to compete with other tools.

An interesting example with Scyther is the *IKEv2-DS* protocol. The Internet Key Exchange version 2, Digital Signatures variant (*IKEv2-DS*) aims at establishing mutual authentication between two parties using an IKE Security Association (SA) that includes shared secret information. The first two exchanges of messages establishing an IKE SA are called the IKE_SA_INIT exchange and the IKE_AUTH exchange. During IKE_SA_INIT, users exchange nonces and establishes a Diffie-Hellman key. Then IKE_AUTH authenticates the previous messages, exchanges the user identities and establish an IKE SA.

Protocol IKEv2-DS:

1. $A \to B : SA1.g^x.Na$
2. $B \to A : SA1.g^y.Nb$
3. $A \to B : \{A.\{SA1.g^x.Na.Nb\}inv(pk(A)).SA2\}_{h(Na.Nb.SA1.g^{xy})}$
4. $B \to A : \{B.\{SA1.g^y.Nb.Na\}inv(pk(B)).SA2\}_{h(Na.Nb.SA1.g^{xy})}$

Where $x.y$ denotes the pair of message x and y. In this given form, *IKEv2-DS* is vulnerable to an authentication attack[11] where the intruder is able to impersonate A when speaking to B. However, he is not able to learn g^{xy}, the key shared by only A and B making this attack unexploitable.

To prevent the attack against *IKEv2-DS*, S. Mödersheim and P. Hankes Drielsma proposed on the Avispa's website[12] to add an extension consisting of two messages, each containing a nonce and a distinguished constant encrypted with the IKE_SA_INIT key. This version is denoted by *IKEv2-DS-fix*.

As C. Cremers already mentioned in [25], specifying explicitly the responder's identify in the first message of the IKE_AUTH exchange also prevents this attack. We denote by *IKEv2-DSv2-fix* this version. This parameter is specified as optional in Sect. 1.2 of [37]. This way, Step 3. of the protocol becomes:

$$A- > B : \{A, \mathbf{B}, \{SA1.g^x.Na.Nb\}inv(pk(A)), SA2\}_{h(Na.Nb.SA1.g^{xy})}$$

As mentioned in the introduction, the difference of modelling between *IKEv2-DS* which was proposed in the Avispa library and *IKEv2-DSv2-fix* which was included in Scyther's library was indeed changing the result of the security analysis since the later was already fixed. It would not have been easy to spot this difference as the two protocols were modeled in different languages and as the parameter added in *IKEv2-DSv2-fix* was supposed optional. Again such tiny changes require the user to deeply understand the input language of each tool and to understand the original specification of the protocol to be noticed.

Moreover, still in [25], C. Cremers also proposed a more detailed version of *IKEv2-DS*, *IKEv2-DSv2-fix* and *IKEv2-MAC* adding other parameters specified in [37] but this time not affecting on the result of the analysis. We also run these modelisations with Scyther and interestingly, these additional parameters slow down the tool when analysing *IKEv2-DS* and *IKEv2-DSv2-fix* but accelerate it when we check *IKEv2-MAC*. This shows how modifications not relevant at the first sight can drastically change the performances and even the results of a tool.

3.3   Further Analyses

In this section, our aim is to measure the impact of the number of variables involved in Exclusive-Or and Diffie-Hellman on each tools.

---

[11] http://www.avispa-project.org/library/IKEv2-DS.html.

[12] http://www.avispa-project.org/library/IKEv2-DSx.html.

Analysis of the Influence of Exclusive-Or Operator: We propose the following unsafe family of protocols called $Pxor_i$.

1. $A \rightarrow B : Na_i$
2. $B \rightarrow A : Na_i \oplus Sb$

where Na_i is result of i fresh nonces xored and Sb is a secret that B wants to share with A. So for instance, if $i = 3$, the protocol $Pxor_3$ is defined such as:

1. $A \rightarrow B : Na_1 \oplus Na_2 \oplus Na_3$
2. $B \rightarrow A : Na_1 \oplus Na_2 \oplus Na_3 \oplus Sb$

With $Na_1 \oplus Na_2 \oplus Na_3 = xor(Na_1, Na_2, Na_3)$. Moreover, we test how the tools handle Exclusive-Or. Thus we also consider a variant $P-nestedxor_i$ in which $(Na_1 \oplus Na_2) \oplus Na_3 = xor(xor(Na_1, Na_2), Na_3)$. This does not make any difference for XOR-ProVerif since the intermediate files produced are strictly the same.

For each tool, Fig. 1a represents timings and Fig. 1b represents memory consumptions in function of the number of nonces sent by A in the $Pxor_i$ protocol. We stopped runs taking more than one hour. All tools are able to find attacks when they did terminate. We can see that CL-Atse is barely not able to deal with more than five variables in an Exclusive-Or. XOR-ProVerif is able to handle up to eight but taking a really long time. However, OFMC seems to perfectly handle this constraint, keeping both his timings and memory consumptions almost constant.

This experimentation demonstrates that the number of variables in Exclusive-Or operators has a clear impact on the tools. It is a factor of complexity explosion like the number of roles, the number of sessions, the number of nonces and the number of participants. OFMC seems to use an efficient strategy to handle a "global" Exclusive-Or.

Figure 1c represents timings for each tool function of the number of nonces sent by A in the $P-nestedxor_i$ protocol. Figure 1d is the same with memory consumptions. All tools are able to find attacks when they did terminate. We can see that CL-Atse has results very close to our experimentation without nested Exclusive-Or. XOR-ProVerif has the exact same behavior as it does not make any difference with prioritized Exclusive-Or or not. This time we can see that OFMC is affected by the number of Exclusive-Or operations growing and is able to handle up to eleven Exclusive-Or.

Analysis of the influence of Diffie-Hellman operator: We propose the following family of unsecure protocols Pdh_i to measure the impact of Diffie-Hellman exponentiations.

1. $A \rightarrow B : g^{Na_i}$
2. $B \rightarrow A : g^{Nb_i}$
3. $A \rightarrow B : \{S\}_{(g^{Na_i})^{Nb_i}}$

The protocol Pdh_i contains i nonces from A and also i nonces from B so that $(g^{Na_i})^{Nb_i} = exp(g, Na_1, \ldots, Na_i, Nb_1, \ldots, Nb_i)$. We also consider the $P-nesteddh_i$ protocol where

$$(g^{Na_i})^{Nb_i} = exp(g, exp(Na_1, exp(\ldots, exp(Na_i, exp(Nb_1, exp(\ldots, Nb_i))))))$$

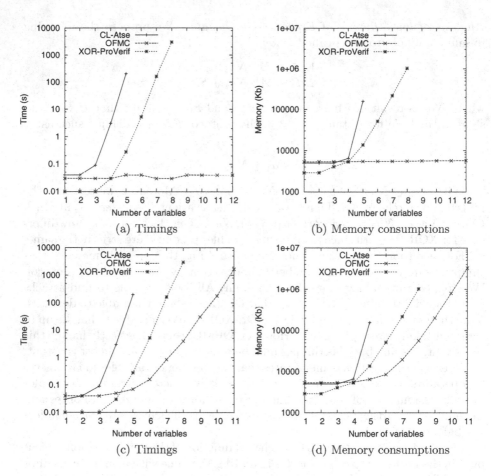

Fig. 1. Performances of the tools on the $Pxor_i$ and $P{-}nestedxor_i$ protocols

Figure 2a represents timings for each tool in function of the number of nonces sent by A and B in the Pdh_i protocol. Figure 2b is the same with memory consumptions. When they did terminate, all tools are able to find attacks. We observe that all tools are able to deal with more variables involved in Diffie-Hellman exponentiations than in Exclusive-Or. This due to the fact that Exclusive-Or has four properties, including commutativity, while Diffie-Hellman only has one (commutativity). DH-ProVerif is able to handle up to eleven nonces in each role before taking too much time. CL-Atse reasonably manages 24 variables with its timing slowly growing and its memory stays constant. OFMC has the exact same behavior as with $Pxor_i$, staying constant in timings and memory usage.

Figure 2c and d respectively represents timings and memory consumptions for each tool function of the number of nonces sent by A and B in the $P{-}nesteddh_i$ protocol. All tools find some attacks if they terminate. We can modelize the nested Diffie-Hellman exponentiations using a rewriting rule directly in ProVerif 1.90

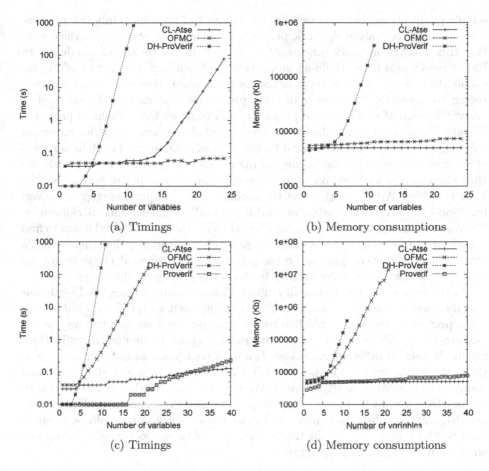

Fig. 2. Performances of the tools on the P_i and $P-nested_i$ protocols

using Pi-calculus and without using DH-ProVerif (the syntax does not allow exponentiation operators with arity greater than two and exclude tests on Pdh_i). Thus we differentiate results from DH-ProVerif, the algorithm from [39] with the results from ProVerif. This time, DH-ProVerif and OFMC are impacted when we increase the number of nonces of the protocol. DH-ProVerif ends up limited by its timing while OFMC fills the memory of the system. Interestingly, this time CL-Atse is perfectly able to handle the nested Diffie-Hellman exponentiations, keeping its timing and memory constant. The modelisation using ProVerif's Pi-calculus language also seems very powerful.

4   Conclusion

In the last decades several automatic verification tools for cryptographics protocols have been developed. They are really useful to help the designer to construct secure protocols against the well known Dolev-Yao intruder. Only few of these tools are able to analyse algebraic properties. In this work we compare the execution time and the memory consumption of the main free tools that can deal with Exclusive-Or and Diffie-Hellman properties. We use a large benchmark of 21 protocols. In this competition there is not a clear winner. However we can see that recent tools can deal with some of these properties. For instance Tamarin offers the verification of new temporal properties and consider Diffie-Hellman property. We also construct two families of protocols to evaluate how the performances of existing tools, that are able to consider the Exclusive-Or and Diffie-Hellman operators, are influenced by the number of operators in the protocol. We clearly see that the complexity is exponential in function of the number of operators used with variables. We also notice that the modelling is an important step in the verification of cryptographic protocols and it can really influence their performance. Moreover each tool has is own strategy based on his theoretical foundations to find attack or to prove the security properties, it is not surprising that there is not a clear winner of our comparison on the set of protocols since algebraic operators introduce a new factor of complexity in the verification procedures.

In the future, we plan to run all Diffie-Hellman examples using the Pi-calculus specification of ProVerif in order to directly compare it with DH-ProVerif on real scale protocols. We also would like to continue our analysis in a fair way as the authors of [26] did. It would be very interesting to push further our investigations on the impact of different parameters on each tool (such as the number of participants or the length of each protocol). Finally, in [21] Chen et al. proposed an improve algorithm of XOR-ProVerif. We plan to compare this new version with the one from [38,39] to measure these improvements. Protocols using elliptic curve cryptography are becoming more and more important and it would be great to analyse them. However, for the time being, none of these tools are able to support such complex algebraic properties.

Acknowledgments. We deeply thank all the tools authors for their helpful advises.

References

1. IEEE 802.11 Local Metropolitan Area Networks: Wireless LAN Medium Acess Control (MAC) and Physical (PHY) Specifications (1999)
2. Armando, A., Basin, D., Boichut, Y., Chevalier, Y., Compagna, L., Cuellar, J., Drielsma, P.H., Heám, P.C., Kouchnarenko, O., Mantovani, J., Mödersheim, S., von Oheimb, D., Rusinowitch, M., Santiago, J., Turuani, M., Viganò, L., Vigneron, L.: The AVISPA tool for the automated validation of internet security protocols and applications. In: Etessami, K., Rajamani, S.K. (eds.) CAV 2005. LNCS, vol. 3576, pp. 281–285. Springer, Heidelberg (2005)
3. Armando, A., Basin, D., Bouallagui, M., Chevalier, Y., Compagna, L., Mödersheim, S., Rusinowitch, M., Turuani, M., Viganò, L., Vigneron, L.: The AVISS security protocol analysis tool. In: Brinksma, E., Larsen, K.G. (eds.) CAV 2002. LNCS, vol. 2404, pp. 349–353. Springer, Heidelberg (2002)
4. Armando, A., Compagna, L.: An optimized intruder model for SAT-based model-checking of security protocols. In: Armando, A., Viganò, L. (eds.) ENTCS, vol. 125, pp. 91–108. Elsevier Science Publishers, March 2005

5. Ateniese, G., Steiner, M., Tsudik, G.: New multiparty authentication services and key agreement protocols. IEEE J. Sel. Areas Commun. **18**(4), 628–639 (2000)
6. Baigneres, T., Junod, P., Lu, Y., Monnerat, J., Vaudenay, S.: A Classical Introduction to Cryptography Exercise Book, 1st edn. Springer Publishing Company, Berlin (2010). Incorporated
7. Basin, D., Mödersheim, S., Viganò, L.: An on-the-fly model-checker for security protocol analysis. In: Snekkenes, E., Gollmann, D. (eds.) ESORICS 2003. LNCS, vol. 2808, pp. 253–270. Springer, Heidelberg (2003)
8. Basin, D.A., Mödersheim, S., Viganò, L.: OFMC: a symbolic model checker for security protocols. Int. J. Inf. Secur. **4**(3), 181–208 (2005)
9. Bellovin, S.M., Miller, F.: Inventor of the one-time pad. Cryptologia **35**(3), 203–222 (2011). An earlier version is available as technical report CUCS-009-11
10. Blanchet, B.: An efficient cryptographic protocol verifier based on prolog rules. In: Proceedings of CSFW 2001, pp. 82–96. IEEE Computer Society Press (2001)
11. Blanchet, B.: Cryptographic Protocol Verifier User Manual (2004)
12. Boichut, Y., Héam, P.-C., Kouchnarenko, O.: TA4SP, 2004. Produit logiciel. TA4SP est un outil de validation de protocoles de sécurité. Grâce à une technique d'approximation appliquée sur le problème d'atteignabilité en réécriture, TA4SP peut prouver qu'une propriété de secret est inviolée pour un nombre de sessions non-borné en sur-approximant la connaissance atteignable de l'intrus. L'outil peut également montrer qu'une propriété est violée en sous-approximant la connaissance de l'intrus. Une démo de l'outil est disponible à l'adresse : http://lifc.univ-fcomte. fr/~boichut/outil/ta4sp.php
13. Boichut, Y., Héam, P.-C., Kouchnarenko, O., Oehl, F.: Improvements on the Genet and Klay technique to automatically verify security protocols. In: Proceedings of AVIS 2004, April 2004
14. Boreale, M., Buscemi, M.G.: Experimenting with sta, a tool for automatic analysis of security protocols. In: Proceedings of the ACM Symposium on Applied Computing, SAC 2002, pp. 281–285. New York, NY, USA, ACM (2002)
15. Boyd, C., Mao, W.: On a limitation of BAN logic. In: Helleseth, T. (ed.) EUROCRYPT 1993. LNCS, vol. 765, pp. 240–247. Springer, Heidelberg (1994)
16. Bozga, L., Lakhnech, Y., Périn, M.: HERMES: an automatic tool for verification of secrecy in security protocols. In: Hunt Jr., W.A., Somenzi, F. (eds.) CAV 2003. LNCS, vol. 2725, pp. 219–222. Springer, Heidelberg (2003)
17. Bull, J., Otway, D.J.: The authentication protocol. Technical report DRA/CIS3/PROJ/CORBA/SC/1/CSM/436-04/03, Defence Research Agency (1997)
18. Burrows, M., Abadi, M., Needham, R.: A logic of authentication. ACM Trans. Comput. Syst. **8**, 18–36 (1990)
19. Cervesato, I.: The dolev-yao intruder is the most powerful attacker. In: Proceedings of the Sixteenth Annual Symposium on Logic in Computer Science — LICS 2001, pp. 16–19. IEEE Computer Society Press, Short (2001)
20. Cheminod, M., Bertolotti, I.C., Durante, L., Sisto, R., Valenzano, A.: Experimental comparison of automatic tools for the formal analysis of cryptographic protocols. In: DepCoS-RELCOMEX 2007, pp. 153–160, Szklarska Poreba, Poland. IEEE Computer Society, 14–16 June 2007
21. Chen, X., van Deursen, T., Pang, J.: Improving automatic verification of security protocols with XOR. In: Breitman, K., Cavalcanti, A. (eds.) ICFEM 2009. LNCS, vol. 5885, pp. 107–126. Springer, Heidelberg (2009)

22. Corin, R., Etalle, S.: An improved constraint-based system for the verification of security protocols. In: Hermenegildo, M.V., Puebla, G. (eds.) SAS 2002. LNCS, vol. 2477, p. 326. Springer, Heidelberg (2002)

23. Cortier, V., Delaune, S., Lafourcade, P.: A survey of algebraic properties used in cryptographic protocols. J. Comput. Secur. **14**(1), 1–43 (2006)

24. Cremers, C.J.F.: The scyther tool: verification, falsification, and analysis of security protocols. In: Gupta, A., Malik, S. (eds.) CAV 2008. LNCS, vol. 5123, pp. 414–418. Springer, Heidelberg (2008)

25. Cremers, C.: Key exchange in IPsec revisited: formal analysis of IKEv1 and IKEv2. In: Atluri, V., Diaz, C. (eds.) ESORICS 2011. LNCS, vol. 6879, pp. 315–334. Springer, Heidelberg (2011)

26. Cremers, C.J.F., Lafourcade, P., Nadeau, P.: Comparing state spaces in automatic security protocol analysis. In: Cortier, V., Kirchner, C., Okada, M., Sakurada, H. (eds.) Formal to Practical Security. LNCS, vol. 5458, pp. 70–94. Springer, Heidelberg (2009)

27. Dalal, N., Shah, J., Hisaria, K., Jinwala, D.: A comparative analysis of tools for verification of security protocols. IJCNS **3**(10), 779–787 (2010)

28. Diffie, W., Hellman, M.: New directions in cryptography. IEEE Trans. Inf. Soc. **22**(6), 644–654 (1976)

29. Dolev, D., Yao, A.C.: On the security of public key protocols. In: Proceedings of the 22Nd Annual Symposium on Foundations of Computer Science, SFCS 1981, pp. 350–357, Washington, DC, USA. IEEE Computer Society (1981)

30. Durante, L., Sisto, R., Valenzano, A.: Automatic testing equivalence verification of spi calculus specifications. ACM Trans. Softw. Eng. Methodol. **12**(2), 222–284 (2003)

31. Clavel, M., Eker, S., Lincoln, P., Meseguer, J.: Principles of maude. Electron. Notes Theoret. Comput. Sci. **4**, 65–89 (1996)

32. Escobar, S., Meadows, C., Meseguer, J.: Maude-NPA: cryptographic protocol analysis modulo equational properties. In: Aldini, A., Barthe, G., Gorrieri, R. (eds.) FOSAD 2007. LNCS, vol. 5705, pp. 1–50. Springer, Heidelberg (2007)

33. Gong, L.: Using one-way functions for authentication. SIGCOMM Comput. Commun. **19**(5), 8–11 (1989)

34. Horng-Twu, L., Wen-Shenq, J., Chi-Kai, L.: An electronic online bidding auction protocol with both security and efficiency. Appl. Math. Comput. **174**, 1487–1497 (2008)

35. Hussain, M., Seret, D.: A comparative study of security protocols validation tools: HERMES vs. AVISPA. In: Proceedings of ICACT 2006, vol. 1, pp. 303–308 (2006)

36. Kaufman, C.: Internet key exchange protocol version 2 (IKEv2). IETF RFC 4306, December 2005

37. Kaufman, C., Hoffman, P., Nir, Y., Eronen, P., Kivinen, T.: Internet key exchange protocol version 2 (IKEv2). IETF RFC 7296, October 2014

38. Küsters, R., Truderung, T.: Reducing protocol analysis with xor to the xor-free case in the horn theory based approach. In: Ning, P., Syverson, P.F., Jha, S. (eds.) ACM Conference on Computer and Communications Security, pp. 129–138. ACM (2008)

39. Küsters, R., Truderung, T.: Using ProVerif to analyze protocols with Diffie-Hellman exponentiation. In: Proceedings of the 22nd Computer Security Foundations Symposium (CSF), pp. 157–171. IEEE Computer Society (2009)

40. Lafourcade, P., Terrade, V., Vigier, S.: Comparison of cryptographic verification tools dealing with algebraic properties. In: Degano, P., Guttman, J.D. (eds.) FAST 2009. LNCS, vol. 5983, pp. 173–185. Springer, Heidelberg (2010)

41. Lowe, G.: Breaking and fixing the Needham-Schroeder public-key protocol using FDR. In: Margaria, T., Steffen, B. (eds.) TACAS 1996. LNCS, vol. 1055, pp. 147–166. Springer, Heidelberg (1996)
42. Lowe, G.: Casper: a compiler for the analysis of security protocols. J. Comput. Secur. 6(1–2), 53–84 (1998)
43. Lowe, G., Roscoe, A.W.: Using CSP to detect errors in the TMN protocol. IEEE Trans. Softw. Eng. 23(10), 659–669 (1997)
44. Lowe, G., Roscoe, B.: Using CSP to detect errors in the TMN protocol. IEEE Trans. Softw. Eng. 23(10), 659–669 (1997)
45. Meadows, C.A.: Analyzing the Needham-Schroeder public key protocol: a comparison of two approaches. In: Martella, G., Kurth, H., Montolivo, E., Bertino, Elisa (eds.) ESORICS 1996. LNCS, vol. 1146, pp. 351–364. Springer, Heidelberg (1996)
46. Meadows, C.: Language generation and verification in the NRL protocol analyzer. In: Proceedings of CSFW 1996, pp. 48–62. IEEE Computer Society Press (1996)
47. Meier, S., Schmidt, B., Cremers, C., Basin, D.: The TAMARIN prover for the symbolic analysis of security protocols. In: Sharygina, N., Veith, H. (eds.) CAV 2013. LNCS, vol. 8044, pp. 696–701. Springer, Heidelberg (2013)
48. Mitchell, J., Mitchell, M., Stern, U.: Automated analysis of cryptographic protocols using Murphi. In: IEEE Symposium on Security and Privacy, May 1997
49. Needham, R., Schroeder, M.: Using encryption for authentication in large networks of computers. IEEE Trans. Softw. Eng. 21(12), 993–999 (1978)
50. Patel, R., Borisaniya, B., Patel, A., Patel, D., Rajarajan, M., Zisman, A.: Comparative analysis of formal model checking tools for security protocol verification. In: Meghanathan, N., Boumerdassi, S., Chaki, N., Nagamalai, D. (eds.) CNSA 2010. CCIS, vol. 89, pp. 152–163. Springer, Heidelberg (2010)
51. Puys, M., Lafourcade, P.: Protocol tool comparison test archive. http://www-verimag.imag.fr/~puys/assets/files/LP15_sources.tar.gz
52. Roscoe, A.W.: Model-Checking CSP. Prentice Hall, Upper Saddle River (1994)
53. Roscoe, A.W.: Modelling and verifying key-exchange protocols using CSP and FDR. In: IEEE Symposium on Foundations of Secure Systems (1995)
54. Ryan, P.Y.A., Schneider, S.A.: An attack on a recursive authentication protocol. a cautionary tale. IEEE Trans. Softw. Eng. 65(1), 7–10 (1998)
55. Schmidt, B., Meier, S., Cremers, C., Basin, D.: Automated analysis of Diffie-Hellman protocols and advanced security properties. In: Computer Security Foundations Symposium (CSF), 2012 IEEE 25th, pp. 78–94, June 2012
56. Schneier, B.: Applied Cryptography, 2nd edn. Wiley, Hoboken (1996)
57. Song, D., Berezin, S., Perrig, A.: Athena: a novel approach to efficient automatic security protocol analysis. IEEE Trans. Softw. Eng. 9(1/2), 47–74 (2001)
58. Tatebayashi, M., Matsuzaki, N., Newman Jr., D.B.: Key distribution protocol for digital mobile communication systems. In: Brassard, G. (ed.) CRYPTO 1989. LNCS, vol. 435, pp. 324–334. Springer, Heidelberg (1990)
59. Turuani, M.: The CL-Atse protocol analyser. In: Pfenning, F. (ed.) RTA 2006. LNCS, vol. 4098, pp. 277–286. Springer, Heidelberg (2006)
60. Vaudenay, S.: A Classical Introduction to Cryptography: Applications for Communications Security. Springer-Verlag New York, Inc., Secaucus, NJ, USA (2005). ISBN: 0387254641, 9780387254647
61. Viganò, L.: Automated security protocol analysis with the AVISPA tool. ENTCS 155, 61–86 (2006)
62. Ylonen, T., Lonvick, C.: The secure shell (SSH) transport layer protocol. IETF RFC 4253, January 2006

AnBx: Automatic Generation and Verification of Security Protocols Implementations

Paolo Modesti(✉)

School of Computing Science, Newcastle University, Newcastle upon Tyne, UK
paolo.modesti@newcastle.ac.uk

Abstract. The *AnBx* compiler is a tool for automatic generation of Java implementations of security protocols specified in a simple and abstract model that can be formally verified. In our model-driven development approach, protocols are described in *AnBx*, an extension of the Alice & Bob notation. Along with the synthesis of consistency checks, the tool analyses the security goals and produces annotations that allow the verification of the generated implementation with ProVerif.

Keywords: Security protocols · Java code generation · Applied formal methods · Verification

1 Introduction

In the Internet era, organisations and individuals heavily depend on the security of the network infrastructure and its software components. Security protocols play a key role in protecting communications and user's digital assets, but evidence shows [1] that despite considerable efforts, their implementation remains challenging and error-prone. In fact, low-level implementation bugs that need to be manually patched, are discovered even in ubiquitous protocols like TLS and SSH which are thoroughly tested. Indeed, a robust implementation requires the specification of the (defensive) consistency checks on the received data that need to be performed to control that the protocol is running according to the specification. However, it is important to recognize that while some checks on reception are trivially derived from the narrations (verification of a digital signature, comparison of the agent's identities), others are more complex and managing them can be a challenging task even for an expert programmer.

To counter this problem, we propose a model-driven development approach that allows automatic generation of a program, from a simpler and abstract model that can be formally verified. In this paper, we present the *AnBx Compiler and Code Generator*[1], a tool for automatic generation of Java implementations of security protocols specified in the simple Alice & Bob (*AnB*) notation [2] (or its extension *AnBx* [3]), suitable for agile prototyping.

In addition to the main contribution of an end-to-end *AnB* to Java compiler, this paper extends our previous work [4] providing a formalization of the compiler, focusing on the generation of consistency checks (enhancing on [5]) and

---

[1] Available at http://www.dais.unive.it/~modesti/anbx/.

© Springer International Publishing Switzerland 2016
J. Garcia-Alfaro et al. (Eds.): FPS 2015, LNCS 9482, pp. 156–173, 2016.
DOI: 10.1007/978-3-319-30303-1_10

on the generation of annotations of the security goals that are necessary for the verification of the implementation with ProVerif [6].

Outline of the Paper. In Sect. 2 we describe the architecture of the *AnBx Compiler and Code Generator.* The translation from *AnB* to the intermediate format and the construction of the implementation are described in Sect. 3. Section 4 focuses on the verification of the implementation and in Sect. 5 we conclude by discussing related and future work.

2 Architecture of the *AnBx* Compiler

In this section, we present an overview of the compiler, which is developed in Haskell, by illustrating all the steps in the automatic Java code generation of security protocols from an *AnBx* or *AnB* model (Figs. 1 and 2).

Pre-Processing and Verification. $AnBx \rightarrow AnB \rightarrow$ (verification).

The *AnBx* protocol is lexed, parsed and then compiled to *AnB*, a format which can be verified with the OFMC model checker [7]. The compiler can also directly read protocols in *AnB*. The *AnBx* language is described in Sect. 3.1.

Front-End. $AnB \rightarrow ExecNarr \rightarrow Opt\text{-}ExecNarr.$

At this stage, if the verification is successful, the *AnB* specification can be compiled into an *executable narration* (*ExecNarr*), a set of actions that operationally encodes how agents are expected to execute the protocol. The core of this phase (Sect. 3) is the automatic generation of the consistency checks derived

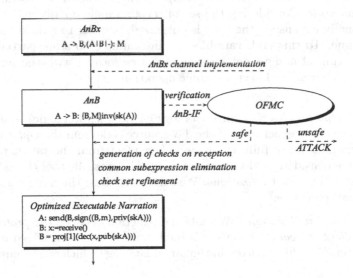

Fig. 1. Compiler front-end: pre-processing, verification, *ExecNarr* optimization

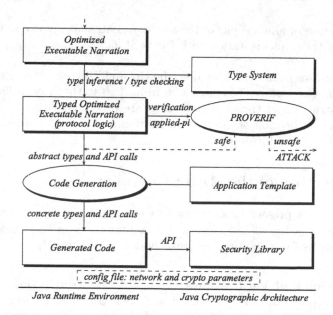

Fig. 2. Compiler back-end (type system, code generator, verification) and run-time support

from the static information of the protocol narrations. Checks are expressed by means of consistency formulas; the tool applies some simplification strategies which offer good results in practice, in order to reduce the number of generated formulas. A further step is the generation of the *optimized executable narration* (*Opt-ExecNarr*) [4], which applies some optimization techniques, including common subexpression elimination (CSE), which in general are useful to generate efficient code. Considering the set of cryptographic operations, which are computationally expensive, the code is optimized, in order to reduce the overall execution time. To this end, variables are instantiated to store partial results and a reordering of assignment instructions is performed with the purpose of minimizing the number of cryptographic operation.

Back-End. *Opt-ExecNarr* → (protocol logic) + (application logic) → *Java*.
The final stage is the generation of the Java source code from the *Opt-ExecNarr*. The previous phases are fully language independent from the target programming language considered. Moreover, we designed a versatile tool that allows for a wide range of user customizations. We summarize here the main components and their characteristics:[2]

Code Generation Strategy. We make a distinction between the *protocol logic* and the *application logic*. The latter is implemented by means of parametrized application template files written in the target language which can be customized

---

[2] A detailed description of the compiler's back-end is available in [8].

by the user. This helps the integration of the generated code in larger applications. The templates are instantiated with the information (the *protocol logic*) derived from the optimized executable narration. We model the *protocol logic* by means of a language independent intermediate format called *Typed-Opt-ExecNarr*, which is, in essence, a typed representation of the *Opt-ExecNarr*. This is useful to parametrize the translation and to simplify the emission of code in other programming languages.

Type System. Building the *Typed-Opt-ExecNarr* requires a type system modelling a typed abstract representation of the security-related portion of a generic procedural language supporting a rich set of abstract cryptographic primitives. The type system infers the type of expressions and variables insuring that the generated code is well typed. It has the additional benefit of detecting at run time whether the structure of the incoming messages is equal to the expected one, according to the protocol specification.

Code Emission. This is performed by instantiating the protocol templates, i.e., the skeleton of the application, using the information derived from the protocol logic. It is worth noting that only at this final stage the language specific features and their API calls are actually bound to the protocol logic. To this end, two mappings are required. One between the abstract and the concrete types; the other one between the abstract actions and the concrete API calls.

Security API. The run-time support relies on the cryptographic services offered by the Java Cryptography Architecture (JCA) . In order to connect to the JCA, we designed an API for security which wraps, in an abstract way, the JCA interface and implements the custom classes necessary to encode the generated programs in Java. The *AnBxJ* library offers a high degree of generality and customization, since the API does not commit to any specific cryptographic solution (algorithms, libraries, providers). Moreover, the library provides access in an abstract way to the communication primitives used to exchange messages in the standard TCP/IP network environment. The generated code comes along with a configuration file that allows the developer to customize the deployment of the application at the cryptographic (keystore location, aliases, cipher schemes, key lengths, etc.) and network level (IP addresses, ports, etc.) without requiring to regenerate the application.

Verification of the Implementation. The *Typed-Opt-ExecNarr* can be translated into Applied pi-calculus and verified with ProVerif [6]. This requires that the *AnB* security goals are analysed and specific annotations modelling the security properties are generated along the compilation chain. The verification of the implementation is described in Sect. 4.

3   Construction of the Implementation

We now describe how protocols in *AnB* can be compiled into *ExecNarr*. The goal is to obtain an operational description of the actions each agent has to perform, including the informative checks on reception of messages.

```
Protocol: CreditCard
Types:
        Agent C,M,A;
        Certified C,M,A;
        Function [Agent,Agent -> Number] ccn
Knowledge:
        C: C,M,A;
        M: C,M,A;
        A: C,M,A;
        C,A share ccn(C,A)
Actions:
        C -> M,(C|A|A): ccn(C,A)
        M -> A,(C|A|A): ccn(C,A)
Goals:
        A weakly authenticates C on ccn(C,A)
        ccn(C,A) secret between C,A
```

Fig. 3. *AnBx* protocol - example

3.1   The *AnBx* Language

The *AnBx* language [3] is built as an extension of *AnB*, whose description and formal semantics are available in [2]. *AnBx* uses channels as the main abstraction for communication, providing different authenticity and/or confidentiality guarantees for message transmission, including a novel notion of *forwarding* channels, enforcing specific security guarantees from the message originator to the final recipient along a number of intermediate forwarding agents. The translation from *AnBx* to *AnB*, can be parametrized using different channel implementations, by means of different cryptographic operations.

The example in Fig. 3 depicts a (hyper-simplified) communication pattern common in e-commerce protocols like iKP [9] and SET [10]. To complete a payment, a customer C needs to send its credit card number ccn(C,A) to the acquirer A, through the merchant M, as these protocols do not contemplate direct exchange of messages between C and A. The goal of the protocol is dual: the secrecy of the credit card should not be compromised and A should be convinced that message has originated from C.

Some peculiarities of the *AnBx* syntax are the following. In Type section Certified C,M,A declares that these agents can digitally sign and encrypt messages. The function ccn with signature [Agent,Agent -> Number] is used to model abstractly a credit card number. Concretely, the statement in the Knowledge section C,A share ccn(C,A) means that C and A know the credit card number before the protocol execution. The action C -> M,(C|A|A): ccn(C,A), means that the payload is digitally signed by C, verifiable by A, and confidential for A.

Goals in *AnBx* specify the security properties that the protocol is meant to convey. They can also be translated into low level goals suitable for the verification with various tools. We support three standard *AnB* goals:

Weak Authentication goals have the form B weakly authenticates A on M and are defined in terms of non-injective agreement [11];

Authentication goals have the form B authenticates A on M and are defined in terms of injective agreement on the runs of the protocol, assessing the freshness of the exchange;

Secrecy goals have the form M secret between A1, ..., An and are intended to specify which agents are entitled to learn the message M at the end of a protocol run.

3.2 Protocol Compilation

The intermediate format used by the compiler (*ExecNarr*) is composed by two sections: a *declaration* and the actual *narration*. The *declaration* includes the initial knowledge of each agent, the names generated by them and the names that are assumed to be initially known only by a subset of agents, similarly to the share construct. The syntax of *ExecNarr*, which extends the one presented in [5], is shown in Table 1. The *agents* are taken from set of agent names **A**, and the *messages* are built upon set of names **N**. We also consider a set of user-defined functions **F**. It is assumed that **A,F,N** are mutually disjoint.

As a first step of the compilation process, we need to derive the *declaration* section from the *AnB* agent's knowledge mapping the Knowledge of the protocol. A function $\tau : \mathbf{M_{AnB}} \to \mathbf{M}$ translates the *AnB* messages to their equivalent in *ExecNarr*, where $\mathbf{M_{AnB}}$ and **M** are the sets of messages in the two formats.

A core component of the translation from *AnB* to the executable narration format is the computation of the checks on reception extending and refining the ideas proposed by Briais and Nestmann [5].

However, we improve [5] on three directions. First, a major contribution of the present paper is the translation of security goals allowing for verification of the implementation of the protocol (Sect. 4). Second, we support a richer language allowing to model a larger class of real-world protocols, introducing operators like *hmac*, *kap*, *kas* and user defined functions. *kap* and *kas* are used to model the basic operations on keys which are available in key agreement protocols like Diffie-Hellman [12]. They satisfy the algebraic property $kas(kap(g, x), y) \approx kas(kap(g, y), x)$, given the pre-shared parameter g. Third, we dramatically improved the performance of the compiler as shown in [4].

The *AnB* actions are translated to produce an operational description of the steps each agent has to perform. Atomic exchanges of the form $A \to B : M$ are compiled to a more specific set of basic actions:

emission $A :$ send(B, E) of a message expression E (evaluating to M);
reception $B : x :=$ receive$()$ of a message and its binding to a fresh variable
　　name x, where $x \in \mathbf{V}$, the set of variables, mutually disjoint from **A**, **F**, **N**;
check $B : \phi$ for the validity of the formula ϕ from the point of view of agent B.

In addition, we define two additional basic actions that may be performed during the protocol execution and goal annotations:

Table 1. Syntax of the executable narrations (extensions with respect to [5] are marked with *. Moreover, previously pairs $(E.F)$ were used instead of tuples $(\star)$.)

expressions **E**

$E, F ::=$	a	*name*
	A	*agent's name*
	x	*variable*
	$hash(E)$	*hashing*
	$pub(E)$	*public key*
	$priv(E)$	*private key*
	$(E_1, ..., E_n)$	*tuple* * $E_i \in$ **E**, $i \in \{1..n\}$
	$\pi_i(E)$	*i−th projection* $^\wedge$
	$enc(E, F)$	*asymmetric encryption*
	$encS(F, F)$	*symmetric encryption* *
	$dec(E, F)$	*asymmetric decryption*
	$decS(E, F)$	*symmetric decryption* *
	$hmac(E, F)$	*hmac* *
	$kap(E, F)$	*key agreement half key* *
	$kas(E, F)$	*key agreement full key* *
	$E(F)$	*function* *

formulae

$\phi ::=$	$[E = F]$	*equality check*
	$[E : \mathbf{M}]$	*well−formedness test*
	$inv(E, F)$	*inversion test*

events*

$Q ::=$	**witness|request**	
	wrequest|secret	

goal labels*

$L ::= l$		*goal label*

goals events*

		$(A_1, ..., A_n$ *are agent's names)*
$\gamma ::= Q(L, E, (A_1, ..., A_n))$		*goal event*

actions

		$(A, B$ *are agent's names)*
$I ::=$	$A : \mathbf{new}\ k$	*fresh name generation*
	$A : send(B, E)$	*message emission*
	$A : x := receive()$	*message reception*
	$A : x := E$	*assignment* *
	$A : \phi$	*check*
	$A : \gamma$	*goal event* *

narrations

$N ::=$	ϵ	*empty narration*
	$I; N$	*non empty narration*

declarations

$D ::=$	$A\ \mathbf{knows}\ M$	*initial knowledge*
		$(M$ *is a ground expression)*
	$A\ \mathbf{generates}\ n$	*fresh name generation*
	$\mathbf{private}\ k$	*private name*

protocol

$P ::= D; P \mid N$		*declarations + narration*

scoping A : new k, represents the creation and scope of private names;
assignment A : $x := E$, the variable x assume the value of the expression E.
goal event A : γ, a goal annotation γ from the point of view of agent A.

Generation of Consistency Checks. Formulas ϕ on received messages are described by a conjunctions of three kinds of checks:

equality $[E = F]$ denoting the comparison of two expressions E and F;
well-formedness $[E : \mathbf{M}]$ denoting the verification of whether the projections and decryption contained in E are likely to succeed;
inversion $inv(E, F)$ denoting the verification that E and F evaluate to inverse messages.

Since consistency checks will have to operate on $(message, expression)$ pairs, the representation of the agent's knowledge must be generalized. The idea is that a pair (M, E) denotes that an expression E is equivalent to the message M. For this reason, it is necessary to introduce the notion of *knowledge sets*, and two operations on them: *synthesis* reflecting the closure of knowledge sets using message constructors; *analysis* reflecting the exhaustive recursive decomposition of knowledge pairs as enabled by the currently available knowledge.

Formally these sets and operations are defined as follows with the necessary adaptations from [5]:

Table 2. Analysis ANA-rules

ANA−INI $\dfrac{(M, E) \in K}{(M, E) \in \mathcal{A}_0(K)}$

ANA−OP1 $\dfrac{(op(M), E) \in \mathcal{A}_n(K)}{(op(M), E) \in \mathcal{A}_{n+1}(K)}$ $op \in \{pub, priv, hash\}$

ANA−OP2 $\dfrac{(op(M, N), E) \in \mathcal{A}_n(K)}{(op(M, N), E) \in \mathcal{A}_{n+1}(K)}$ $op \in \{hmac, kap, kas\}$

ANA−FUN $\dfrac{(M(N)), E) \in \mathcal{A}_n(K) \quad M \in \mathbf{F}}{((M(N)), E) \in \mathcal{A}_{n+1}(K)}$

ANA−PROJ $\dfrac{((M_1, ..., M_m), E) \in \mathcal{A}_n(K)}{((M_i, \pi_i(E)) \in \mathcal{A}_{n+1}(K)}$ $i \in \{1..m\}$

ANA−DEC $\dfrac{(enc(M, N), E) \in \mathcal{A}_n(K) \quad (inv(N), F) \in \mathcal{S}(\mathcal{A}_n(K))}{(M, dec(E, F) \in \mathcal{A}_{n+1}(K)}$

ANA−DECS $\dfrac{(encS(M, N), E) \in \mathcal{A}_n(K) \quad (inv(N), F) \in \mathcal{S}(\mathcal{A}_n(K))}{(M, decS(E, F) \in \mathcal{A}_{n+1}(K)}$

ANA−DEC−REC $\dfrac{(op(M, N), E) \in \mathcal{A}_n(K) \quad (inv(N), F) \notin \mathcal{S}(\mathcal{A}_n(K))}{(op(M, N), E) \in \mathcal{A}_{n+1}(K)}$ $op \in \{enc, encS\}$

ANA−NAM−REC $\dfrac{(M, E) \in \mathcal{A}_n(K) \quad M \in \mathbf{N} \cup \mathbf{A}}{(M, E) \in \mathcal{A}_{n+1}(K)}$

Table 3. Synthesis SYN-rules

$$\text{SYN-OP1} \quad \frac{(M, E) \in \mathcal{S}(K)}{(op(M), op(E)) \in \mathcal{S}(K)} \; op \in \{pub, priv, hash\}$$

$$\text{SYN-OP2} \quad \frac{(M, E) \in \mathcal{S}(K) \quad (N, F) \in \mathcal{S}(K)}{(op(M, N), op(E, F)) \in \mathcal{S}(K)} \; op \in \{hmac, kas, kap\}$$

$$\text{SYN-ENC} \quad \frac{(M, E) \in \mathcal{S}(K) \quad (N, F) \in \mathcal{S}(K)}{(op(M, N), op(E, F)) \in \mathcal{S}(K)} \; op \in \{enc, encS\}$$

$$\text{SYN-TUPLE} \quad \frac{(M_1, E_1) \in \mathcal{S}(K) \quad \ldots \quad (M_m, E_m) \in \mathcal{S}(K)}{((M_1, ..., M_m), (E_1, ..., E_m)) \in \mathcal{S}(K)} \; i \in \{1..m\}$$

$$\text{SYN-FUN} \quad \frac{(M, E) \in \mathcal{S}(K) \quad (M, F) \in \mathcal{S}(K) \quad M \in \mathbf{F}}{(M(N), (E(F)) \in \mathcal{S}(K)}$$

$$\text{SYN-KAP} \quad \frac{(M, E) \in \mathcal{S}(K) \quad (N, F) \in \mathcal{S}(K) \quad M \in \mathbf{N}}{(kap(M, N), kap(E, F)) \in \mathcal{S}(K)}$$

$$\text{SYN-KA-EQ} \quad \frac{(kas(kap(M, N), O), kas(kap(E, F), G) \in \mathcal{S}(K) \quad M \in \mathbf{N}}{(kas(kap(M, O), N), kas(kap(E, G), F) \in \mathcal{S}(K)}$$

Definition 1 (Knowledge). Knowledge sets $K \in \mathbf{K}$ are finite subsets of $\mathbf{M} \times \mathbf{E}$. The analysis $\mathcal{A}(K)$ of K is $\bigcup_{n \in \mathbb{N}} \mathcal{A}_n(K)$ where the sets $\mathcal{A}_i(K)$ are the smallest sets satisfying the ANA-rules in Table 2.

The synthesis $\mathcal{S}(K)$ of K is the smallest subset of $\mathbf{M} \times \mathbf{E}$ containing K and satisfying the SYN-rules in Table 3. In addition, we define a variant of the synthesis $\mathcal{S}^\star(K)$ of K as the smallest subset of $\mathbf{M} \times \mathbf{E}$ containing K and satisfying the SYN-rules in Table 3 excluding the SYN-ENC rule.

With respect to the original work [5] we defined $\mathcal{S}^\star$ and we added the SYN-rules SYN-OP2, SYN-FUN, SYN-TUPLE, SYN-KAP, SYN-KA-EQ and the ANA-rules ANA-OP2, ANA-FUN, ANA-PROJ in order to support a more expressive language like AnB. These new rules are necessary to generalize the notion of synthesis and analysis with functions and operators defined in AnB, and previously unavailable in the original work. It is worth noting that the SYN-KA-EQ rule is necessary to model the algebraic equivalence $kas(kap(g, x), y) \approx kas(kap(g, y), x)$. More equational theories could be supported by adding ad-hoc rules.

During the protocol execution the initial knowledge set is extended, according to the information learned by the reception actions: the expected message and the corresponding expression.

Definition 2 (Consistency Checks). Let K be a knowledge set. Its consistency formula $\Phi(K)$ is defined as follows:

$$\Phi(K) := \bigwedge_{(M, E) \in K} [E : \mathbf{M}]$$
$$\wedge \bigwedge_{(M, E_i) \in K \wedge (M, E_j) \in \mathcal{S}^\star(K) \wedge E_i \neq E_j} [E_i = E_j]$$
$$\wedge \bigwedge_{(M, E_i) \in K \wedge (inv(M), E_j) \in \mathcal{S}(K)} inv(E_i, E_j)$$

The first conjunction clause checks that all expressions can be evaluated, the second checks that if there are several ways to build a message M, then all the corresponding expressions must evaluate to the same value. We can see here that $\mathcal{S}^*$ is introduced to avoid computing any equality check which requires synthesizing new terms using symmetric and asymmetric encryption. In fact, in concrete implementations, non-deterministic encryption schemes are employed and therefore, those checks are going to fail anyway. It is important to underline that this does not undermine the robustness of the application because we just prune checks failing due to the over approximation of the abstract model. The third conjunction clause checks that if it is possible to generate a message M and its inverse $inv(M)$, then the corresponding expressions must also be mutually inverse. The generation of the consistency formulas implies comparing pairs taken from K, with pairs taken from the synthesis of K. Knowledge sets can often be simplified without loss of information, i.e. without undermining the computation of the consistency formula.

Definition 3 (Irreducibles). *Let K be a knowledge set, $OP_1=\{pub, priv, hash\}$ the set of the unary operators, $OP_2 = \{enc, encS, hmac, kap, kas\}$ the set of binary operators and $\mathbf{F}$ the set of user-defined functions. The set of irreducibles $\mathcal{I}(K)$ is defined as*

$$\mathcal{I}(K) = irr\left(\mathcal{A}(K)\right), \text{ where}$$
$$
\begin{aligned}
irr(K) \quad := \quad & \{(M, E) \in K \mid M \in \mathbf{A} \cup \mathbf{N}\} \\
& \cup \quad \{((M_1, ..., M_n), E) \in K \mid \forall F\,(M_i, F) \notin \mathcal{S}(K)\ \forall i \in \{1..n\}\} \\
& \underset{op \subset OP_1 \cup \mathbf{F}}{\cup} \{(op\,(M), E) \in K \mid \forall F\,(M, F) \notin \mathcal{S}(K)\} \\
& \underset{op \in OP_2}{\cup} \{(op\,((M, N), E) \in K \mid \forall F\,(M, F) \notin \mathcal{S}(K) \land \forall G\,(N, G) \notin \mathcal{S}(K)\}
\end{aligned}
$$

Let $\sim$ denote the equivalence relation on $\mathbf{M} \times \mathbf{E}$ induced by $(M, E) \sim (N, F)$ $\Longleftrightarrow M = N$. $rep\,(K)$ denotes the result of deterministically selecting one representative element for each equivalent class induced by $\sim$ on K.

Compilation. The above notions are the elements required to compile the *AnB* protocol to *ExecNarr*. The translation function keeps track of the global information regarding variables used, private names, generated names, and agents' local knowledge. To model the latter we define a function $\boldsymbol{k} : \mathbf{A} \to \mathbf{K}$, mapping agents' names to their current knowledge.

The compilation of $A \to B : M$ checks that M can be synthesized by A, instantiate a new variable x and adds the pair (M, x) to the knowledge of B. The consistency formula $\Phi(\mathcal{A}(K'_B))$ of the analysis of the updated knowledge K'_B defines the checks ϕ to be performed by B at run-time.

Our compilation process extends the one formalized in [5] in two fundamentals aspects. First, it considers an extended language as described above. Second, it handles the generation of events related to security goals that was previously not considered. The compilation can be summarized as follows: if $A \neq B$ and $\exists E.\,(\tau(M), E) \in \mathcal{S}\,(\boldsymbol{k}\,(A))$, we can compile the *AnB* action $A \to B : M$ as a sequence of basic actions in *ExecNarr*. In detail:

$A : \gamma_A$
$A : \mathtt{send}(B, E)$
$B : x := \mathtt{receive}()$
$B : \phi$
$B : \gamma_B$

where x is a fresh variable storing the incoming message, $\boldsymbol{k}(A)$ and $\boldsymbol{k}(B)$ are the partial mappings of the knowledge set for the two agents, $K'_B = \boldsymbol{k}(B) \cup \{(M, x)\}$ is the updated knowledge of the agent B, $\phi = \Phi(\mathcal{A}(K'_B))$ is the formula representing the consistency checks, γ_A and γ_B are sets of goal annotations, computed as we explain in the next section. The updated knowledge of the agent B, in the reduced form, $\boldsymbol{k}'(B) = rep(\mathcal{I}(K'_B))$, is made available for the compilation of the next protocol action.

4 Verification of the Implementation

4.1 Compiling Security Goals

The standard approach of verification tools like OFMC [7] and ProVerif [6] is to model secrecy goals as reachability properties and authentication goals as correspondence assertions. In order to verify the implementation, AnB security goals must be analysed and specific annotations (events) modelling the security properties need to be generated along the compilation chain. To build the annotations, our approach is inspired by the translation from AnB to IF done in OFMC [13]. However, since IF is not suitable to encode consistency checks in an imperative style as the one used by $ExecNarr$, we found it practical to translate our encoding into Applied pi-calculus which can be verified by ProVerif.

Let $\mathbf{G}$ be the set of goals of the AnB protocol. Abstractly, *authentication goals* can be expressed in the general form $g := ((A_1, A_2), goaltype, M)$ where A_2 is the "originator/sender" agent, A_1 is a "recipient/receiver" agent, and M is the message that the goal g is meant to convey. In $ExecNarr$, the structure of a single goal annotation γ for an agent A is $Q(L, E, (A_1, A_2))$, where Q is a goal event (**wrequest** or **request** or **witness**), L is a goal label, E is an expression that represents the message M from the perspective of A, and A_1, A_2 are the agent's names. Goal labels must be unique for each goal and corresponding assertions must share the same label. Instead *secrecy goals* have the abstract form $g := ((A_1, ...A_n), secret, M)$ where $A_1, ...A_n$ is a list of agents' names (the secrecy set), and M is the message meant to stay secret among the agents. In $ExecNarr$ the structure of a single goal annotation γ for an agent A is $Q(L, E, (A_1, ...A_n))$ where Q is a goal event **secret**, L is a goal label, E is an expression that represents the message M from the point of view of A, and $A_1, ...A_n$ the secrecy set. Since annotations for the secrecy goals are generated in a different way, we first discuss only the authentication goals.

Authentication Goals. Initially, we consider two identical copies of the $\mathbf{G}$ set, named G_S^0 and G_R^0. During the compilation process, these two sets are analysed and consumed, from the point of view of the sender and the receiver respectively. Consumed means that for each action $A \rightarrow B : M$, the compiler considers only the goals for which it is possible to synthesize the message specified in the goal according to the current agent's knowledge and for those generates the corresponding annotations. Once these messages are synthesized, and the annotation is generated, these goals are removed from the goal sets. We recall here that for goals expressed by means of a correspondence assertion, one *begin* event must be generated on the sender side and one *end* event must generated on the receiver side.

We compile all the protocol actions in sequence with the following procedure. Given a protocol action $A \rightarrow B : M$, an authentication goal $g :=$ $((B', A'), goaltype, M')$ and a sender goal set G_S, a subset G'_S is computed:

$$G'_S = \{g \in G_S | \exists E. (\tau(M'), E) \in \mathcal{S}(k(A)) \wedge A = A'\}$$

This is the set of goals where the message M' can be synthesized by A. Then for each $g \in G'_S$ the compiler generates a *begin* event. We denote γ_A the set of all generated events on the A side at this step. For example, if g is a weak authentication goal, the following event is generated: witness(_wauth_MSGBA,E,(B',A)), where the event type Q=witness and goal label L=_wauth_MSGBA.

Similarly, given the receiver set of goal G_R, a subset G'_R is computed:

$$G'_R = \{g \in G_R | \exists E. (\tau(M'), E) \in \mathcal{S}(k'(B)) \wedge B = B'\}$$

It should be noted that this time we synthesize M' from $k'(B)$, the updated local knowledge of B in the reduced form, which includes $\{(M, x)\}$, the incoming message M and the associated variable x. Therefore, we try to generate the *end* event as soon as the receiving agents can synthesize the goal message, but we position them, in the generated code, after the last usage of the message (checks included). For each $g \in G'_R$ the compiler generates an *end* event. We denote γ_B the set of all generated event on the B side. For example, if g is a weak authentication goal, the following event is generated: wrequest(_wauth_MSGBA,E,(B,A')), where the event type Q=wrequest and goal label L=_wauth_MSGBA.

The labels of the two events must be identical, in order to link them, when proving the agreement. To this end, we underline that in order to have a precise verification of the security goals, it is crucial the position where these annotations are placed into the generated code. This guarantees that the goals are "reachable" (in ProVerif) it also makes the verification more efficient, as it strengthens the corresponding property [14].

Modelling the injective agreement is similar, we just replace the wrequest predicate with request. It should be noted that the generation of the two corresponding assertions (*begin*/*end* events) in general implies compiling two different actions. This is the reason why we consider two sets of goals G_S and G_R. The authentication goal in Fig. 3 is a clear example of this as the two agents never exchange a message directly. In fact, managing only a single set of authentication goals may result in an imprecise translation in the cases where only one of the agents involved in the action, can synthesize the goal expression but not the other. After compiling this protocol action, we compute two new sets of goals $G''_R = G_R \setminus G'_R$, $G''_S = G_S \setminus G'_S$, and then apply the procedure to the next action, and so on.

Secrecy Goals. In order to verify secrecy goals, verification tools investigate whether an expression can become available to the attacker. At the current step of the compilation we generate one `secret` event for every agent belonging to the secrecy set $\{A_1, .., A_n\}$, provided the secret message M' can be synthesized by the agent. For agent A_i is checked if $\exists E. (\tau (M'), E)$. Then an event of the form `secret(<label>,E,(A1,..,An))` is generated and appended at the end of the actions for each agent. The label must be the same for all events associated with this goal.

4.2 Translation into Applied pi and Verification with ProVerif

After the generation of the *ExecNarr*, the compiler performs an optimization step and generates a typed representation of the implementation called *Typed-Opt-ExecNarr*. This language-independent format is used for the code emission in the target language (Java) which is done mapping one action of *Typed-Opt-ExecNarr* to one action in Java. The verification of the soundness of the translation up to this step is done with ProVerif. The translation into Applied pi requires several steps: (1) the generation of a prelude that includes cryptographic primitives, constructors, destructors and security goals used in the protocol, the definition of (2) a specific process which models the agents' actions for each agent, (3) a main process than orchestrates the agent's processes, and (4) an initialization process that initialize the whole system. The generation of the prelude is rather standard with cryptographic primitives defined as usual in ProVerif.

For the definition of *authentication goals* we consider the annotations of *end* events $Q (L, E, (A_1, A_2))$ and for each of them we generate the following goal definition: "`query m:bitstring, a1:bitstring, a2:bitstring`" + *inj* + "`event(`" + Q + L + "`(m,a1,a2)) ==> `" + *inj* + "`event(witness`" + L + "`(m,a1,a2))`" where *inj*= "`inj-`" if $Q=$ "`request`" (strong authentication), otherwise is the empty string (weak authentication). It should be noted that since this is a general definition of the goal, we can freely use generic parameters as `m,a1,a2`. For the definition of the *secrecy goals* `secret` $(L, E, (A_1, ...A_n))$ we define: "`free`" + L + "`:bitstring[private].query attacker(`" + L + "`)`".

For the generation of the agent's process, the translation of actions is described in Table 4. Secrecy events are translated into outputs of encrypted terms. We encrypt the label L with the expression E which is used as key. If the key is compromised the expression becomes known by the attacker, and then L; therefore, the goal is violated.

In Fig. 4, we show a fragment of the translation of the three processes in Applied pi of the example Fig. 3. For each agent a process is generated. Process M does not contain events annotations because M acts only as a blind forwarder of the message from C to A. Agent C registers a `witness` event linked to the credit card number `CcnCA` and outputs a signed and encrypted message on the

Table 4. Translation of executable narrations into Applied pi (where $+$ is the concatenation operator, *ch* is the plain channel, *eq* is the equality function)

Typed-Opt-ExecNarr	*Applied pi*
$A : \textbf{new } k$	$\textbf{new } k$
$A : send(B, E)$	$out\,(ch, E)$
$A : x := receive()$	$in\,(ch, x)$
$A : x := E$	$\textbf{let } x = E \textbf{ in}$
$A : E = F$	$\textbf{if } eq\,(E, F) \textbf{ then}$
$A : wff(E)$	$\textbf{if } eq\,(E, E) \textbf{ then}$
$A : inv(E, F)$	$\textbf{if } eq\,(decS\,(encS\,(E, F)\,, F))\,, E)\ \textbf{then}$
$A : Q\,(L, F, (A_1, \ldots, A_n))$	$\begin{cases} out\,(ch, encS\,(L, E)) & if\ Q = \textbf{secret} \\ \textbf{event } Q + L\,(E, A_1, ..., A_n) & otherwise \end{cases}$

```
(* Process M *)
let process_M(A:bitstring,C:bitstring,M:bitstring,InvpkM:bitstring,InvskM:
    bitstring,honestC:bitstring,honestA:bitstring) =
in(ch,VAR_M_R0:bitstring);
out(ch,VAR_M_R0);
if C = honestC && A = honestA then
out(ch,encS(InvskVSMM,InvskM));
out(ch,encS(InvpkVPMM,InvpkM));0.
(* Process C *)
let process_C(A:bitstring,C:bitstring,M:bitstring,CcnCA:bitstring,pkA:
    bitstring,InvpkC:bitstring,InvskC:bitstring,honestM:bitstring,honestA:
    bitstring) =
event witness_wauth_CCNCAAC(CcnCA,A,C);
out(ch,enc(sign((A,CcnCA),InvskC),pkA));
if M = honestM && A = honestA then
out(ch,encS(CCNCACA,CcnCA));
out(ch,encS(InvskVSCC,InvskC));
out(ch,encS(InvpkVPCC,InvpkC));0.
(* Process A *)
let process_A(A:bitstring,C:bitstring,M:bitstring,CcnCA:bitstring,skC:
    bitstring,InvpkA:bitstring,InvskA:bitstring,honestC:bitstring,honestM:
    bitstring) =
in(ch,VAR_A_R1:bitstring);
let VAR_A_DDAR1VPAUSC:bitstring = verify(dec(VAR_A_R1, InvpkA), skC) in
if eq(A,proj_1_2(VAR_A_DDAR1VPAUSC)) then
if eq(CcnCA,proj_2_2(VAR_A_DDAR1VPAUSC)) then
if eq(decS(encS(dec(VAR_A_R1,InvpkA),dec(VAR_A_R1,InvpkA)),dec(VAR_A_R1,
    InvpkA)),dec(VAR_A_R1,InvpkA)) then
if C = honestC && M = honestM then
out(ch,encS(CCNCACA,CcnCA));
out(ch,encS(InvskVSAA,InvskA));
out(ch,encS(InvpkVPAA,InvpkA));
event wrequest_wauth_CCNCAAC(CcnCA,A,C); 0.
```

Fig. 4. Translation into Applied pi of the example (fragment)

public channel ch. More interestingly, A receives a message on the public channel, decrypts the message and verifies the digital signature of A. Then C checks if the payload is equal to the information already possessed and then, if the check is successful, registers a `wrequest` event linked to the credit card number. If the check fails, the correspondence cannot be proved, and therefore there is an attack. Each agent's process is parametrized and actions are translated according to Table 4. The parameters of the process are the free names of each process, plus the honestX parameters which are used to distinguish the runs of the honest agents from the runs which may include the intruder (in this case goals are trivially violated). For the generation of the main process, we consider the parallel execution of an arbitrary number of sessions. The process that initializes the system declares the agent names, sends them on the plain channel and makes them available to the attacker along with the public keys. Moreover, the shared values (as the credit card number) are declared. These parameters are passed to the main process and then to the single processes. An unbounded number of instances of the initialization process are generated to define the most general instantiation of the protocol.

4.3   Experimental Results and Tool Evaluation

To experiment and validate our approach we considered a test protocol suite, which includes, along with the AnB examples in the OFMC distribution, complex e-commerce protocols like SET [10] and iKP [9]. We compared, for this set of protocols, the results of the analysis performed by OFMC and ProVerif, in order to check if they provide the same assessments in terms of protocol safety or detection of (known) attacks. Although this is not a formal proof of correctness, we think that this comparison may provide a significant experimental evidence of the soundness of the translation steps along the compilation chain from AnB to Applied pi. No new attacks, in Dolev-Yao intruder model, should have been introduced. We found that the two tools provide the same results, with the following caveats. Firstly, ProVerif cannot prove injective agreements if freshness is achieved using sequence numbers. However, if non-injective agreements can be proved, and the sequence number is used as a parameter in annotations, the injectivity, given the uniqueness of the number, can also be derived, but, for a fully automated proof, it would be necessary to use tools able to model set membership, for example Set-pi [15]. It should be noted that this is not a limitation of the Applied pi language itself but a consequence of how ProVerif models sets. Secondly, it is worth noting that while ProVerif verifies for an unbounded number of sessions, for large protocols like SET and iKP OFMC struggles to verify two sessions. Therefore, a direct comparison in these cases may not be immediate. On the performance side we found that ProVerif is generally faster than OFMC, but in a few cases is unable to terminate the analysis. In these cases a few techniques like reordering of terms in a message or tagging or mentioning explicitly the arguments in new instructions may help ProVerif to terminate. However, it should be noted that in the latter case the analysis preformed by ProVerif could be less precise, therefore, the previous techniques should be preferable.

On the formal side, the soundness of the translation from $AnBx$ to AnB, for a specific channel implementation, has been proven in [16]. At the moment, we do not verify the concrete Java code which may be part of the future work. However, we believe that the verification of $Typed\text{-}Opt\text{-}ExecNarr$ is a crucial step for the validation of the protocol implementation, being the last step before code emission.

5   Related Work and Conclusions

The tool presented in this paper allows for the specification of security protocols in *AnBx*, an extension of the Alice & Bob notation, and automatically generates Java implementations, including the checks on receptions, which are crucial for building robust code. Some tools proposed in the past required the manual encoding of consistency checks and, in contrast with those using process calculi as an input language [17–19], we think that an intuitive specification language makes the model-driven approach more suitable for a larger audience of developers. JavaSPI [20], an evolution of Spi2Java, uses Java both as a modelling and as an implementation language. Our abstract specification is succinct, while, for example, the Spi calculus requires long specification files and type annotations [18], which are also required in [21]. Instead, apart from a few naming conventions, our tool delegates the duty to generate well-typed code entirely to the type system.

Two recent works considered the generation of implementations from an Alice & Bob specification. The first one, SPS [22], uses the notion of *formats* to abstract the structure of real-world protocols and computes the checks on reception proving the correctness of the translation with respect to the semantics of [2]. The tool automatically generates JavaScript specifications for the execution environment of the FutureID project [23], which may require some manual encoding. The other one [24] proposes a translation from an Alice & Bob specification into an intermediate representation verifiable with Tamarin [25]; the paper illustrates how to derive the checks but the tool does not generate concrete implementations in a programming language. Instead, our tool generates with one-click Java code that is directly runnable, thanks to the support of the integrated *AnBxJ* security library.

We can currently verify the abstract model with OFMC, and deriving annotations from the security goals the implementation (up to the code emission) with ProVerif. For future work, it would be important to verify the final Java code, along with trying to build a mechanized proof of correctness of the translation chain. Another possible extension could be the generation of interoperable implementations. However, *AnBx* is meant more as a design language rather than a mere specification language and therefore, from this point of view, is more amenable for designing new applications or re-engineering existing protocols. A further opportunity could be to plug the tool into an existing Integrated Development Environment (IDE) such as Eclipse [26] experimenting with professional programmers the effectiveness of the model-driven approach proposed by the *AnBx compiler* in a more realistic software development environment.

Acknowledgements. This work was partially supported by the EU FP7 Project no. 318424, "FutureID: Shaping the Future of Electronic Identity" (futureid.eu). The author thanks Michele Bugliesi, Thomas Groß and Sebastian Mödersheim for useful discussions and Bruno Blanchet for his support on the use of the ProVerif tool.

References

1. Avalle, M., Pironti, A., Sisto, R.: Formal verification of security protocol implementations: a survey. Formal Aspects Comput. **26**(1), 99–123 (2014)
2. Mödersheim, S.: Algebraic properties in Alice and Bob notation. In: International Conference on Availability, Reliability and Security (ARES 2009), pp. 433–440 (2009)
3. Bugliesi, M., Modesti, P.: AnBx - security protocols design and verification. In: Armando, A., Lowe, G. (eds.) ARSPA-WITS 2010. LNCS, vol. 6186, pp. 164–184. Springer, Heidelberg (2010)
4. Modesti, P.: Efficient Java code generation of security protocols specified in *AnB/AnBx*. In: Mauw, S., Jensen, C.D. (eds.) STM 2014. LNCS, vol. 8743, pp. 204–208. Springer, Heidelberg (2014)
5. Briais, S., Nestmann, U.: A formal semantics for protocol narrations. Theor. Comput. Sci. **389**, 484–511 (2007)
6. Blanchet, B.: An efficient cryptographic protocol verifier based on prolog rules. In: IEEE Computer Security Foundations Workshop, pp. 0082–0082. IEEE Computer Society (2001)
7. Basin, D., Mödersheim, S., Viganò, L.: OFMC: a symbolic model checker for security protocols. Int. J. Inf. Secur. **4**(3), 181–208 (2005)
8. Modesti, P.: Efficient Java code generation of security protocols specified in AnB/AnBx. Technical report CS-TR-1422, School of Computing Science, Newcastle University (2014)
9. Bellare, M., Garay, J., Hauser, R., Herzberg, A., Krawczyk, H., Steiner, M., Tsudik, G., Van Herreweghen, E., Waidner, M.: Design, implementation, and deployment of the iKP secure electronic payment system. IEEE J. Sel. Areas Commun. **18**(4), 611–627 (2000)
10. Bella, G., Massacci, F., Paulson, L.: Verifying the SET purchase protocols. J. Autom. Reasoning **36**(1), 5–37 (2006)
11. Lowe, G.: A hierarchy of authentication specifications. In: CSFW 1997, pp. 31–43. IEEE Computer Society Press (1997)
12. Denker, G., Millen, J.: CAPSL and CIL language design. Technical report SRI-CSL-99-02, SRI International Computer Science Laboratory (1999)
13. Mödersheim, S.: Algebraic properties in Alice and Bob notation (extended version). Technical report RZ3709, IBM Zurich Research Lab (2008)
14. Blanchet, B., Smyth, B., Cheval, V.: ProVerif 1.91: automatic cryptographic protocol verifier, user manual and tutorial (2015)
15. Bruni, A., Modersheim, S., Nielson, F., Nielson, H.R.: Set-pi: set membership pi-calculus. In: IEEE Computer Security Foundations Symposium (CSF), pp. 185–198 (2015)
16. Bugliesi, M., Calzavara, S., Mödersheim, S., Modesti, P.: Security protocol specification and verification with AnBx. Technical report CS-TR-1479, School of Computing Science, Newcastle University (2015)
17. Tobler, B., Hutchison, A.: Generating network security protocol implementations from formal specifications. In: Nardelli, E., Talamo, M. (eds.) Certification and Security in Inter-Organizational E-Service. IFIP On-Line Library in Computer Science, vol. 177, pp. 33–54. Springer, Heidelberg (2005)
18. Backes, M., Busenius, A., Hriţcu, C.: On the development and formalization of an extensible code generator for real life security protocols. In: Goodloe, A.E., Person, S. (eds.) NFM 2012. LNCS, vol. 7226, pp. 371–387. Springer, Heidelberg (2012)

19. Pironti, A., Pozza, D., Sisto, R.: Formally based semi-automatic implementation of an open security protocol. J. Syst. Softw. **85**(4), 835–849 (2012)
20. Avalle, M., Pironti, A., Pozza, D., Sisto, R.: JavaSPI: a framework for security protocol implementation. Int. J. Secure Softw. Eng. **2**(4), 34–48 (2011)
21. Millen, J., Muller, F.: Cryptographic protocol generation from CAPSL. Technical report SRI-CSL-01-07, SRI International, December 2001
22. Almousa, O., Mödersheim, S., Viganò, L.: Alice and Bob: reconciling formal models and implementation. In: Bodei, C., Ferrari, G.-L., Priami, C. (eds.) Degano Festschrift. LNCS, vol. 9465, pp. 66–85. Springer, Heidelberg (2015)
23. FutureID Consortium: FutureID Project. http://www.futureid.eu
24. Basin, D., Keller, M., Radomirović, S., Sasse, R.: Alice and Bob meet equational theories. In: Martí-Oliet, N., Ölveczky, P.C., Talcott, C. (eds.) Meseguer Festschrift. LNCS, vol. 9200, pp. 160–180. Springer, Heidelberg (2015)
25. Schmidt, B., Meier, S., Cremers, C., Basin, D.: Automated analysis of Diffie-Hellman protocols and advanced security properties. In: 2012 IEEE 25th Computer Security Foundations Symposium (CSF), pp. 78–94. IEEE (2012)
26. Eclipse Foundation: Eclipse IDE. http://www.eclipse.org

Evaluating Obfuscation Security:
A Quantitative Approach

Rabih Mohsen[1(✉)] and Alexandre Miranda Pinto[2,3]

[1] Department of Computing, Imperial College London, London, UK
r.mohsen11@imperial.ac.uk
[2] Information Security Group, Royal Holloway University of London, London, UK
alex.miranda.pinto@gmail.com
[3] Instituto Universitário da Maia, Maia, Portugal

Abstract. State of the art obfuscation techniques rely on an unproven concept of security, therefore it is very hard to evaluate their protection quality. In previous work we introduced algorithmic information theory as a theoretical foundation for code obfuscation security. We propose Kolmogorov complexity, estimated by compression, as a software complexity metric to measure regularities in obfuscated programs. In this paper we provide a theoretical validation for its soundness as a software metric, so it can have as much credibility as other complexity metrics. Then, we conduct an empirical evaluation for 43 obfuscation techniques, which are applied to 10 Java byte code programs of SPECjvm2008 benchmark suite using three different decompilers as a threat model, aiming to provide experimental evidence that support the formal treatments.

1 Introduction

Man-at-the-end (MATE) attacks are performed by an adversary who has physical access to a device or software and can compromise it. Malicious reverse engineering attack, is a typical MATE attack, which violates the confidentiality rights of the vendor by extracting software intellectual property (such as algorithms) or sensitive data (such as license codes or cryptographic keys). Software protection techniques such as code obfuscation, are vital to defend programs against vicious reverse engineering attacks. An obfuscating transformation attempts to manipulate code in such a way that it becomes unintelligible to human and automated program analysis tools, while preserving their functionality.

Collberg et al. [6] were the first to define obfuscation in terms of a semantics-preserving transformation function. Barak et al. [2] provided a formal definition of obfuscation based on virtual black box model, in an attempt to achieve a well-defined security. However, they found a counterexample which showed that this kind of "secure" definition cannot be met. Intuitively, they proved the existence of a set of programs or functions that are impossible to obfuscate. On the other hand, Preda and Giacobazzi [15] proposed a semantics based approach to define obfuscation security using abstract interpretations theory, aiming to provide a formal tool for comparing obfuscations with respect to their potency. A more recent

© Springer International Publishing Switzerland 2016
J. Garcia-Alfaro et al. (Eds.): FPS 2015, LNCS 9482, pp. 174–192, 2016.
DOI: 10.1007/978-3-319-30303-1_11

study conducted by Garg et al. [8] provided promising positive results, using indistinguishability obfuscation, for which there are no known impossibility results.

Our motivation is derived from the difficulty of evaluating the strength of seemingly resilient obfuscating transformations. There is a need to evaluate how obfuscating and deobfuscating transformations affect the understanding of the program. Many obfuscation transformation techniques were proposed, which intuitively make the program difficult to understand and harder to attack, with no provable properties presented to measure. Several attempts were made to provide concrete metrics for evaluating obfuscation such as in [6], using classical complexity measures. However, most of these metrics are still context dependent and differ among development platforms, therefore it is very hard to standardise them. This reason and the fact that there are currently no provable security metrics to measure the quality of the code obfuscation, leads to the following questions:

- Is there any theory that can provide an intuitive way to define and explain obfuscation security?
- Can we derive from that theory a quantitative metric, with practical relevance, which can be used to measure the protection level in code obfuscation?
- How to evaluate the usefulness of this metric?

We tried to answer the first question in [14] by providing a theoretical foundation for obfuscation theory based on *algorithmic information theory*, and we proposed a novel metric for code obfuscation that is based on Kolmogorov complexity. In this paper, we aim to answer the remaining questions. First, we apply Weyuker's validation framework [17] to check whether Kolmogorov complexity is theoretically sound as software metric, then we derive a normalised version of Kolmogorov complexity that is approximated by compression. To provide the empirical validation, we conducted an experiment, using the proposed metric, on obfuscated Java jar files of SPECjvm2008 benchmark suite by applying a number of most widely used obfuscation techniques. Specifically, we investigate the quality of obfuscation techniques in two obfuscators: *Sandmark*[1] an open source suite, and *Dasho*[2] a commercial tool. Moreover, we employed three decompilers as a model of attack to study the resilience of code obfuscation.

The theoretical results show that Kolmogorov complexity is theoretically sound with respect to Weyuker's validation framework. The empirical results show that obfuscation techniques managed to produce a substantial increase in the proposed metric comparing to original unobfuscated programs, which confirms our formal definition [14] about code obfuscations. Furthermore, all decompilation attacks demonstrate a different level of success at reducing the complexity of obfuscated programs; however not to the level where it matches the complexity of original unobfuscated programs. We also compared our results, in particular, Sandmark obfuscation techniques with the recent results of Ceccato et al. [4] using Cyclomatic complexity measure [13]. We find that our metric is

---

[1] http://sandmark.cs.arizona.edu.
[2] http://www.preemptive.com/products/dasho.

more sensitive then Cyclomatic measure at detecting any increase in complexity comparing to original unobfuscated code.

The remainder of this paper is structured as follows. In Sect. 2, we provide an overview of related work. Section 3 provides the preliminaries and background theory about Kolmogorov complexity. In Sect. 4 we provide the motivation behind our approach. Section 5 presents the theoretical validation, and proposes a normalised version of Kolmogorov complexity as metric to measure code obfuscation. Section 6 describes the experimental design, and discusses the experimental results. Finally, Sect. 7 concludes and provides the future work.

2   Related Work

The first attempt to evaluate obfuscation was conducted by Collberg et al. [6]; they relied on classical software complexity metrics to evaluate obfuscation such as Cyclomatic Complexity, and Nesting Complexity. Anckaert et al. [1] suggested a framework of four program properties that reflect the quality of code obfuscation: code, control flow, data and data flow, then they applied software complexity metrics to measure these properties; however they did not perform any validation on the proposed metrics. Ceccato et al. [5] experimentally assessed one obfuscation technique (identifier renaming) using statistical reasoning. They measured the success and the efficiency of an attacker by considering the human factor in their threat model, without introducing any new metrics. In a recent study by Ceccato et al. [4] a set of software metrics (modularity, size and complexity of code) were applied to a set of obfuscated programs to measure their effectiveness. Their results show that a limited number of obfuscated techniques, involved in their study, were effective in making code metrics change substantially from original to obfuscated code, in Sect. 6.2 we discuss the similarity with our results.

Jbara and Feitelson [10], argued that the most of complexity metrics are syntactic features that ignore the programs global structure. Program global structure may have effect on program understanding, they suggested the use of code regularity that is estimated by compression to measure program comprehension. They conducted a controlled experiment using cognitive tasks on a set of program functions. The results established a positive relation between code regularity and program comprehension. The code regularity, according to Jbara and Feitelson, is estimated by compression, which is also used to approximate Kolmogorov complexity [11]. Their intuitions and results agree with our observation and theoretical treatments in [14] for code obfuscation. However, our work differs from their work in two ways: we provide a sound theoretical foundation and validation based on algorithmic information theory (Mutual algorithmic informationKolmorgorov complexity) for code regularity, and justify its use in code obfuscation security. On the other hand, they only used compression to measure code comprehension in empirical sense, without applying any theoretical validation. Secondly, we conducted an experiment on a set of obfuscated programs, hoping to provide empirical evidence that support our theoretical work, whereas they did not apply their experiment to study the effect of compression on obfuscated code.

3   Preliminaries and Notations

We use U as the shorthand for a universal Turing machine, x for a finite-length binary string and $|x|$ its length. We use the notation $O(1)$ for a constant, $p(n)$ for a polynomial function with input $n \in \mathbb{N}$. Symbol $\|$ is used to denote the concatenation between two programs or strings. $\mathcal{P}$ is a set of binary programs and $\mathcal{P}'$ is a set of binary obfuscated programs, and $\mathcal{L} = \{\lambda_n : \lambda_n \in \{0,1\}^+, n \in \mathbb{N}\}$ is a binary set of security (secret) parameters that is used in obfuscation process. Given two sets, I an input set and O an output set, a program functionality (meaning) is a function $[\![.]\!] : \mathcal{P} \times I \to O$ that computes the program's output given an input and terminates.

3.1   Kolmogorov Complexity

Kolmogorov complexity (also known as Algorithmic complexity) is used to describe the complexity or the degree of randomness of a binary string. It was independently developed by A.N. Kolmogorov, R. Solomonoff, and G. Chaitin in the late 1960s [12]. Intuitively, Kolmogorov complexity of a binary string p is the length of the shortest binary program that describes p, and is computed on a Universal Turing Machine. We consider only the prefix version of Kolmogorov complexity (prefix algorithmic complexity) which is denoted by $K(.)$. *Complexity* and *Kolmogorov complexity* terms are sometimes used interchangeably; for more details on prefix Kolmogorov complexity and algorithmic information theory, we refer the reader to [12]. The necessary parts of this theory are briefly presented in the following.

Definition 1. ([12]) *Let $U(P)$ denote the output of U when presented with a program $P \in \{0,1\}^+$.*

1. The *Kolmogorov complexity* $K(x)$ of a binary string x is defined as: $K(x) = \min\{|P| : U(P) = x\}$.
2. The *Conditional Kolmogorov Complexity* relative to y is defined as: $K(x\,|\,y) = \min\{|P| : U(P, y) = x\}$.

Definition 2. ([12]) Mutual algorithmic information of two binary programs x and y is given by: $I_K(x; y) = K(y) - K(y\,|\,x)$.

Theorem 1 (chain rule [12]). *For all x, $y \in \mathbb{N}$*

1. $K(x; y) = K(x) + K(y\,|\,x) + O(\log K(x; y))$.
2. $K(x) - K(x\,|\,y) = K(y) - K(y\,|\,x)$ *i.e.* $I_K(x; y) = I_K(y; x)$, *up to an additive term* $O(\log K(x; y))$.

Theorem 2 ([12]). *There is a constant c such that for all x and y*

$$K(x) \leq |x| + 2\log|x| + c \text{ and } K(x\,|\,y) \leq K(x) + c.$$

Kolmogorov complexity is uncomputable due to the undecidability halting program, however it can be approximated based on compression as shown in [11], Theorem 2 and in [12], this helps to intuitively understand this notion and makes this theory relevant for real world applications. The theorem states that $K(x)$ is the lower bound [11] of all the lossless compressions of x; therefore, we say that every compression $C(x)$ of x gives an estimation of $K(x)$.

4   Obfuscation Using Kolmogorov Complexity

The main purpose of code obfuscation is to confuse an adversary, making the task of reverse engineering extremely difficult. Code obfuscation introduces noise and dummy instructions that produce irregularities in the targeted obfuscated code. We believe that these make the code difficult to comprehend, that is, obfuscated. Classical complexity metrics have a limited power for measuring and quantifying irregularities in obfuscated code, because most of these metrics are designed to measure certain aspects of code attributes such as finding bugs and code maintenance. Code regularity (and irregularity) can be quantified, as was suggested in [10], using Kolmogorov complexity and compression. Code regularity means a certain structure is repeated many times, and thus can be recognized. Conversely, irregularities in code can be explained as the code exhibiting different types of structure over the code's body.

The main intuition behind our approach is based on the following argument: if an adversary fails to capture some patterns (regularities) in an obfuscated code, then the adversary will have difficulty comprehending that code: it cannot provide a valid, brief, or simple description. On the other hand, if these regularities are simple to explain, then describing them becomes easier, and consequently the code will not be difficult to understand.

```
while(i<n){          while(i<n){            while(i<n){
  i=i+1                i=i+1                  i=i+1
  x=x+i}               if 7*y*y-1==x*x{//F    if 7*y*y-1==x*x{//F
                         y=x*i                  y=x*(i+1)
                       else                   else
                         x=x+4*i}               x=x+4*i}
                       if 7*y*y-1==x*x{       if x*x-34*y*y==-1{//F
                         y=x*i                  y=x*i
                       else                   else
                         x=x-2*i;}              x=x-2*i}
                       if 7*y*y-1==x*x{       if (x*x+x)mod2==0{//T
                         y=x*i                  x=x-i
                       else                   else
                         x=x-i;}}               y=x*(i-1)}}
```

(a) Sum code   (b) One opaque predicate   (c) Three opaque predicate

Fig. 1. Obfuscation example: (a) is the original code for the sum of n integers; (b) is an obfuscated version of (a) with one opaque predicate and data encoding which has some patterns and regularities; (c) is another obfuscated version of (a) with three opaque predicate and data encoding, which has less patterns and regularities comparing to (b).

Example: We demonstrate our motivation using the example in Fig. 1. We obfuscate the program in Fig. 1(a), which calculates the sum of the first n positive integers, by adding opaque predicates[3] with bogus code and data encoding. If we apply Cyclomatic complexity, a classical complexity measure, to Fig. 1(b) the result will be 7. Cyclomatic complexity is based on control flow graph (CFG), and is computed by: $E - N + 2$, where E is the number of edges and N is the number of nodes in CFG. Figure 1(b) contains $N = 8$ nodes, $E = 13$ edges then the Cyclomatic complexity is $(13 - 8 + 2) = 7$. We can see some regularity here: there is one opaque predicate repeated three times. Furthermore, the variable y is repeated three times in the same place of the If-branch.

We take another obfuscated version in Fig. 1(c) (of the same program); this code is obfuscated by adding three different opaque predicates. The patterns and regularities becomes less in this version comparing to Fig. 1(b); however the Cyclomatic complexity is still the same 7, and it does not account for the changes that occurred in the code. Assuming the opaque predicates of Fig. 1(c) are equally difficult to break, attacking this code requires at least twice more effort than the code in Fig. 1(b), as we need to figure out the value of two more opaque predicates.

Furthermore, Fig. 1(b) can be compressed at higher rate than Fig. 1(c); again, this is due to the inherent regularity in Fig. 1(b). We argue that an obfuscated program which is secure and confuses an adversary will exhibit a high level of irregularity in its source code, and thus it requires a longer description to characterize all its features. This can be captured by the notion of Kolmogorov complexity, which quantifies the amount of information in an object.

4.1   Applying Kolmogorov Complexity to Code Obfuscation

So far, we argued that Kolmogorov complexity can be used to determine regularities in code obfuscation. The question that makes sense to ask is: At which level of Kolmogorov complexity can we claim an obfuscated code is secure against a specific adversary? It is vital to provide first some sort of formal definition of code obfuscation, that captures the desired security properties. Although this task is quite difficult and cumbersome, we provided an intuitive definition in [14] that is inspired by practical uses of obfuscation. We believe that it is the first step toward establishing a solid foundation for code obfuscation. The rationale behind this definition is that an obfuscated program must be more difficult to understand than the original program. This uses the notion of c-unintelligibility:

Definition 3. (Unintelligibility)([14]) A program P' is said to be c-unintelligible with respect to another program P if it is c times more complex than P, i.e. the added complexity is c times the original one, and thus more difficult to understand. Formally: $K(P') \geq (c+1)K(P)$, for some constant $c > 0$.

---

[3] An opaque predicate is an algebraic expression which always evaluates to same value (true or false) regardless of the input.

Definition 4. A *c-Obfuscator* $\mathcal{O} : \mathcal{P} \times \mathcal{L} \rightarrow \mathcal{P}'$ is a mapping from programs with security parameters $\mathcal{L}$ to their obfuscated versions such that $\forall P \in \mathcal{P}, \forall \lambda \in \mathcal{L} . \mathcal{O}(P, \lambda) \neq P$ and satisfies the following properties:

- **Functionality**: $O(P, \lambda)$ and P compute the same function, such that $\forall i \in I$. $[\![P]\!](i) = [\![\mathcal{O}(P, \lambda)]\!](i)$.
- **Polynomial Slowdown**: the size and running time of $\mathcal{O}(P, \lambda)$ are at most polynomially larger than the size and running time of P.
- **Unintelligibility**: $\mathcal{O}(P, \lambda)$ is c-unintelligible with respect to P.

We could use the unintelligibility property to answer the aforementioned question. If we need to secure a program against an adversary, whether it is human or an automatic reverse engineering tool, we may require an obfuscator to add c amount of irregularities that could foil that adversary.

4.2   Security Model

To properly define security we need to specify the capabilities of our attacker. The most basic case we are trying to capture is that of a human who seeks to obtain some original code from an obfuscated version of it, without the assistance of any automated tools. The difficulty of the analyst's task is measured by the amount of information that s/he lacks to obtain the target code. If the obfuscation is weak, this will be small. A good obfuscation will force the analyst to obtain more information to reach its target, possibly some of the randomness used to execute the obfuscation in the first place.

At the other extreme, we have an analyst with access to the complete range of analysis tools. It can compute any function[4] of the obfuscated code, and eventually produce a modified version thereof. Ultimately, it will seek to produce a deobfuscated version of the program, that is, well-structured code which is similar to the original program and has less noise. In this set of functions, we include, for example, automated reverse-engineering analysis techniques such as static program analysis (e.g., data flow, control flow, alias analysis, program slicing, disassemblers, and decompilers) and dynamic program analysis (e.g., dynamic testing, profiling, and program tracing).

While the first adversary is too limited to be realistic, the powers of the second are too broad to be useful. Every obfuscated program that is obtained by a deterministic transformation (taking clear code and auxiliary randomness as input) can be reversed by undoing the exact same steps in the opposite order. Therefore, for each instance there will be at least one computable function that is able to return the original code. To achieve a meaningful model we have to establish limits to the adversary power and exclude such situations that would make any obfuscation trivially impossible.

We do this by letting the adversary run functions of the obfuscated code, but only from a list chosen before it receives the challenge obfuscation (i.e., independent from the challenge). Besides, adversaries are parameterized by the amount

---

[4] Any *computable* function, that is.

of information they use: this includes their own code, that of any algorithm they choose to run and any other auxiliary information. The adversary wins if it produces a candidate deobfuscation that is close to the original and this does not require too much information. Formally, for a security parameter $0 \leq \epsilon \leq 1$, the adversary wins if:

- It receives obfuscated code $P' = \mathcal{O}(P, \lambda)$ and produces deobfuscation P^*
- $P^* = P$, and the Kolmogorov complexity of the adversary's information, Q, is less than $(1 - \epsilon)K(P)$.

This definition is compatible with the definition of security in [14]: if the last condition is true, the adversary successfully produce P from P^* using information Q. Therefore, $K(P|P') \leq K(Q) < (1 - \epsilon)K(P)$ and so $I_K(P : P') > \epsilon K(P)$.

5   Theoretical Metric Validation

Obfuscated programs are software in the first place. Measuring obfuscation means we are quantifying some software properties that may reflect the code security. Although the security property is captured using unintelligibility according to the above definition, Kolmogorov complexity requires validation to ensure its acceptance, usefulness and soundness as a software metric. Theoretical validation is considered as a necessary step before empirical validation. Several properties have been suggested for theoretical validating of software complexity measures such as Weyuker [17] and Briand et al. [3]. Among the proposed models, we found Weyuker's axioms are more suitable for validating Kolmogorov complexity. Weyuker's validation properties, despite the criticisms that were received [16], have been broadly applied to certify many complexity measures, and are still an important basis and general approach to certify a complexity measure. Weyuker proposed nine properties or axioms for complexity validation, which we use to validate Kolmogorov complexity. There are some concepts presented in Weyuker's properties that require some clarification in the context of Kolmogorov complexity such as functional equivalence, composition of two programs, permutation of statements order and renaming. Consider two programs P and Q that belong to a set of binary strings $\{0, 1\}^+$.

- Functional equivalence: P and Q are said to have the same functionality if they are semantically equivalent i.e. given identical input, the output of the two programs are the same, i.e. $\forall i \in I. [\![P]\!](i) = [\![Q]\!](i)$.
- Composition : Although Weyuker did not include any formal relation to identify the composition of two programs, we consider the composition in the context of Kolmogorov complexity as the joint Kolmogorov complexity, which can be expressed as the concatenation of P and Q programs before applying the complexity measure. $K(P; Q) = K(P \parallel Q)$ where $\parallel$ is the concatenation between P and Q.
- Permutation: A program $P \in \{0, 1\}^+$ can be composed of concatenated sub-binary strings $p_i \subset P$, for example it may represent program instructions, such that: $P = p_1 \parallel ... \parallel p_n$. The permutation involves changes in the order or the structure of how these binary substrings are represented in P.

– Renaming: Renaming refers to syntactic modification of a program's identifiers, variables and modules names.

Weyuker validation properties are presented in the following, where C_o is a complexity measure that maps a program to a non-negative number.

Definition 5. [17] (Weyuker's validation properties) A complexity measure C_o : $P \rightarrow \mathbb{R}$ is a mapping from a program to a non-negative real number and has the following properties:

1. **Not constant:** $\exists P, Q. \; C_o(P) \neq C_o(Q)$. This property states the complexity measure *is not constant*.
2. **Non-coarse:** Given a nonnegative number c, there are only a finite number of programs such that $C_o(P) = c$.
3. **Non-uniqueness:** $\exists P, Q. \; P \neq Q \wedge C_o(P) = C_o(Q)$. This property again states that the measure is nontrivial, in that there are multiple programs of the same size.
4. **Functionality:** $\exists P, Q. \; \forall i \in I. [\![P]\!](i) = [\![Q]\!](i)) \wedge C_o(P) \neq C_o(Q)$. It expresses that there are functionally equivalent programs with different complexities.
5. **Monotonicity:** $\forall P, Q. \; C_o(P) \leq C_o(P \parallel Q) \wedge C_o(Q) \leq C_o(P \parallel Q)$. This property checks for monotonic measures. It states that adding to a program makes it increase its complexity.
6. **Interaction matters (a):** $\exists P, Q, R. \; C_o(P) = C_o(Q) \wedge C_o(P \parallel R) \neq C_o(Q \parallel R)$. This property explains the interaction of two equal complexity programs with an auxiliary concatenated program. It states that a program R may produce different complexity measure when it is added to two equal complexity programs P and Q.

   Interaction matters (b): $\exists P, Q, R. \; C_o(P) = C_o(Q) \wedge \; C_o(R \parallel P) \neq C_o(R \parallel Q)$. This property is similar to the previous except that the identical code occurs at the beginning of the program.
7. **Permutation is significant:** Let $\pi(P)$ be a permutation of P's statements order. Then, $\exists P. \; C_o(P) \neq C_o(\pi(P))$. This expresses that changing the order of statements may change the complexity of the program.
8. **Renaming:** If P is a renaming of Q, $P = Rename(Q)$, then $C_o(P) = C_o(Q)$. This property asserts that uniformly renaming variable names should not change a program's complexity.
9. **Interaction may increase complexity:** $\exists P, Q. \; C_o(P) + C_o(Q) \leq C_o(P \parallel Q)$. This property states that a merged program of two programs can be more complex than its component parts.

The Renaming property as was suggest by Weyuker is not desirable for code obfuscation. Functionally it is true, a renaming of variables does not in any way alter the structure of the code. However, it is easy to see that it can make human understanding much more difficult. A good programming practice is to use clear names for variables and methods, that explain accurately what they do and go a long way towards reducing the necessity of comments in the code. Conversely, long random names obscure their meaning forcing the analyst to follow the program's logic to understand their functionality. From a Kolmogorov point of view, meaningful names have a smaller complexity than long ones, and a program with renamed variables might well be more complex which suits our intuitition regarding its comprehensibility. We consider this proposition no further.

Weyuker argued that property 9 helps to account for a situation that a program's complexity increases as more additional components are introduced, due to the potential interaction among these parts. Briand et al. [3] provided a modified version of this property (stronger version) called **Disjoint Module Additivity**, which establishes a relation between a program and the complexity of its parts. Given two disjoint modules m_1, m_2 such that $P = m_1 \cup m_2$ and $m_1 \cap m_2 = \emptyset$ where P is the whole program, then $C_o(m_1) + C_o(m_2) = C_o(P)$. Below we check whether these properties are satisfied by Kolmogorov complexity.

Proposition 1 (Not constant). $\exists P, Q. K(P) \neq K(Q)$.

Proof. By simple counting, there are at most 2^n programs with complexity at most n. Therefore, there must be programs with complexity larger than n and so there must be programs with distinct complexities.

Proposition 2 (Non-coarse). *Given a nonnegative number c, there are only a finite number of programs such that $\exists d. |\{P : \exists c. K(P) = c\}| \leq d$.*

Proof. According to Theorem 7.2.4 in [7] the number of strings (in our context programs) of Kolmogorov complexity less than or equal to k is upper bounded by 2^k, i.e. $|S = \{\forall P \in \{0,1\}^* : K(P) \leq k\}| \leq 2^k$, which means set S is finite.

Proposition 3 (Non-uniqueness). $\exists P, Q. P \neq Q \wedge K(P) = K(Q)$.

Proof. It is possible to construct a prefix-free code with 2^n strings of length up to n, e.g. the code composed only of all the strings of length n. By basic properties of Kolmogorov complexity, these have complexity up to $n + O(1)$. If the proposition is false, there is at most one minimal program of each size. Therefore, there could be at most $n-1$ non-empty strings of length smaller than $n + O(1)$ with complexity up to $n + O(1)$, which is a contradiction. Thus, there must be strings with the same complexity.

Proposition 4 (Functionality). $\exists P, Q. (\forall i \in I. [\![P]\!](i) = [\![Q]\!](i)) \wedge K(P) \neq K(Q)$.

Proof. In general, one same function can be produced by several different implementations, that might bear little resemblance (e.g. different sorting algorithms, all producing the same result). Therefore, in general their complexities will be different. For an extreme example, consider program P and let $Q \| R$, where R is an added program that does not touch on any of the variables, memory or other resources of P and does not return results. It takes resources and does work, but ultimately Q just returns what P returns. Then, $\forall i \in I. [\![P]\!](i) = [\![Q]\!](i)$ and $K(Q) = K(P) + K(Q|P) \geq K(P)$. And because Q has to be independent from P in order to use other resources, it must be that $K(Q|P) = K(Q)$ and the inequality is strict.

Proposition 5 (Monotonicity). $\forall P, Q.\, K(P) \leq K(P\|Q) \wedge K(Q) \leq K(P\|Q).$

Proof. We need to prove that $K(P \| Q)$ is greater than $K(P)$ and $K(Q)$. By Theorem 1, $K(P, Q) = K(P) + K(Q|P) + c$ where c is an additive constant. Up to a logarithic term, $K(P \| Q) = K(P, Q) = K(P) + K(Q|P)$. By definition, $K(Q|P) \geq 0$ and so $K(P) \leq K(P \| Q)$. The proof is equal for $K(Q)$.

Proposition 6 (Interaction matters). *(a)* $\exists P, Q, R.\, K(P) = K(Q) \wedge K(P \| R) \neq K(Q \| R)$ *and (b)* $\exists P, Q, R.\, K(P) = K(Q) \wedge K(R \| P) \neq K(R \| Q).$

Proof. Assume the existence of two binary programs P, Q such that $K(P) = K(Q)$ and $I(P, Q) = O(1)$. Let $R = P$. Then, we have that up to small approximation factors $K(P \| R) = K(P, R) = K(P) + K(R|P) = K(P) + O(1)$. On the other hand, $K(Q \| R) = K(Q, R) = K(Q) + K(R|Q) = K(P) + K(R)$ where the last equality follows from the definition of mutual information. If R must be different than either P, Q, then we can repeat the same proof by picking a program R that has high $I(P, R)$ but small $I(Q, R)$, for example, a truncation of P.

Proposition 7 (Permutation). *Given a permutation* π, $\exists P.\, K(P) \neq K(\pi(P)).$

Proof. Fix a program P with n distinct lines, each at most m bits long. There are $n!$ permutations of P, and because the lines are all distinct these lead to $n!$ different permuted programs. We show that there must be a program Q corresponding to some permutation $Q = \pi(P)$ such that $K(Q) > K(P)$. By construction, $|P| = mn$ and so there are at most 2^{mn} strings with complexity smaller or equal to P. By Stirling's approximation, $\ln n! = n \ln n - n + O(\ln n)$. Pick n such that $\ln n > \ln(2) \cdot m + 1$, which implies $n \ln n - n > \ln(2) \cdot mn \Rightarrow n! > 2^{mn}$. Then, there are more permuted programs that strings less complex than P and so at least one permutation leads to a program more complex than P.

Proposition 8 (Disjoint Module Additivity). $\exists P, Q.\, K(P) + K(Q) = K(P \| Q).$

Proof. $K(P; Q) = K(P) + K(Q|P)$ by Theorem 1. Assume $P \cap Q = \emptyset$, then $K(Q|P) = K(Q)$ since the two programs are fully independent; therefore $K(P; Q) = K(P \| Q) = K(P) + K(Q)$ up to logarithmic precision.

The above results show that Kolmogorov complexity satisfies all Weyuker's properties in Definition 5, with two weak exceptions that have been addressed above. Therefore, we conclude Kolmogorov complexity is a suitable complexity measure for software based on Weyuker's validation framework.

5.1   Normalized Kolmogorov Complexity

Kolmogorov Complexity is an absolute measure, which is problematic when we want to compare two programs with different sizes. For example consider a program P of 1000 bits size that can be compressed to 500 bits, take another program Q of 10^6 bits size, which is compressed to 1000 bits. By using the absolute measure of Kolmogorov complexity, Q is more complex than P. However, P can be compressed to almost half of its size, where Q can be compressed to $\frac{1}{1000}$ of its size, which clearly indicates that Q has more regularities than P, and hence that makes P more complex than Q. In order to overcome this issue, we suggest a normalized version of Kolmogorov Complexity that is relativized by the upper bound of Kolmogorov complexity i.e. the maximum complexity a certain obfuscated code can achieve. Kolmogorov complexity is upper bounded by the length of its program, the subject of measure, according to Theorem 2; this bound can be used as the maximum Kolmogorov complexity. Normalized Kolmogorov complexity can be useful demonstrating the divergence of obfuscated code complexity before and after a given attack, in terms of information content (high variability of text content), from the maximum value of that complexity.

Definition 6. The normalised Kolmogorov complexity NK of a program P is given by:

$$NK(P) = \frac{K(P)}{|P| + 2\log(|P|)}$$

where $|P|$ is the length of P

A high value of NK means that there is a high variability of program content structure, i.e. high complexity. A low value of NK means high redundancy, i.e. the ratio of repeating fragments, operators and operands in code. Since Kolmogorov complexity can be effectively approximated by compression [11], it is possible to estimate NK by using a standard compressor instead of a minimal program:

$$NC(P) = \frac{C(P)}{|P| + 2\log(|P|)},$$

implying $0 \leq NC \leq 1$.

We can say that if the size of compressed obfuscated code is equal to the size of obfuscated code itself, then the obfuscated code is considered highly random, and is difficult to comprehend by an attacker. This can be justified in light of our discussion of code regularity in Sect. 4.

6   Experiment Evaluation

The recent empirical result [10] shows that data compression is a promising software metric technique to estimate human comprehension in software. So far, we present a theoretical validation that complements this result, and we propose formal definition that reflects the natural intuition of code obfuscation unintelligibility. Therefore, it is necessary to validate this formal treatment empirically, and to check whether code obfuscation techniques increase the complexity (NC measure) of software. Furthermore, we need to examine the extent to which current obfuscation techniques resist reverse engineering tools (decompilers) i.e. prevent reducing the complexity of obfuscated code.

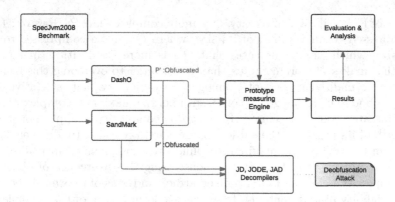

Fig. 2. High level overview of the experimental procedure

Specifically, we aim to answer the following questions:

– What is the effectiveness of obfuscation algorithms using the NC measure, by
  type: control flow, data and layout obfuscation?
– Is there any change in NC measure between a clear code and its obfuscated
  version using different obfuscation algorithms? Does that change, if it occurs,
  imply an increase in NC measure?
– What is the impact of deobfuscation (decompilers) on code obfuscation
  resilience?

We answered the above questions by conducting an experiment on an obfuscated version of SPECjvm2008 (Java Virtual Machine Benchmark) programs.
We obfuscated 10 real-world applications of SPECjvm2008 benchmark suite,
ranging in size from medium to large, and containing several real life applications and benchmarks, focusing on core Java functionality. Each one was written
in the Java source language and compiled with `javac` to Java byte code, where
the obfuscation took place on this level. A brief description of SPECjvm2008 is
given in Table 1, the full description and documentation of SPECjvm2008 suite
can be found on the benchmark's webpage[5]. The complete list of the obfuscation algorithms that were used in our experiment is provided in Table 2, the full
description of each obfuscation techniques can be found on their website.

We select two obfuscators of the most prominent tools: one commercial
DashO evaluation copy with all main features turned on, and a free source version of *SandMark* (see Table 2). The original benchmark `jar` files were obfuscated
by using 43 different obfuscation techniques of *DashO* and *Sandmark* obfuscators. We apply three Java decompilers to investigate the resilience, and assess to
which extent the applied obfuscation techniques can resist decompilation attacks.
Our choice was based on a study by Hamilton and Danicic [9], who investigated
the effectiveness of Java decompilers using an empirical evaluation on a group of
currently available Java bytecode decompilers. We selected, based on that experiment, three Java decompilers that score the best among all the decompilers in

---

[5] http://www.spec.org/jvm2008/.

Table 1. SPECjvm2008 benchmark brief description

Benchmark	Description
compiler	A java decompiler using the OpenJDK (JDK 7 alpha) front end compiler
compress	Compresses data, using a modified Lempel-Ziv method (LZW)
crypto	Provides three different ciphers (AES,RSA, signverify) to encrypt data
derby	An open-source database written in pure Java
mpegaudio	MPEG-3 audio stream decoder
scimark	A floating point benchmark
serial	serializes and deserializes primitives and objects, using data from the JBoss benchmark
startup	Starts each benchmark for one operation
Sunflow	Tests graphics visualization using multi-threaded global illumination rendering system
xml	Has two sub-benchmarks: XML.transform and XML.validation.

terms of effectiveness and correctness: JD[6], JAD[7] and JODE[8]. We applied *bzip2* compressor to compute *NC*, which is one of the most effective lossless compressor to approximate Kolmogorov complexity, according to [12].

We automate the whole testing proposed, using a scripting code that was written in python to glue the command line versions of Sandmark, Dasho obfuscation, decompilation, and our proposed metric. All of the above components are integrated into our prototype, Fig. 2 shows an overview of the tool-set and the experimental procedure.

6.1 Results and Analysis

The results are reported in forms of charts. Figure 3 shows the results of *NC* according to obfuscation transformation algorithms and decompilation. The bottom line of Fig. 3 with error bars represents the baseline measurement of SPECjvm2008 benchmark before obfuscation process taking place, the error bars are the standard deviation of *NC* among different programs of SPECjvm2008. We used the baseline as a reference comparison line to other results, for example to show if any changes in *NC* occur due to obfuscation techniques and decompilation. To facilitate reading Fig. 3 , we produced artificial gaps among the different obfuscation techniques groups. For convenience presenting the obtained results, we clustered all the obfuscation transformation algorithms into three types of

---

[6] http://java.decompiler.free.fr.

[7] http://varaneckas.com/jad/.

[8] http://jode.sourceforge.net/.

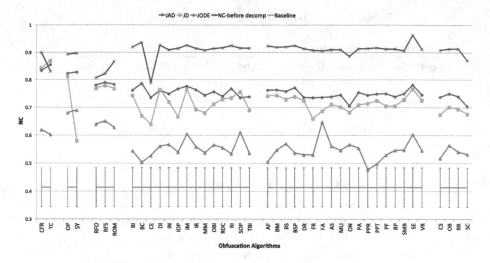

Fig. 3. NC measure per obfuscation technique

Table 2. Obfuscation techniques and their abbreviations used in the experiment, (C) stands for control flow, (D) Data and (L) Layout obfuscation.

Obfuscator	Obfuscated technique	Abbr	Obfuscator	Obfuscated technique	Abbr
Dasho-(C)	DControlFlow	CFR	Sandmark-(D)	BlockMarker	BM
Dasho-(C)	tryCatch10	TC	Sandmark-(D)	BludgeonSignature	BS
Dasho-(D)	Optimisation	OP	Sandmark-(D)	BooleanSplitter	BSP
Dasho-(D)	Synthetic	SY	Sandmark-(D)	DuplicateRegister	DR
Dasho-(L)	FlattenHierarchyOverInduction	RFO	Sandmark-(D)	FalseRefactor	FR
Dasho-(L)	FlattenhierarchySimple	RFS	Sandmark-(D)	FieldAssignment	FA
Dasho-(L)	OverInductionMaintainhierarchy	ROM	Sandmark-(D)	IntegerArraySplitter	AS
Sandmark-(C)	BranchInverter	BI	Sandmark-(D)	MergeLocalIntegers	MLI
Sandmark-(C)	BuggyCode	BC	Sandmark-(D)	OverloadNames	ON
Sandmark-(C)	ClassSplitter	CE	Sandmark-(D)	ParamAlias	PA
Sandmark-(C)	DynamicInliner	DI	Sandmark-(D)	PromotePrimitiveRegisters	PPR
Sandmark-(C)	Inliner	IN	Sandmark-(D)	PromotePrimitiveTypes	PPT
Sandmark-(C)	InsertOpaquePredicates	IOP	Sandmark-(D)	PublicizeFields	PF
Sandmark-(C)	InterleaveMethods	IM	Sandmark-(D)	ReorderParameters	RP
Sandmark-(C)	Irreducibility	IR	Sandmark-(D)	StaticMethodBodies	SMB
Sandmark-(C)	MethodMerger	MM	Sandmark-(D)	StringEncoder	SE
Sandmark-(C)	OpaqueBranchInsertion	OBI	Sandmark-(D)	VariableReassigner	VR
Sandmark-(C)	RandomDeadCode	RDC	Sandmark-(L)	ConstantPoolReorder	CS
Sandmark-(C)	ReorderInstructions	RI	Sandmark-(L)	Objectify	OB
Sandmark-(C)	SimpleOpaquePredicates	SOP	Sandmark-(L)	RenameRegisters	RR
Sandmark-(C)	TransparentBranchInsertion	TBI	Sandmark-(L)	SplitClasses	SC
Sandmark-(C)	ArrayFolder	AF			

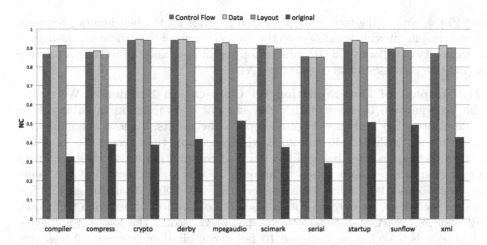

Fig. 4. Averaged NC measure per obfuscation transformation. C: Control Flow, D: Data and L: Layout obfuscation

transformations: *Control-flow*, *Data* and *Layout*, see Table 2 and Fig. 4, then we report the average *NC* for each type transformation over the benchmark programs.

The Impact of Obfuscation on Complexity. In this section we answered the first two empirical questions. First we investigate the obfuscation effectiveness: Around 50 % of obfuscation techniques, of different obfuscation types, have scored similar complexity values (*NC=0.91*) with very minor difference, all of these techniques are part of Sandmark obfuscator framework. This could indicate a common design pattern among these techniques, which needs further investigation. Dasho's obfuscation techniques show a different behavior, only data obfuscation type have a similar complexity values. We also found that *StringEncoder* and *BuggyCode* performed better than all the obfuscation techniques in terms of *NC*, where *ClassSplitter* and *RenameFlattenHierarchyOverInduction* scored the lowest among all obfuscation techniques. Aggregating the obfuscation techniques according to their types, shows a very minor difference using the proposed metric see Fig. 4. Data obfuscation and control flow obfuscation performed roughly the same. That was a bit surprising, as we expected the data obfuscation to outperform control-flow obfuscation. This is due to the nature of data obfuscation that adds a lot of noise to program data structure comparing to control flow obfuscation, which only complicates the structure of Control Flow Graph (CFG).

We used the results in Figs. 3 and 4 to investigate whether code obfuscation changes the complexity of original unobfuscated code. For visual inspection, we see a change in *NC* over all the obfuscation transformation algorithms comparing to the unobfuscated benchmark programs' scores. In Fig. 3, we notice a substantial increase in *NC* all over the obfuscation algorithms comparing to the baseline. We also see a clear increase in complexity of obfuscations per type, see Fig. 4, comparing to the unobfuscated code for all the benchmark programs. These results provide an answer to the second question that there are changes in complexity of software due to obfuscation techniques, and these changes produce a positive increase in the complexity (NC).

The Impact of Decompilation on Obfuscation Resilience. We answer the last question by investigating the effect of decompilation as an attack on code obfuscation resilience. Figure 3 reports the results, it shows three different lines labeled with JAD, JD and JODE which resemble the average NC of obfuscation techniques after being subjected to decompilation for all the benchmark programs. Most of obfuscation techniques, in this study, shows high resilience against JD and JAD, and a weak resilience against JODE. Analysing each obfuscation technique, we observe a high resilience of Dasho's obfuscation techniques against JD, apart of *Synthetic* technique which scores the lowest complexity. *Synthetic* is a technique designed to fail decompilation; however JD was very effective at thwarting this technique. *StringEncoder* has the highest resilience against JD where *ClassSplitter* demonstrates the lowest resilience. *tryCatch10* shows a high resilience against JD and JAD, as they are ineffective against the intensive use of try-catch blocks. JODE performed better than other decompilers at reducing the complexity of obfuscation transformations on individual technique, as we see in Fig. 3. JODE was very effective at reducing the complexity of *tryCatch10* obfuscated programs comparing to JAD and JD. We notice that JODE managed to reduce the NC to the benchmark baseline level in Fig. 3. We investigate this matter in more details, and we find the main reason for this decrease in complexity: JODE failed to produce a complete decompilation when it decompiles the programs that were obfuscated with arbitrary bytecode, such as *BuggyCode*, we also realized the same problem with JAD too. Surprisingly JODE failed to replace java.lang.Integer object to the correct int in the source code for *PromotePrimitiveRegisters*, and *PromotePrimitiveTypes* obfuscation, which agrees with Hamilton and Danicic [9] observation that JODE sometimes fails at resolving and inferring the correct types. Nevertheless, JODE decompiled the other obfuscated programs with a reasonable accuracy. In general, all decompilation attacks have managed to reduce NC to a certain degree, where JODE outperformed all of the decompilers at reducing the complexity of obfuscated programs.

6.2   Comparing with Ceccato et al. Results

We compare some of our results, in particular Sandmark obfuscation techniques, with Ceccato et al. [4] results using Cyclomatic complexity measure. In [4], most obfuscations report a Cyclomatic complexity similar to the clear code, only few cases show higher increase in complexity. In our study, we find that most of Sandmark obfuscated programs reported a significant increase in NC complexity.

We further investigated this matter, and observed in Ceccato et al. study that Cyclomatic complexity only accounts for changes in obfuscated programs that involve changes in Control Flow Graph (CFG), i.e. adding or changing basic blocks or edges to CFG, such as some of control flow obfuscation type. We also notice that the obfuscated techniques, which did not report any increase in Cyclomatic complexity, according to Ceccato et al., report a similar NC complexity increase in our study. However that was because Cyclomatic measure did not detect any changes in the obfuscation process, whereas NC is more sensitive than Cyclomatic measure at detecting any increase in obfuscation complexity comparing to original unobfuscated code.

7   Conclusion and Future Work

Compression can be ultimately represented by Kolmogorov complexity; however, this poses the following two questions: How good is Kolmogorov complexity as a metric for code obfuscation? How can we verify the validity of this metric to measure code obfuscation? In previous work [14] we provided a theoretical foundation for the use of Kolmogorov complexity as a metric to measure the security of code obfuscation, without having to rely on classical complexity metrics, and we detailed the intuitions supporting this choice. In this paper we addressed some remaining questions, with efforts divided in two main parts: the first part shows that Kolmogorov complexity is a sound metric to measure software with respect to the properties of Weyuker's validation framework; the second part presents the empirical results which show that obfuscation techniques managed to produce a substantial increase in the proposed metric comparing to original unobfuscated programs, which confirms our formal definition about code obfuscations.

   In our experiment, we used an attack model where the adversary can only use static analysis techniques; the metric we proposed does not certify code obfuscations against dynamic analysis tools such as profiling, debugging and dynamic slicers. We plan to extend our framework to certify dynamic code obfuscation as future work.

References

1. Anckaert, B., Madou, M., De Sutter, B., De Bus, B., De Bosschere, K., Preneel, B.: Program obfuscation: a quantitative approach. In: Proceedings of QoP 2007, pp. 15–20. ACM Press, New York, USA, October 2007
2. Barak, B., Goldreich, O., Impagliazzo, R., Rudich, S., Sahai, A., Vadhan, S.P., Yang, K.: On the (im)possibility of obfuscating programs. In: Kilian, J. (ed.) CRYPTO 2001. LNCS, vol. 2139, pp. 1–18. Springer, Heidelberg (2001)
3. Briand, L.C., Morasca, S., Basili, V.R.: Property-based software engineering measurement. IEEE Trans. Softw. Eng. 22(1), 68–86 (1996)
4. Ceccato, M., Capiluppi, A., Falcarin, P., Boldyreff, C.: A large study on the effect of code obfuscation on the quality of java code. Empirical Softw. Eng. 1–39 (2014)
5. Ceccato, M., Di Penta, M., Nagra, J., Falcarin, P., Ricca, F., Torchiano, M., Tonella, P.: The effectiveness of source code obfuscation: an experimental assessment. In: ICPC, pp. 178–187 (2009)

6. Collberg, C., Thomborson, C., Low, D.: A taxonomy of obfuscating transformations (1997)
7. Cover, T.M., Thomas, J.A.: Elements of Information Theory. Wiley, Hoboken (2006)
8. Garg, S., Raykova, M., Gentry, C., Sahai, A., Halevi, S., Waters, B.: Candidate indistinguishability obfuscation and functional encryption for all circuits. In: FOCS (2013)
9. Hamilton, J., Danicic, S.: An evaluation of current java bytecode decompilers. In: SCAM 2009, pp. 129–136. IEEE Computer Society, Washington, DC, USA (2009)
10. Jbara, A., Feitelson, D.G.: On the effect of code regularity on comprehension. In: Proceedings of the 22nd International Conference on Program Comprehension, ICPC, pp. 189–200. ACM, New York, NY, USA (2014)
11. Kieffer, J.C., Yang, E.H.: Sequential codes, lossless compression of individual sequences, and Kolmogorov complexity. IEEE Trans. Inf. Theor. **42**(1), 29–39 (1996)
12. Li, M., Vitnyi, P.M.B.: An Introduction to Kolmogorov Complexity and Its Applications, 3rd edn. Springer, Heiderlberg (2008)
13. McCabe, T.J.: A complexity measure. IEEE Trans. Softw. Eng. **2**(4), 308–320 (1976)
14. Mohsen, R., Pinto, A.M.: Algorithmic information theory for obfuscation security. In: SECRYPT 2015 - Proceedings of the 12th International Conference on Security and Cryptography, Colmar, Alsace, France, pp. 76–87, 20–22 July 2015
15. Dalla Preda, M., Giacobazzi, R.: Semantics-based code obfuscation by abstract interpretation. J. Comput. Secur. **17**(6), 855–908 (2009)
16. Tian, J., Zelkowitz, M.V.: A formal program complexity model and its application. J. Syst. Softw. **17**(3), 253–266 (1992)
17. Weyuker, E.J.: Evaluating software complexity measures. IEEE Trans. Softw. Eng. **14**(9), 1357–1365 (1988)

Spam Emails, Botnets and Malware

Fast and Effective Clustering of Spam Emails Based on Structural Similarity

Mina Sheikhalishahi[1], Andrea Saracino[2]([⊠]), Mohamed Mejri[1],
Nadia Tawbi[1], and Fabio Martinelli[2]

[1] Department of Computer Science, Université Laval, Quebec City, Canada
mina.sheikh-alishahi.1@ulaval.ca,
{mohamed.mejri,nadia.tawbi}@ift.ulaval.ca
[2] Istituto di Informatica e Telematica, Consiglio Nazionale delle Ricerche, Pisa, Italy
{andrea.saracino,fabio.martinelli}@iit.cnr.it

Abstract. Spam emails yearly impose extremely heavy costs in terms of time, storage space and money to both private users and companies. Finding and persecuting spammers and eventual spam emails stakeholders should allow to directly tackle the root of the problem. To facilitate such a difficult analysis, which should be performed on large amounts of unclassified raw emails, in this paper we propose a framework to fast and effectively divide large amount of spam emails into homogeneous campaigns through structural similarity. The framework exploits a set of 21 features representative of the email structure and a novel categorical clustering algorithm named Categorical Clustering Tree (CCTree). The methodology is evaluated and validated through standard tests performed on three dataset accounting to more than 200k real recent spam emails.

1 Introduction

Spam emails constitute a notorious and consistent problem still far from being solved. In the last year, out of the daily 191.4 billions of emails sent worldwide in average [20], more than 70 % are spam emails. Spam emails cause several problems, spanning from direct financial losses, to misuses of Internet traffic, storage space and computational power [22]. Moreover, spam emails are becoming a tool to perpetrate different cybercrimes, such as phishing, malware distribution, or social engineering-based frauds.

Given the relevance of the problem, several approaches have already been proposed to tackle the spam email issue. Currently, the most used approach for fighting spam emails consists in identifying and blocking them on the recipient machine through filters, which generally are based on machine learning techniques or content features, such as keywords, or non ascii characters [5,8,25].

This research has been partially supported by EU Seventh Framework Programme (FP7/2007–2013) under grant no 610853 (COCO Cloud), MIUR-PRIN Security Horizons and Natural Sciences and Engineering Research Council of Canada (NSERC).

© Springer International Publishing Switzerland 2016
J. Garcia-Alfaro et al. (Eds.): FPS 2015, LNCS 9482, pp. 195–211, 2016.
DOI: 10.1007/978-3-319-30303-1_12

Unfortunately, these countermeasures just slightly mitigate the problem which still impose non negligible cost to users and companies [22].

To effectively fight the problem of spam emails, it is mandatory to find and persecute the spammers, generally hiding behind complex networks of infected devices which send spam emails against their user will, i.e. botnets. Thus, information useful in finding the spammer should be inferred analyzing text, attachments and other elements of the emails, such as links. Therefore, the early analysis of correlated spam emails is vital [2,7]. However, such an analysis, constitutes an extremely challenging task, due to the huge amount of spam emails, which vastly increases hourly (8 billions per hour) [20] and for the high variance that related emails may show, due to the use of obfuscation techniques [19]. To simplify this analysis, huge amount of spam emails, generally collected through honey-pots, should be divided into spam campaigns [29]. A *spam campaign* is the set of messages spread by a spammer with a specific purpose [6], like advertising a product, spreading ideas, or for criminal intents.

This paper proposes a methodology to fast and effectively group large amount of spam emails by structural similarity. A set of 21 discriminative structural features are considered to obtain homogeneous email groups, which identify different spam campaigns. Grouping spam emails on the base of their similarities is a known approach. However, previous works mainly focus on the analysis of few specific parameters [2,21,29,30], showing results whose accuracy is still somehow limited. The proposed approach in this work is based on a *categorical hierarchical clustering* algorithm named *Categorical Clustering Tree (CCTree)*, introduced in [27], which builds a tree whose leaves represent the various spam campaigns. The algorithm clusters (groups) emails through structural similarity, verifying at each step the homogeneity of the obtained clusters and dividing the groups not enough homogeneous (pure) on the base of the attribute which yields the greatest variance (entropy). The effectiveness of the proposed approach has been tested against 10k spam emails extracted from a real recent dataset [1], and compared with other well-known categorical clustering algorithm, reporting the best results in terms of clustering quality (i.e. purity and accuracy) and time performance.

The contributions of this paper can be summarized as follows:

- We present a framework to effectively and efficiently analyze and cluster large amounts of raw spam emails into spam campaigns, based on a Categorical Clustering Tree (CCTree) algorithm.
- We introduce a set of 21 categorical features representative of email structure, briefly discussing the discretization procedure for numerical features.
- The performance of CCTree has been thoroughly evaluated through *internal evaluation*, to estimate the ability in obtaining homogeneous clusters and *external evaluation*, for the ability to effectively classify similar elements (emails), when classes are known beforehand. Internal and external evaluation have been performed respectively on a dataset of 10k unclassified spam emails and 276 emails manually divided in classes.

- We propose and validate through analysis on 200k spam emails, a methodology to choose the optimal CCTree configuration parameters based on detection of max curvature point (knee) on an homogeneity-number of clusters graph.
- We compare the proposed methodology with two general categorical clustering algorithms, and other methodologies specific for clustering spam emails.

The rest of the paper is structured as follows. Section 2, reports the formal description and the theoretical background of the Categorical Clustering Tree algorithm. Section 3 describes the proposed framework, detailing the extracted features and reporting implementation details. Section 4 reports the experiments to evaluate the ability of CCTree in clustering spam emails, comparing the results with the ones of two well known categorical clustering algorithms. Also the methodology to set the CCTree parameters is reported and validated. Section 5 discuss limitations and advantages of the proposed approach reporting result comparison with some related work. Other related work on clustering spam emails is presented in Sect. 6. Finally Sect. 7 briefly concludes proposing future research directions.

2   Categorical Clustering Tree

In this section we recall notions on the Categorical Clustering Tree (CCTree) algorithm, presented in [27], recalling terminology and construction methodology.

2.1   CCTree Construction

The CCTree is constructed iteratively through a decision tree-like structure, where the leaves of the tree are the desired clusters. An example of CCTree is reported in Fig. 1. The root of the CCTree contains all the elements to be clustered. Each element is described through a set of *categorical* attributes, such as the *Language* of a message. Being categorical each attribute may assume a finite set of discrete values, constituting its domain. For example the attribute

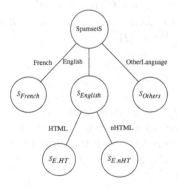

Fig. 1. A small CCTree.

Language may have as domain: {*English, French, Spanish*}. At each step, a new level of the tree is generated by splitting the nodes of the previous levels, when they are not homogeneous enough. *Shannon Entropy* [26] is used both to define a homogeneity measure called *node purity*, and to select the attribute used to split a node. In particular non-leaf nodes are divided on the base of the attribute yielding the maximum value for Shannon entropy. The separation is represented through a branch for each possible outcome of the specific attribute. Each branch or edge extracted from parent node is labeled with the selected feature which directs data to the child node. The process of CCTree construction can be formalized as follows.

Input: Let D be a set of data points, containing N tuples on a set A of d attributes, and let S be a set of stop conditions.

Attributes: An ordered set of d attributes $A = \{A_1, A_2, \ldots, A_d\}$ is given, where each attribute is an ordered set of mutually exclusive values. Thus, the j'th attribute could be written as $A_j = \{v_{1j}, v_{2j}, \ldots, v_{(rj)j}\}$, where r_j is the number of features of attribute A_j.

Data Points: A set D of N data points is given, where each data point is a vector whose elements are the features of attributes.

Stop Conditions: A set of stop conditions $S = (\{\mu, \varepsilon\})$ is given. μ is the "minimum number of elements in a node", i.e. when the number of elements in a node is less than μ, then the node is not divided even if not pure enough. ε represents the "minimum desired purity" for each cluster, i.e. when the purity of a node is better or equal to ε, it will be considered as a leaf. To calculate the node purity, a function based on Shannon entropy is defined as follows:

Let N_{kj_i} represents the number of elements having the k'th value of j'th attribute, in node i. Let N_i be the number of elements in node i. Thus, considering $p(v_{kj_i}) = \frac{N_{kj_i}}{N_i}$, the purity of node i, denoted by $\rho(i)$, is defined as:

$$\rho(i) = -\sum_{j=1}^{d} \sum_{k=1}^{r_j} p(v_{kj_i}) log(p(v_{kj_i}))$$ where d is the number of attributes, and r_j is the number of features of j'th attribute.

Output: The final output of the CCTree algorithm is a set of clusters, constituted by the leaves of the CCTree. For additional information on the CCTree algorithm we refer the reader to [27].

3   Framework

The presented framework acts in two steps. At first raw emails are analyzed by a parser to extract vectors of structural features. Afterward the collected vectors (elements) are clustered through the introduced CCTree algorithm. This section reports details on the proposed framework for analysis and clustering spam emails and extracted features.

3.1   Feature Extraction and Definition

To describe spam emails, we have selected a set of 21 categorical attributes, which are representative of the structural properties of emails. The reason is that the general appearance of messages belonging to the same spam campaign mainly remain unchanged, although spammers usually insert random text or links [6]. The selected attributes extends the set of structural features proposed in [18] to label emails as spam or ham. The attributes and a brief description are presented in Table 1.

Table 1. Features extracted from each email.

Attribute	Description
RecipientNumber	Number of recipients addresses.
NumberOfLinks	Total links in email text.
NumberOfIPBasedLinks	Links shown as an IP address.
NumberOfMismatchingLinks	Links with a text different from the real link.
NumberOfDomainsInLinks	Number of domains in links.
AvgDotsPerLink	Average number of dots in link in text.
NumberOfLinksWithAt	Number of links containing "@".
NumberOfLinksWithHex	Number of links containing hex chars.
SubjectLanguage	Language of the subject.
NumberOfNonAsciiLinks	Number of links with non-ASCII chars.
IsHtml	True if the mail contains html tags.
EmailSize	The email size, including attachments.
Language	Email language.
AttachmentNumber	Number of attachments.
AttachmentSize	Total size of email attachments.
AttachmentType	File type of the biggest attachment.
WordsInSubject	Number of words in subject.
CharsInSubject	Number of chars in subject.
ReOrFwdInSubject	True if subject contains "Re" or "Fwd".
NonAsciiCharsInSubject	Number of non ASCII chars in subject.
ImagesNumber	Number of images in the email text.

Since the clustering algorithm is *categorical*, all selected features are categorical as well. It is worth noting that some features are meant to represent *numerical* values, e.g. AttachmentSize, instead that categorical ones. However, it is always possible to turn these features from numerical into categorical, defining intervals and assigning a feature value to each interval defined in such a way. We chose these intervals on the base of the *ChiMerge* discretization method [15], which returns outstanding results for discretization in decision tree-like problems [10].

3.2   Implementation Details

On the implementation side, an email parser has been developed in Java to automatically analyze raw mails text and extract the features in form of vectors. The software exploits the JSoup [14] for HTML parsing, and of the LID[1] Python tools for language recognition. The LID software exploits the technique of n-grams to recognize the language of a text. For each language that LID has to recognize, a database of words must be provided to the software, in order to extract n-grams. The language on which LID has been trained are the following: English, Italian, French, German, Spanish, Portuguese, Chinese, Japanese, Persian, Arabic, Croatian.

We have implemented the CCTree algorithm using the MATLAB[2] software, which takes as input the matrix of emails features extracted by the parser.

It is worth noting that the complete framework, i.e. feature extraction and clustering module, are totally portable on different operative system. In fact, both the feature extraction module and the clustering module (i.e. MATLAB) are Java-based and executable on the vast majority of general purpose operative system (Java, UNIX, iOS, etc.). Also the Python module for language analysis it is portable. Moreover, LID has been made as a disposable component, i.e. if the Python interpreter is missing, the analysis is not stopped. For the emails where the language is not inferable, the UKNOWN_LANGUAGE value for the attribute is used instead.

4   Evaluation and Results

This section reports the experimental results to evaluate the quality of the CCTree algorithm on the problem of clustering spam emails. A first set of experiments has been performed on a dataset of 10k recent spam emails (first week of February 2015 [1]), to estimate the capability of the CCTree algorithm in obtaining homogeneous clusters. This evaluation is known as *Internal Evaluation* and estimates the quality of the clustering algorithm, measuring how much each element of the resulting cluster is similar to the elements of the same cluster and dissimilar from the elements of other clusters. A second set of experiments aims at assessing the capability of CCTree to correctly classify data using a small dataset with benchmark classes known beforehand. This evaluation is named *External Evaluation* and measures the similarity between the resulting clusters of a specific algorithm and the desired clusters (classes) of the pre-classified dataset. For external evaluation, CCTree has been tested against a dataset of 276 emails, manually labeled in 29 classes[3]. The emails have been manually divided, looking both at the structure and the semantic of the message. Thus, emails belonging to one class can be considered as part of a single spam campaign. The results of CCTree are compared with those of two categorical clustering

---

[1] http://www.cavar.me/damir/LID/.

[2] http://mathworks.com.

[3] Available at: http://security.iit.cnr.it/images/Mails/cctreesamples.zip.

algorithms, namely COBWEB and CLOPE. COBWEB and CLOPE have been selected among the others, since they are well known to be respectively very accurate and extremely fast. The comparison has been done both for internal and external evaluation on the same aforementioned datasets. A time performance analysis is also reported. It is worth noting that the three algorithms are all implemented on Java-based tools, hence the validity of time comparison.

COBWEB [9] is a categorical clustering algorithm, which builds a dendrogram where each node is associated with a conditional probability which summarizes the attribute-value distributions of objects belonging to a specific node. Differently from the CCTree algorithm, also includes a merging operation to join two separate nodes in a single one. COBWEB is computationally demanding and time consuming, since it re-analyzes at each step every single data point. However, the COBWEB algorithm is used in several fields for its good accuracy, in a way that its similarity distance measure, named Category Utility, is used to evaluate categorical clustering accuracy [3]. The WEKA [12] implementation of COBWEB has been used for the experiments.

CLOPE [32] is a fast categorical clustering algorithm which maximizes the number of elements with the same value for a subset of attributes, attempting to increase the homogeneity of each obtained cluster. Also for CLOPE we have used the WEKA implementation for the performed experiments.

4.1 Internal Evaluation

Internal evaluation measures the ability of a clustering algorithm in obtaining homogeneous clusters. A high score on internal evaluation is given to clustering algorithms which maximize the *intra-cluster similarity*, i.e. elements within the same cluster are similar, and minimize the *inter-cluster similarity*, i.e. elements from different clusters are dissimilar. The cluster dissimilarity is measured by computing the distances between elements (data points) in various clusters. The used distance function changes for the specific problem. In particular, for elements described by categorical attributes, the common geometric distances, e.g. Euclidean distance, cannot be used. Hence, in this work the *Hamming* and *Jaccard* distance measures [13] are applied. Internal evaluation can be performed directly on the dataset on which the clustering algorithm operates, i.e. the knowledge of the classes (desired clusters) is not a prerequisite. The internal evaluation indexes are the Dunn Index [4] and the Silhouette [23], defined as follows:

Dunn Index. Let Δ_i be the diameter of cluster C_i, that can be defined as the maximum distance of elements of C_i: $\Delta_i = \max_{x,y \in C_i , x \neq y}\{d(x,y)\}$, where $d(x,y)$ measures the distance of pair x and y, and $|C|$ shows the number of elements belonging to cluster C. Also, let $\delta(C_i, C_j)$ be the inter-cluster distance between clusters C_i and C_j, which is calculated as the pairwise distance between elements of two clusters. Then, on a set of k clusters, the *Dunn index* [11], is defined as: $DI_k = \min_{1 \leq i \leq k}\{\min_{1 \leq j \leq k}\{\frac{\delta(C_i,C_j)}{\max_{1 \leq t \leq k} \Delta_t}\}\}$.

A higher Dunn index value means a better cluster quality. It is worth noting that the value of Dunn index is negatively affected by the greatest diameter between the elements of all generated clusters ($\max_{1\leq t\leq k}\Delta_t$). Hence, even a single resulting cluster with poor quality (non homogeneous), will cause a low value of the Dunn index.

Silhouette. Let $d(x_i)$ be the average *dissimilarity* of data point x_i with other data points within the same cluster. Also, let $d'(x_i)$ be the lowest average dissimilarity of x_i to any other cluster, except the cluster that x_i belongs to. Then, the *silhouette* $s(i)$ for x_i is defined as:

$$s(i) = \frac{d'(i) - d(i)}{\max\{d(i), d'(i)\}} = \begin{cases} 1 - \frac{d(i)}{d'(i)} & d(i) < d'(i) \\ 0 & d(i) = d'(i) \\ \frac{d'(i)}{d(i)} - 1 & d(i) > d'(i) \end{cases}$$

where the definition result in $s(i) \in [-1, 1]$. As much as $s(i)$ is closer to 1, the more the data point x_i is appropriately clustered. The average value of $s(i)$ over all data of a cluster, shows how tightly related are data within a cluster. Hence, the more the average value of $s(i)$ is close to 1, the better is the clustering result. For easy interpretation, the silhouette of all clustered points is also represented through a *silhouette plot*.

Performance Comparison. As discussed in Sect. 2, CCTree algorithm requires two stop conditions as input, i.e. the minimum number of elements in a node to be split (μ), and minimum purity in a cluster (ε). Henceforth, the notation `CCTree`(ε, μ) will be used to refer the specific implementation of the CCTree algorithm.

Figure 2 graphs the internal evaluation measurements of CCTree with five different values of ε, when the minimum number of elements μ has been set to 1. It is worth noting that if $\mu = 1$, the only stop condition affecting the result is the node purity. Thus, we first fix $\mu = 1$ to find the best amount of required node purity for our dataset.

As shown in Fig. 2, the purity value reach the maximum and stabilize when $\varepsilon = 0.001$. More strict purity requirements (i.e., $\varepsilon < 0.001$) do not further increase the precision. This value of ε will be fixed for the following evaluations.

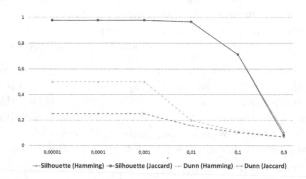

Fig. 2. Internal evaluation at the variation of the ε parameter.

Fixing the node purity $\varepsilon = 0.001$, we look for the better value for the μ parameter to be able to compare CCTree performance with accurate COBWEB and fast CLOPE. To this end, we provide four different values of minimum number of elements in a cluster. Table 2 presents the Silhouette and Dunn index results for proposed values of μ, namely 1, 10, 100, and 1000. In addition, the last two rows of Table 2 reports the resulting number of clusters and the *time* required to generate the clusters. Table 2 also reports the comparison with the two categorical clustering algorithms COBWEB and CLOPE, previously described. The first two columns from left, show comparable results in term of clustering precision for the silhouette index. In fact, COBWEB and CCTree have both a good precision, when the CCTree purity is set to $\varepsilon = 0.001$ and the minimum number of elements is set to $\mu = 1$ (CCTree(0.001,1)). COBWEB performs slightly better on the silhouette index, for both distance measures. However, the difference (less than 2 percent) is negligible by considering that COBWEB creates almost twice more the number of clusters rather than CCTree(0.001,1). It can be inferred that a higher number of small clusters improves the internal homogeneity (e.g., a cluster with one element is totally homogeneous). However, as it will be detailed in the following, a number of clusters, strongly greater than the expected number of groups, is not desirable. Moreover, CCTree(0.001,1) returns better result for the Dunn index, with respect to COBWEB. We recall that the value of Dunn index is strongly affected by the cluster homogeneity of the worst resulting cluster. The value returned for CCTree(0.001,1) shows that all the returned clusters globally have a good homogeneity, compared to COBWEB, i.e. the worst cluster for CCTree(0.001,1) is much more homogeneous than the worst cluster for COBWEB. The rightest column of Table 2 reports the results for the CLOPE clustering algorithm. CLOPE is a categorical clustering algorithm, known to be fast in creating as much as possible pure clusters. The accuracy of CLOPE is quite limited for Silhouette, and zero for the Dunn index.

Table 2. Internal evaluation results of CCTree, COBWEB and CLOPE.

Algorithm	COBWEB	CCTree - $\varepsilon = 0.001$				CLOPE
		$\mu = 1$	$\mu = 10$	$\mu = 100$	$\mu = 1000$	
Silhouette (Hamming)	0.9922	0.9772	0.9264	0.7934	0.5931	0.2801
Silhouette (Jaccard)	0.9922	0.9777	0.9290	0.8021	0.6074	0.2791
Dunn (Hamming)	0.1429	0.5	0.1	0.0769	0.0769	0
Dunn (Jaccard)	0.1327	0.25	0.1	0.0879	0.0857	0
Clusters	1118	619	392	154	59	55
Time (s)	17.81	0.6027	0.3887	0.1760	0.08610	3.02

A graphical description of the accuracy difference between the clustering of Table 2 can be inferred from the Hamming Silhouette plots of Fig. 3. The plots are horizontal histograms in which every bar represents the silhouette result, $s(i) \in [-1, 1]$, for each data point x_i, as from the aforementioned definition. Both

COBWEB and `CCTree(0.001,1)` show no negative values, with the majority of data points scoring $s(i) = 1$. In fact, for `CCTree(0.001, 1000)` the worst data points do not score less than -0.5, whilst for CLOPE some data points have a silhouette of -0.8, which will cause a strong non-homogeneity in their clusters. Also, the number of data point with positive values are much more for `CCTree(0.001,1000)`, than for CLOPE. Finally, Table 2 also reports the time elapsed for the clustering performed by the algorithms. It can be observed that COBWEB pay its accuracy with an elapsed time of 17 s on the dataset of 10k emails, against the 3 s of the much more inaccurate CLOPE. The CCTree algorithm outperforms both COBWEB and CLOPE, requiring only 0.6 s in the most accurate configuration (`CCTree(0.001,1)`). From internal evaluation we can thus conclude that the CCTree algorithm obtains clusters whose quality is comparable with the ones of COBWEB, requiring even less computational time than the fast but inaccurate algorithm CLOPE.

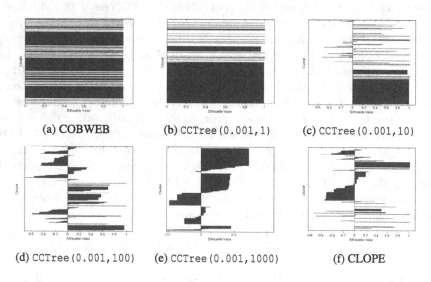

(a) COBWEB   (b) `CCTree(0.001,1)`   (c) `CCTree(0.001,10)`

(d) `CCTree(0.001,100)`   (e) `CCTree(0.001,1000)`   (f) CLOPE

Fig. 3. Silhouette plot.

4.2   CCTree Parameters Selection

Through internal evaluation and the results reported in Tables 2 and 3, we showed the dependence of the internal evaluation indexes and number of clusters to the values of μ and ε parameters. We will briefly discuss here some guidelines to correctly choose the CCTree parameters to maximize the clustering effectiveness.

Concerning the ε parameter, we showed in Sect. 4 that it is possible to find the optimal value of ε by setting $\mu = 1$ and varying the ε to find the fixed point in terms of accuracy, i.e. the optimal ε was considered the one for which the lesser amount of ε is not improving the accuracy.

Fixed the parameter ε, the parameter μ must be selected to balance the accuracy with the number of generated clusters. As the number of cluster is affected by the μ parameter, it is possible to choose the optimal value of μ knowing the optimal number of clusters. The problem of estimating the optimal number of clusters for hierarchical clustering algorithms, has been solved in [24], by determining the point of maximum curvature (*knee*) on a graph showing the inter-cluster distance in function of the number of clusters. Recalling that silhouette index is inversely related to inter-cluster distance, it is sound to find the knee on the graph of Fig. 4 computed with the silhouette (Hamming) on the dataset used for internal evaluation, with seven different values of μ. The graph reports the values computed on the same dataset used for internal evaluation. For the sake of representation, we do not show in this graph plots for μ greater than 100. Applying the L-method described in [24], it is possible to find that the knee is located at $\mu = 10$. A further insight can be taken from the results of Table 3 and Fig. 5, reporting the analysis on three additional datasets of spam emails coming from three different weeks of March 2015 from the spam honeypot in [1]. The sets have comparable size with the one of the dataset used for internal evaluation (first week of February 2015), with respectively 10k, 10k and 9k spam emails. From both the table and the graph it is possible to infer how the same trend for both silhouette value and number of clusters holds for all the tested datasets. Hence we verify (i) the validity of the knee methodology, (ii) the possibility of using the same CCTree parameters for datasets with the same data type and comparable size.

To give statistical validity to the performed analysis on parameter determinacy, we have analyzed a dataset of more than 200k emails collected from October 2014 to May 2015 from the honey pot in [1]. The emails have been divided in 20 datasets, containing 10k spam emails each. Each set represents one week

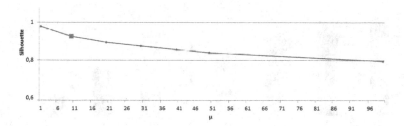

Fig. 4. Silhouette in function of the number of clusters for different values of μ.

Table 3. Silhouette values and number of clusters in function of μ for four email datasets.

Data	$\mu = 1$		$\mu = 10$		$\mu = 100$		$\mu = 1000$	
	Silhouette	Clusters	Silhouette	Clusters	Silhouette	Clusters	Silhouette	Clusters
February	0.9772	610	0.9264	385	0.7934	154	0.5931	59
March I	0.9629	635	0.9095	389	0.7752	149	0.6454	73
March II	0.9385	504	0.8941	306	0.8127	145	0.6608	74
March III	0.9397	493	0.8926	296	0.8102	131	0.6156	44

of spam emails. Figure 5 shows the average values for number of clusters and silhouette computed on the 20 dataset varying the value of the μ parameter with the values of the former experiments (i.e. 1, 10, 100, 1k). The standard deviation is also reported as error bars. It is worth noting that, the standard deviation for the values of $\mu = \{1, 10\}$ on 20 datasets is slightly higher than 2 %, while it reaches 4 % for $\mu = 100$ and 8 % for $\mu = 1000$, which is in line with the results of Table 3. Comparable results are also obtained for the number of clusters where the highest value for standard deviation is, as expected, for $\mu = 1$, amounting to 108, which again is in line with the results of Table 3. Thus, for all the 20 analyzed datasets, spanning eight months of spam emails, we can always locate the knee for silhouette and number of clusters when $\mu = 10$ (Fig. 6).

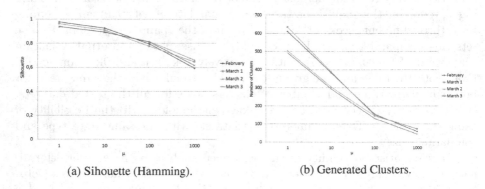

(a) Sihouette (Hamming).   (b) Generated Clusters.

Fig. 5. Trends of silhouette value and cluster number for four spam campaigns.

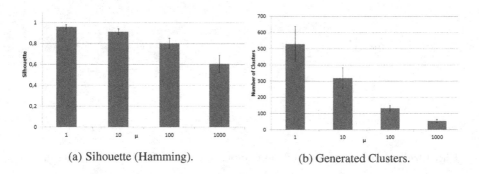

(a) Sihouette (Hamming).   (b) Generated Clusters.

Fig. 6. Average and standard deviation for silhouette value and amount of generated clusters in function of the μ parameter for 20 datasets.

4.3 External Evaluation

The external evaluation is a standard technique to measure the capability of a clustering algorithm to correctly classify data. To this end, external evaluation is performed on a small dataset, whose classes, i.e. the desired clusters, are known beforehand. A common index used for external evaluation is the F-measure [17], which coalesces in a single index the performance about correctly classified elements and misclassified ones.

Formally, let the sets $\{C_1, C_2, \ldots, C_k\}$ be the desired clusters (classes) for the dataset D, and let $\{C'_1, C'_2, \ldots, C'_l\}$ be the set of clusters returned by applying a clustering algorithm on D. Then, the F-measure $F(i)$ for each cluster C_i and the global F-measure F_c on the dataset are defined as follows:

$$F(i) = \max_{i,j} \frac{2|C_i \cap C'_j|}{|C_i| + |C'_j|} \qquad F_c = \sum_{i=1}^{k} F(i) \frac{|C_i|}{|\cup_{j=1}^{k} C_j|}$$

The F-measure result is returned in the range [0,1], where 1 represents the ideal situation in which the cluster C_i is exactly equal to one of the resulted clusters.

Experimental Results. For the sake of external evaluation, 276 spam emails collected from different spam folders of different mailboxes has been manually analyzed and classified. Emails have been divided in 29 groups (classes) according to the structural similarity of raw email message. The external evaluation set has no intersection with the one used for internal evaluation.

Table 4. External evaluation results of CCTree, COBWEB and CLOPE.

Algorithm	COBWEB	CCTree - $\varepsilon = 0.001$				CLOPE
		$\mu = 1$	$\mu = 5$	$\mu = 10$	$\mu = 50$	
F-Measure	0.3582	0.62	0.6331	0.6330	0.6	0.0076
Clusters	194	102	73	50	26	15

The results of external evaluation are reported in Table 4. Building on the results of internal evaluation, the value of node purity has been set to $\varepsilon = 0.001$ to obtain homogeneous clusters. The values of μ have been chosen according to the following rationale. $\mu = 1$ represents a CCTree instantiation in which the μ parameter does not affect the result. On the other hand $\mu = 50$ returns a number of clusters comparable with the 29 clusters manually collected. Higher values of μ do not modify the result for a dataset of this size. The best results are returned for $\mu = \{5, 10\}$. The F-measure for these two values is higher than 0.63, with a negligible difference, even if the number of generated clusters is higher than the expected one.

Table 4 also reports the comparison with the COBWEB and CLOPE algorithms. As shows CCTree algorithm outperforms COBWEB and CLOPE for the F-measure index, showing thus a higher capability in correctly classifying spam emails. We recall that for internal evaluation, COBWEB returned slightly better results than CCTree. The reason of this difference is resulted from the number of resulting clusters. COBWEB, in fact, always returns a high number of clusters (Table 4). This generally yields a high cluster homogeneity (several small and homogeneous clusters). However, it not necessarily implies a good classification capability. In fact, as shown in Table 4, COBWEB returns almost 200 clusters on a dataset of 276 emails, which is six times the expected number of clusters (i.e., 29 clusters). This motivates the lower F-measure score for the COBWEB algorithm. It is worth noting that the CCTree outperform COBWEB even if the minimum number of elements per node is not considered (i.e., $\mu = 1$). On the other hand, CLOPE also performs poorly on F-measure for the 276 emails dataset. The CLOPE algorithm, in fact, only produced 15 clusters, i.e. less than half of the expected ones, with an F-measure score of 0.0076.

5   Discussion and Comparisons

Combining the analysis of 21 features, the proposed methodology, becomes suitable to analyze almost any kind of spam emails. This is one of the main advantages with respect to other approaches, which mainly exploit one or two features to cluster spam emails into campaigns. These features are links [2,16], keywords [5,8,25], or images [33] alternatively. The analysis of these methodologies remains limited to those spam emails that effectively contain the attributed features. However, emails without links and/or images are a consistent percentage of spam emails. In fact, from the analysis of the dataset used for internal evaluation, 4561 emails out of 10165 do not contain any link. Furthermore, only 810 emails are containing images. To verify the clustering capability of these methodologies we have implemented three programs to cluster the emails of the internal evaluation dataset on the base of the contained URLs, reported domains and links of remote images. The emails without links and pictures have not been considered. Table 5 reports the generated number of clusters for each methodology. It is worth noting that on large dataset these cluster methodologies are highly inaccurate, generating a number of campaigns close to the number of analyzed elements, hence, almost every cluster has a single element. For comparison purpose we reported the results of the most accurate implementation of CCTree and of COBWEB, which we recall being able to produce extremely homogeneous cluster, reporting a Silhouette value of 99 %. We point out that, comparing Silhouette is meaningless, due to the different sets of used features. Comparisons with other methodologies such as the FPTree-based approaches

Table 5. Campaigns on the February 2015 dataset from five clustering methodologies.

Cluster methodology	Analyzed emails	Generated campaigns
Link based clustering	4561	4449
Domain based clustering	4561	4547
Image based clustering	810	807
COBWEB (21 features)	10165	1118
CCTree (0.001,10)	10165	392

[6,7], which require the extraction and analysis of a different set of features, are left as a future work.

6 Related Work

Another clustering approach exploiting a pairwise comparisons of email subjects is presented in Wei et al. [31]. The proposed methodology introduces a set of eleven features to cluster spam emails through two clustering algorithms. At first an agglomerative hierarchical algorithm is used to cluster the whole data set based on subject pairwise comparison. Afterward, the *connected component graph* algorithm is used to improve performance. The authors of [29] applied a methodology based on k-means algorithm, named O-means clustering, which exploits twelve features extracted from each email. The O-mean algorithm works on the hypothesis that the number of clusters is known beforehand, which is not always a working hypothesis. Furthermore, the authors use Euclidean distance, which for several features that they apply, it does not bring meaningful information. Differently from this approach the CCTree exploits the more general distance measure, i.e. Shannon entropy. Moreover the CCTree does not require the desired number of clusters as input parameter. An application of the presented approach in a goal-based spam classification problem, is discussed in [28].

Frequent Pattern Tree (FP-Tree), is another technique applied to detect spam campaigns in large datasets. The authors of [6,7] extract set of features from each spam message. The FP-Tree is built based on the frequency of features. The sensitive representation of both message layout and URL features, causes that two spam emails with small difference be assigned to different campaigns. For this reason, FP-Tree approach becomes prone to text obfuscation techniques [19], used to deceive anti-spam filters and to emails with dynamically generated links. Our methodology, based on categorical features which do not consider text and link semantics is more robust against these deceptions.

7 Conclusion and Future Directions

In this paper we proposed a methodology, based on a categorical clustering algorithm named CCTree, to cluster large amount of spam emails in campaigns, grouping them by structural similarity. The set of features representing message structure, have been precisely chosen and the intervals for each feature has been found through discretization approach. The CCTree algorithm has been extensively tested on two dataset of spam emails, to measure both the capability in generating homogeneous clusters and the specificity in recognizing predefined groups of spam emails. The guideline for selecting CCTree parameters is provided, whilst the determinacy of selected parameter for the similar data set with the same size has been proven statistically. Considering the proven accuracy and efficiency, the proposed methodology may stand as a valuable tool to help authorities in rapidly analyzing large amount of spam emails, with the purpose of finding and persecuting spammers.

As a future work we plan to extend the proposed framework, to target specific attacks brought through spam emails. In particular we argue that it is possible to extract from the CCTree structure, rules to recognize emails related to well known cyber-crimes such as phishing or scam. The framework will be used to rapidly detect and group spam campaigns related to attributed cyber-crimes, among large sets of real spam emails.

References

1. Spam archive. http://untroubled.org/spam/
2. Anderson, D., Fleizach, C., Savage, S., Voelker, G.: Spamscatter: Characterizing internet scam hosting infrastructure. In: Proceedings of 16th USENIX Security Symposium (2007)
3. Andritsos, P., Tsaparas, P., Miller, R.J., Sevcik, K.C.: LIMBO: scalable clustering of categorical data. In: Bertino, E., Christodoulakis, S., Plexousakis, D., Christophides, V., Koubarakis, M., Böhm, K. (eds.) EDBT 2004. LNCS, vol. 2992, pp. 123–146. Springer, Heidelberg (2004)
4. Bezdek, J., Pal, N.: Cluster validation with generalized dunn's indices. In: Proceedings of Second New Zealand International Two-Stream Conference on Artificial Neural Networks and Expert Systems, pp. 190–193 (1995)
5. Blanzieri, E., Bryl, A.: A survey of learning-based techniques of email spam filtering. Artif. Intell. Rev. **29**(1), 63–92 (2008)
6. Calais, P., Pires, D., Guedes, D., Meira, W., Hoepers, C., Steding-Jessen, K.: A campaign-based characterization of spamming strategies. In: CEAS (2008)
7. Dinh, S., Azeb, T., Fortin, F., Mouheb, D., Debbabi, M.: Spam campaign detection, analysis, and investigation. Digit. Invest. **12**(1(0)), S12–S21 (2015). DFRWS 2015 Europe Proceedings of the Second Annual DFRWS Europe
8. Drucker, H., Wu, D., Vapnik, V.: Support vector machines for spam categorization. IEEE Trans. Neural Netw. **10**(5), 1048–1054 (1999)
9. Fisher, D.: Knowledge acquisition via incremental conceptual clustering. Mach. Learn. **2**(2), 139–172 (1987)
10. Garcia, S., Luengo, J., Saez, J.A., Lopez, V., Herrera, F.: A survey of discretization techniques: taxonomy and empirical analysis in supervised learning. IEEE Trans. Knowl. Data Eng. **25**(4), 734–750 (2013)
11. Halkidi, M., Vazirgiannis, M.: Clustering validity assessment: finding the optimal partitioning of a data set. In: Proceedings of IEEE International Conference on Data Mining, ICDM 2001, pp. 187–194 (2001)
12. Hall, M., Frank, E., Holmes, G., Pfahringer, B., Reutemann, P., Witten, I.H.: The weka data mining software: an update. SIGKDD Explor. Newslett. **11**(1), 10–18 (2009)
13. Han, J., Kamber, M., Pei, J.: Data Mining: Concepts and Techniques, 3rd edn. Morgan Kaufmann Publishers Inc., San Francisco (2011)
14. Hedley, J.: Jsoup cookbook (2009). http://jsoup.org/cookbook
15. Kerber, R.: Chimerge: discretization of numeric attributes. In: Proceedings of the Tenth National Conference on Artificial Intelligence, AAAI 1992, pp. 123–128. AAAI Press (1992)
16. Li, F., Hsieh, M.: An empirical study of clustering behavior of spammers and groupbased anti-spam strategies. In: CEAS 2006 Third Conference on Email and AntiSpam, pp. 27–28 (2006)

17. Manning, C.D., Prabhakar, R., Schütze, H.: Introduction to Information Retrieval. Cambridge University Press, New York (2008)
18. Martin, S., Nelson, B., Sewani, A., Chen, K., Joseph, A.D.: Analyzing behavioral features for email classification. In: CEAS (2005)
19. Pu, C., Webb, S.: Observed trends in spam construction techniques: a case study of spam evolution. In: CEAS, pp. 104–112 (2006)
20. Radicati, S.: Email statistics report 2013–2017 (2013). http://goo.gl/ggLntn
21. Ramachandran, A., Feamster, N.: Understanding the network-level behavior of spammers. ACM SIGCOMM Comput. Commun. Rev. **36**(4), 291–302 (2006)
22. Rao, J., Reiley, D.: On the spam campaign trail, the economics of spam. J. Econ. Perspect. **26**(3), 87–110 (2012)
23. Rousseeuw, P.J.: Silhouettes: a graphical aid to the interpretation and validation of cluster analysis. J. Comput. Appl. Math. **20**, 53–65 (1987)
24. Salvador, S., Chan, P.: Determining the number of clusters/segments in hierarchical clustering/segmentation algorithms. In: Proceedings of the 16th IEEE International Conference on Tools with Artificial Intelligence, ICTAI 2004, pp. 576–584. IEEE Computer Society, Washington, DC (2004)
25. Seewald, A.: An evaluation of naive bayes variants in content-based learning for spam filtering. Intell. Data Anal. **11**(5), 497–524 (2007)
26. Shannon, C.E.: A mathematical theory of communication. SIGMOBILE Mob. Comput. Commun. Rev. **5**(1), 3–55 (2001)
27. Sheikhalishahi, M., Mejri, M., Tawbi, N.: Clustering spam emails into campaigns. In: Library, S.D. (ed.) 1st International Conference on Information Systems Security and Privacy (2015)
28. Sheikhalishahi, M., Saracino, A., Mejri, M., Tawbi, N., Martinelli, F.: Digital waste sorting: a goal-based, self-learning approach to label spam email campaigns. In: Foresti, S. (ed.) STM 2015. LNCS, vol. 9331, pp. 3–19. Springer, Heidelberg (2015)
29. Song, J., Inque, D., Eto, M., Kim, H., Nakao, K.: O-means: an optimized clustering method for analyzing spam based attacks. IEICE Trans. Fundam. Electron. Commun. Comput. Sci. **94**, 245–254 (2011)
30. Tretyakov, K.: Machine learning techniques in spam filtering. In: Data Mining Problem-Oriented Seminar, MTAT, vol. 3, pp. 60–79. Citeseer (2004)
31. Wei, C., Sprague, A., Warner, G., Skjellum, A.: Mining spam email to identify common origins for forensic application. In: Proceedings of the 2008 ACM Symposium on Applied Computing, SAC 2008, pp. 1433–1437 (2008)
32. Yang, Y., Guan, X., You, J.: Clope: A fast and effective clustering algorithm for transactional data. In: Proceedings of the Eighth ACM SIGKDD International Conference on Knowledge Discovery and Data Mining, KDD 2002, pp. 682–687. ACM, New York, USA (2002)
33. Zhang, C., Chen, W., Chen, X., Warner, G.: Revealing common sources of image spam by unsupervised clustering with visual features. In: Proceedings of the 2009 ACM Symposium on Applied Computing, SAC 2009, pp. 891–892. ACM, New York, USA (2009)

A Closer Look at the HTTP and P2P Based Botnets from a Detector's Perspective

Fariba Haddadi[(✉)] and A. Nur Zincir-Heywood

Faculty of Computer Science, Dalhousie University, Halifax, NS, Canada
{haddadi,zincir}@cs.dal.ca

Abstract. Botnets are one of the main aggressive threats against cyber-security. To evade the detection systems, recent botnets use the most common communication protocols on the Internet to hide themselves in the legitimate users traffic. From this perspective, most recent botnets are HTTP based and/or Peer-to-Peer (P2P) systems. In this work, we investigate whether such structural differences have any impact on the performance of the botnet detection systems. To this end, we studied the differences of three machine learning techniques (Decision Tree, Genetic Programming and Bayesian Networks). The investigated approaches have been previously shown effective for HTTP based botnets. We also analyze the detection models in detail to highlight any behavioural differences between these two types of botnets. In our analysis, we employed four HTTP based publicly available botnet data sets (namely Citadel, Zeus, Conficker and Virut) and four P2P based publicly available botnet data sets (namely ISOT, NSIS, ZeroAccess and Kelihos).

Keywords: Botnet detection · HTTP · P2P · Machine learning

1 Introduction

In the past couple of years, parties involved in information technology have experienced enormous growth in cybersecurity. Technology as one side of this domain has changed at an outstanding rate and threats, on the other hand, have evolved significantly. In this scope, botnets are considered as one of the most aggressive threats that are responsible for a large volume of malicious activities.

A botnet is a network of compromised hosts (i.e. bots) that are under the remote control of an offender, called botmaster. Bots are unwillingly and unknowingly utilized by the botmaster to carry out a diverse range of malicious activities from the distributed-denial-of-service (DDoS) attacks to identity thefts and spamming. On the other hand, masters have utilized various protocols (e.g. IRC, HTTP and DNS), topologies (i.e. centralized and de-centralized) and techniques (e.g. encryption and fluxing) since 2003. Such diverse structures have assisted the botmasters to evolve and defeat the detection systems of this field.

Botmaster forms the botnet through five phases called the initial infection, the secondary injection, the connection, the malicious C&C (Command and Control)

© Springer International Publishing Switzerland 2016
J. Garcia-Alfaro et al. (Eds.): FPS 2015, LNCS 9482, pp. 212–228, 2016.
DOI: 10.1007/978-3-319-30303-1_13

and the maintenance and update phases. Since a botnet can upgrade its structure (or any algorithm that is used by botnets) in the fifth phase of the lifecycle, automatic pattern discovery could potentially enable security systems to adapt to such changes in the botnet evolution. In this case, many detection approaches have been proposed based on various machine learning (ML) techniques. These approaches can be surveyed from the data perspective (i.e. the type of network data being analyzed and its representation) and the ML algorithms employed. From the data perspective, network traces should be represented to the algorithms through feature sets. Many of the approaches analyzed specific parts/packets of the network trace such as DNS queries, HTTP requests and their corresponding responses. Others utilized the flow[1] definition to aggregate discrete network packets into a collection for the analysis purposes. Network packets include two main parts: (i) Packet header, which includes the control information of the protocols used on the network, and (ii) Packet payload, which includes the application information used on the network. To be able to analyze communication information such as the domain names, payload information should be available in clear text. However, given that most recent botnets utilize encryption methods to encode the communication information, detection systems should be able decrypt the information. Using such approaches may not be practical given that the decryption process increases the computing complexity significantly. Moreover, the encryption methods/algorithms can be modified/changed on the fly. On the other hand, flow-based detection approaches can be very much useful since the features are only extracted from the packet header.

In our previous work, we have proposed to employ the flow features of the Tranalyzer flow exporter for botnet detection purposes. The effectiveness of this feature set was evaluated on eight HTTP-based botnets using ML techniques. However, botnets with the P2P topology (which may/may not use HTTP as their communication protocol) are also among the most recent aggressive types of botnets. Hence, in this work, we aim to evaluate the proposed approach as well as the suggested feature set against the P2P botnets. We also investigate whether the suggested approach can be as effective on the P2P botnets as it was on HTTP-based botnets. To this end, we use Tranalyzer [1] to extract the flow features from four P2P botnet data sets as well as four HTTP botnet data sets. Three ML algorithms (C4.5 decision tree, Bayesian Networks and the Symbiotic Bid-Based Genetic Programming (SBB)) are employed to build the detection system models. Furthermore, beside evaluating the effectiveness of the proposed approach, we also aim to analyze the trained detection models in order to highlight the behavioural differences of the HTTP and the P2P botnets. Last but not the least, a multi-class classification approach is designed to investigate whether each botnet would have enough discrepancy from the classifier's perspective to be distinguished from the others.

---

[1] Flow is defined as a logical equivalent for a call or a connection in association with a user specified group of elements [14]. The most common way to identify a traffic flow is to use a combination of five properties (aka 5-tuple) from the packet header, namely source/destination IP addresses and port numbers as well as the protocol.

The rest of the paper is structured as follows: The background and the related work on botnet traffic analysis are summarized in Sect. 2. Our methodology is discussed in Sect. 3. Evaluation and results are provided in Sect. 4. Finally, conclusions are drawn in Sect. 5.

2   Background and Related Work

A bot program is a self-propagating malware that infects vulnerable hosts known as bots (zombies) and is designed to perform specific malicious tasks after being triggered. Hosts can get infected with malwares in different ways such as visiting an untrusted malicious website or opening a malicious email attachment. Usually bots receive commands from the master through a communication server and carry out malicious tasks such as Distributed Denial of Service (DDoS), spamming, phishing and identity theft attacks [5,15].

Botnet architecture is categorized in different ways. In one method, centralized and de-centralized are considered as the two main categories of botnets. In the centralized model, command and data exchange between the master and bots is managed at the central C&C server. The C&C server uses different services/protocols to manage the botnet. IRC, HTTP and DNS are the most common protocols in this architecture, which is based on a client-server scheme. Easy implementation of the centralized communication channels and low latency are the two main advantages of this structure. The low latency is caused by the clear connections between the clients and the C&C servers. This feature is very important for the malicious tasks such as DDoS, which require the bots and the servers to be highly synchronized. However, the main disadvantage of this architecture is the single point of failure issue that is caused by the C&C servers. In this case, if the C&C servers are discovered by the botnet detection systems, the whole botnet can then be taken down. Having said this, discovering the botnets with centralized architecture is relatively easier since all the connections are going through specific C&C servers.

On the other hand, in the de-centralized category, botnets either use the P2P architecture or utilize techniques such as fluxing with the C&C based communication servers to compensate the characteristics of the centralized architecture. In the P2P structure, bots can act as both clients and servers. They do not contact any specific server for commands directly but receive the commands from their peers. Botnets with the de-centralized architecture are more resilient than centralized botnets. In other words, discovering and removing a bot from a P2P botnet or a C&C server from the list of all possible servers hardly affect the botnet mission. Moreover, analyzing botnets behaviour with the de-centralized architecture and detecting them is more complicated because of the distributed structure. However, the implementation complexity and latency of botnets in this category is notable comparing to the centralized structure.

The HTTP botnets and P2P botnets (which may or may not use HTTP as their communication protocol) are considered as the two main recent types of botnets. Hence, in this work, we aim to investigate these types of botnets in terms of any discrepancy in designing the detection systems and their performances. Wurzinger et al. proposed an approach to detect botnets based on the correlation of commands and responses in the monitored network traces [17]. To identify traffic responses, they located the corresponding commands in the preceding traffic. Then, using these command and response pairs, the detection model was built focusing on IRC, HTTP and P2P botnets. Data sets used in this work were collected by running bot binaries in a controlled environment. Traffic features such as the number of non-ASCII bytes in the payload were analyzed to characterize bot behavior. Zhang et al. proposed a botnet detection system to identify P2P botnets based on a two phase analysis of the traffic [18]. In the first phase, P2P hosts are identified regardless of being malicious or legitimate. To do this, Netflow features are extracted and then filtered based on the IP addresses associated with resolved DNS responses. In the second phase, the remaining flows are analyzed to differentiate the P2P botnet traffic from other legitimate P2P traffic. Wang et al. proposed a fuzzy pattern recognition approach (called BBDP) to detect HTTP and IRC botnet behavioral patterns [16]. It is known that botnets query several domain names in a given period of time to identify their C&C server, and then form a TCP connection with the C&C server. So, Wang analyzed the features of DNS queries (such as the number of failed DNS responses) and TCP flows to detect botnet malicious domain names and IP addresses. To accelerate the detection process and be able to detect botnets in real-time, traffic reduction and parallel processing were utilized. Their results showed up to 95 % detection rate for their system. Kirubavathi et al. designed specifically an HTTP-based botnet detection system using a multilayer Feed-Forward Neural network [12]. Given that HTTP-based botnets do not maintain a connection with the C&C server but periodically make a request to the C&C server (over the HTTP) to download the instructions, they extracted features related to TCP connections in specific time intervals based on the packet headers. To collect data to evaluate their system, botnets were simulated in the lab. Zhao et al. investigated a botnet detection system based on flow intervals [19]. Flow features of traffic packets were utilized with several ML algorithms where the decision tree classifier was finally selected as the preferred classifier to detect botnets. They focused on P2P botnets (such as Waledac) that employ the HTTP protocol and a fast-flux based DNS technique. Their proposed detection approach resulted in up to 99 % detection rates with false positive rate around 2 %. Beigi et al. investigated the effectiveness of flow-based feature sets employed in previous botnet detection studies and evaluated them using their own feature selection algorithm [3]. Their results indicated that the Byte-based group of features has less effect while the packet-based group has more impact. In their evaluation, IRC, HTTP and P2P botnet data sets were utilized. In our previous work, a machine learning based detection system was designed and evaluated on several HTTP botnets [10]. In addition to different machine learning algorithms, five flow feature sets were benchmarked and investigated in detail. The result of those analysis showed that the C4.5 classifier can detect HTTP based botnets using Tranalyzer feature set with up to 100 % detection rate. The proposed approach was also compared against the Snort intrusion detection system, a machine learning packet based system and BotHunter botnet detection system [8]. The comparison results showed that the approach outperforms the other three detection systems considering several performance criteria such as complexity and detection rate. Moreover, the performance of the proposed approach was evaluated over a period of time. The results indicated that not only the approach performs well facing the new versions of the botnet it is trained for but also, it can identify the change of topology by observing the changes in the performance [11].

In summary, some systems/approaches [16,17] require both the payload and the header section of the packets to extract the necessary features while others [10,19] only need the header of the packets (e.g. flow based systems). The importance of the approaches in the second group can be better understood knowing that the most recent aggressive botnets employ encryption to better hide themselves and their information from the detection systems. Our proposed approach stands in this group. Moreover, there are several studies on flow based botnet detection systems where each proposed their own set of features [18,19]. Some studies have analyzed the feature selection algorithms to extract the most effective feature sets [3]. Such feature selection processes can cause the models to be focused on specific type(s) of botnet(s) which may not be very effective for other types. Hence, using a ML algorithm that has the ability to perform attribute selection as an implicit property of constructing the classifier may be a better way to approach feature selection while utilizing all the possible extracted flow features. This is the main idea behind our previously proposed approach [10].

3   Methodology

As discussed in Sect. 1, flow based botnet detection systems are beneficial since most of the recent botnet traffic communications (placed in the packet payloads) are encrypted and such systems do not require payload information at all. On the other hand, using ML based techniques to build the detection system potentially provides the system with the ability to cope with the botnet upgrades using minimum apriori knowledge. In our previous work, we benchmarked five flow feature sets and five ML techniques in order to find the best performing combination [10]. Although the combination of Tranalyzer feature set with the C4.5 classifier was proposed as the final and best combination, the evaluation was only done on eight HTTP based botnets. Given that in addition to HTTP botnets, P2P botnets are also among the most recent destructive active botnets, we aim to examine the proposed system on the P2P architectures as well. To this end, four HTTP botnets and four P2P botnets are collected and three best-performed classifiers from our previous works [9,10] (i.e. C4.5 decision tree, Bayesian Networks and SBB) are selected and evaluated in this research. Moreover, for the feature extraction purpose, Tranalyzer flow exporter is utilized. Finally, additional experiments and model analysis are performed to reveal the behavioural differences between these two categories of botnets.

3.1 Learning Algorithms

The candidate ML algorithms in this work are C4.5 decision tree, Bayesian Networks and SBB.

C4.5 is an extension to ID3 algorithm that aims to find the small decision trees (using pruning) and then convert the trained tree into an if-then rule set. The algorithm employs a normalized information gain criterion to select attributes from a given set of attributes to determine the splitting point of the decision tree. In other words, the attribute with the highest information gain value is chosen as the splitting point. A more detailed explanation of the algorithm can be found in [2].

Bayesian Networks are graphical representations for probabilistic relationships among the variables given a set of discrete features. The graph nodes that are associated with the attributes, are connected through the links that correspond to the direct influence from one feature to the other. Given the Bayesian networks' structure, the conditional probability distribution of the graph is then computed. The learning process aims to find a Bayesian Network structure that describes the training data in the best possible way. Detailed explanation on Bayesian Networks can be found in [2].

SBB is a form of linear genetic programming with a co-evolutionary architecture [13]. Three populations are co-evolved in this algorithm: A point population, a team population and a learner population. The learner population represents a set of learners, which associate a GP-bidding behaviour with an action. The team population comprises a set of learners and finally the point population denotes a subset of training data exemplars. Evaluating a team on the points, all of the team's learner programs are executed while only the learner with the highest bid suggests its action as the team's action. The bidding procedure employs linear GP in addition to a sigmoid function to standardize the bid values between zero and one.

3.2 Traffic Employed

In this paper, eight publically available botnet traffic traces are employed for evaluation while four of them represent HTTP botnets behaviour and the rest represents P2P botnets behaviour. To the best of our knowledge, the P2P botnet data sets employed in this research are the only ones that are publicly available at this time. Furthermore, the HTTP botnet data sets are not only publicly available but also are different from the data sets used in our previous work [10]. By choosing different data sets in this work, we intend to explore and evaluate how much the performance of the proposed approach depends on the data sets and how well it generalizes.

Conficker (CAIDA), Zeus (NIMS), Citadel (NIMS), Virut (CVUT) are the sample data sets of the HTTP category. Conficker (CAIDA) is the Conficker botnet data set collected and published by the CAIDA organization. The data set is a three-day capture of Conficker version A and B which is anonymized. In other words, the payload information is removed and the CAIDA network addresses are masked. A more detailed description of the CAIDA Conficker data set can be found at [4]. Moreover, Zeus (NIMS) and Citadel (NIMS) are the Zeus and Citadel botnet data sets that are generated in the NIMS[2] lab sandbox. To generate these botnet traffic traces, Zeus botnet toolkit version 2.1.0.1 and Citadel botnet toolkit version 1.3.5.1 are utilized. In the sandbox testbed, 12 windows bots and one C&C server are configured and set up. Finally, Malware capture facility Project at the Czech Technical University in Prague (CVUT) have collected several malware traffic logs [6]. Virut (CVUT) is one of the data sets from this collection. Detailed information of this capture can be found at [7].

On the other hand, NSIS (CVUT), ZeroAccess (CVUT), Kelihos (CVUT) and ISOT (Uvic) are representative of P2P botnets used in this work. NSIS (CVUT), ZeroAccess (CVUT) and Kelihos (CVUT) are from the CVUT malware capture facility project [6] and ISOT (Uvic) is made publically available by the University of Victoria [19]. ISOT (Uvic) data set has combined two separate data sets of botnet malicious traffic from the French chapter of honeynet project on Strom and Waledac botnets. This combination of two botnets traffic represents the malicious side of the ISOT (Uvic) data sets.

In order to differentiate botnet behaviour from legitimate behaviour, a data set must include legitimate data samples, representing legitimate behaviours. In this case, ISOT (UVIC) data set includes traffic traces from two legitimate resources, the traffic Lab at Ericsson Research in Hungary and the Lawrence Berkeley National Laboratory (LBNL) in USA, to be representative of legitimate behaviours. However, all other seven data sets either do not have any legitimate traffic included or include some background traffic which may or may not represent legitimate behaviours. Given that other researchers in the literature have also used the LBNL traffic traces to represent the normal behaviour, we utilized and combined these traffic traces with the other seven data sets (all except the ISOT (Uvic)). Therefore, all of the data sets employed in this work share the same type of legitimate behaviour. Since we are not using the source/destination IP addresses and source/destination port numbers, different ranges of these four features will not affect the results.

ML approaches require the training and testing data sets to be presented by feature sets. However, network traces are formed by network packets and therefore, need to be processed in order to be represented by features. Although fields of the network packets can be utilized as features (in packet based detection approaches), aggregating the network packets into flows and extracting the flow features has been shown effective in the recent literature. Hence, in this research, Tranalyzer flow exporter is employed in the feature extraction phase. In general, flow exporters summarize network traffic utilizing the network packet headers only. These tools collect packet information with common characteristics such as IP addresses and port numbers, aggregate them into flows and then calculate some statistics such as the number of packets per flow etc. Tranalyzer is a lightweight uni-directional flow exporter that employs an extended version of

---

[2] Network Information Management and Security: https://projects.cs.dal.ca/projectx/.

NetFlow feature set to support 93 flow features. More detailed information on the tool and its feature set can be found in [1,10].

4   Evaluation and Results

As discussed earlier, in this paper, we aim to investigate any differences in terms of detection performances and solutions between HTTP and P2P botnets as well as the generalization of the approach from one data set to another. To this end, eight botnet data sets (four in each category) are evaluated using three ML algorithms, namely C4.5, Bayesian networks and SBB.

To prepare the data sets, Conficker (CAIDA), Kelihos (CVUT), NSIS (CVUT), Virut (CVUT), ZeroAccess (CVUT), Citadel (NIMS) and Zeus (NIMS) network traces are combined with LNBL legitimate network traces similar to the approaches used in the literature [19]. Tranalyzer flow exporter is then employed to extract the features and finally, uniform sampling was used to create balanced (in terms of malicious vs non-malicious samples) data sets for training purposes. We employed all of the numeric features provided by the Tranalyzer as inputs to the ML classifiers except the IP addresses and port numbers. The reasons behind this are: IP addresses can be anonymized whereas port numbers can be assigned dynamically. Thus, employing such features may decrease the generalization abilities of the detection systems for unseen behaviors. Table 1 shows the number of flow samples of all the eight data sets in addition to the original size of the data sets (traffic trace files before adding the LBNL traces).

Table 1. Specification of the data sets employed

Data set	Size	Sample count (# of flows)
Conficker (CAIDA)	183 GB	4135673
Kelihos (CVUT)	409 MB	1098448
NSIS.ay (CVUT)	281 MB	26294
ZeroAccess (CVUT)	59.2 MB	214442
Virut (CVUT)	109 MB	305664
Citadel (NIMS)	40.4 MB	12662
Zeus (NIMS)	18.7 MB	21356
ISOT (Uvic)	10.6 GB	197462

4.1   Performance Metrics

Performance. In traffic classification, two metrics are typically used in order to quantify the performance of the classifiers: Detection Rate (DR) and False Positive Rate (FPR). DR reflects the number of the correctly classified specific botnet samples in a given data set using $DR = \frac{TP}{TP+FN}$ where TP (True Positive) is the number of botnet traffic samples that are classified correctly, and FN (False Negative) is the number of botnet samples that are classified incorrectly (as legitimate samples). On the other hand, FPR shows the number of legitimate samples that are classified incorrectly as the botnet samples using $FPR = \frac{FP}{FP+TN}$ where TN (True Negative) is the number of legitimate traffic samples that are classified correctly.

Complexity. Classifier complexity can be measured by different criteria such as memory consumption, time or the learned model by the learning algorithms. In this work, two complexity criteria are utilized: **(1) training (computation) time** is employed where this is estimated on a common computing platform. **(2) solution complexity**, is measured using the tree size for C4.5 and the program size of the solution team for SBB. It should be noted here that a direct comparison between solutions from different representations is impossible since the underlying units of measurement are different in different ML algorithms.

4.2   Results

Table 2 shows the results of the three classifiers on all four HTTP data sets. Comparing the results of the three classifiers on the HTTP botnets, C4.5 and SBB performed the same. To this end, we expand our evaluations over time and solution complexity. Table 3 shows that there is no consistent pattern in the time complexity as C4.5 had the highest and the lowest training time of the table on Conficker (CAIDA) and Citadel (NIMS) data sets, respectively.

Table 2. Classification results of the HTTP botnets

Classifier	Data set	DR	Botnet		Legitimate	
			TPR	FPR	TNR	FNR
C4.5	Zeus (NIMS)	99.93 %	99.9 %	0.1 %	100 %	0.1 %
	Citadel (NIMS)	99.90 %	99.9 %	0.1 %	99.9 %	0.1 %
	Conficker (CAIDA)	99.95 %	100 %	0.1 %	99.9 %	0 %
	Virut (CVUT)	99.88 %	99.9 %	0.1 %	99.9 %	0.1 %
Bayesian Networks	Zeus (NIMS)	98.45 %	96.9 %	0 %	100 %	3.1 %
	Citadel (NIMS)	98.76 %	97.5 %	0 %	100 %	2.5 %
	Conficker (CAIDA)	98.62 %	99.1 %	1.9 %	98.1 %	0.9 %
	Virut (CVUT)	94.64 %	94.5 %	5.2 %	94.8 %	5.5 %
SBB	Zeus (NIMS)	99.97 %	99.94 %	0 %	100 %	0.06 %
	Citadel (NIMS)	100 %	100 %	0 %	100 %	0 %
	Conficker (CAIDA)	99.06 %	99.01 %	0.9 %	99.01 %	0.9 %
	Virut (CVUT)	98.29 %	98.25 %	1.77 %	98.33 %	1.75 %

Table 3. Complexity analysis of the classifiers on the HTTP botnets

Classifier	Data set	Time complexity (sec)	Solution complexity
C4.5	Zeus (NIMS)	2.11	41
	Citadel (NIMS)	1.06	31
	Conficker (CAIDA)	7454.18	1317
	Virut (CVUT)	215	481
SBB	Zeus (NIMS)	279.6	38
	Citadel (NIMS)	295.55	30
	Conficker (CAIDA)	235.439	58
	Virut (CVUT)	214.76	17

Table 4. Classification results of the P2P botnets

Classifier	Data set	DR	Botnet		Legitimate	
			TPR	FPR	TNR	FNR
C4.5	ZeroAccess (CVUT)	99.94 %	100 %	0.1 %	99.9 %	0 %
	Kelihos (CVUT)	99.93 %	99.9 %	0.1 %	99.9 %	0.1 %
	NSIS (CVUT)	99.23 %	99.3 %	0.8 %	99.2 %	0.7 %
	ISOT (Uvic)	99.83 %	99.8 %	0.2 %	99.8 %	0.2 %
Bayesian Networks	ZeroAccess (CVUT)	99.29 %	99.7 %	1.1 %	98.9 %	0.3 %
	Kelihos (CVUT)	93.16 %	93.8 %	7.4 %	92.6 %	6.2 %
	NSIS (CVUT)	95.94 %	93.6 %	1.8 %	98.2 %	6.4 %
	ISOT (Uvic)	96.49 %	99.2 %	6.2 %	93.8 %	0.8 %
SBB	ZeroAccess (CVUT)	99.39 %	99.63 %	0.84 %	99.16 %	0.37 %
	Kelihos (CVUT)	97.74 %	99.19 %	3.7 %	96.29 %	0.8 %
	NSIS (CVUT)	94.09 %	92.11 %	3.9 %	96.1 %	7.8 %
	ISOT (Uvic)	93.12 %	97.36 %	11.11 %	88.89 %	2.64 %

However, in terms of solution complexity, SBB consistently provides solutions with lower complexity. This confirms the results of our previous work on HTTP botnets [9].

On the other hand, Table 4 shows the evaluation results of the P2P data sets. In this case, C4.5 outperformed the other two classifiers. Unlike our experiments on HTTP botnets, SBB could not keep up with C4.5 and showed the lowest DR and the highest FPR. However, complexity analysis (Table 5) resulted in the same pattern as our HTTP botnets, indicating that SBB offers solutions with lower complexity.

Although SBB finds solutions with lower complexity in both types of botnets (HTTP and P2P), a high performance is still the primary goal in malware detection systems. Hence, SBB's lower performance on P2P botnets makes C4.5 the desirable classifier in this work. Comparing the C4.5 classification results of the HTTP and the P2P botnets, the classifier performed equally well on both types

Table 5. Complexity analysis of the classifiers on the P2P botnets

Classifier	Data set	Time complexity (sec)	Solution complexity
SBB	ZeroAccess (CVUT)	279.6	38
	Kelihos (CVUT)	295.55	30
	NSIS (CVUT)	235.439	58
	ISOT (Uvic)	214.76	17
C4.5	ZeroAccess (CVUT)	94.85	135
	Kelihos (CVUT)	1149.57	849
	NSIS (CVUT)	5.38	275
	ISOT (Uvic)	82.57	525

of botnet. Hence, in terms of detection capability and performance, we can conclude that our ML detection approach (combination of Tranalyzer flow exporter and C4.5 classifier), which was previously suggested for HTTP botnets, can be a valid choice for the P2P botnet detection systems as well. Moreover, some of the data sets employed in this paper are used by other researchers in the literature. For example, Zhao et al. achieved DRs between 97.9 to 99.9 % on the ISOT (Uvic) data set [19] and Beigi et al. obtained DRs between 75 % to 99 % on different combination of data sets including ISOT (Uvic), Virut (CVUT), ZeroAccess (CVUT) and NSIS (CVUT) [3]. This shows the performance achieved by our ML detection approach is not only comparable to other approaches in the literature but also outperformed those approaches in some cases.

Comparing the C4.5 complexity results, we notice higher complexity (time and solution) on the P2P botnets. However, this might be very much caused by the differences of the botnets' behaviour or even the data sets with different number of samples. Hence, to shed more light into this, we analyzed and compared the trained C4.5 classification models to understand if there are any obvious characteristics in the models that can specifically point out the differences of the P2P and the HTTP botnets. Table 7 shows the top features (on the first three levels of the trees) of the C4.5 decision trees with the highest information gain. The description of the features named in this work can be found in Table 6 while the description of all the features supported by Tranalyzer are available at [1]. This analysis indicates that: (i) Packet-based and Byte-based features (such as minPktSz or UppQuartilePl) are used by C4.5 for both types of botnets. (ii) Various connection-based features (such as ConnSrcDst or ConnSrc) are utilized for all of the P2P botnets. (iii) TTL-based features (such as ipMinTTL) are mostly used by the P2P botnets. (iv) Inter-arrival based features are only used for the HTTP botnets.

Going one step further, we also analyzed the features that are most frequently utilized by C4.5 in Table 8. The analysis also confirms that the packet-based and the byte-based features are frequently used for both types of botnets. On the other hand, the inter-arrival based features are only selected and used for

Table 6. Brief description of some of the Tranalyzers' features

Feature	Description
connSrc	Number of connections from source IP to different hosts
connDst	Number of connections from destination IP to different hosts
connSrcDst	Number of connections between source IP and destination IP
numBytesSnt	Number of transmitted bytes
numBytesRcvd	Number of received bytes
bytePS	Send bytes per second
minPktSz	Minimum layer3 packet size
maxPktSz	Maximum layer3 packet size
numPktsSnt	Number of transmitted packets
numPktsRcvd	Number of received packets
RangePl	Range of packet lengths
pktPS	Send packets per second
UppQuartilePl	Upper quartile of packet lengths
pktAsm	Packet stream asymmetry
tcpOptPktCnt	TCP options Packet count
tcpWS	TCP Window Scale
tcpAvcWinSz	TCP average window size
tcpInitWinSz	TCP initial window size
tcpPSeqCnt	TCP packet seq count
tcpRTTAckTripAve	TCP Ack Trip Average
ipMinTTL	IP Minimum TTL
ipMaxTTL	IP Maximum TTL
ipTTLChg	IP TTL Change count
MinIat	Minimum inter-arrival time
skewIat	Skewness of inter-arrival times
lowQuartileIat	Lower quartile of inter-arrival times
tcpMSS	TCP Maximum Segment Length
ipMaxdIPID	IP Maximum delta IP ID

the HTTP botnets. Finally, the connection-based features are utilized for the P2P botnets more than the HTTP botnets. However, unlike our observation on features with the highest information gain, TTL-based features are used for both types of botnets. In short, connection-based features seem to be more important for the P2P botnet detection. This might be because of the frequent connections between the peers on the network. Intuitively, this makes sense to us. On the other hand, inter-arrival based features are more likely to be significant in HTTP botnet detection. This might be because of the automated way that C&C servers

Table 7. Features with the highest information gain

Type	Data set	Features
P2P	ZeroAccess (CVUT)	ConnSrcDst, minPktSz, ConnSrc, tcpWS, ipMinTTL
	Kelihos (CVUT)	ipMinTTL, pktPS, tcpAveWinSz, tcpOptPktCnt, Duration, ipTTLChg, connDst
	NSIS (CVUT)	minPktSz, pktPS, connSrcDst, pktAsm, connSrc, numBytesRcvd
	ISOT (Uvic)	connSrcDst, UppQuartilePl, connDst, ipMinTTL
HTTP	Zeus (NIMS)	tcpInitWinSz, pktPS, MinIat, SkewIat, pktPS, numPktsSnt
	Citadel (NIMS)	tcpRTTAckTripAve, bytPS, MinIat, ipMaxTTL, connDst
	Conficker (CAIDA)	numPktsRcvd, numBytesSnt, minPktSz, Duration
	Virut (CVUT)	maxPktSz, tcpPSeqCnt, pktPS, lowQuartileIat, pktAsm, RangePl, connDst

Table 8. Features with the highest frequency

Type	Data set	Features
P2P	ZeroAccess (CVUT)	connSrc, connDst, numBytesSnt, ipMinTTL, minPktSz, numBytesRcvd
	Kelihos (CVUT)	numBytesRcvd, numBytesSnt, connSrc, MinPktSize, connDst, tcpInitWinSz
	NSIS (CVUT)	ipMinTTL, connDst, MinPktSz, numBytesSnt, connSrc, numBytesRcvd
	ISOT (Uvic)	connSrcDst, ipMinTTL, MaxPktSz, numBytesRcvd, connDst, numBytesSnt
HTTP	Zeus (NIMS)	pktPS, ipMaxIPID, pktAsm, MinIat, ipMaxTTL
	Citadel (NIMS)	MinIat, ipMaxTTL, numBytesSnt, minPktSz, RangeIat
	Conficker (CAIDA)	ipMinTTL, TcpInitWinSz, Duration, ipMaxdIPID, connDst, tcpMSS
	Virut (CVUT)	ipMinTTL, numpktRcvd, connDst, TcpInitWinSz, connSrc, MaxPktSz

and the bots are configured to communicate. In other words, bots and servers are setup to talk based on specific time intervals. Moreover, as our previous works have also indicated, packet based and byte based features are important given that botnets behave differently in terms of the number of packets and bytes sent/received compared to the behaviours of the legitimate users.

Although we have observed discrepancy between the HTTP and the P2P botnet detection models in terms of features with the highest information gain or frequency, all the aforementioned important categories of features were used by the C4.5 classifier for both types of botnets in order to build the detection model. In other words, they all have been appeared in the decision trees of both types of botnets at some point. Hence, we cannot exclusively assign/relate any categories of features to P2P or HTTP botnets. This might be caused by the fact that P2P botnets can use HTTP protocol as the base of communication (forming some similarities). Kelihos and ZeroAccess are good examples of such kind of P2P botnets, which are employed in this work.

In summary, we aimed to evaluate the combination of Tranalyzer feature set and C4.5 classification algorithm on P2P botnets given that this combination was shown to be effective on HTTP botnets. The analysis, evaluation and results show that this approach is as effective for P2P botnets as it was for HTTP botnets. Moreover, we could not highlight any obvious differences between the HTTP and P2P classification models to demonstrate the differences of botnet behaviours. Thus, the new research question to answer is: How would this combination handle a traffic trace that consists of P2P botnets, HTTP botnets and legitimate traces? In other words, can this combination differentiate botnet behaviours (P2P and HTTP) from legitimate behaviours? To this end, we generated a new balanced data set combining all the eight botnet data sets employed in this work labeled as "botnet" and the LBNL legitimate data set labeled as "legitimate". We refer to this data set as HPL (HttpP2pLegitimate) with 3005999 botnet samples and 3005999 legitimate samples. Table 9 shows the results of this classification indicating that C4.5 can classify the HTTP and the P2P botnet behaviours from legitimate behaviours using Tranalyzer feature set. Features with the highest information gain in this classification model are: numBytesSnt, tcpPSeqCnt, connSrcDst, connDst, ipOptCnt, connSrc, minPkt8z, ipMinTTL, MinIat.

The result also shows that the HTTP and the P2P botnets do have some similarities since C4.5 can put them together as one class. This can be based on the HTTP protocol that is used by the P2P botnets or the similar automated nature of botnet behaviours in general. Hence, to understand if these botnets have enough distinct behaviours that can be used to differentiate them despite the similarities, we run another experiment. In this new experiment, we generated a multi-class data set, called HPL-multiClass which has nine classes: one legitimate class and eight botnet classes (four HTTP and four P2P classes). Since some of the data sets used in this work are much larger than the others (such as Conficker), we kept the new multi-class data set unbalanced, which consists of all of the samples mentioned in Table 1. The result of this experiment is shown

Table 9. HTTP and P2P botnets versus legitimate behaviour

Classifier	Data set	DR	Botnet		Legitimate		Complexity	
			TPR	FPR	TNR	FNR	Time	Solution
C4.5	HPL	99.9 %	99.99 %	0.1 %	99.9 %	0.1 %	13171.78	5781

Table 10. HPL-multiClass classification results

Type	Data set	TPR	FPR
P2P	ZeroAccess (CVUT)	99.8%	0%
	Kelihos (CVUT)	99.8%	0%
	NSIS (CVUT)	96.8%	0%
	ISOT (Uvic)	99.4%	0%
HTTP	Zeus (NIMS)	92.8%	0%
	Citadel (NIMS)	91.0%	0%
	Conficker (CAIDA)	100%	0%
	Virut (CVUT)	99.8%	0%
Legitimate	LBNL	99.9%	0.1%
	Overall DR = 99.88%		
	Score = 97.7%		

in Table 10, indicating that C4.5 performed well while being able to differentiate eight different botnet behaviours from legitimate behaviours (with overall DR of 99.88%). However, given that this is an unbalanced multi-class classification, a classwise average DR can better demonstrate the performance. To this end, we utilized *Score* measure, which summarizes the classwise detection rates of a classifier over all classes. Score criteria is defined as, Eq. 6, [13]:

$$Score = \frac{1}{|C|} \sum_{c \in C} DET_c \qquad (1)$$

where $DETc$ is the detection rate for class c. Based on Score, we conclude that the HTTP, P2P botnets and legitimate traces employed in this work can be differentiated with the accuracy of 97% despite the similarities shown in the previous experiment (Table 9). Moreover, the results indicate that the TPR of Zeus (NIMS), Citadel (NIMS) and NSIS (CVUT) are not as high as the other five botnets. Analyzing the confusion matrix showed that: (i) almost all the Zeus (NIMS) miss-classified samples are classified as Citadel (NIMS), (ii) almost all of the Citadel (NIMS) miss-classified samples are classified as Zeus (NIMS), and (iii) most of the NSIS (CVUT) miss-classified samples are classified as Legitimate, Conficker (CAIDA), Virut (CVUT) and Kelihos(CVUT). We believe that the Citadel and Zeus miss-classification pattern is caused by the fact that Citadel botnet is an enhanced version of the Zeus botnet, and therefore they share some similarities in behaviours. On the other hand, NSIS (CVUT) miss-classification pattern showed that this botnet has some similarities with HTTP botnets in terms of behaviour, which should be further investigated.

5   Conclusions

A Botnet, which is a network of infected hosts remotely controlled by a botmaster, is considered as one of the main cybersecurity challenges given the variety, the high infection rate and the extended range of malicious tasks. Being able to upgrade any part of the structure on the fly is one of the reasons why this type of malware could sustain itself since 2003. To this end, detection systems also require automatic and intelligent mechanisms to cope with the updates. In this work, we employed three machine learning algorithms, namely C4.5, Bayesian Networks and SBB, to generate botnet detection models for several types of botnets such as Zeus, Citadel, Virut, Conficker, Kelihos and ZeroAccess. These botnets can be categorized into two main groups: HTTP and P2P. To represent the traffic traces, Tranalyzer flow exporter was utilized which aggregate the packets into traffic flows and extract their features.

Our main objective in this work was to investigate the possibility of detecting P2P botnets with our previously proposed approach on HTTP botnets. As the results indicate, the combination of Tranalyzer feature set and the C4.5 ML algorithm can also be effective in P2P botnet detection. We obtained the DR of up to 99.95 %. Additionally, similarities and differences of these botnets were further investigated by two multi-botnet classification scenarios. Again the detection performances were very promising, reaching up to 99.9 %. Moreover, the detection models are analyzed and compared using the features selected and utilized by the C4.5 decision trees in order to highlight the behavioural differences between the HTTP and the P2P botnets, if possible. In this case, the features with the highest information gain and the highest frequency are investigated. The analysis showed that some of the features could potentially be more useful in P2P botnet detection (such as connection-based features) while some others can be better to describe the HTTP botnets (such as inter-arrival based features). This is to say that these features cannot be specifically assigned to one type of botnet (HTTP or P2P). However, the degree of importance might be different.

Acknowledgments. This research is supported by the Canadian Safety and Security Program(CSSP) E-Security grant. The CSSP is led by the Defense Research and Development Canada, Centre for Security Science (CSS) on behalf of the Government of Canada and its partners across all levels of government, response and emergency management organizations, nongovernmental agencies, industry and academia.

References

1. Tranalyzer. http://tranalyzer.com/
2. Alpaydin, E.: Introduction to Machine Learning. MIT Press, Cambridge (2004)
3. Beigi, E.B., Jazi, H., Stakhanova, N., Ghorbani, A.: Towards effective feature selection in machine learning-based botnet detection approaches. In: Communications and Network Security (CNS) (2014)

4. CAIDA Conficker. http://www.caida.org/data/passive/telescope-3days-conficker-dataset.xml
5. Feily, M., Shahrestani, A.: A survey of botnet and botnet detection emerging security information. In: Systems and Technologies (2009)
6. Garcia, S.: Malware capture facility project, cvut university, February 2013. https://agents.fel.cvut.cz/malware-capture-facility
7. Garcia, S., Grill, M., Stiborek, J., Zunino, A.: An empirical comparison of botnet detection methods. Comput. Secur. **45**, 100–123 (2014)
8. Haddadi, F., Cong, D.L., Porter, L., Zincir-Heywood, A.N.: On the effectiveness of different botnet detection approaches. In: ISPEC (2015)
9. Haddadi, F., Runkel, D., Zincir-Heywood, A., Heywood, M.: On botnet behaviour analysis using GP and C4.5. In: Gecco Companion (2014)
10. Haddadi, F., Zincir-Heywood, A.N.: Benchmarking the effect of flow exporters and protocol filters on botnet traffic classification. IEEE Syst. J. **PP**(99), 1–12 (2014). doi:10.1109/JSYST.2014.2364743. http://ieeexplore.ieee.org/xpls/abs_all.jsp?arnumber=6963332&tag=1
11. Haddadi, F., Zincir-Heywood, A.N.: Botnet detection system analysis on the effect of botnet evolution and feature representation. In: Gecco Companion (2015)
12. Kirubavathi, V., Nadarajan, R.: Http botnet detection using adaptive learning rate multilayer feed-forward neural network. In: Information Security Theory, Practice: Security, Privacy and Trust in Computing Systems and Ambient Intelligent Ecosystems (2012)
13. Lichodzijewski, P., Heywood, M.I.: Coevolutionary bid-based genetic programming for problem decomposition in classification. Genet. Program. Evolvable Mach. **9**, 331–365 (2008)
14. RFC 2722, October 1999. http://tools.ietf.org/html/rfc2722
15. Vuong, S.T., Alam, M.S.: Advanced methods for botnet intrusion detection systems. In: Intrusion Detection Systems (2011)
16. Wang, K., Huang, C., Lin, S., Lin, Y.: A fuzzy pattern-based filtering algorithm for botnet detection. Comput. Netw. **55**, 3275–3286 (2011)
17. Wurzinger, P., Bilge, L., Holz, T., Goebel, J., Kruegel, C., Kirda, E.: Automatically generating models for botnet detection. In: Backes, Michael, Ning, Peng (eds.) ESORICS 2009. LNCS, vol. 5789, pp. 232–249. Springer, Heidelberg (2009)
18. Zhang, J., Perdisci, R., Lee, U.S.W., Luo, Z.: Detecting stealthy p2p botnets using statistical traffic fingerprints. In: Dependable Systems and Networks (DSN) (2011)
19. Zhao, D., Traore, I., Sayed, B., Lu, W., Saad, S., Ghorbani, A., Garant, D.: Botnet detection based on traffic behavior analysis and flow intervals. Comput. Secur. J. **39**, 2–16 (2013). doi:10.1016/j.cose.2013.04.007. http://www.sciencedirect.com/science/article/pii/S0167404813000837. Part A

Obfuscation Code Localization Based on CFG Generation of Malware

Nguyen Minh Hai[1], Mizuhito Ogawa[2]([✉]), and Quan Thanh Tho[1]

[1] Ho Chi Minh City University of Technology, Ho Chi Minh City, Vietnam
{hainmmt,qttho}@cse.hcmut.edu.vn
[2] Japan Advanced Institute of Science and Technology, Nomi, Japan
mizuhito@jaist.ac.jp

Abstract. This paper presents a tool BE-PUM (Binary Emulator for PUshdown Model generation), which generates a precise control flow graph (CFG), under presence of typical obfuscation techniques of malware, e.g., *indirect jump, self-modification, overlapping instructions*, and *structured exception handler (SEH)*, which cover *packers*. Experiments are performed on 2000 real-world malware examples taken from *VX Heaven* and compare the results of a popular commercial disassembler IDA Pro, a state-of-the-art tool JakStab, and BE-PUM. It shows that BE-PUM correctly traces CFGs, whereas IDA Pro and JakStab fail. By manual inspection on 300 malware examples, we also observe that the starts of these failures exactly locate the entries of obfuscation code.

Keywords: Concolic testing · Binary code analysis · Malware · Obfuscation

1 Introduction

Recently, control flow graphs (CFGs) attract attention in malware detection at industry levels, e.g., VxClass at Google. They use semantic fingerprints [24,29,36] to overcome the limitation on advanced polymorphic viruses of bits-based fingerprints [15,35], which are popular in commercial antivirus software. Semantic fingerprints consist of code and control flow graph fragments, which are obtained by disassembly. Then, the similarity is detected by statistical methods.

Beyond detection, malware classification requires more precise control flow graphs to observe what kinds of obfuscation/infection techniques are used. However, precise disassembly is not easy. For instance, commercial disassemblers, e.g., IDA Pro and Capstone, are easily cheated by typical obfuscation techniques, like *indirect jump, structured exception handler, overlapping instructions*, and *self-modification*. Typical self-modification is a self-decryption, and often by modifying encryption keys, a polymorphic virus mutates. Worse, recent *packers*, e.g., UPX, Themida, Telock, PECompact, Yoda, give us easy generation of polymorphic viruses.

Our ultimate goal is malware classification by their obfuscation techniques. As the first step, the aim of this research is to generate a precise CFG of

© Springer International Publishing Switzerland 2016
J. Garcia-Alfaro et al. (Eds.): FPS 2015, LNCS 9482, pp. 229–247, 2016.
DOI: 10.1007/978-3-319-30303-1_14

x86/Win32 binary under presence of typical obfuscation techniques, which includes precise disassembly. As a byproduct, we observe that when the results of IDA Pro and BE-PUM differ, they locate the entries of the obfuscation code.

Corresponding to the nature of dynamic parsing of x86, we apply on-the-fly CFG generation. To handle self-modification, we regard a CFG node as a pair of a location and an instruction, such that a modified code is regarded as a different node. They are also applied in McVeto [37], but different from its CEGAR approach, we apply dynamic symbolic execution (concolic testing) in a breadth-first manner to decide the next destinations of multiple paths at a conditional jump [12]. Concolic testing requires a binary emulator. Our choice is to restrict the binary emulation to a user process, and APIs are handled by stubs. This gives the flexibility to handle anti-debugging and trigger-based behavior [9], at the cost of manual stub construction and approximation.

The framework is implemented as BE-PUM (Binary Emulator for PUshdown Model generation), and experiments are performed on 2000 real-world malware taken from VX Heaven[1] to compare the results of a popular commercial disassembler IDA Pro, a state-of-the-art tool JakStab, and BE-PUM. It shows that BE-PUM correctly traces CFGs, whereas IDA Pro and JakStab fail. By manual inspection on 300 malware examples, we also observe that the starts of the failures exactly locate the entries of obfuscation code.

Contributions. Each element of the techniques in BE-PUM is not new, e.g., on-the-fly control flow graph generation [37,38], dynamic symbolic execution (concolic testing) [12,13], and formal x86 (32bit) semantics [7]. Dynamic symbolic execution for precise CFG generation is also not new, e.g., for C [34] and x86 binaries of system software [28]. Our contributions are:

- We compose them as a tool BE-PUM to generate precise CFG of x86 binary under the presence of obfuscation techniques, and its precision and practical efficiency are confirmed by empirical study.
- A preliminary BE-PUM was presented in [27], which supports 18 x86 instructions, no Windows APIs, and no self-modifying code. Current BE-PUM is extended to support about 200 x86 instructions and 310 Win32 APIs.
- We observe that when the results of IDA Pro and BE-PUM differ, they correctly locate the entry points of obfuscation codes.

CFGs generated by disassembler tools can be used to build models for model checking malware [4,16,18,19,32,33]. For instance, a CFG generated by IDA Pro was used for this purpose in [32,33]. Our approach immediately boosts such model checking by providing more precise models.

Another popular method to detect malware behavior is dynamic execution on binary emulators. However, malware behavior observation is sometimes not enough for classifying techniques. Even worse, dynamic execution may miss hidden behavior of malware. For instance, malware detects that they are in a sandbox by anti-debugging techniques, e.g., observing response time, checking

---

[1] http://vx.netlux.org.

behavior of rarely used Windows APIs, and calling the API "IsDebuggerPresent". Another difficulty is trigger-based behaviors [9, 25, 31], e.g., attacks triggered by specific date and time. We believe that semantic understanding of malware will compensate these limitations.

2 Typical Obfuscation Techniques and Their Difficulty

Roughly speaking, malware techniques consist of three steps.

1. Obfuscation, e.g., complex control flow to get rid of the bit-based detection, and anti-debugging to hide malicious intention during sandbox emulation.
2. Infection/spreading techniques, e.g., attacking Windows security holes.
3. Malicious behavior, e.g., information leak.

We focus on the first step. Nowadays, at least 75 % of malware uses a packer [30]. The original aim of a packer is the code compaction, and later includes obfuscation techniques to evade reverse engineering for software license protection. Most of control flow obfuscation are combinations of techniques below.

- **Indirect jump.** This technique stores the target of the jump in a register, a memory address, or a stack frame (jumping with ret), of which these values are often modified with arithmetic operations. It also appears as *overlapping instruction* [21], which confuses the boundary of instructions at the binary level.
- **Structured exception handler (SEH).** When exceptions like *division by zero* and *write on protected area* occur, the control is spawn to a system error handler and the stack is switched to another memory area in the user process. When the system error handler ends, the control returns to the user process, and the stack is recovered to the original. An SEH is an exception handler in a user process, prepared for post processing of an exception. SEH techniques often modify the return address at fs: [0x00].
- **Self modifying code (SMC).** During the execution, binary code loaded on memory is modified. Often, it appears as *Self decryption*, in which the execution of a header part modifies the later part of binary code.
- **Entry point obscuring.** The entry point is set to outside the .code section.

IDA Pro is the most popular commercial disassembler, which combines recursive disassembly and linear sweep. We show obfuscation examples, in which IDA Pro is confused.

Indirect Jump. Indirect jump hides the control flow by storing the target of a jump in a register or memory. *Virus.Adson.1559* shows a typical approach to dynamically load a library by calling Windows API *GetProcAddress* for retrieving the address of the target API. By calling convention of the API, the return value of *GetProcAddress* is stored in the register *eax* and it calls the API by jumping to the value of *eax*.

```
004024A6   50                   PUSH EAX ; FindFirstFileA
004024A7   FFB5 36324000        PUSH DWORD PTR SS:[EBP+403236]
                                   ; Kernel32 Handle
004024AD   FF95 3A324000        CALL DWORD PTR SS:[EBP+40323A]
                                   ; Call GetProcAddress
004024B3   FFE0                 JMP EAX ; Call FindFirstFileA
```

IDA Pro fails to resolve the next address at $004024B3$, and JakStab as well.

Overlapping Instruction. From $0040B332$ to $0040B334$ and $0040B326$ to $0040B32C$ in *Virus.Bagle.bf* (from the VX Heaven), it pops the value $0040B08F$ from the stack (as *esp* points to $0012FFA4$) to *ecx* and increments its value. Then, it pushes the value $0040B090$ of *ecx* to the stack again. At $0040B32C$, ret jumps to $0040B090$, where the binary code is EB 13 EB 02 and interpreted as jmp 0x0040b0a5, whereas IDA-Pro jumps to $0040B08F$ and fails to interpret E8 EB 13 EB 02.

		IDA-Pro	Correct CFG
0040B08A	E89E020000	call sub_40B32D	
0040B08F	E8EB13EB02	call near ptr 32BC47Fh	
0040B090	EB13FB02		jmp 0x0040b0a5
...			
0040B326	EB03	jmp short loc_40B32B	jmp 0x0040b32b
0040B32B	51	push ecx	pushl
0040B32C	C3	retn	ret
...			
0040B332	59	pop ecx	popl
0040B333	41	inc ecx	incl
0040B334	EBF0	jmp short loc_40B326	jmp 0x0040b326

3   CFG Reconstruction Techniques

3.1   Concrete Model and Its On-the-fly Generation

The execution of binary code is dynamic, i.e., interpret a binary sequence that starts from a memory address pointed by the register eip, which decides the next address to set eip. Corresponding to such nature, our CFG construction is designed in an on-the-fly manner. In the figure below, when a CFG node is a conditional jump, we apply concolic testing to decide next destinations.

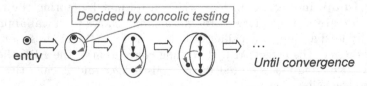

The state of a binary program can be regarded as an environment consisting of values of registers, flags, and a memory status (which includes the status of the stack). Our concrete model represents such a state by a pair $\langle (k, asm), \psi(\bar{\alpha}) \rangle$ of a CFG node and a path condition $\psi(\bar{\alpha})$ of a path $\bar{\alpha}$ reaching from the initial CFG node to (k, asm). This path condition encodes the environment after the execution from the entry point. We adopt a pair of a location and an instruction as a CFG node to handle self-modifying code. When self-modification occurs, we distinguish (k, asm) and (k, asm') as different CFG nodes. This idea is also used in McVeto [37]. We fix the notation as.

- k is an address in M and k_0 is the entry address,
- asm is an x86 assembly instruction,
- asm obtained by disassembly of a binary sequence starting from $k \in M$ is referred by $asm = instr(Env_M, k)$,
- $(m, asm') = next(k, asm)$ with $k = Env_R(eip)$ and $asm = instr(Env_M, k)$ is decided by a transition $Env \rightarrow Env'$ (described in Fig. 1) as $m = Env'_R(eip)$ and $asm' = instr(Env'_M, m)$.

3.2 Concolic Testing and Multiple Path Detection

Symbolic execution [22] is a traditional technique to symbolically execute a program, which maintains a symbolic state $\langle p, \psi \rangle$ where p is a CFG node and ψ is a path formula of the path from the initial CFG node to p. A path formula ψ describes the precondition of the execution path to p, starting from the precondition at the program entry. If ψ is satisfiable (often checked by SAT/SMT solvers), the path is *feasible*.

In binary code, for data instructions (e.g., MOV, ADD, XOR), the next location is statically decided by the length of the instruction. However, for control instructions (e.g., JMP, CMP), it may be dynamically decided, especially at indirect (conditional) jumps. Using symbolic execution, there are two ways to explore possibly multiple destinations of a CFG node (in the figure below).

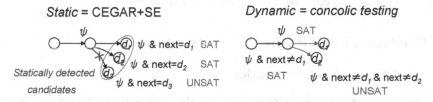

- **Static symbolic execution (SSE)**, in which next destination candidates are statically detected, and the feasibility of each destination p' is checked by the satisfiability of $\psi \wedge \text{next} = p'$. To refine statically detected candidates, it can be combined with CEGAR, like in McVeto [37].
- **Dynamic symbolic execution (DSE)**, in which the feasibility is checked by testing with a satisfiable instance of ψ (*concolic testing*), which requires a binary emulator. This will continue until $\psi \wedge \text{next} = p' \wedge \text{next} = p'' \dots$ becomes UNSAT for explored next destinations $p', p'', \dots$, like in [12].

We describe a path formula as a pair of an environment of parameters (e.g., registers, flags) and a Presburger formula consisting of constants and symbolic values of inputs, which is obtained by deploying the current values of parameters as the updates of their initial values. It ignores system status and kernel procedures, and focuses only on a user process.

3.3   API as Stub

Concolic testing requires a binary emulator, and our choice is to restrict a binary emulation to a user process, and APIs are handled by stubs. This gives the flexibility in symbolic execution, at the cost of manual stub construction and an approximation. Current BE-PUM implements the stubs for 310 APIs. The output of an API in the stub is given either by Java API or as a symbolic value. Note that a stub keeps a post-condition as the same as the pre-condition, but updates the environment by its output.

– For typical APIs functions, such that *FindFirstFileA*, *GetModuleHandle*, *FindNextFileA*, we rely on JNA (Java Native Access), which allows Java programs to call native shared libraries. Each system call is treated as if a single instruction such that (i) the update of the path formulas and the environments follow to the technical specification at Microsoft Developer Network.3; and (ii) the return value is obtained by executing Java API. Note that most of major APIs (though not all APIs) are covered by Java API.
– Sometimes, specific APIs are used for obfuscation techniques, e.g., anti-debugger or anti-debugging, and trigger-based behavior. For them, we must avoid execution of the API, since it will make us fall into the "trap" of the malware. For example, some malware performs anti-emulator by calling the system call like *IsDebuggerPresent* or *CheckRemoteDebuggerPresent*. If this API is executed under an emulator, a specific value will be returned, and the malware changes its behavior to hide its intention. For them, instead of calling Java API, we simply adopt a symbolic value as an output of the API, like in [9]. This is also effective for trigger-based behavior.

4   Control Flow Graph Reconstruction

4.1   X86 Operational Semantics

Our x86 binary semantics are inspired by [7]. We assume that a target X86 binary program $Prog_{x86}$ is loaded on a memory area, referred as M. The instruction pointer eip and the stack pointer esp are special registers that point to the current address of instructions and the top of the stack, respectively. The former is initially set to the entry address of $Prog_{x86}$. The stack is taken in M, where the stack top frame is pointed by the register esp and the stack bottom is pointed by the register ebp. In Windows, the stack area is taken between the *stack base* and the *stack limit*, which has the length of 1M bytes (and can be enlarged); but we ignore these boundaries.

Definition 1. *A memory model is a tuple (F, R, S, M), where F is the set of 9 system flags (AF, CF, DF, IF, OF, PF, SF, TF, and ZF), R is the set of 16 registers (eax, ebx, ecx, edx, esi, edi, esp, edp, cs, ds, es, fs, gs, ss, eip, and eflags), M is the set of memory locations to store, and $S(\subseteq M)$ is the set of contiguous memory locations for a stack (associated standard push/pop operations).*

For $k = Env_R(eip) \in M$, let $instr(Env_M, k)$ be a mapping that disassembles a binary code at the memory location k and return an instruction (with its arguments). An operational semantics of binary codes $Prog_{x86}$ is described as transitions in Fig. 1 among environments Env, which consists of a flag valuation Env_F, a register valuation Env_R, a stack valuation Env_S, and a memory valuation Env_M (on $M \setminus S$).

In BE-PUM, each register in R is represented by a 32-bit vector. Meanwhile, system flags in F are simply represented as boolean variables. Each memory location in M is represented by a 8-bit vector, in which the arithmetic operations are bit-encoded. BE-PUM dynamically identifies the instruction boundary as a sequence of 8-bit vectors (instead of a fixed 32-bit segment in the preliminary version [27]), which helps us to handle *overlapping instructions*.

$$\frac{Env_R(eip) = k, instr(Env_M, k) =" call\ r", \\ m' = k + |call\ r|, m = Env_R(r), push(S, m') = S'}{(Env_F, Env_R, Env_S, Env_M) \to (Env_F, Env_R[eip \leftarrow m], esp \leftarrow esp - 4], Env_{S'}, Env_M)} \, [Call]$$

$$\frac{Env_R(eip) = k, instr(Env_M, k) =" ret", empty(S)}{(Env_F, Env_R, Env_S, Env_M) \to \bot} \, [Return\ (empty\ stack)]$$

$$\frac{Env_R(eip) = k, instr(Env_M, k) =" ret", \neg empty(S), pop(S) = (S', m)}{(Env_F, Env_R, Env_S, Env_M) \to (Env_F, Env_R[eip \leftarrow m], esp \leftarrow esp + 4], Env_{S'}, Env_M)} \, [Return]$$

$$\frac{Env_R(eip) = k, instr(Env_M, k) =" jmp\ r", Env_R(r) = m}{(Env_F, Env_R, Env_S, Env_M) \to (Env_F, Env_R[eip \leftarrow m], Env_S, Env_M)} \, [(Indirect)Jump]$$

$$\frac{R(eip) = k, instr(Env_M, k) =" jmp\ m", M(m) = m'}{(Env_F, Env_R, Env_S, Env_M) \to (Env_F, Env_R[eip \leftarrow m'], Env_S, Env_M)} \, [Jump]$$

$$\frac{\begin{array}{l} Env_R(eip) = k, instr(Env_M, k) =" cmp\ r_1\ r_2", m = k + |cmp\ r_1\ r_2|, \\ c = Env_R(r_1) - Env_R(r_2), sf = (c < 0), zf = (c = 0), \\ cf = ((Env_R(r_1) >= 0) \wedge (Env_R(r_2) < 0)) \vee ((c < 0) \wedge ((Env_R(r_1) >= 0) \vee (Env_R(r_2) < 0))), \\ of = ((Env_R(r_1) < 0) \wedge (Env_R(r_2) >= 0) \wedge (c > 0)) \vee ((Env_R(r_1) >= 0) \wedge (Env_R(r_2) < 0) \wedge (c < 0)) \end{array}}{(Env_F, Env_R, Env_S, Env_M) \to (Env_F[CF \leftarrow cf, OF \leftarrow of, SF \leftarrow sf, ZF \leftarrow zf], Env_R[eip \leftarrow m], Env_S, Env_M)} \, [Cmp]$$

$$\frac{Env_R(eip) = k, instr(Env_M, k) =" mov\ t\ r", \\ r \in R, w = Env_R(r), m = k + |mov\ t\ r|}{(Env_F, Env_R, Env_S, Env_M) \to (Env_F, Env_R[eip \leftarrow m], Env_S, Env_M[t \leftarrow w])} \, [Move]$$

Fig. 1. Some of rules of operational semantics for control instructions

Figure 1 shows some examples of the description of the operational semantics of x86 instructions, which follows the technical description at *Intel Software Developer's Manual*. For instance, in the instruction *Call*, the register *eip* points to the address k in memory M of the next instruction, and $instr(Env_M, k)$ maps the binary code at k to the next instruction *callr*. The return address of *callr* is calculated by adding the size of the instruction *callr* to the current address k and is pushed onto the top of the stack S. The address of next instruction is updated with the value m of memory pointed by the address r.

4.2   Concrete Model with Path Conditions and CFG Reconstruction

Definition 2. *We borrow notations from* Definition 1. *A control flow graph (CFG) node is a pair of a location k and an assembly instruction asm. A configuration of a concrete model is a pair $\langle (k, asm), \psi(\bar{\alpha}) \rangle$ where (k, asm) is a CFG node, $\bar{\alpha}$ is a path (a sequence of CFG nodes) from the initial CFG node (k_0, asm_0) to (k, asm), and $\psi(\bar{\alpha})$ is a path condition given by*

$$\begin{cases} \psi(\epsilon) := \textbf{true} \\ \psi(\bar{\alpha}') := \psi(\bar{\alpha}) \wedge (SideCond \wedge PostCond) \ if \ \bar{\alpha}' = \bar{\alpha}.next(k, asm) \end{cases}$$

for the side conditions SideCond appearing in $Env \to Env'$ and the strongest post condition PostCond at (k, asm), which is a Presburger formula consisting of constants and symbolic values of inputs.

We obtain a CFG of an x86 binary program $Prog_{x86}$ by extracting (k, asm) from a configuration $\langle (k, asm), \psi(\bar{\alpha}) \rangle$ in Definition 2. There are several reasons for causing branching on a CFG. $next(k, asm)$ may have multiple possibility depending on an initial environment, which may be given by external system status. In current BE-PUM implementation, possible $next(k, asm)$'s are explored by repeated concolic testing with its satisfiable instances. This exploration continues until it reaches to UNSAT by adding the refutations of already explored next destinations.

5   BE-PUM Implementation

5.1   BE-PUM Architecture

BE-PUM implements CFG reconstruction (in Definition 2) based on concolic testing. It applies *JakStab 0.8.3* [20] as a preprocessor to compute a single-step disassembly $instr(Env_M, k)$, and an SMT *Z3.4.3* as a backend engine to generate a test instance for concolic testing.

The figure below shows the architecture of BE-PUM, which consists of three components: *symbolic execution, binary emulation*, and *CFG storage*. The symbolic execution picks up one from the frontiers (symbolic states at the ends of explored execution paths), and it tries to extend one step. If the instruction is a data instruction (i.e., only Env_M is updated and the next location is statically decided), it will simply disassemble the next instruction. If the instruction is a control instruction (e.g., conditional jumps), the concolic testing is applied to decide the next location. Note that some variable does not appear in the path-condition, the SMT will not return its value. If the concolic testing needs this value, BE-PUM terminates. However, in our observation, this is unlikely. When either a new CFG node or a new CFG edge is found, they are stored in CFG storage and a configuration is added to the frontiers. This procedure continues until either the exploration has converged (which will be discussed later), or reaching to unknown instructions, system calls, and/or addresses.

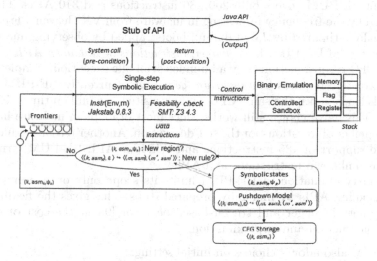

The next figure shows the implementation of a stub in BE-PUM, which consists of three components: a *pre-condition* P, the *binary emulation*, and a *post condition* P'. Currently, the BE-PUM implementation passes P to P' as identical, but with the update of the environment by an output of an API, which is obtained together with the return address by executing native shared library in JNA.

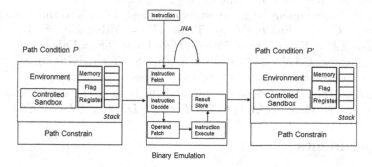

Note that exceptions, like the *division by zero*, are detected at the binary emulator, which pass them to the Windows system error handler.

5.2   Strategy and Limitations

There are several limitations in our implementation.

- X86 instructions are about 1000 and Windows APIs are more than 4000. Current BE-PUM covers only 200 x86 instructions and 310 APIs. They are selected by the frequency appearing in malware from VX Heaven.[2] Frequency is initially estimated by JakStab, and bootstrapped by observing unexpected termination of BE-PUM by *unknown instructions* or *unknown API*.
- Since CFG reconstruction is by a bounded symbolic execution, complete CFG reconstruction requires *loop invariant generation*. Currently, BE-PUM simply unfolds loops and if the same CFG node is visited one million times, it terminates. This naive choice still works, since most of loops in malware have the fixed number of iterations for the self-decryption. Another reason is, due to the limited support of x86 instructions and Windows API, BE-PUM terminates more by unknown instructions and APIs.
- The binary emulation in BE-PUM limits its scope only on a user process, and handling APIs by manually prepared stubs. This gives the flexibility to handle anti-debugger and trigger-based behavior [9], at the cost of manual stub construction and approximation.

  BE-PUM also adopts choices on initial setting.

- When BE-PUM starts to generate a model of binary code, the stack S is initially pushed (i) the address of the file name of the code; (ii) the address of the system exception handler; and (iii) the return address, which is randomly selected from the memory image of *kernel32*. The former two obey to the standard manner of Win32, and the last is based on the assumption that a code is often started by a call from somewhere in *kernel32*. This frequently holds and is often used by malware, e.g., *Aztec* [23].
- The initial environment (e.g., registers and flags) follows to the reference[3].
  - **Flags**: $CF = $ **False**, $PF = $ **True**, $AF = $ **False**, $ZF = $ **True**, $SF = $ **False**, $TF = $ **False**, $DF = $ **False**, $OF = $ **False**, $IF = $ **False**.
  - **Registers**: $EAX, CS, DS, ES, FS, GS, SS, EFFLAGS$ are set to symbolic values, EIP and EDX to the address of the entry point, ESP and EBP to the addresses of the top and the base of the stack, respectively. The rest is set as $ECX = 0, EBX = 7EFDE00, EDI = 0, ESI = 0$.

6   Experiments

We perform experiments of CFG reconstruction for 2000 real-world malware, taken from *VX Heaven*, and 6 non-malware examples. We compare the results of BE-PUM with IDA Pro and JakStab for the coverage of nodes, edges, and processing time. Our experiments are performed on Windows XP with AMD Athlon II X4 635, 2.9 GHz and 8 GB. Note that BE-PUM may have stopped with an *unknown instruction* or *API*.

---

[2] http://vx.netlux.org.
[3] https://code.google.com/p/corkami/wiki/InitialValues.

6.1   Model Generation Performance

In general, the number of reachable nodes of BE-PUM is better than IDA Pro and JakStab. Since IDA Pro uses syntactic analysis, it is easily confused by indirect jumps and encrypted codes. JakStab also fails since its static analysis cannot effectively analyze. BE-PUM encounters the problem at the cost of higher processing time than JakStab and IDA Pro due to its concolic testing.

As a statistical observation of the experimental result, we show the averages of the ratios among tools.

- The ratio between the numbers of CFG edges and CFG nodes, which shows detection of multiple paths. The ratios for JakStab, IDA Pro, and BE-PUM are 1.05, 2.05, and 1.24, respectively. This shows that IDA Pro detects multiple paths better, but they could be infeasible paths.
- The ratio between the numbers of explored CFG nodes by two tools. Between BE-PUM and JakStab is 11.59, and between BE-PUM and IDA Pro is 6.61. Notable examples in Table 1 are, *Virus.Artelad.2173*, *Email-Worm.LoveLetter.b*, *Virus.Pulkfer.a*, and *Email-Worm.Klez.h*, in which nodes are about 10 times more by BE-PUM. Since the numbers of CFG nodes and edges by BE-PUM are almost the same, BE-PUM fails to find multiple paths. This can occur when the loop counter is set to a constant and the loop continues to decrypt/modify some fragment. Further investigation is needed on these examples.

With closer look, Table 1 shows 28 malware examples among 2000 and 6 non-malware examples, in which the unit of **Time** is the millisecond. Among 2000, BE-PUM successfully converges with 250 examples, and it is interrupted on many viruses by *unknown instructions* (e.g., *Email-Worm.Bagle*) and *unsupported APIs* (e.g., *Virus.Cabanas*) due to the limited support of instructions and APIs. It is also interrupted by *unknown addresses* (e.g., *Virus.Seppuku* except for *Seppuku.1606*) due to jumping to an address outside the file area (e.g. the address of an unknown API or a system file).

IDA Pro sometimes detects more nodes. It is partially because IDA Pro covers most of x86 instructions, whereas BE-PUM covers only 200. Another reason is that IDA Pro is cheated by obfuscation and continues to generate unrelated assembly code, e.g., *Benny.3219.a/b* and *Eva.a/b*, whereas BE-PUM terminates with a precise CFG. This also occurs in non-malware examples. IDA Pro often has better results than BE-PUM because of its full support of Windows APIs. For example, with *Winever.exe*, BE-PUM fails to resolve the return address of Windows API *ShellAboutW@shell32.dll*.

```
01001284   56                PUSH ESI
01001285   56                PUSH ESI
01001286   8D45 BC           LEA EAX,DWORD PTR SS:[EBP-44]
01001289   50                PUSH EAX
0100128A   56                PUSH ESI
0100128B   FF15 3C100001     CALL ShellAboutW@Shell32.dll
```

Table 1. Part of experimental results for model generation

Example	Size	JakStab			IDA Pro			BE-PUM		
	KByte	Nodes	Edges	Time	Nodes	Edges	Time	Nodes	Edges	Time
Virus.Artelad. 2173	23	134	154	10ms	159	162	1133ms	1610	1611	236468ms
Email-Worm. LoveLetter.b	60	1027	1026	297	984	1011	10	7558	7602	1073984
Virus.Pulkfer.a	129	907	924	10	805	823	20	8347	8353	44672
Email-Worm. Klez.h	137	192	178	20	50	56	1	5652	5651	46344
Email-Worm. Coronex.a	12	26	27	500	148	157	204	308	339	1000
Trojan-PSW. QQRob.16.d	25	89	100	766	17	15	382	91	105	953
Virus.Aztec	8	104	111	1973	223	215	495	300	313	44384
Virus.Belial.a	4	41	42	407	118	116	198	128	134	985
Virus.Benny. 3219.a	8	138	153	890	599	603	415	149	164	2438
Virus.Benny.3223	12	42	47	328	770	781	135	149	164	2218
Virus.Bogus.4096	38	87	98	546	88	86	269	88	98	656
Virus.Brof.a	8	17	17	343	98	102	167	137	147	1484
Virus.Cerebrus. 1482	8	6	5	156	164	165	70	179	198	735
Virus.Compan.a	8	25	26	360	83	81	176	91	98	484
Virus.Cornad	4	21	20	141	68	72	67	94	100	344
Virus.Eva.a	8	14	13	329	381	392	145	249	277	13438
Virus.Htrip.a	8	10	10	359	145	143	172	148	157	2187
Virus.Htrip.d	8	10	10	265	164	162	124	165	173	2296
Virus.Seppuku. 1606	8	131	136	1968	381	390	965	339	364	8372
Virus.Wit.a	4	54	60	360	153	151	172	185	203	2641
Email-Worm. Bagle.af	21	123	143	937	142	151	461	140	166	2157
Email-Worm. Bagle.ag	17	127	147	828	13	12	413	127	147	1047
Virus.Cabanas.a	8	3	2	156	1	1	78	68	72	1532
Virus.Cabanas.b	8	3	2	140	9	7	70	63	66	1781
Virus.Canabas. 2999	8	2	1	656	7	6	85	358	401	8703
Virus.Seppuku. 1638	8	139	144	2266	414	412	112	689	712	13000
Virus.Seppuku. 3291	8	26	25	187	556	554	66	253	270	12156
Virus.Seppuku. 3426	8	27	27	188	30	28	61	299	317	13484
non-malware binary										
hostname.exe	8	329	360	2412	343	389	33	326	357	235610
winver.exe	6	162	166	422	310	345	24	232	240	122484
systray.exe	4	110	136	532	115	138	14	123	139	16125
regedt32.exe	3	52	54	266	56	61	11	61	69	22844
actmovie.exe	4	164	179	281	187	215	51	180	196	243469
nddeapir.exe	4	164	179	500	187	215	24	180	196	223297

However, in *systray.exe*, BE-PUM is better than IDA Pro, since IDA Pro fails
to resolve obfuscation techniques, like an indirect return at

010010BD	C2 0400	RETN	4

and an indirect jump at

010010CA	6A 00	PUSH	0
010010CC	BF 5C100001	MOV EDI,	0100105C
010010D1	57	PUSH	EDI
010010D2	FFD6	CALL	ESI

6.2   Example of Obfuscation Localization and Classification

We show a case-study of *Seppuku.1606*. Most of malware in VX Heaven are traditional and some have known assembly source (e.g., for *Aztec*, *Bagle*, *Benny*,
and *Cabanas*), where *Seppuku.1606* has no available assembly source. We manually traced the result of *BE-PUM* with the help of *Ollydbg*, and found code
fragments for SEH technique and self-modification.

An intended exception occurs at 00401035 by reading the memory address
77E80000 pointed by register *esi*, and then storing that value in the register **eax**.
Since 77E80000 is protected, this raises an exception caught by an SEH.

00401028	33C0	xor	eax, eax
0040102A	64FF30	push	dword ptr fs:[eax]
0040102D	648920	mov	fs:[eax], esp
00401030	BE0000E877	mov	esi, 77E80000h
00401035	66AD	lods	ds:[esi]

The self-modification occurs at 004010*EB* that *Seppuku.1606* overwrites the
opcode at 00401646 from *E8FFFFF9B5* to *E800000000*, which means the mod
ification from *Call* 00401000 to *Call* 0040164*B*.

004010E4	57	PUSH EDI	
004010E5	8B8589144000	MOV EAX,DWORD PTR SS:[EBP+401489]	
004010EB	AB	STOS DWORD PTR ES:[EDI]	
004010EC	83C404	ADD ESP,4	

In the correct CFG, the path from 0040164*B* finally reaches the exit point
after a call of an API *MessageBoxA*. BE-PUM correctly traces this behavior,
where IDA Pro fails at 00401646 with `call sub_401000`.

```
00401000  60                PUSHA
00401001  E800000000        CALL $+5
 . . . . .
00401646  E800000000        CALL Virus_Wi.0040164B
0040164B  6A10              PUSH 10
0040164D  6800204000        PUSH Virus_Wi.00402000
00401652  6827204000        PUSH Virus_Wi.00402027
00401657  6A00              PUSH 0
00401659  E80D000000        CALL <JMP.&USER32.MessageBoxA>
0040165E  6A00              PUSH 0
00401660  E800000000        CALL <JMP.&KERNEL32.ExitProcess>
```

The CFG generated by IDA Pro has a wrong path at the instruction $004010EB$, whereas BE-PUM successfully continued as this point. We observe that $004010EB$ is in fact the entry point of the self-modification. A similar situation occurs for all of other 285 obfuscation samples (Sect. 6.3).

6.3 Manual Obfuscation Classification

We expect that when the results of IDA Pro and BE-PUM differ, they will locate the entry points of obfuscation code. To confirm this idea, we choose 300 viruses among 2000 from VX Heaven, and generate CFGs by BE-PUM and IDA Pro. They are automatically compared, and the former is manually investigated at the point that the difference occurs with the help of Ollydbg. We observe that 293 viruses contain obfuscation code and they are classified into

- *249 indirect jumps*: Virus.Delf.n, Virus.Delf.r, Virus.Delf.w, Worm.Randin.b, Worm.Limar, Worm.Delf.q, Worm.Delf.o, ...
- *110 SEH*: Virus.Eva.a Virus.Eva.b, Virus.Eva.c, Virus.Eva.e, Virus.Eva.f, Virus.Eva.g, Virus.Rever, ...
- *30 self-modifying code*: Virus.Cabanas.2999 Virus.Rever, Net-Worm.Sasser.b, Net-Worm.Sasser.c, Virus.Pesin.a, ...
- *6 encryption:* Virus.Cabanas.2999, Virus.Savior.1828, Net-Worm.Sasser.a, Net-Worm.Sasser.f, Virus.Glyn, Virus.Hader.2701.

and all of the cases, when the results of IDA Pro and BE-PUM differ, they exactly locate where obfuscation starts. There are 7 viruses without obfuscation code, and IDA Pro and BE-PUM report the same result.

As an example of indirect jumps (by `retn`, similar to Virus.Bagle.bf in Sect. 2), we observe Virus.HLLW.Rolog.f.

	BE-PUM	IDA Pro
00437001 60	PUSHAD	
00437002 E8 03000000	CALL 0043700A	
00437007 E9 EB045D45		JMP 45A074F7
00437008 EB04	JMP 0043700E	
0043700A 5D	POP EBP	
0043700B 45	INC EBP	
0043700C 55	PUSH EBP	
0043700D C3	RETN	

At 00437002, the Call instruction put the return address 00437007 into the stack. From 0043700A to 0043700D, 00437007 in the top stack frame is popped to the register *ebp*, incremented, and pushed again. Thus, at 0043700D, it must return to 00437008, instead of 00437007.

BE-PUM correctly read JMP 0043700E, whereas IDA Pro is confused as JMP 45A074F7. JakStab also handles this obfuscation.

7 Related Work

There are two main targets of binary code analysis. The first one is *system software*, which is compiled code but its source is inaccessible, due to legacy software and/or commercial protection. It is often large, but relatively structured from the compiled nature. The second one is *malware*, which is distributed in binary only. It is often small, but with tricky obfuscation code. For the former, a main obstruction is scalability. *IDA Pro*[4] and *Capstone*[5] are the most popular disassemblers. Other remarkable approaches include *OSMOSE* [5] built on *BINCOA* [6], *BitBlaze* [13], *Veritesting* [1] built on *BAP* [10], and *SAGE* [28].

There are various model generation tools for binary executables. Destinations of indirect jumps can be identified by either static or dynamic method. BE-PUM stands in between, using both methods. For instance, CodeSurfer/x86 [2], McVeto [37], and JakStab [20]) adopt a static approach, while *OSMOSE* [5], BIRD [26], Renovo [17], Syman [38], and SAGE [28] choose a dynamic one. Generally, dynamic methods seems more effective on malware analysis [11].

Static methods are abstract interpretation (static analysis) for an over approximation, and symbolic execution to check feasibility of an execution path for an under-approximation. JakStab and McVeto apply CEGAR to refine over approximations. McVeto also uses symbolic execution to check the path feasibility (named a *concrete trace*). X-Force [14] executes dynamically, which is implemented on PIN from Intel. It explores different execution paths by systematically forcing the branch outcome of conditional transfer instructions. BE-PUM uses dynamic symbolic execution, instead of dynamic execution. BitBlaze [13] also combine static and dynamic analyses on binary. It is based on Value Set Analysis (VSA) [3] for handling indirect jumps. It also adopts existing disassemblers

---

[4] https://www.hex-rays.com/products/ida/.
[5] http://www.capstone-engine.org/.

like IDA Pro, and handling obfuscated code relies on them. Moser [12] developed a system for Windows to explore multiple paths. In [12], it is mentioned not to cover self-modification. MineSweeper [9] uses symbolic values for APIs to detect trigger-based behavior. In [9], it is mentioned not to cover indirect jumps. Syman [38] emulates the full Windows OS. Such detailed information makes symbolic execution complex and models easily explode even for small binary code. OSMOSE and CodeSurfer/x86 reduce to 32-bit vector models, called DBA (Dynamic Bit-vector Automaton) [5]. *CoDisasm* [8] is proposed very recently, which disassembles based on analyses of dynamic traces by decomposing into *waves*. It also can handle overlapping instructions and self-modification, and further comparison is needed.

In summary, BE-PUM is the most similar to McVeto. However, McVeto finds candidates of the destinations by static analysis (which are possibly infinitely many), and chooses one and checks the satisfiable condition of the path at the destination to conclude whether it is reachable (concrete trace). BE-PUM solves the path condition at the source of an indirect jump, and applies concolic testing (over binary emulator) to decide (one of) the destination. Unfortunately, we could not find access to the McVeto implementation, and we did not compare with experiments. McVeto seems not to support APIs, which limits to analyze SEH techniques. Concolic testing is easier to adopt stubs for APIs. The table below summarizes the comparison, in which ? means not confirmed yet.

	Indirect jump	Overlapping instruction	SEH	SMC self-decryption	Packer
IDA Pro	No	No	No	No	No
JakStab	Static analysis	Static	No	No	No
MineSweeper	No	No	No	No	No
X-Force	Dynamic emulation	Yes	No	Yes	?
McVeto	Symbolic execution	Yes	No	Yes	?
CoDisasm	Dynamic analysis	Yes	?	Yes	Yes
BE-PUM	Concolic testing	Yes	Yes	Yes	Yes

8 Conclusion

This paper introduced a tool BE-PUM (Binary Emulator for PUshdown Model generation), which generates a precise control flow graph (CFG) of malware under presence of typical obfuscations, based on dynamic symbolic execution on x86 binaries. Experiments are performed over 2000 malware examples taken from VX-Heaven database. Although each element of the techniques in BE-PUM is not new, the combination works in practical efficiency, and is effective such that when the results of IDA Pro and BE-PUM differ, they correctly locate the entry points of the obfuscation code. This is confirmed by manual classification of 300 examples.

A precise CFG is a backbone model for model checking. Future work includes to clarify the target properties of model checking to automatic classification of obfuscation techniques. We have some observations.

- *Indirect jump* comes together with arithmetic operations on a register or a memory address that appears as an argument of a jump instruction, or a `pop-inc-push` sequence for the overlapping instruction technique (as in *Bagle.bf* and *Heher.j*).
- *SEH* set up the return address in SEH by the specific sequence of instructions `push fs:[0]` and `mov esp, fs:[0]`.
- *SMC* comes together with a loop of XORing and a sequence in the CFG that has previously visited locations with modified instructions.

Another future work is loop handling. BE-PUM applies concolic testing to decide the destinations, but symbolic execution is a bounded search. Current BE-PUM simply unfolds loops, relying on the observation that most of loops in malware have the fixed number of iterations for self-decryption. *Loop invariant generation* is an ultimate solution; before that we are planning to apply constant propagation to detect a constant loop counter, which would improve in practice.

Acknowledgments. This work is supported by JSPS KAKENHI Grant-in-Aid for Scientific Research(B) 15H02684 and AOARD-144050 (14IOA053). It is also funded by Ho Chi Minh City University of Technology under grant number TNCS-2015-KHMT-06.

References

1. Avgerinos, T., Rebert, A., Cha, S.K., Brumley, D.: Enhancing symbolic execution with veritesting. In: 36th ICSE, pp. 1083–1094 (2014)
2. Balakrishnan, G., Gruian, R., Reps, T., Teitelbaum, T.: CodeSurfer/x86—a platform for analyzing x86 executables. In: Bodik, R. (ed.) CC 2005. LNCS, vol. 3443, pp. 250–254. Springer, Heidelberg (2005)
3. Balakrishnan, G., Reps, T.: Wysinwyx: what you see is not what you execute. ACM TOPLAS **32**(6), 206–263 (2010)
4. Balakrishnan, G., Reps, T., Kidd, N., Lal, A.K., Lim, J., Melski, D., Gruian, R., Yong, S., Chen, C.-H., Teitelbaum, T.: Model checking x86 executables with CodeSurfer/x86 and WPDS++. In: Etessami, K., Rajamani, S.K. (eds.) CAV 2005. LNCS, vol. 3576, pp. 158–163. Springer, Heidelberg (2005)
5. Bardin, S., Herrmann, P.: OSMOSE: automatic structural testing of executables. In: STVR, pp. 29–54 (2011)
6. Bardin, S., Herrmann, P., Leroux, J., Ly, O., Tabary, R., Vincent, A.: The BINCOA framework for binary code analysis. In: Gopalakrishnan, G., Qadeer, S. (eds.) CAV 2011. LNCS, vol. 6806, pp. 165–170. Springer, Heidelberg (2011)
7. Bonfante, G., Marion, J.-Y.,-Plantey, D.R.: A computability perspective on self-modifying programs. In: SEFM, pp. 231–239 (2009)
8. Bonfante, G., Fernandez, J., Marion, J.-Y., Rouxel, B., Sabatier, F., Thierry, A.: CoDisasm: medium scale concatic disassembly of self-modifying binaries with overlapping instructions. In: CCS (2015, to appear)

9. Brumley, D., et al.: Automatically identifying trigger-based behavior in malware. In: Lee, W., Wang, C., Dagon, D. (eds.) Botnet Analysis and Defense, pp. 65–88. Springer, Heidelberg (2008)

10. Brumley, D., Jager, I., Avgerinos, T., Schwartz, E.J.: BAP: a binary analysis platform. In: Gopalakrishnan, G., Qadeer, S. (eds.) CAV 2011. LNCS, vol. 6806, pp. 463–469. Springer, Heidelberg (2011)

11. Kolbitsch, C., Livshits, B., Zorn, B.G., Seifert, C.: Rozzle: de-cloaking internet malware. In: IEEE Symposium on Security and Privacy, pp. 443–457 (2012)

12. Moser, A., et al.: Exploring multiple execution paths for malware analysis. In: IEEE Symposium on Security and Privacy, pp. 231–245 (2007)

13. Bitblaze, D.S., et al.: A new approach to computer security via binary analysis. In: ICISS (2008)

14. Peng, F., et al.: Force-executing binary programs for security applications. In: USENIX Security, pp. 829–844 (2014)

15. Filiol, E.: Malware pattern scanning schemes secure against black-box analysis. J. Comput. Virol. 2, 35–50 (2006)

16. Holzer, A., Kinder, J., Veith, H.: Using verification technology to specify and detect malware. In: Moreno Díaz, R., Pichler, F., Quesada Arencibia, A. (eds.) EUROCAST 2007. LNCS, vol. 4739, pp. 497–504. Springer, Heidelberg (2007)

17. Kang, M., Poosankam, P., Yin, H.: Renovo: a hidden code extractor for packed executables. In: Recurring Malcode, pp. 46–53 (2007)

18. Kinder, J., Katzenbeisser, S., Schallhart, C., Veith, H.: Detecting malicious code by model checking. In: Julisch, K., Kruegel, C. (eds.) DIMVA 2005. LNCS, vol. 3548, pp. 174–187. Springer, Heidelberg (2005)

19. Kinder, J., et al.: Proactive detection of computer worms using model checking. IEEE Trans. Dependable Secure Comput. 7, 424–438 (2010)

20. Kinder, J., Zuleger, F., Veith, H.: An abstract interpretation-based framework for control flow reconstruction from binaries. In: Jones, N.D., Müller-Olm, M. (eds.) VMCAI 2009. LNCS, vol. 5403, pp. 214–228. Springer, Heidelberg (2009)

21. Kinder, J.: Static analysis of x86 executables. Ph.D thesis, Technische Universitat Darmstadt (2010)

22. King, J.C.: Symbolic execution and program testing. CACM 19(7), 385–394 (1976)

23. Labir, E.: VX reversing I, the basics. CodeBreakers-J. 1(1), 17–47 (2004)

24. Lakhotia, A., Preda, M.D., Giacobazzi, R.: Fast location of similar code fragments using semantic 'juice'. In: PPREW, pp. 25–30 (2013)

25. Moser, A., Kruegel, C., Kirda, E.: Limits of static analysis for malware detection. In: ACSAC, pp. 215–225 (2007)

26. Nanda, S., Li, W., Lam, L., Chiueh, T.: BIRD: binary interpretation using runtime disassembly. In: CGO, pp. 358–370 (2006)

27. Nguyen, M.H., Nguyen, T.B., Quan, T.T., Ogawa, M.: A hybrid approach for control flow graph construction from binary code. In: APSEC, pp. 159–164 (2013)

28. Godefroid, P., Lahiri, S.K., Rubio-González, C.: Statically validating must summaries for incremental compositional dynamic test generation. In: Yahav, E. (ed.) Static Analysis. LNCS, vol. 6887, pp. 112–128. Springer, Heidelberg (2011)

29. Preda, M.D., Giacobazzi, R., Lakhotia, A., Mastroeni, I.: Abstract symbolic automata: mixed syntactic/semantic similarity analysis of executables. In: POPL, pp. 329–341 (2015)

30. Roundy, K.A., Miller, B.P.: Binary-code obfuscations in prevalent packer tools. ACM Comput. Surv. 46, 215–226 (2014)

31. Sharif, M., Lanzi, A., Giffin, J., Lee, W.: Impeding malware analysis using conditional code obfuscation. In: NDSS (2008)

32. Song, F., Touili, T.: Pushdown model checking for malware detection. In: Flanagan, C., König, B. (eds.) TACAS 2012. LNCS, vol. 7214, pp. 110–125. Springer, Heidelberg (2012)
33. Song, F., Touili, T.: LTL model-checking for malware detection. In: Piterman, N., Smolka, S.A. (eds.) TACAS 2013 (ETAPS 2013). LNCS, vol. 7795, pp. 416–431. Springer, Heidelberg (2013)
34. Person, S., Dwyer, M.B, Elbaum, S.G.,Pasareanu, C.S.: Differential symbolic execution. In: SIGSOFT FSE, pp. 226–237 (2008)
35. Szor, P.: The Art of Computer Virus Research and Defense. Addison-Wesley Professional, Reading (2005)
36. Dullien, T., Kornau, T., Weinmann, R.-P.: A framework for automated architecture-independent gadget search. In: WOOT (2009)
37. Thakur, A., Lim, J., Lal, A., Burton, A., Driscoll, F., Elder, M., Andersen, T., Reps, T.: Directed proof generation for machine code. In: Touili, T., Cook, B., Jackson, P. (eds.) CAV 2010. LNCS, vol. 6174, pp. 288–305. Springer, Heidelberg (2010)
38. Izumida, T., Futatsugi, K., Mori, A.: A generic binary analysis method for malware. In: Echizen, I., Kunihiro, N., Sasaki, R. (eds.) IWSEC 2010. LNCS, vol. 6434, pp. 199–216. Springer, Heidelberg (2010)

Short Papers

Runtime Monitoring of Stream Logic Formulae

Sylvain Hallé[✉] and Raphaël Khoury

Laboratoire d'informatique formelle, Université du Québec à Chicoutimi,
Chicoutimi, Canada
shalle@acm.org, rkhoury@uqac.ca

Abstract. We introduce a formal notation for the processing of event traces called Stream Logic (SL). A monitor evaluates a Boolean condition over an input trace, while a filter outputs events from an input trace depending on some monitor's verdict; both constructs can be freely composed. We show how all operators of Linear Temporal Logic, as well as the parametric slicing of an input trace, can be written as Stream Logic constructs.

1 Introduction

Trace validation is performed in various areas of computer science. For example, in programming, analyzing a trace of events can be used to determine the success of a test run [2] or for debugging purposes to ensure that methods of an object have been called in the correct order [7]; similarly, a trace can represent a recorded interaction between a client and a web service and one can verify that each client interacts properly with the server according to some predefined protocol [6]. Providing a verdict dynamically, as the events are produced by the system, is its realtime counterpart called *runtime monitoring*.

Several notations have been developed to describe the set of valid traces specific to each use case. Regular expressions are supported by tools like MOP [7]; Monpoly [4], BeepBeep [6] and ProM [8] employ Linear Temporal Logic (LTL) or first-order extensions thereof; Logscope [5] and RuleR [3] use a language based on μ-calculus.

Reasoning about properties on traces can sometimes prove difficult. It is well known, for example, that there exist properties for which neither a "true" nor a "false" verdict can be given for any finite prefix of a trace; however, depending on the notation used, identifying such properties may be complex. Hence in LTL, apart from trivial cases that are easy to spot (the formula $\mathbf{G}\,\mathbf{F}\,p$ is one such example), the general problem reduces to satisfiability solving and belongs to the PSPACE-complete class.

In this paper, we propose a reformulation of formal trace specifications using different base concepts, with runtime monitoring and partial evaluation of trace prefixes in mind. The result is a formal notation for the processing of event

The authors acknowledge the financial support of the Natural Sciences and Engineering Research Council of Canada (NSERC).

J. Garcia-Alfaro et al. (Eds.): FPS 2015, LNCS 9482, pp. 251–258, 2016.
DOI: 10.1007/978-3-319-30303-1_15

traces called Stream Logic (SL), detailed in Sect. 2. SL defines two basic objects, called *monitors* and *filters*. A monitor evaluates a Boolean condition over an input trace, while a filter outputs events from an input trace depending on some monitor's verdict, and both constructs can be freely composed. The formal semantics of SL is defined, and a few syntactical identities are also presented.

We then proceed to highlight some of the advantages of SL over other notations. In Sect. 3, we show how SL subsumes LTL by emulating each of its operators, and describe how conclusions about a monitor's possible outcome can be drawn through purely syntactical manipulations. Finally, Sect. 4 describes a proof-of-concept implementation of a Stream Logic processor showing the feasibility of the approach on a number of use cases. In particular, our SL interpreter provides order-of-magnitude speed gains compared to a tool applying the classical recursive semantics of LTL to monitor a trace.

2   A Calculus for Event Streams

In this section, we describe the formal notation and semantics of Stream Logic, a language for expressing both conditions and filters on finite traces of events. We shall first present each concept intuitively in Sect. 2.1, and then show in Sect. 2.2 the formal semantics of the complete system.

2.1   Basic Constructs

A trace of events is a finite sequence of atomic events, represented as $a, b, \ldots$, taken from some finite set of symbols. Traces will be designated as $\overline{m} = m_1, m_2, \ldots, m_n$. We assume there is a set of predicates $p, q, r, \ldots$, which each return either true ($\top$) or false ($\bot$) for each possible event. When the context is clear, an event symbol a will also stand for the predicate that returns true whenever its input is symbol a, and false otherwise. For a trace $\overline{m} = m_1, m_2, \ldots$, we let $\overline{m}^k$ be the trace obtained from $\overline{m}$ and starting at the k-th symbol: $m_k, m_{k+1}, \ldots$.

Monitors. The first fundamental concept of SL is that of a monitor. A monitor φ takes a trace $\overline{m} = m_1, m_2, \ldots m_n$ as an input, and returns as an output a sequence $\overline{v} = v_1, v_2, \ldots$, where $v_i \in \{\top, \bot\}$. This is noted $\overline{m} : \varphi$. Informally, a monitor is fed messages from $\overline{m}$ one by one, and at any moment, can be queried for its current state, which by definition is the last symbol appended to $\overline{v}$. Hence a monitor queried multiple times without being fed any new message in between will return the same symbol. By definition, a monitor that has not been fed any message returns a third, special value noted ?.

In the following, we will consider a few simple monitors. The first is the "true" monitor, which outputs the sequence $\top, \top, \ldots$. We will abuse notation and use the $\top$ symbol to designate this monitor. Similarly, we have the monitors $\bot$ and ?. Finally, we have the constant monitor, noted c for some constant, which, for any trace $\overline{m} = m_1, m_2, \ldots$, outputs the sequence $\overline{v} = v_1, v_2, \ldots$, where $v_i = \top$ if $m_i = c$, and $v_i = \bot$ if $m_i \neq c$.

These monitors can be combined to produce compound results using the classical Boolean connectives. Given a trace $\overline{m} = m_1, m_2, \ldots$ and two monitors φ and ψ producing sequences $\overline{v}_\varphi$ and $\overline{v}_\psi$, the monitor $\varphi \wedge \psi$ produces the sequence $\overline{v}_{\varphi \wedge \psi}$ that is the pairwise conjunction of symbols in each monitor's output sequence. The case of disjunction and negation monitors can be defined in the expected way.

Clearly, if φ has read k symbols, its output can contain at most k symbols. However, as we shall see, each monitor need not to produce their output symbols at the same time. The conjunction monitor can only output symbol i if monitors φ and ψ have both output symbol i; otherwise, the conjunction monitor must delay the output of symbol i until both values are available (or until a conclusion can be drawn anyway, such as when one of the monitors returns $\bot$). This entails that a monitor can be fed an input message, and not produce the corresponding output symbol immediately.

We also introduce additional binary connectives for monitors. The first is operator $\wedge_1$. Informally, the monitor $\varphi \wedge_1 \psi$ returns the value of the *first* of φ or ψ that is no longer undefined. In the case where φ and ψ both take a value at the same time, $\wedge_1$ behaves like $\wedge$. Connective $\vee_1$ is defined similarly with respect to $\vee$.

Filters. The second important construct in SL is the filter. The filter is an operator which, given some monitor φ and an input trace $\overline{m}$, returns a subtrace retaining only the symbols that match a specific condition. Formally, let $\overline{m} = m_1, m_2, \ldots$ be a message trace, and $\overline{v} = v_1, v_2, \ldots$ be the output sequence for monitor φ on that trace. The expression

$$\overline{m} : \frac{\infty}{\varphi}$$

constructs from $\overline{m}$ the subtrace made only of symbols m_i such that $v_i = \top$. Hence, the filter $\frac{\infty}{c \vee d}$ produces the subtrace made only of symbols c or d.

The ∞ symbol in the top part of the fraction indicates that one is to take all messages from $\overline{m}$ that satisfy φ. We can also indicate to return only one particular message by replacing ∞ by a number. Hence $\frac{k}{\varphi}$ returns only the k-th message that satisfies φ (i.e. $\overline{m}'_k$).

Filters and monitors can be chained; that is, the output of a filter can be given as the input for a monitor, or another filter. If f is a filter and φ is a monitor, then $\overline{m} : f : \varphi$ is the monitor that evaluates φ on trace $\overline{m}$, but is being fed only the input symbols that are returned by f.

Consider for example the following monitor, assuming an input sequence $\overline{m}$:

$$\frac{1}{b \wedge \left(\frac{2}{\top} : c\right)} : \top$$

The filter this time retains for the input trace only symbols m_i that satisfy two conditions. The first is that $m_i = b$. The second is itself a compound monitor, that is given as its input trace the sequence $\overline{m}' = m_i, m_{i+1}, \ldots$. This sequence

Table 1. The formal semantics of SL. In this recursive definition, f and f' are arbitrary filters and φ and ψ are arbitrary monitors.

$$\llbracket \overline{m}, \top \rrbracket_i \triangleq \begin{cases} \top & \text{if } 1 \le i \le |\overline{m}| \\ \epsilon & \text{otherwise} \end{cases}$$

$$\llbracket \overline{m}, p \rrbracket_i \triangleq \begin{cases} \epsilon & \text{if } i > |\overline{m}|, \text{ otherwise} \dots \\ \top & \text{if } \overline{m}_i \text{ satisfies } p \\ \bot & \text{if } \overline{m}_i \text{ does not satisfy } p \end{cases}$$

$$\llbracket \overline{m}, \neg\varphi \rrbracket_i \triangleq \begin{cases} \bot & \text{if } \llbracket \overline{m}, \varphi \rrbracket_i = \top \\ \top & \text{if } \llbracket \overline{m}, \varphi \rrbracket_i = \bot \\ \epsilon & \text{otherwise} \end{cases}$$

$$\llbracket \overline{m}, \varphi \wedge \psi \rrbracket_i \triangleq \begin{cases} \bot & \text{if } \llbracket \overline{m}, \varphi \rrbracket_i = \bot \text{ or } \llbracket \overline{m}, \varphi \rrbracket_i = \bot \\ \top & \text{if } \llbracket \overline{m}, \varphi \rrbracket_i = \top \text{ and } \llbracket \overline{m}, \varphi \rrbracket_i = \top \\ \epsilon & \text{otherwise} \end{cases}$$

$$\left\llbracket \overline{m}, \frac{k}{\varphi} \right\rrbracket \triangleq \begin{cases} \llbracket \overline{m}^2, \frac{k-1}{\varphi} \rrbracket & \text{if } \llbracket \overline{m}, \varphi \rrbracket_1 = \top \\ \llbracket \overline{m}^2, \frac{k}{\varphi} \rrbracket & \text{otherwise} \end{cases}$$

$$\llbracket \overline{m}, f : \varphi \rrbracket \triangleq \llbracket \llbracket \overline{m}, f \rrbracket, \varphi \rrbracket$$

first goes through a filter that retains only its second message (i.e. m_{i+1}), and passes it on to the constant monitor c; this monitor outputs the symbol $\top$ only if $m_{i+1} = c$. Hence the filter will return the first message m_i such that $m_i = b$ and $m_{i+1} = c$. The end monitor outputs the $\top$ symbol whenever it receives a message from that filter. The end result is that the monitor returns $\top$ as soon as the property "some b is immediately followed by a c" is observed at least once.

2.2   Semantics

Now that we have described intuitively the basic constructs of SL, we shall formally define the semantics of the language; this is done in Table 1. The notation $\llbracket \overline{m}, \varphi \rrbracket$ designates the output trace produced by feeding the input trace $\overline{m}$ to monitor φ. Similarly, the notation $\llbracket \overline{m}, f \rrbracket$ defines the output trace produced by feeding $\overline{m}$ to filter f. Since $\llbracket \cdot \rrbracket$ represents a trace, we use the subscript notation $\llbracket \cdot \rrbracket_i$ to denote the i-th event of that output.

An interesting side effect of this semantics is that it defines a form of buffering for events to be processed by monitors or filters, without the need for managing these buffers explicitly in the notation. As an example, let us consider the filter expression $\frac{\infty}{\frac{1}{c} : \top}$. Let us first apply the finite semantics to determine the output of this filter on the input trace made of the single symbol a. Working from the inside expression outwards, one realizes that $\llbracket a, \frac{1}{c} \rrbracket = \epsilon$; this propagates outwards and leads to the conclusion that the filter outputs nothing. However, while the top-level filter outputs nothing after receiving the first event, one can see that it outputs a after receiving c. In other words, events are implicitly "buffered" by some monitors and some filters until some condition allows them to be released.

3   Applications

In this section, we show potential uses of SL in various applications. We concentrate on a reduction to Linear Temporal Logic, the possibility of simplifying monitor expressions, and the characterization of monitorable properties in a purely syntactical way.

3.1   Linear Temporal Logic

As a first application of SL, we show how temporal operators from Linear Temporal Logic can be rewritten using the concepts of filters and monitors.

The first case is the $\mathbf{F}$ ("eventually") operator, which we can write as:

$$\mathbf{F}\,\varphi \triangleq \frac{1}{\varphi} : \top$$

In this case, the filter $\frac{1}{\varphi}$ will create a subtrace retaining only the first message that satisfies φ and discarding all others. On that trace, we evaluate the expression $\top$, which will return true as soon as it reads one message from the trace (otherwise the whole expression evaluates to ?).

This translation also conveys the intuitive meaning of the operator: until a message satisfying φ is read, $\mathbf{F}\,\varphi$ is not *yet* true, but can become so in the future (and can never become false). Despite the existence of a single undefined value, the filter tells us whether this value can turn true in the future (when the expression at the right of the filter is $\top$), or turn false in the future (when the expression at the right of the filter is $\bot$), and hence "simulate" four-valued, finite-trace semantics for LTL.

Similarly, for $\mathbf{X}$, the monitor simply returns the value of φ on the trace made of the second message, which is written as:

$$\mathbf{X}\,\varphi \triangleq \frac{2}{\top} : \varphi$$

Finally, operator $\mathbf{U}$ ("until") requires slightly more work:

$$\varphi\,\mathbf{U}\,\psi \triangleq \frac{1}{\neg\varphi} : \bot \;\wedge_1\; \frac{1}{\psi} : \top$$

The translation of $\mathbf{U}$ builds two subtraces from an input trace $\overline{m}$. The first one retains the first message of $\overline{m}$ that does not satisfy φ. The left-hand side of $\wedge_1$ hence returns $\bot$ as soon as a message from $\overline{m}$ is read that does not satisfy φ. Similarly, the right-hand side of $\wedge_1$ returns $\top$ as soon as a message from $\overline{m}$ is read that satisfies ψ. Using these definitions, one can recursively translate any LTL expression into an equivalent filter expression.

3.2   Identities and Monitor Simplification

A number of identities on filters and monitors can be derived from the semantics defined in the previous section.

The first identities apply on filters. For instance, it is clear that the monitor $\perp$, when used as the condition for a filter, will result in nothing being output; this can be expressed as:

$$\overline{m} : \frac{k}{\perp} \equiv \epsilon \tag{1}$$

Dually, passing an input trace through a constant filter, is equivalent to this constant filter.

$$f : \perp \equiv \perp \tag{2}$$

Identities can also be defined for monitors. For example, it is straightforward to conclude that a monitor φ given the empty trace is equivalent to the constant monitor ?, which never outputs any event.

$$\epsilon : \varphi \equiv ? \tag{3}$$

These are a few examples of syntactical identities that can be derived from monitors and filters. These identities can be then applied in a straightforward way to perform simplification of filter and monitor expressions to reason about their possible verdicts. As an example, consider the LTL formula $\mathbf{G}\,\mathbf{F}\,p$. In the context of monitoring finite prefixes of traces, a monitor for this formula must return ? on every message it reads. Realizing this fact using standard techniques involves, for example, the construction of the corresponding Büchi automaton and the discovery that neither state is labelled as accepting. However, writing this expression in SL yields:

$$\overline{m} : \frac{1}{\left(\frac{1}{p}\perp\right)}\perp \equiv \overline{m} : \frac{1}{\perp}\perp \text{ by (2)}$$

$$\equiv \epsilon : \perp \text{ by (1)}$$

$$\equiv ? \text{ by (3)}$$

Hence we have seen how, by purely syntactical means, it is possible to simplify the original monitor down to the *constant* ?. This shall be distinguished from the monitor that performs a computation that just happens to return ? all the time.

4   Implementation and Experiments

To assess the feasibility of the approach, we implemented a runtime monitor/filter based on the concepts described in this paper. The implementation

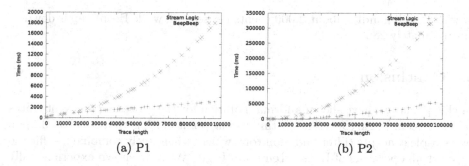

Fig. 1. Total running time with respect to messages received for various traces on sample properties.

is made of 1,600 lines of Java code independent of any external library, and is publicly available online.[1]

We ran a simple benchmark comparing our proof-of-concept implementation of Stream Logic with the latest version of BeepBeep[2], another Java-based runtime monitor written by one of the authors. BeepBeep was chosen among other existing monitors for a number of reasons: first, it is capable of accepting events made of parameter-value pairs in XML format; second, it is also implemented in Java (eliminating differences caused by the implementation language) and has roughly the same size in lines of code; finally, it uses a completely different evaluation algorithm, described in [6], which uses the recursive semantics of Linear Temporal Logic to monitor specifications.

We followed the same methodology as described in [1]. We built a dataset consisting of traces of randomly-generated events, with each event being made of up to ten random parameters, labelled $p_0, \ldots, p_9$ each carrying five possible values. Each trace has a length between 1 and 100,000 events, and 50 such traces were produced. Two properties were then verified on these traces. Property #1 is $\mathbf{G}\, p_0 \neq 0$, and simply asserts that in every event, parameter p_0, when present, is never equal to 0. Property #2 is $\mathbf{G}\,(p_0 = 0 \rightarrow \mathbf{X}\, p_1 = 0)$: it expresses the fact that whenever $p_0 = 0$ in some event, the next event is such that $p_1 = 0$.

Each property was written both as an SL expression and as an LTL formula, and these were sent respectively to our proof-of-concept implementation of an SL engine and to BeepBeep. The running time for evaluating these properties on each trace was computed and plotted in Fig. 1.

Two major observations can be made from these preliminary results. First, the SL engine, globally, performs faster than BeepBeep for a majority of properties and traces: in the case of P1, BeepBeep averages 5,000 events per second, and SL obtains roughly 25,000. However, the gap between both tools widens, both as the trace lengthens and as the property to process becomes more complex. In the case

---

[1] https://bitbucket.org/sylvainhalle/streamlogic.
[2] http://sourceforge.net/projects/beepbeep, version 1.7.6.

of P2, SL still handles about 2,000 events per second, while BeepBeep is down at approximately 280.

5 Conclusion

In this paper, we have shown a formal notation for the processing of event traces called Stream Logic (SL). The distinguishing point of SL is that it is based upon two simple concepts (filter and monitor), which, when freely combined, suffice to support all operators of Linear Temporal Logic. We have shown experimentally on a sample dataset how the application of the formal semantics of SL yields an evaluation algorithm with better running time compared to the traditional LTL evaluation algorithm presented in past literature. The promising results obtained on the proof-of-concept implementation discussed in this paper lead to a number of extensions and improvements over the current method. In particular,we shall investigate whether there exists a characterization of monitorable or enforceable properties based on syntactical properties of SL expressions.

References

1. Barre, B., Klein, M., Soucy-Boivin, M., Ollivier, P.-A., Hallé, S.: MapReduce for parallel trace validation of LTL properties. In: Qadeer, S., Tasiran, S. (eds.) RV 2012. LNCS, vol. 7687, pp. 184–198. Springer, Heidelberg (2012). doi:10.1007/978-3-642-35632-2_20
2. Barringer, H., Havelund, K.: TRACECONTRACT: a scala DSL for trace analysis. In: Butler, M., Schulte, W. (eds.) FM 2011. LNCS, vol. 6664, pp. 57–72. Springer, Heidelberg (2011)
3. Barringer, H., Rydeheard, D., Havelund, K.: Rule systems for run-time monitoring: from eagle to RuleR. J. Logic Comput. 20(3), 675–706 (2010)
4. Basin, D., Klaedtke, F., Müller, S.: Policy monitoring in first-order temporal logic. In: Touili, T., Cook, B., Jackson, P. (eds.) CAV 2010. LNCS, vol. 6174, pp. 1–18. Springer, Heidelberg (2010)
5. Groce, A., Havelund, K., Smith, M.H.: From scripts to specifications: the evolution of a flight software testing effort. In: Kramer, J., Bishop, J., Devanbu, P.T., Uchitel, S. (eds.) ICSE (2), pp. 129–138. ACM (2010)
6. Hallé, S., Villemaire, R.: Runtime enforcement of web service message contracts with data. IEEE Trans. Serv. Comput. 5(2), 192–206 (2012)
7. Meredith, P.O., Jin, D., Griffith, D., Chen, F., Rosu, G.: An overview of the MOP runtime verification framework. STTT 14(3), 249–289 (2012). doi:10.1007/s10009-011-0198-6
8. Verbeek, H.M.W., Buijs, J.C.A.M., van Dongen, B.F., van der Aalst, W.M.P.: XES, XESame, and ProM 6. In: Soffer, P., Proper, E. (eds.) CAiSE Forum 2010. LNBIP, vol. 72, pp. 60–75. Springer, Heidelberg (2010)

MIME: A Formal Approach to (Android) Emulation Malware Analysis

Fabio Bellini, Roberto Chiodi, and Isabella Mastroeni(✉)

Dipartimento di Informatica, Università di Verona, Verona, Italy
{fabio.bellini,roberto.chiodi}@studenti.univr.it,
isabella.mastroeni@univr.it

Abstract. In this paper, we propose a new dynamic and configurable approach to anti-emulation malware analysis, aiming at improving transparency of existing analyses techniques. We test the effectiveness of existing widespread free analyzers and we observe that the main problem of these analyses is that they provide static and immutable values to the parameter used in anti-emulation tests. Our approach aims at overcoming these limitations by providing an abstract non-interference-based approach modeling the fact that parameters can be modified dynamically, and the corresponding executions compared.

Keywords: Anti-emulation malware · Abstract non-interference · Program analysis

1 Introduction

The recent technological escalation led to a massive diffusion of electronic devices with permanent Internet connection. One of the most widespread mobile OS is Android, that have reached more than 1 billion device activations in the last year, with an average of 1.5 million activations per day. By installing software coming from untrusted markets, a user may cause/introduce lots of vulnerabilities on his system, such as privilege escalation, remote control, financial charge and data leakage [18]. For instance, one in five Android users faces a mobile threat, and the half of them installs trojans designed to steal money.

The Problem. In order to study malware payloads, it is necessary to analyze malicious software by using specific tools, based on emulation and virtualization, which statically and dynamically analyze the code. The problem is that some malware try to avoid these analyses by exploiting environment detection tricks allowing them to understand whether they are emulated or not. These techniques are called *anti-emulation checks* [6,15]. If an anti-emulation check detects the presence of a virtual environment, the malware changes its behavior

This work is partly supported by the MIUR FIRB project FACE (Formal Avenue for Chasing malwarE) RBFR13AJFT.

J. Garcia-Alfaro et al. (Eds.): FPS 2015, LNCS 9482, pp. 259–267, 2016.
DOI: 10.1007/978-3-319-30303-1_16

showing only harmless executions or simply aborting the computation. In [11] it has been proposed a method to automatize the creation of red pills, generating thousands of mnemonic opcodes that trigger different behaviors in real and emulated environments. Futhermore, lots of anti-emulation checks were find out for many different emulation environments like QEMU, Bochs and VMWare [4,8,13,14,16]. On the other hand, several tools were developed to reduce discrepancies between real and emulated environments, trying to obtain *perfect transparency* [3,7,17]. Recently, the security focus moved to the Android mobile environment, where virtualization on devices is inefficient and not widespread nowadays. There are currently some Android analyzers available that scan applications trying to extract their main features like permissions, services or used networks, for detecting malicious actions. The problem, is that also Android malware started to embed anti-emulation checks, making them resilient to analyses, and, in [12], it is shown how simple is to bypass analyzers by using trivial anti-emulation checks.

Our Approach. We test 28 samples belonging to 15 different known malware families on 9 analysis frameworks available online, such as Andrubis and Virus-Total. We analyze the obtained results, providing a more specific perspective on the connection between the state-of-the-art of anti-emulation techniques and our samples sources. This work allows us to identify the limitations of the existing analyzers, such as the lack of versatility and customization, usually caused by the general trend to prefer better performance instead of stronger protection. Moreover, we observe that there are no formal frameworks allowing us to semantically understand the problem of anti-emulation. A semantic comprehension would allow us to compare different techniques, and to understand how we can tune our analysis in order to adapt it to different attacking scenarios. In the existing literature, the only attempt to formalize the notion of anti-emulation is given as an *interference* between the environment and the program execution [6]. The problem with this notion is that it is too strong, since benign applications may change behaviors depending on the environment. Hence, we propose a formal definition of anti-emulation, given in terms of abstract non-interference [5], a weakening of non-interference based on abstract interpretation [2], where both the property that can/cannot interfere, and the output observation are modeled as properties of the concrete behavior. This formal framework is used for better understanding how we can make *anti*-anti-emulation checks stronger depending on the platform we work on, allowing us to improve existing analysis tools and providing a first overview of an ideal analysis framework called *Multiple Investigation in Malware Emulation* (MIME).

2   Limitations of Existing Android Malware Analyses

We started the test phase analyzing the anti-emulation checks in Android well-known malware families. In our work, we consider: *BadNews, BaseBridge, BgServ, DroidDream Light, Droid KungFu* – 1, 2, 3, 4, Sapp, Update –, *FakeMart, Geinimi,*

Jifake, OBad and *ZSone*. For each malware family, we chose two different variants to verify how frameworks react to small code differences that are not related to malware payload – only in Jifake and Droid KungFu Update this was not possible, because only one version was available. We submitted all these samples to 9 different analyzers, free and available with Web interface: *AndroTotal Andrubis, APKScan, Dexter, ForeSafe, Mobile-SandBox, VirusImmune, VirusTotal* and *VisualThreat*. In our tests, we submitted samples which were statically and dynamically analyzed or scanned by a pool of anti-virus software: all the previous frameworks could cover one or more of these categories. By summarizing, we collected 252 different combinations malware-analyzer that are fully available in [1]. In order to avoid emulation, most of malware check several environment issues, such as constants in Android Build class and/or other information as IMEI[1], IMSI[2] and telephone sensors management. Thus, in order to verify the behavior and, consecutively, the presence of anti-emulation checks in those malware, we mainly need dynamic analysis: this means that the most complete results come from Andrubis, APKScan, ForeSafe and VirusTotal. Nevertheless, we observe that even these frameworks use trivial anti-emulation-related parameters, such as IMEI, IMSI, etc. Other kinds of malware anti-emulation checks are also in general used, as shown in the following example.

```
deviceId=android.provider.Settings.System.getString(context1.
     getContentResolver(),"android_id");
if (deviceId == null){
        deviceId = "Emulator";
}
```

Listing 1.1. Geinimi anti-emulation check inspecting the android id value

We can observe that, most of the actual frameworks do not provide the possibility to dynamically customize the configuration of the virtual machine (in the following denoted VM), making easy for a malware to detect the virtual environment. Finally, the analyzers we considered in the test phase, do not allow multiple execution in different virtual environments, but always provide the same configuration for the VM, hence, if different executions in different environments are required, it is necessary to manually upload the samples in several frameworks. All these limitations make the analysis of anti-emulation malware often imprecise (being detected) and/or expensive.

3 Formal Definition of Anti-emulation

We show here that the existing notion of anti-emulation [6] is too strong for really capturing the problem, and we propose a model based on *abstract* non-interference. In non-interference we have some information to protect that has

---

[1] International Mobile Equipment Identity.
[2] International Mobile Subscriber Identity.

not to interfere with the observable information. In the anti-emulation field, the information to protect is the "kind" (virtual or not) of execution environment: when a malware uses anti-emulation techniques there is a flow of information from the "kind" of execution environment to the malware.

Abstract Non-interference. Suppose the variables of program split in private (H) and public (L). Let ρ a property characterizing the *attacker observation*, while ϕ is the property stating what, of the private data, can flow to the output observation, also called *declassification*. A program P satisfies ANI if $\forall h_1, h_2 \in$ H, $\forall l \subseteq$ L: $\phi(h_1) = \phi(h_2) \Rightarrow \rho(\llbracket P \rrbracket(h_1, l)) = \rho(\llbracket P \rrbracket(h_2, l))$. Whenever the attacker is able to observe the output property ρ, then it can observe nothing more than the property ϕ of the input [5,9,10].

Observational Semantics and Formal Definition of Anti-Emulation. We focus on Android applications which are written in Java and compiled to *Dalvik* byte-code, with the possibility to use a large part of the standard Java library. Let **App** be the set of Android applications. According to the definition in [6], we model the behavior of a program **A** as a function depending on the input memory $\sigma \in$ **Mem** and on the environment **E** $\in$ **Env**. An environment provides "all the aspects of the system the program might query or discover, including the other software installed, the characteristics of hardware, or the time of day" [6]. In order to describe the actions performed by a program we consider a set of *Events $\mathcal{E}$* describing the relevant actions performed by the application during its execution. Let $\Sigma = \mathcal{E} \times$ **Mem** be the set of program states then, the observational semantics is: $\llbracket \cdot \rrbracket$: **App** $\longrightarrow$ (**Env** $\times$ **Mem** $\to \wp(\Sigma^*)$). Given **A** $\in$ **App**, $\llbracket A \rrbracket$ is a function providing the trace of events executed by the program **A** depending on an hosting environment **E** and on an initial input σ. The only formal characterization of anti-emulation [6] says that **P** uses *anti-emulation techniques* if its execution under a real environment $\mathbf{E_r}$ changes its behavior under an emulated environment $\mathbf{E_e}$, although input σ is the same and environments are very similar: $\llbracket P \rrbracket(\mathbf{E_e}, \sigma) \neq \llbracket P \rrbracket(\mathbf{E_r}, \sigma)$. In this case, $\neq$ denotes the fact that the two executions are "observationally" different.

The ANI-Based Approach. Our approach, is based on what we observe of the program executions, i.e., on the granularity of the set $\mathcal{E}$ modeling the events, namely the actions, considered suspicious. In particular, we have to identify the set $\mathcal{M} \subseteq \mathcal{E}$ of the suspicious/malicious events. We denote $\mathcal{B} \stackrel{\text{def}}{=} \mathcal{E} \setminus \mathcal{M}$ the set of all the supposed benign events. The set $\mathcal{M}$ can be extracted depending on known information regarding the sample that we want to analyze. For instance, when considering applications handling images could be *malicious* the action of sending an SMS, while this action is perfectly acceptable for instant messaging applications. Alternatively, we can use the common payloads investigated in [18].

Let $\mathbb{E} \subseteq$ **Env** the admitted range of variation for (virtual and real) environments, $\sigma \in$ **Mem** an input for the application **A**, let $X \subseteq \Sigma^*$ and $X_{|\mathbb{E}} \subseteq \mathcal{E}$ the set of events in the traces in X

$$Sel_\mathbb{E}(\langle \mathbf{E}, \sigma \rangle) = \begin{cases} \langle \mathbb{E}, \sigma \rangle & \text{if } \mathbf{E} \in \mathbb{E} \\ \langle \mathbf{E}, \sigma \rangle & \text{otherwise} \end{cases} \qquad Obs_{\mathscr{M}}(X) = \begin{cases} \texttt{True} & \text{if } X \cap \mathscr{M} \neq \emptyset \\ \texttt{False otherwise} \end{cases}$$

$Sel_\mathbb{E}$ decides whether an environment is in the considered range $\mathbb{E}$ or not, while $Obs_{\mathscr{M}}$ checks whether the application shows only benign behaviors or even malicious ones.

The core of the abstract non-interference-based model of anti-emulation is the flow of information between the execution environment and the application behavior. Our definition strongly depends on the set $\mathscr{M}$. Thus, fixed the set $\mathscr{M}$ and given the abstractions $Sel_\mathbb{E}$ and $Obs_{\mathscr{M}}$ defined above, an application $\mathtt{A}$ does not use *anti-emulation* with respect to $\mathbb{E}$ and $\mathscr{M}$ if:

$$\forall \langle E_1, \sigma_1 \rangle, \langle E_2, \sigma_2 \rangle \in \mathtt{Env} \times \mathtt{Mem.} \; \mathtt{Sel}_\mathbb{E}(\langle E_1, \sigma_1 \rangle) = \mathtt{Sel}_\mathbb{E}(\langle E_2, \sigma_2 \rangle) \Rightarrow \\ Obs_{\mathscr{M}}(\llbracket \mathtt{A} \rrbracket(\langle E_1, \sigma_1 \rangle)) = \mathtt{Obs}_{\mathscr{M}}(\llbracket \mathtt{A} \rrbracket(\langle E_2, \sigma_2 \rangle)) \tag{1}$$

The malware does not contain any anti-emulation check, with respect to the environment range $\mathbb{E}$ and the malicious actions set $\mathscr{M}$, if by varying the environment inside $\mathbb{E}$ we observe only malicious actions (the malware does not contain anti-emulation checks) or only benign actions (the model does not capture the correct anti-emulation checks of the malware analyzed).

4 Multiple Investigation in Malware Emulation (MIME)

We propose an analyzer architecture based in a configurable VM called MIME – Multiple Investigation in Malware Emulation. Existing analyses use an environment setting which is static and immutable, in the sense that they cannot be configured depending on the application contexts. Moreover, from our empirical studies, we observed that the problem of existing analyses is that parameters are set to fixed, and often trivial, values. This means that a truly transparent analyzer should be able to provide values that the malware expects from a real environment. Unfortunately, it is quite unrealistic to find a value robust to different malware. The idea we propose is to consider the ANI definition of anti-emulation, where we look for anti-emulation checks by analyzing malware several times, and each time under different environment settings. In other words, we let the input environment to vary, by setting a list of anti-emulation parameters (such as IMEI, IMSI, . . .), and we observe how the corresponding execution is affected. Our goal is the automation of this formal model by making systematic the variation of the environment setting and automatic the corresponding executions and comparisons. The main idea of MIME is to perform several executions depending a configurable environment, which is systematically modified until we find an anti-emulation check (detected by an evaluation function) or until we exhaustively explore the space of environments we consider. In Fig. 1, we show the proposed analysis architecture.

Configuring MIME Architectures. We choose a pool of n anti-emulation-connected input parameters. We associate with each parameter a list of pre-arranged values, in order to automatize the environment setting. It is worth

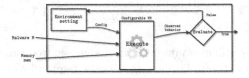

Fig. 1. Simple architecture of a MIME customizable analyzer.

noting, that both the set of parameters and the corresponding values can be easily customized. In the MIME strategy, we represent these parameters like *rotors*, and each value corresponds to a position: by changing only one position at a time, we can detect which are the malware reactions. In general, let p_i the i-th parameter, let R_i be the rotor for p_i, and let V_i be the set of values for p_i. This idea, in our formal model corresponds to consider a set $\mathbb{E}_i$ for each parameter p_i, which simply corresponds to the execution environment where the parameter p_i is set to one of the values in V_i, while all the other parameters are set to a default/trivial initial value (for IMEI it may be all 0s). This choice is necessary since we aim at understanding precisely whether the parameter p_i, and not others, may affect execution. In this case, we consider Eq. 1, with input abstraction $Sel_{\mathbb{E}_i}$. Namely, the MIME strategy proposes to verify n times the Eq. 1, each time with respect one parameter p_i, i.e., with respect to $\mathbb{E}_i$. Now, the evaluation function returns a boolean value identifying the presence of at least one malicious action in $\mathcal{M}$.

Using MIME for Analyzing Anti-Emulation Malware. Let us explain how the MIME strategy aims at improving the transparency of existing analyses. It is clear that the price to pay is in the performance of the analysis. Let `Rotors` be the matrix of all rotors, each rotor i has a number of possible different values max_i. Suppose to have $n + 1$ rotors, then we define `max` as maximal value in $\{ max_i \, | \, i \in [0, n] \}$. Let M be the analyzed malware, and `mem` the machine state memory. `Config` is the array containing the $n + 1$ positions of the rotors used for

```
Function: Mime
Input: M, Rotors[n+1][max],mem
result = null;
for each k in [0,n] Config[k]=0; //Environment reset (rotors initial pos)
trace = Execute(M,Config,mem);
val_0=Evaluate(trace);
for each k in [0,n] Config[k]=max_k; //Environment setting to max rotors pos
trace = Execute(M,Config,mem);
val_m = Evaluate(trace);
if (val_0 != val_m) result = to_string(Catching_anti_emu(M, Rotors,mem));
if (val_0 == val_m)
    if (val_0) result = malware; // M is a malware without anti-emulation
    else result = pot_not_malware; //M is not recognized as malware
Output: result
```

Listing 1.2. MIME approach in anti-emulation malware recognition.

setting the environment. `Execute` corresponds to the observation of the malware execution, formally it corresponds to the observed semantics $[\![\cdot]\!]$ where `Config` corresponds precisely to its environment input. `Evaluate` corresponds to the evaluation function that, as we noticed before, is modeled by the output abstraction $Obs_{\mathcal{M}}$. Finally, `position_anti_emu` is the array of the rotor positions where an anti-emulation check is detected by the evaluation. Listing 1.2 implements the idea that we first compute the default configuration of rotor parameters, whose evaluation `val_0` is `true` if a malicious action in $\mathcal{M}$ is observed. Then we execute the malware in the smarter configuration possible in our model, where the rotors are set to the maximal values, and we evaluate in `val_m` whether the corresponding execution exhibits malicious events. If the two values are different it means that somewhere in the code, there is an anti-emulation check, and therefore we launch the function `Catching_anti_emu`. If the two values are both equal to `true` then it means that the malware does not use anti-emulation checks. Finally, if the values are both equal to `false`, and we knew that it was a malware, it means that it uses an anti-emulation check based on different parameters or it uses a conjunctive combination of tests on the known parameters. We lose this situation since we check parameters one at time. However, to the best of our knowledge, based on the experimental results, this last situation is not used by anti-emulation checks. Listing 1.3 shows `Catching_anti_emu`. In this case, we have to vary the environment setting looking for the parameters responsible of the anti-emulation check. Since we aim at observing the interference of each single parameter on the malware behavior, we let only one rotor at time to change value, while all the others are set to default initial values. For this reason, each time we finish to analyze the interference of one rotor, we reset it before changing rotor. We always check all the rotors since there may be more than one anti-emulation check. `val` becomes `true` if some malicious action is detected, at this point since we know that there was also an harmless execution (the routine is called only in this case), it means that the current rotor contains an anti-emulation check in the current position, that we store in `position_anti_emu`. At the end of the execution, this vector contains all the rotor positions, namely

```
Function: Catching_anti_emu
Input: M, Rotors[n+1][max],mem
position_anti_emu[n] = null;
for each i in [0,n] {
    for each k in [0,n] Config[k]=0; //Environment reset
    for each j in [0, max_i-1]{
        Config[j]=Rotors[i,j];
        trace = Execute(M,Config,mem);
        val = Evaluate (trace);
        if (val) position_anti_emu[i] = j; break;
        else     j = j+1;
    }
    i = i+1; //change rotor
}
Output: position_anti_emu
```

Listing 1.3. Catching anti-emulation checks in MIME.

the parameters values, used in anti-emulation checks. If at the end this vector is all `null`, then it means that the anti-emulation checks involve unobserved parameters or are based on different techniques.

5   Future Works

We develop our approach in the Android word however, our approach to anti-emulation can be easly generalized to any platform. In this case, it is necessary to change the `Evironment setting` and the VM, in order to let it analyze desktop malware. Until now, no implementation of our approach has been made, so a possible future implementation of MIME will be useful to successfully analyze anti-emulation malware. This would help also in understanding the scalability problem. Finally, our ANI model of anti-emulation is strongly related to the definition of the $\mathcal{M}$ set of the malicious events. We would like to improve this model and study in depth the relation between the $\mathcal{M}$ set and the anti-emulation checks detection in malware, characterizing the amount of both false positives and negatives.

References

1. Bellini, F., Chiodi, R., Mastroeni, I.: Mime: a formal approach for multiple investigation in (android) malware emulation analysis. Technical report RR 97/2015 (2015). http://hdl.handle.net/11562/926789
2. Cousot, P., Cousot, R.: Abstract interpretation: a unified lattice model for static analysis of programs by construction or approximation of fixpoints. In: Conference Record of POPL 1977, pp. 238–252. ACM (1977)
3. Dinaburg, A., Royal, P., Sharif, M., Lee, W.: Ether: malware analysis via hardware virtualization extensions. In: Proceedings of CCS 2008, pp. 51–62. ACM (2008)
4. P. Ferrie. Attacks on virtual machine emulators. Symantec Corporation, Mountain View (2007)
5. Giacobazzi, R., Mastroeni, I.: Abstract non-interference: parameterizing non-interference by abstract interpretation. In: Proceedings of POPL 2004, pp. 186–197. ACM (2004)
6. Kang, M.G., Yin, H., Hanna, S., McCamant, S., Song, D.: Emulating emulation-resistant malware. In: Proceedings of VMSec 2009, pp. 11–22. ACM (2009)
7. Lindorfer, M., Kolbitsch, C., Milani Comparetti, P.: Detecting environment-sensitive malware. In: Sommer, R., Balzarotti, D., Maier, G. (eds.) RAID 2011. LNCS, vol. 6961, pp. 338–357. Springer, Heidelberg (2011)
8. Liston, T., Skoudis, E., On the cutting edge: Thwarting virtual machine detection (2006). http://handlers.sans.org/tliston/ThwartingVMDetection_Liston_Skoudis.pdf
9. Mastroeni, I.: On the rôle of abstract non-interference in language-based security. In: Yi, K. (ed.) APLAS 2005. LNCS, vol. 3780, pp. 418–433. Springer, Heidelberg (2005)
10. Mastroeni, I.: Abstract interpretation-based approaches to security - A survey on abstract non-interference, its challenging applications. In: Semantics, Abstract Interpretation, Reasoning about Programs: Essays Dedicated to David A. Schmidt on the Occasion of his 60th Birthday, pp. 41–65 (2013)

11. Paleari, R., Martignoni, L., Fresi Roglia, G., Bruschi, D.: A fistful of red-pills: how to automatically generate procedures to detect cpu emulators. In: Procedings of WOOT 2009, p. 2. USENIX Association (2009)
12. Petsas, T., Voyatzis, G., Athanasopoulos, E., Polychronakis, M., Ioannidis, S.: Rage against the virtual machine: hindering dynamic analysis of android malware. In Proceedings of EuroSec 2014, pp. 5:1–5:6. ACM (2014)
13. D. Quist, V. Smith. Detecting the presence of virtual machines using the local data table. Offensive Computing (2006). http://index-of.es/Misc/vm.pdf
14. Raffetseder, T., Kruegel, C., Kirda, E.: Detecting system emulators. In: Garay, J.A., Lenstra, A.K., Mambo, M., Peralta, R. (eds.) ISC 2007. LNCS, vol. 4779, pp. 1–18. Springer, Heidelberg (2007)
15. Rutkowska, J.: Red pill... or how to detect vmm using (almost) one cpu instruction (2004). http://www.securiteam.com/securityreviews/6Z00H20BQS.html
16. Vishnani, K., Pais, A.R., Mohandas, R.: Detecting & defeating split personality malware. In: Proceedings of SECURWARE 2011, pp. 7–13 (2011)
17. Yan, L.K., Jayachandra, M., Zhang, M., Yin, H.: V2e: combining hardware virtualization and software emulation for transparent and extensible malware analysis. Sigplan Not. 47(7), 227–238 (2012)
18. Zhou, Y., Jiang, X.: Dissecting android malware: characterization and evolution. In: Proceedings of SP 2012, pp. 95–109. IEEE Computer Society (2012)

Information Classification Enablers

Erik Bergström[✉] and Rose-Mharie Åhlfeldt

Informatics Research Centre, University of Skövde, 541 28 Skövde, Sweden
{erik.bergstrom,rose-mharie.ahlfeldt}@his.se

Abstract. This paper presents a comprehensive systematic literature review of information classification (IC) enablers. We propose a classification based on the well-known levels of management: strategic, tactical and operational. The results reveal that a large number of enablers could be adopted to increase the applicability of IC in organizations. The results also indicate that there is not one single enabler solving the problem, but rather several enablers can influence the adoption.

Keywords: Information classification · Systematic literature review · ISMS

1 Introduction

To organize information security, Information Security Management Systems (ISMS) such as the ISO 27000-series can be used. ISMS can offer support in planning, implementing and maintaining information security. A central ISMS activity is asset management, where organizational assets are identified by an inventory, and appropriate protections are defined [31]. All information found should have an owner, and the acceptable use of the asset should be identified, documented and implemented. To be able to ensure that information receives an appropriate protection, IC is performed on each asset [31]. The information is normally classified according to its criticality, and value for the organization from a confidentiality, integrity, and availability perspective. A higher classification implies that more protective measures are needed. IC is important, not only for determining the value of information assets, but also because it serves as the input to the risk analysis [43]. IC stems from the military sector, where possibly the most well-known variant exists: top secret, secret and unclassified. IC follows the information lifecycle, and classifications can change over time, making it ever-present in an organization.

Several studies highlight that many organizations are struggling with IC, even though it is not a new concept [17,24,25,35], and even a compulsory activity for some governmental agencies [43]. A literature study focusing on issues in the IC process identified a number of problems ranging from technological to human and organizational issues [8]. A frequently mentioned problem is the classification scheme itself, and the lack of more detailed guidelines, making it hard to implement [24]. The ISO 27000-series does not include any scheme or

© Springer International Publishing Switzerland 2016
J. Garcia-Alfaro et al. (Eds.): FPS 2015, LNCS 9482, pp. 268–276, 2016.
DOI: 10.1007/978-3-319-30303-1_17

model, but rather some guidelines [43]. It is not expected that organizations could use exactly the same scheme and approach for IC, but the way from standard to implementation is for many very difficult, making ISMS fail at an early stage.

Research about IC in general is limited [43], and to the best of our knowledge, no other surveys with an enabler focus have been carried out. This work is a continuation of the issue study by Bergström and Åhlfeldt [8], but here, the aim is to identify the enablers for the IC process, by presenting and classifying the existing body of literature to explore what decreases the inhibitors and enables successful implementation. The study has been performed as a Systematic Literature Review (SLR), where the results have been classified and analysed. In this work, the SLR guidelines presented in [37] have been used to answer the following research question: *what are the main enablers in the IC process?*

2 Method

SLR was used as a way to ensure that the search and retrieval process was unbiased and accurate. There has been some critique against SLRs [12], and the authors acknowledge that the search and retrieval process in SLRs is not the most important step, but the reading and understanding of the subject area. IC is a well-established term used, e.g., in the ISO 27000-series, but there are some synonyms that were found in the pilot searches. The search string (("security classification "OR" information classification "OR" data classification") AND "information security") was used for full-text searches in the following databases without any limitations: the ACM Guide to Computing Literature, IEEE Xplore, ScienceDirect (Elsevier), Springer Link and Inspec (Ovid). The search returned 1545 publications that were downloaded and aggregated into a reference manager. A first rough sorting was performed by looking at the title, abstract and searches in the full text document in order to find out where the word classification was used. Exclusion criteria used in this first sorting was duplicate hits, unavailable publications, non-English results, search terms only in author biography or reference list, faulty results and results from completely other contexts than the aim of the study. After this sorting, 254 papers remained, and after a final full-text review, 49 papers describing enablers for IC were left.

Initially, the results were coded with open coding following the recommendations from Strauss and Corbin [52], that led to a categorization in 25 different categories. Following this, it was decided to classify these categories into fewer broader categories, or themes, using thematic coding, to decrease interpretation of the "secondary" papers that were not primarily about IC. In thematic coding, the analysis frequently takes its start from a list of known or anticipated themes [5], in this case, three broader themes emerged: *strategic, tactical* and *operational*, that are well-known levels of management [51].

3 Classification and Analysis of Literature

The classification into themes has been performed according to where in the organization the implementation of the enabler would be carried out.

Strategic. It is essential that when IC is introduced in an organization, it needs to get accepted and embraced, and to get there, support is needed from others in the organization [25]. *Key influencers* need to be brought into the process early [25], so that they can be a part of the design of the classification strategy [17]. That means, for example, management, human resources, loss prevention, and legal should be involved since they will share the result of the classification [32]. Another approach is to target only senior personnel since their decisions are more influential, and it can limit the numbers in the decision process [19]. It is also important to acknowledge that one key factor of a successful implementation is to have *top management support* [38,49], even if they are not directly involved in the development of the IC scheme.

It is important to remember that IC should be employed from cradle to grave [29]. From an asset management perspective, this means that also retention, destruction and archiving of the data need consideration [39]. In other words, *Information Lifecycle Management* (ILM) needs to be considered from an IC perspective [1], so that, for instance, the proper value of the information is used, and that information is stored correctly according to its value [4]. Applying ILM in association with IC might also help in identifying the information capital in an organization [3].

Several papers emphasize the importance of using the *same IC scheme* for all information in the whole organization [18,22,50], or even between different organizations that are in a similar context, such as, for instance, the intelligence community [23]. In an organization where *legislation* can be used to motivate IC, it can be seen as one of the most effective tools in getting the necessary muscle and support to get it implemented [25].

Tactical. A well mentioned enabler is to *simplify the IC scheme* itself so that it becomes generally understood [17,21,25,27,44,46,49]. Few describe explicitly what actually makes the scheme simple, but Photopoulos [46] mentions a minimal number of levels should be adopted for simplicity and effectiveness, and not to use overly granulated guidelines. Fibikova and Müller [21] agree with simplifying the scheme, but not to oversimplify it. One way of simplifying the scheme is to use visual aids. Everett [19] suggests the use of this to highlight, how different documents should be handled when they are removed such as shredded or not. It is also possible to use icons, as they themselves draw attention, and through familiarity, associated controls are brought into mind [30]. A set of icons for IC are proposed by Hilton [30], that as well stresses that they can be used for conveying messages in a multilingual environment.

Another approach to IC is to not classify all information in a process, but rather to *classify networks* [17] or *classify applications* [21] according to their sensitivity instead of the information. Several authors recommend a *data-centric approach* where one starts with a hard look at what data the business must protect and why instead of going for all information in the organization [3,7,34,35].

Collette [17] recommends the use of *best practices*, because they can elevate the authority of the security office in designing the scheme. Bunker [13] emphasizes the need of building a *security culture*, by using regular updates, and to use newsletters focusing on the individual rather than the organization. There is a need of explaining the *why*, and the *how* on an ongoing basis, to use FAQs, to create *easy routes* to contact security personnel [19], and to use an information *security awareness* program [34]. There are also some recommendations concerning how the scheme is communicated [10,44,55], and when it needs to be reviewed or audited [6,10,33]. An understanding of what is realistically achievable is important, and it is better to do some classification than none [25]. One way to start can be to run a successful *pilot project* to show a "quick win" that demonstrates the benefits to the organization [49].

Finally, when virtualization is introduced, or when information is moved to the cloud, more care and thought around classification must be put in place [18,26,56], and it is recommended to classify [42] since each classification might have distinct security requirements that need to be passed to the cloud provider [15]. Service contracts should specify the ownership of the information [42], but Wilson [56] points out that regardless, transparency might decrease contrary to the in-house equivalent.

Operational. The most frequently mentioned enabler is *staff training* [16,20,29, 30,36,45,46,48,56], or *learning* [45,47]. There are different views on how much, and when training should be offered as a mandatory prerequisite [23,33], or through periodical campaigns [40].

There are numerous references to tools alleviating IC in a general way [14, 32,40,41]. Several mentions automatic or semiautomatic *classification tools*, or the need of developing tools [4,13,28,53,54], but it is also acknowledged that ultimately, classification is a subjective business best done collaboratively [25].

Labeling is a part of the IC process, and is applied after the classification in a similar fashion as the famous "Top Secret" label used on paper, but electronically. The label itself is an enabler [9], and it can e.g. prevent users from sharing data in an unauthorized manner [7], help organizations meet legal and regulatory requirements [19], enable automation [57], and be extra important when transitive information is created, or information moves rapidly in an organization [44]. A simple way of ensuring staff to stick to the classification is by providing templates, which include relevant protection markers [19]. There are also suggestions on what the label should consist of, e.g., an ownership part, audit trail, and a change log [11], and time-related parameters [17]. The lack of labels can also be used as a label [32].

Increased granularity, e.g. classification on paragraph level [27] is tightly coupled with access control mechanisms, which are out of scope here, but as it decides the approach to the classification it is worth to mention. The granularity is also coupled to collaborative working environments, where information might need a finer granularity on the classification to enable effective sharing of information [1,14], e.g. in governmental settings [2].

4 Discussion and Conclusions

Table 1 shows an overview of the enablers. The enablers should not be measured quantitatively, but rather be seen as a more frequently mentioned enabler. Hence, operational enablers are, for instance, not more important than strategic ones.

Table 1. Overview of the key enablers found in the publications, classified according to the proposed themes strategic, tactical and operational.

Themes	Publications	Key Enablers
Strategic	[1,3,4,17–19,22,23,25,29,32,38, 39,49,50]	Key influencers, management support, ILM, same scheme, and legislation.
Tactical	[3,6,7,10,13,15,17–19,21,25– 27,30,33–35,42,44,46,49,55,56]	Simplifying the scheme, classify applications/networks, awareness, security culture, best practices, and pilot project.
Operational	[1,2,4,7,9,11,13,14,16,17,19,20, 23,25,27–30,32,33,36,40,41,44– 48,53,54,56,57]	Staff training, learning, automatic or semiautomatic classification tools, labeling, and granularity.

The inclusive SLR approach was a good choice, and the results also include less scientific publications that were more practitioner-oriented and contained more hands-on-oriented enablers. One aspect of IC is that the process is somewhat an art form, and practitioners understanding of the process, and what they see as enablers should be of interest to the scientific community. A complicating factor among practitioner driven work in the information security field is the potential reluctance to share experiences and results, especially negative ones.

One interesting result is the discussion on support from key influencers, and top-level management. For example, ISO/IEC 27002, mentions that all owners of information should be accountable for the classification. That implies that at least, all staff handling information in a way that could change the classification, should know about classification and be able to perform it, but since IC is a subjective business, this pose a tremendous challenge for organizations.

Many state that the scheme should be simplified, but not too simplified. Of course, the exact layout depends on the organization, and the context, but what is a good balance? Several that ask for a higher granularity are from the military sector, so it might not apply to others that do not have the same need of information sharing, and a simpler approach could be adopted. There are a number of publications stating that the focus should be on a part of all information, e.g., the most confidential and proprietary information. This is a good suggestion, but without asset management, and inventory, the organization might not even know what information they possess.

ISO 27002 mentions the information lifecycle as a part of asset management, but does not give any guidance on how to implement it, and how to connect it to the scheme. A more explicit connection could be beneficial, maybe by highlighting the current stage of an asset explicitly in the scheme.

Because of the nature of IC, one suggestion is to turn to practitioners to try to gather best-practices, and experiences. The ISO/IEC 27002 standard is very general and brief on IC, and a clearer process description along with an example scheme could enable the implementation. IC is a multifaceted problem, and there is not one single enabler that will solve all of them. More likely, a unique combination of enablers will be the solution for an organization. However, it is highly possible that most organizations could benefit from a few of them, and more case studies are needed to evaluate this, and to identify which ones are more important. There are many promising enablers identified here, for instance, the use of visual aids, simplified schemes, and the introduction of ILM in the scheme.

References

1. Adiraju, S.K.: Security considerations in integrating the fragmented, outsourced, ITSM processes. In: Third International Conference on Services in Emerging Markets, pp. 175–182 (2012)
2. Ager, T., Johnson, C., Kiernan, J.: Policy-based management and sharing of sensitive information among government agencies. In: Military Communications Conference, pp. 1–9 (2006)
3. Aksentijevic, S., Tijan, E., Agatic, A.: Information security as utilization tool of enterprise information capital. In: Proceedings of the 34th International Convention, pp. 1391–1395 (2011)
4. Al-Fedaghi, S.: On information lifecycle management. In: Asia-Pacific Services Computing Conference, pp. 335–342 (2008)
5. Ayres, L.: Thematic Coding and Analysis. The Sage encyclopedia of qualitative research methods, Thousand Oaks (2008). pp. 868–869
6. Baškarada, S.: Analysis of data. Information Quality Management Capability Maturity Model, pp. 139–221. Vieweg+Teubner, Wiesbaden (2009)
7. Bayuk, J.: Data-centric security. Comput. Fraud Secur. 2009(3), 7–11 (2009)
8. Bergström, E., Åhlfeldt, R.-M.: Information classification issues. In: Bernsmed, K., Fischer-Hübner, S. (eds.) NordSec 2014. LNCS, vol. 8788, pp. 27–41. Springer, Heidelberg (2014)
9. Bernard, R.: Information lifecycle security risk assessment: A tool for closing security gaps. Comput. Secur. 26(1), 26–30 (2007)
10. Bezuidenhout, M., Mouton, F., Venter, H.S.: Social engineering attack detection model: Seadm. In: Information Security for South Africa, pp. 1–8 (2010)
11. Blazic, A.J., Saljic, S.: Confidentiality labeling using structured data types. In: Fourth International Conference on Digital Society, pp. 182–187 (2010)
12. Boell, S., Cezec-Kecmanovic, D.: Are systematic reviews better, less biased and of higher quality? In: European Conference on Information Systems (2011)
13. Bunker, G.: Technology is not enough: taking a holistic view for information assurance. Inf. Secur. Tech. Rep. 17(1–2), 19–25 (2012)

14. Burnap, P., Hilton, J.: Self protecting data for de-perimeterised information sharing. In: Third International Conference on Digital Society, pp. 65–70 (2009)
15. Chaput, S., Ringwood, K.: Cloud compliance: A framework for using cloud computing in a regulated world. In: Antonopoulos, N., Gillam, L. (eds.) Cloud Computing: Principles, Systems and Applications. Computer Communications and Networks, 14th edn, pp. 241–255. Springer, Heidelbreg (2010)
16. Clark Iii, C., Chaffin, L., Chuvakin, A., Dunkel, D., Fogie, S., Gregg, M., Grossman, J., Hansen, R., Petkov, P.D., Rager, A., Schiller, C.A., Paladino, S.: InfoSecurity 2008 Threat Analysis. Syngress, Burlington (2008)
17. Collette, R.: Overcoming obstacles to data classification [information security]. Computer Economics Report 28(4), 8–11 (2006). (Int. Ed.)
18. Escalante, D., Korty, A.J.: Cloud services: policy and assessment. EDUCAUSE Rev. 46(4), 60–61 (2011)
19. Everett, C.: Building solid foundations: the case for data classification. Comput. Fraud Secur. 2011(6), 5–8 (2011)
20. Feuerlicht, J., Grattan, P.: The role of classification of information in controlling data proliferation in end-user personal computer environment. Comput. Secur. 8(1), 59–66 (1989)
21. Fibikova, L., Müller, R.: A simplified approach for classifying applications. In: Pohlmann, N., Reimer, H., Schneider, W. (eds.) ISSE 2010 Securing Electronic Business Processes, chapter 4, pp. 39–49. Vieweg+Teubner (2011)
22. Freeman, E.: Information and computer security risk management. In: Ghosh, S., Turrini, E. (eds.) Cybercrimes: A Multidisciplinary Analysis, 8th edn, pp. 151–163. Springer, Heidelberg (2011)
23. Gantz, S.D., Philpott, D.R.: FISMA and the Risk Management Framework. Syngress, Boston (2013)
24. Ghernaouti-Helie, S., Simms, D., Tashi, I.: Protecting information in a connected world: A question of security and of confidence in security. In: 14th International Conference on Network-Based Information Systems, pp. 208–212 (2011)
25. Glynn, S.: Getting to grips with data classification. Database Netw. J. 41(1), 8–9 (2011)
26. Gorge, M.: Are we being 'greenwashed' to the detriment of our organisations' security? Comput. Fraud Secur. 2008(10), 14–18 (2008)
27. Handel, M.J., Wang, E.Y.: I can't tell you what i found: problems in multi-level collaborative information retrieval. In: Proceedings of the 3rd International Workshop on Collaborative Information Retrieval, pp. 1–6. ACM (2011)
28. Hayat, Z., Reeve, J., Boutle, C., Field, M.: Information security implications of autonomous systems. In: Military Communications Conference, pp. 897–903. IEEE Press (2006)
29. Heikkila, F.M.: E-discovery: Identifying and mitigating security risks during litigation. IT Prof. 10(4), 20–25 (2008)
30. Hilton, J.: Improving the secure management of personal data: privacy on-line is important, but it's not easy. Inf. Secur. Tech. Rep. 14(3), 124–130 (2009)
31. ISO, IEC 27002: Information technology -security techniques- code of practice for information security controls (2013)
32. Johnson, M.E., Goetz, E., Pfleeger, S.L.: Security through information risk management. IEEE Secur. Priv. 7(3), 45–52 (2009)
33. Kaiser, F.M.: The impact of overclassification on personnel and information security. Gov. Inf. Q. 3(3), 251–269 (1986)

34. Kajava, J., Anttila, J., Varonen, R., Savola, R., Röning, J.: Senior executives commitment to information security – from motivation to responsibility. In: Wang, Y., Cheung, Y., Liu, H. (eds.) CIS 2006. LNCS (LNAI), vol. 4456, pp. 833–838. Springer, Heidelberg (2007)

35. Kane, G., Koppel, L.: Information Protection Playbook. Elsevier, Boston (2013)

36. King, P.: In the new converged world are we secure enough? Inf. Secur. Tech. Rep. 12(2), 90–97 (2007)

37. Kitchenham, B., Charters, S.: Guidelines for performing systematic literature reviews in software engineering. Report, Keele University and Durham University Joint Report (2007)

38. Ku, C.Y., Chang, Y.W., Yen, D.C.: National information security policy and its implementation: a case study in Taiwan. Telecommun. Policy 33(7), 371–384 (2009)

39. Kumar, R., Logie, R.: Creating an information-centric organisation culture at SBI general insurance. In: Sadiq, S. (ed.) Handbook of Data Quality: Research and Practice, 16th edn, pp. 369–395. Springer, Heidelberg (2013)

40. McCormick, M.: Data theft: A prototypical insider threat. In: Stolfo, S.J., Bellovin, S., Keromytis, A.D., Hershkop, S., Smith, S., Sinclair, S. (eds.) Insider Attack and Cyber Security: Beyond the Hacker. Advances in Information Security, vol. 39, 4th edn, pp. 53–68. Springer, Heidelberg (2008)

41. Newman, A.R.: Confidence, pedigree, and security classification for improved data fusion. In: Proceeding of the Fifth International Conference on Information Fusion, vol. 2, pp. 1408–1415 (2002)

42. Onwubiko, C.: Security issues to cloud computing. In: Antonopoulos, N., Gillam, L. (eds.) Cloud Computing: Principles, Systems and Applications. Computer Communications and Networks, 16th edn, pp. 271–288. Springer, Heidelberg (2010)

43. Oscarson, P., Karlsson, F.: A national model for information classification. In: Workshop on Information Security and Privacy (2009)

44. Parker, D.B.: The classification of information to protect it from loss. Inf. Sys. Secur. 5(2), 9–15 (1996)

45. Parker, D.B.: The strategic values of information security in business. Comput. Secur. 16(7), 572–582 (1997)

46. Photopoulos, C.: Managing Catastrophic Loss of Sensitive Data. Syngress, Burlington (2008)

47. Puhakainen, P., Siponen, M.: Improving employees' compliance through information systems security training: an action research study. MIS Q. 34(4), 757–778 (2010)

48. Rakers, J.: Managing professional and personal sensitive information. In: Proceedings of ACM SIGUCCS Fall Conf.: Navigation and Discovery, pp. 9–14. ACM (2010)

49. Saxby, S.: News and comment on recent developments from around the world. Comput. Law Secur. Rev. 24(2), 95–110 (2008)

50. Smith, E., Eloff, J.H.P.: Security in health-care information systems current trends. Int. J. Med. Inform. 54(1), 39–54 (1999)

51. Solms, R., Solms, S.H.: Information security governance: a model based on the direct-control cycle. Comput. Secur. 25(6), 408–412 (2006)

52. Strauss, A., Corbin, J.: Basics of Qualitative Research: Techniques and Procedures for Developing Grounded Theory. Sage Publications Inc, Thousand Oaks (1998)

53. Tsai, W.T., Wei, X., Chen, Y., Paul, R., Chung, J.Y., Zhang, D.: Data provenance in soa: security, reliability, and integrity. SOCA 1(4), 223–247 (2007)

54. Virtanen, T.: Design criteria to classified information systems numerically. In: Dupuy, M., Paradinas, P. (eds.) Trusted Information: The New Decade Challenge Part 8. IFIP, vol. 65, 22nd edn, pp. 317–325. Springer, Heidelberg (2001)

55. Wiles, J., Gudaitis, T., Jabbusch, J., Rogers, R., Lowther, S.: Low Tech Hacking. Syngress, Boston (2012)

56. Wilson, P.: Positive perspectives on cloud security. Inf. Secur. Tech. Rep. **16**(3–4), 97–101 (2011)

57. Wrona, K., Hallingstad, G.: Controlled information sharing in NATO operations. In: Military Communications Conference, pp. 1285–1290 (2011)

Information Flow Control on a Multi-paradigm
Web Application for SQL Injection Prevention

Meriam Ben-Ghorbel-Talbi, François Lesueur[(⊠)], and Gaetan Perrin

Université de Lyon, CNRS, INSA-Lyon, LIRIS, UMR5205, 69621 Lyon, France
{meriam.talbi,francois.lesueur,gaetan.perrin}@insa-lyon.fr

Abstract. In this paper, we propose an integrated framework to control information flows in order to prevent security attacks, namely, SQL injections threatening data confidentiality. This framework is based on the Prerequisite TBAC model, a new Tuple-Based Access Control model designed to control data dissemination in databases, and that guarantees a controlled declassification. To track information flow in the application part, we propose to propagate dynamically security labels through the system using Paragon, a typed-security language that extends Java with information flow policy specification.

Keywords: Information flow · TBAC · Declassification

1 Introduction

When trying to control information flows in a program, most propositions focus on only one part: either security-typed languages for imperative programs or Multi-Level Security databases for the declarative parts. Although programs are in fact constructed using both imperative and declarative programming, few previous work study both at the same time. In this paper, our contribution is two-fold: we propose an integrated framework to follow information flows from the moment they enter the system until they leave it, possibly being stored and manipulated in the database in the meantime. Moreover, this framework is based on Dissemination Control to circumvent the threats of uncontrolled declassification. We argue that the combination of these contributions allows to greatly reduce the burden of the application developer: the end-to-end aspect allows to dynamically tag data entering the system (proxy service) rather than variables in the code and then to control output only when it leaves the system, the application part can be mostly unchanged. The dynamic aspect allows the developer not to specify security labels on its variables, inside his code, but in the database at the tuple level. Dissemination control prevents erroneous declassifications, since data entering the system are tagged with their allowed ways of being declassified and the developer can declassify according to these tags without worrying of a confidentiality breach. Hence, our framework can be used to prevent information leakage, such as SQL injections.

© Springer International Publishing Switzerland 2016
J. Garcia-Alfaro et al. (Eds.): FPS 2015, LNCS 9482, pp. 277–285, 2016.
DOI: 10.1007/978-3-319-30303-1_18

In this paper, we propose to use TBAC [1], a new Tuple-Based Access Control model designed to control the information flow in databases. The objective of TBAC is to provide a mechanism that controls the dissemination of tuples according to the authorizations defined by their producers. It is designed in the same spirit as the decentralized information models [2] in the sense that users are allowed to specify their own security policy on their data. To deal with declassification we propose to extend the TBAC model family by a new instance, which we call *Prerequisite* TBAC, that provides means to define which conditions have to be satisfied to declassify data and by which subjects. In order to control the dissemination throughout the system, namely in the application part, we propose to use Paragon [3], a typed-security language that extends Java by adding the ability to label data information flow policies. Paragon is well adapted to our requirements and provides expressive information-flow policies to deal with the declassification issue. Moreover, it supports runtime policies which is an important feature to implement the dynamic aspect of our approach.

2   Related Work

Several works in the literature have proposed information flow control solutions based on the multilevel security policy model (MLS). Work in databases have proposed MLS DBMS to enforce information flow control [4–6]. In these models objects are passive entities such as relations, tuples, or rows. Subjects are active entities such as users or programs. Many MLS database systems have been also proposed, such as Oracle Label Security (OLS) [7], PostgreSQL [8], Sybase Secure SQL Server [9]. Work in programming languages, such as Flow-Caml [10], have addressed information-flow control by proposing security-typed languages. They use tainting mechanisms by labeling variables as tainted or untainted in order to control programs inputs and outputs. The basic concept of these languages is to statically analyze the source code of a program at compile time in order to check that all the performed operations respect the security policy.

Recently, more research has focused on the Decentralized Label Model (DLM) to deal with decentralized systems requirements. An application of the DLM model to programming languages was proposed in [11] called Jif, for Java Information Flow. Jif extends Java by adding labels that express restrictions on how information may be used. Paragon [3] is another security-typed extension to Java, which builds on the recent policy language Paralocks proposed in [12]. The main strength of Paragon over Jif is that it is more general in the sense that the DLM policy lattice is a sub-lattice of Paralocks.

However, few work have addressed the end-to-end information flow control issue: to our best knowledge, the IFDB model [13] is the only one that proposes to track flows and enforce security policy both in the DBMS and the application platform. It introduces the query by label concept: each query has an associated label, which is the label of the process issuing the query. This label is used as a filter. Authority is bound to principals, such as users and roles, and each process runs with the authority of a particular principal. Authority can be delegated and given to users, application procedures, and also to stored procedures and views in order to allow declassification. Other work have been proposed in this same optics, and have pointed out the need to deal with a uniform information flow control between databases and applications. As mentioned in [14], most common web attacks are attacks across component boundaries (e.g. injection attacks, cross-site scripting attacks). In [15] authors have designed DBTaint system. It extends the database to associate each piece of data with a taint tag and propagates these tags during database operations. In [16], information-flow policies are specified in the database query interfaces and enforced in the web scripting language by a static type checker. In [17], authors present LabelFlow, an extension of PHP that tracks the propagation of information dynamically throughout the application, transparently both in the PHP runtime and through the database. IFDB is the most close to our approach as it is based on the DLM model. But, contrary to the IFDB model which tracks flows on a per-process granularity in the application-side, we aim to deal with a fine-grained flow control both in the DBMS and the application platform as in [15–17]. Moreover, we aim to deal with the declassification in the security policy in order to specify how data can be declassified, which is not the case in these previous work.

3   System Architecture

As shown is Fig. 1, the security policy is sticked to data as labels (called *s-tags*), all throughout the framework, so that data are filtered when they leave the entire system and not only the database. Moreover, we specify the declassification policy in the label itself, thus data can be declassified according to their labels, which guarantees a controlled declassification.

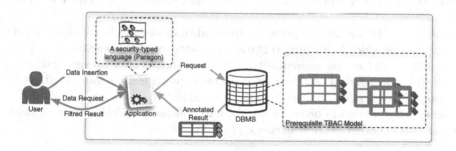

Fig. 1. System architecture

3.1   The Security Model

We propose to deal with the security policy using a new instance of the TBAC model [1], which we call the *Prerequisite* TBAC. This new instance provides facilities to control the dissemination of data based on the policy attached to them and also allows to express some form of authorized declassification. In this model, we consider that a user is allowed to access a data if and only if the prerequisites expressed by the data owners have been previously satisfied. These prerequisites are linked to data and express which treatments these data must go through and by which subjects. Formally, we consider that Pre is the set of expressible prerequisites, U is the set of users, and each tuple t is annotated by an s-tag t_{auth}. An s-tag is a disjunction of atomic $tags$, each atomic tag being defined as $((p, U_v), U_r)$, meaning that someone in U_r can read if someone in U_v validate all the prerequisites in p, where $p \subseteq Pre$, $U_v \subseteq U$, $U_r \subseteq U$. An empty prerequisite means that users in U_r can access this tuple without any prerequisite.

3.2   The Application-Side

To track information flow in the application-side, we use Paragon which builds on two basic components: actors and parameterized locks. Actors can be principals or specific communication channels. Locks are a boolean variables used to communicate the security relevant state of the program to the policy. A policy is composed of a set of clauses and each clause must have a head specifying to which actors the information may flow, and may have a body that specifies in which conditions data may flow to these actors. Note that, Paragon policies are similar to our policy definition: the prerequisite conditions and Locks have the same semantic and are both used to specify how to declassify data.

Runtime Policy. After receiving data from the database, we instantiate the policies of the variables in the application code using s-tags that are attached to the query result. Hence, s-tags will be propagated from the database to the application and they will be sticked to data until they leave the entire system.

Downgrading. In our model, prerequisite conditions are specified using locks in the application-side. According to the system state, or after some data transformation that validates the prerequisite conditions, locks will be opened and hence data will be declassified. As we said previously, prerequisite conditions have to be removed from s-tags as soon as they are validated. Thus, we have to define a *downgrade* function in order to re-annotate policies by deleting opened locks. We call this function *explicit declassification*.

Filtering. In Paragon, Input-Output channels are actors so that they can be labeled with a security policy. Thus, to automatically control data that flow to the user, we just need to tag Output channels with a policy containing the current user's credentials as authorized actor. Hence, only data that satisfy the security policy will flow from the application to the user.

3.3   The Database Side

The TBAC model has been defined in [1] where different instances have been proposed. The TBAC models family evolves around the propagation and combination of access rights on tuples to provide information flow control in a relational ecosystem. In this paper, we propose a new instance, called *Prerequisite* TBAC, to deal with the declassification policy.

Propagation. TBAC uses the provenance framework described in [18] to propagate and combine *s-tags*. In databases, SPJRU queries are used for computations and are the place for access rights propagation and combination. *Select* and *Rename* are transparent as they do not alter the set of *s-tags*. *Project* and *Union* can merge several original tuples into the same one. Each tuple t in the result can be equivalently derived from a set T of tuples (two in the case of $\cup$) which have to be combined additively, thus, access to t should be granted if access is granted to at least one tuple from T. *Join* combines two original tuples into a composite one: access to a joined tuple needs access rights to all the original ones.

We can restate the SPJRU semantics from an access control point of view informally by *one may access to a piece of information if he is authorized to access to the original tuples which contribute to it.* More formally, if we consider two tuples a and b, where $a_{auth} = \{tag_{a_1} \vee \ldots \vee tag_{a_n}\}$ and $b_{auth} = \{tag_{b_1} \vee \ldots \vee tag_{b_m}\}$, annotations are combined with relational queries as follows:

- If $t = a \bowtie b$, access to t requires access to both a and b. Then, t's annotation is defined as a disjunction of a conjunction of atomic tags as follows:
  $t_{auth} = \{(tag_{a_1} \wedge tag_{b_1}) \vee \ldots (tag_{a_1} \wedge tag_{b_m}) \vee \ldots (tag_{a_n} \wedge tag_{b_m})\}$. For each conjunction of atomic tags we have: $((p_{a_i}, U_{va_i}), U_{ra_i}) \wedge ((p_{b_j}, U_{vb_j}), U_{rb_j}) = \{((p, U_v), U_r) | p = p_{a_i} \cup p_{b_j}, U_v = U_{va_i} \cap U_{vb_j}, U_r = U_{ra_i} \cap U_{rb_j}\}$.
- If $t = a \cup b$, access to t requires access to any of a and b and t's annotation is defined by $t_{auth} = \{tag_{a_1} \vee \ldots \vee tag_{a_n} \vee tag_{b_1} \vee \ldots \vee tag_{b_m}\}$. Simplification must be applied for tags having the same prerequisite sets as follows:
  $\{((p, U_v), U_r) | U_v = U_{va_i} \cup U_{vb_j}, U_r = U_{ra_i} \cup U_{rb_j}\}$.

Implicit Declassification is used when the query validates automatically the prerequisite condition. For instance, if a prerequisite requires the data to be aggregated and if the query is an aggregation then the declassification can be automatically triggered. If the current user is allowed to validate this prerequisite, then it is replaced by an empty one, allowing users in the second part of the rule to access this tuple. We consider that, a user u is authorized to validate the prerequisite when either:

- u is expressed in the first part of the rule as a prerequisite user or,
- the prerequisite user specified in the first part of the rule is equal to *all* (i.e. every user is authorized to validate the prerequisite).

Pre-Filtering is used in order to optimize the query result by sending only data that can be accessed or declassified by the current user in the application-side. The pre-filtering function f is applied on every tuple composing the result to a query. For a user u requesting a tuple t, f returns *true* if and only if:

- u is authorized to validate the prerequisite conditions, which means that explicit declassification is required in the application-side in order to access data,
- u is expressed in the second part of the rule as an authorized user with no invalidated prerequisites left.

4   Implementation

We present here a first implementation attempt of our approach. As shown in Fig. 2, we have three components: the database, implemented using HSQLDB (HyperSQL DataBase), that stores data and *s-tags* at the tuple-level; the application, implemented in Java, that interacts with the database to request and insert data; and the proxy, implemented in Paragon, that controls I/O channels, by adding *s-tags* before inserting data in the database, and by filtering data before they leave the application.

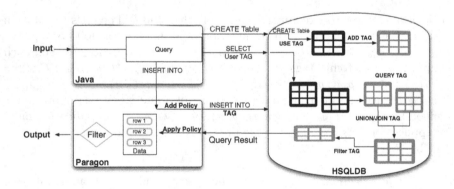

Fig. 2. The implementation architecture

Modifications in the Database. HSQLDB is a relational database software written in Java. We have extended it to deal with *s-tags*. For this purpose, we have implemented a custom SQL parser that modifies all SQL queries at runtime:

- When tables are created, we intercept the query to add the *USETAG* command that adds automatically a new column called *STAG*. This column is used to store the security policy at the tuple level.

– When data are requested, we first add the *UserTAG* command to the SQL query to specify the current user credentials. Then, we intercept the query result and we run our algorithm that combines *s-tags* according to the SQL query. After the *s-tags* calculation, we run our pre-filtering function that decides which tuples can be sent to the application-side, according to the current user credentials.

The Application. We have developed a basic application in Java that plays the role of an interface between the user and the database in order to insert and request data. This application is a ToDo list, where users can signin, create, show one or all their tasks. A given task can be assigned to one or many users, and users can specify their security preferences in order to share their tasks or to allow other users to see some details about them (e.g. the title, or the number of their tasks).

The Proxy. Paragon is used to develop the proxy that controls input/output channels. Using *.pi* files that tie paragon files (*.para*) with java program, it is possible to specify the policy annotations only in the application part where data flows from the application to the database and inversely. To control input channels, entering data are intercepted before inserting them to the database. Hence, the INSERT command is modified in order to add *s-tags* that are derived according to the security policy specified in the application-side. We currently use a default policy: users are only allowed to access to tasks that are assigned to them. To control output channels, the proxy has to dynamically instantiate the policy of the variables constituting the query result by their *s-tags*. Thus, for each tuple in the query result, we convert its corresponding *s-tag* to a paragon policy and we assign it to data. In addition, a new policy is created using the current user credentials and assigned to the output channel. Data are, hence, filtered accordingly. This is possible using the Paragon runtime library that allows to support dynamic features.

Testing SQLI Attacks. SQL Injection Attacks are used by attackers in order to violate data confidentiality and integrity. They use different techniques to modify or inject an SQL query in the application input that is sent and executed in the database. To validate our approach, we have tested some SQLI attacks and the query result was successfully blocked by our proxy. As we said earlier, in our model, we only deal with attacks threatening data confidentiality. For instance, in our application, a user, say *Bob*, can use an SQLI attack in order to show all tasks that are stored in table *Tasks*. Even, if the SQLI succeeds in the database-side and the whole table is returned, the output result shown to *Bob* is filtered and only tuples having *Bob* as authorized user are kept, namely only tasks assigned to *Bob*. Obviously *Bob* will see all fields composing the tuple, even if he is actually not supposed to see them. It is our design choice to use a tuple granularity instead of labeling fields, but, this can be an interesting issue to be investigated as future work.

5 Conclusion

Our framework provides end-to-end security guarantees on declassification, by specifying in the labels themselves how data can be declassified and by which users. This is an important feature that allows to greatly reduce the burden of the application developer and thus to prevent security attacks. As we said in this paper, few existing works have addressed the end-to-end information flow control, and they do not deal with controlled declassification as it is the case in our work. We have focused on attacks threatening data confidentiality and we have proposed a proof of concept implementation to demonstrate that our approach is feasible. Note that, our aim was to let the application part as unchanged as possible, in order to facilitate the integration of our approach in existing programs. For this purpose, we have proposed: a custom SQL parser that modifies SQL queries at runtime to add and combine *s-tags*, resp. when data are inserted and requested from the database; and a proxy service that is in charge to label data entering the system, to dynamically propagate the *s-tags* from the database to the application, and then to control output when data leave the system. Currently we are working on extending our prototype to deal with all the features of our model, namely the implicit and explicit declassification, in the database and the proxy-side, respectively. As future work, we aim to design a complete prototype and to evaluate its performance.

Acknowledgments. This work has been partially funded by the French ANR KISS project under grant No. ANR-11-INSE-0005.

References

1. Thion, R., Lesueur, F., Talbi, M.: Tuple-based access control: a provenance-based information flow control for relational data. In: SEC@SAC (2015)
2. Myers, A.C., Liskov, B.: A decentralized model for information flow control. In: SOSP (1997)
3. Broberg, N., van Delft, B., Sands, D.: Paragon for practical programming with information-flow control. In: Shan, C. (ed.) APLAS 2013. LNCS, vol. 8301, pp. 217–232. Springer, Heidelberg (2013)
4. Lunt, T.F., Denning, D.E., Schell, R.R., Heckman, M., Shockley, W.R.: The seaview security model. IEEE Trans. Softw. Eng. 16(6), 593–607 (1990)
5. Sandhu, R., Chen, F.: The multilevel relational data model. ACM Trans. Inf. Syst. Secur. 1, 93–132 (1998)
6. Smith, K., Winslett, M.: Entity modeling in the MLS relational model. In: VLDB (1992)
7. Jeloka, S.: Oracle Label Security Administrator' s Guide, 11g Release 2 (11.2). Technical report, ORACLE (2013)
8. PostgreSQL Global Development Group: PostgreSQL 9.1 Documentation (2011)
9. Sybase Inc. Building Applications for Secure SQL Server: Sybase Secure SQL Server Release 10.0. Technical report (1993)
10. Simonet, V.: FlowCaml in a nutshell. In: Proceedings of the first APPSEM-II Workshop (2003)

11. Myers, A.C.: JFlow: practical mostly-static information flow control. In: POPL (1999)
12. Broberg, N., Sands, D.: Paralocks - role-based information flow control and beyond. In: POPL (2010)
13. Schultz, D., Liskov, B.: IFDB: decentralized information flow control for databases. In: CCS (2013)
14. Schoepe, D., Hedin, D., Sabelfeld, A.: SeLINQ: tracking information across application-database boundaries. In: ICFP (2014)
15. Davis, B., Chen, H.: DBTaint: cross-application information flow tracking via databases. In: WebApps (2010)
16. Peng, L., Zdancewic, S.: Practical information flow control in web-based information systems. In: CSFW (2005)
17. Chinis, G., Pratikakis, P., Athanasopoulos, E., Ioannidis, S.: Practical information flow for legacy web applications. In: ICOOOLPS. ACM (2013)
18. Green, T.J., Karvounarakis, G., Tannen, V.: Provenance semirings. In: Proceeding of the 26th Symposium on Principles of Database Systems (PODS) (2007)

Searchable Encryption in Apache Cassandra

Tim Waage[✉], Ramaninder Singh Jhajj, and Lena Wiese

Institute of Computer Science, University of Göttingen,
Goldschmidtstrasse 7, 37077 Göttingen, Germany
{tim.waage,lena.wiese}@uni-goettingen.de, r.jhajj@stud.uni-goettingen.de

Abstract. In today's cloud computing applications it is common practice for clients to outsource their data to cloud storage providers. That data may contain sensitive information, which the client wishes to protect against this untrustworthy environment. Confidentiality can be preserved by the use of encryption. Unfortunately that makes it difficult to perform efficient searches.

There are a couple of different schemes proposed in order to overcome this issue, but only very few of them have been implemented and tested with database servers yet. While traditional databases usually rely on the SQL model, a lot of alternative approaches, commonly referred to as NoSQL (short for "Not only SQL") databases, occurred in the last years to meet the new requirements of the so called "Web 2.0", especially in terms of availability and partition tolerance. In this paper we implement three different approaches for searching over encrypted data in the popular NoSQL database Apache Cassandra (offered by many cloud storage providers) and run tests in a distributed environment. Furthermore we quantify their performances and explore options for optimization.

Keywords: Searchable encryption · Benchmarking · Apache Cassandra

1 Introduction

Industry is moving towards distributed data storage due to the increased amount of data being produced every day and the requirements of Web 2.0 services, needing high availability, consistency and partition tolerance [1] as well as good properties concerning scalability on commodity hardware. NoSQL databases running in distributed cloud environments were designed to meet those requirements. They provide ease of use and flexibility at low costs, without needing the customer to worry about the consumption of resources for storing and sharing data. Furthermore cloud service providers often provide such storage space which can be booked flexibly on demand.

However, outsourcing sensitive data to third party storage providers has always been a security risk, in the private sector (e.g. sharing of photos or health information, messaging) as well as in the business sector (e.g. classified documents or confidential mailing). Not only adversaries with physical access to data servers are potentially dangerous, (honest but) curious or malicious database administrators of hosting providers also may snoop on sensitive data and

© Springer International Publishing Switzerland 2016
J. Garcia-Alfaro et al. (Eds.): FPS 2015, LNCS 9482, pp. 286–293, 2016.
DOI: 10.1007/978-3-319-30303-1_19

thereby pose a thread. NoSQL databases usually do not provide any mechanisms to ensure confidentiality of the data items they are storing. Thus this lack of security features often impedes a wider use of cloud storage.

Encryption is always a handy countermeasure in such untrustworthy environments. It can ensure confidentiality of the externally stored data records against any illegitimate read accesses, but it is usually connected to some limitations concerning the interacting possibilities with the encrypted data, in particular when it comes to searching. Several symmetric *searchable encryption* schemes have been proposed to overcome this issue [2], but to our knowledge none of them have been tested with existing cloud database technologies. Thus in this paper we make the following contributions:

- We implement three schemes for searchable encryption [3–5].
- We quantify the performance of all schemes in a small distributed environment consisting of two nodes.
- Furthermore we evaluate their usability in practice and discuss performance optimizations.

2   Apache Cassandra

Apache Cassandra [6] can be considered as key-value store, as well as (wide) column family store. Its data model was designed to represent loosely structured data items like they are typical for the Web 2.0. It is currently the most popular database in its category[1]. Based on a strictly symmetric peer-to-peer concept Cassandra uses the Gossip protocol for coordination purposes in a distributed installation. It makes use of the local file system and runs in a single Java process per node. Concerning the CAP Theorem [1,7] Cassandra offers availability and partition-tolerance.

In contrast to most traditional relational SQL-based systems Cassandra does not provide user, role or access rights management. Frontends have to offer this functionality, if desired (for example, the cloud storage interface). Storing the data in an encrypted form can provide a much higher level of security, but Cassandra does not provide any native mechanisms for doing so.

3   The Searchable Encryption Schemes

This section gives a brief overview of the different ideas of the searchable encryption schemes that we used: the CGK scheme [4] proposed by Curtmola et al., the HK scheme [5] proposed by Hahn and Kerschbaum as well as the SWP Scheme [3] proposed by Song et al. As the amount of space for this article is limited we refer the reader to the original papers for more detailed information on how the schemes work. For security definitions, see [2].

---

[1] SolidIT: DB-Engines   Ranking.   http://db-engines.com/en/ranking,   accessed 13/07/2015.

3.1 CGK [4] - Index per Keyword

The approach of Curtmola et al. is very promising in terms of search time. It relies on an index consisting of an array A which stores lists of document identifiers from document set D containing unique words and a lookup table T to identify the first element in A for a particular word being searched. The index is created per unique word from the document set D instead of per document. The CGK scheme[2] is the first of its kind to achieve optimal search time and the index generated is linear in the number of distinct words per document. Due to the way data is indexed, updates are expensive which makes this scheme more suitable for 'write once' databases. The non-adaptive version provides IND-CKA1 (indistinguishable under chosen keyword attacks) security, the adaptive version IND-CKA2.

3.2 HK [5] - Index per Document

The also IND-CKA2 secure HK algorithm works with two indices: γ_f and γ_w. The main idea is to store all unique words per document (in contrast to CGK) in the forward index γ_f using a special encrypted form similar to SWP. In addition γ_w is an inverted index storing the outcome of previous searches for providing future results in constant time. The encryption process needs as much iterations as there are unique words per document. Thus it can be very fast depending on the given dataset. On the other hand that means it can by design only deliver information on whether a searchword occurs in a document or not.

3.3 SWP [3] - Sequential Scan

The sequential scan based SWP algorithm[3] is almost the only choice when it is desired to avoid having an index (e.g. for practical reasons) [2]. The basic idea is to encrypt words of a fixed size n and embed a hash value within the ciphertext using a specific form. During search the hash value gets extracted again. If the value is of that special form there is a match. SWP does not require any sort of state information, thus it is instantaneously ready to encrypt or search and easy to implement for many scenarios. In contrast to most index based schemes it also delivers information about the exact number (and positions) of matches in documents. On the downside as being typical for linear scan algorithms, encryptions and searches take linear time and thus potentially very long for large datasets. SWP is IND-CPA (indistinguishable under chosen plaintext attacks) secure.

4 Implementation

We implemented all three schemes in Java 8. Concerning the necessary cryptographic primitives we used the implementations of two different crypto providers:

---

[2] Whenever we refer to the CGK Algorithm in this paper, we mean its "non-adaptive" version.

[3] Whenever we refer to the SWP Algorithm in this paper, we mean its "final scheme".

the Java Cryptography Extension (JCE) as well as the Legion of Bouncy Castle package (BC)[4]. In case both providers offered the desired functionality, we always chose the one that performed faster. In order to connect to Apache Cassandra we used the Java Driver 2.1 in combination with the current version 3 of the Cassandra Query Language (CQL).

5 Benchmarks

We employ the popular scenario of using searchable encryption for data in a mailbox. We use a subset of the TREC 2005 Spam Track Public Corpus[5]. We assume average mailbox sizes of 1,000 mails up to 10,000 mails. Hence, we start our measurements with the first 1,000 mails of the corpus and increase that number up to 10,000 mails to see how the schemes and database scale. Thereby the number of plaintext words increases from roughly 700,000 to over 7 million with around 40 % of the words being unique in the sense of the HK scheme. Note that every word in a mail counts, even words like "a", "the", "in" and so on. That means a search is possible for every word, too.

Cassandra is a key-value store, which means the mail documents have to be mapped somehow to a key-value format. We do that as follows. All the mails are written into one table of one keyspace. Thereby the file path of a mail within the data set is used as unique key and the encrypted mail content as its value. Of course more sophisticated structures would be possible, e.g. splitting up the mails into sender, receiver, body and so on, then use appropriate extra keys. However for the sake of simplicity we use this basic format, since there is no reason to expect doing it otherwise would have a serious impact on the results.

In our experimental setup the client connects to a distributed Cassandra Cluster consisting of two nodes, each equipped with a Intel Core i7 3770 CPU (@ 3.4 GHz) and 16 GB RAM, running Ubuntu 14.04 LTS and Apache Cassandra 2.1.4. All measurements include the time caused by the required network traffic.

5.1 Encrypting

In our first test we measure the time taken by the encryption process, which also includes the time needed for outputting the results (encrypted files itself as well as lookup tables, indices etc. where necessary) to the database.

As can be seen in Fig. 1 the time needed for encryption grows linearly in all schemes. The HK scheme is the fastest with the SWP scheme being not significantly slower. Both schemes beat the CGK scheme roughly by a factor of 4.5. Its creation of the array A of linked lists is much more complex than the encryption steps of the other schemes. Thus the SWP and HK schemes manage to encrypt between 95.000 and 130.000 words per second, the CGK algorithm reaches only circa 23.000 words per second, which can still be considered feasible in practice.

---

[4] The Legion of the Bouncy Castle. http://bouncycastle.org, accessed 13/07/2015.

[5] Available   at   http://plg.uwaterloo.ca/~gvcormac/trecspamtrack05,   accessed 13/07/2015.

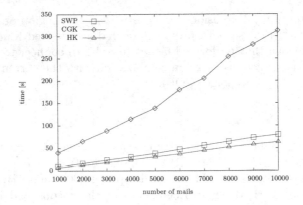

Fig. 1. Time needed for encryption with increasing data set size

5.2 Searching

In our second test we measure the time taken by the search process for one single word, since all three schemes do not provide a better way than using a trivial "AND"-combination for multiple words. In order to allow a fairer comparison we slightly modified the SWP scheme by allowing to abort the search within a document as soon as the first match occurs and continue with the next document. Thus it delivers the same information as the other schemes, namely whether a document contains the search word or not.

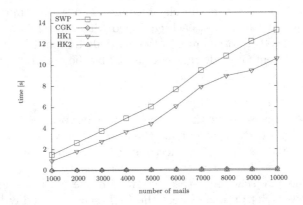

Fig. 2. Time needed for searching with increasing data set size

Figure 2 presents the results. The high encryption effort of the CGK scheme pays off in sublinear search time (0.13 s when searching 10.000 mails). Due to its index γ_w only the HK scheme can be faster (constant search time), but only if searching for the same word again (HK2). It performs orders of magnitude worse when searching a word for the first time (HK1). Then it is almost as slow as the SWP scheme. Note that the SWP scheme as slowest one in our test still manages to search over half a million words per second.

6 Options for Optimization

During our tests we noticed that all schemes leave room for optimizations in practice, which we describe briefly.

The CGK scheme creates an array A in which it stores a list of document identifiers for each distinct word. While creating the index, if the insert command is executed separately for each node from the number of lists, this results in a significant performance hit in terms of time taken to build the index. In order to optimize this, we used bulk insertions of the nodes into the database to reduce the number of interactions with the servers. For our data set we found the optimal value to be 500 nodes to be inserted at a time, which results in almost 65 % improvement compared to single insertions.

The HK scheme barely allows performance optimizations in terms of speed, like the previous schemes do. A potential problem in practice rather is the index size of γ_f. As it can become quite large, one solution to prevent it from growing too fast is reducing the output length of the used pseudo random number generator (in the original work referred to as G). That causes the encrypted representations stored in γ_f to be smaller without being a security issue. In doing so we achieved up to 20 % less disk space consumption for γ_f.

As mentioned earlier the SWP scheme uses words of a fixed length n, achieved by splitting and/or padding the original plaintext words. As the algorithm needs as much iterations as there are words to encrypt, a large n improves the overall performance (less iterations needed), while a small n can save disk space (less padding needed). For our individual data set we found the optimal value to be $n \geq 8$, which was 35 % faster compared to $n = 4$.

7 Related Work

Since the presentation of the SWP [3] scheme for sequential scan on encrypted data, numerous variations have been proposed. A recent survey [2] provides an excellent source for comparing the different schemes. The main differentiation is between symmetric and asymmetric primitives used. Asymmetric searchable encryption (public key encryption with keyword search or short "PEKS") is commonly used in a setting where multiple users can write the encrypted data by using the public key while search can be done by a single reader having the private key. Yet, that is more inefficient than the symmetric variants.

The sequential scan introducing SWP scheme has also been applied as a search function over relational data in CryptDB [8]. Most of the subsequent schemes follow an index-based approach (besides the tested CGK and HK scheme e.g. [9–11]), because it proved to be efficient in particular for large data sets although the index size might become too large to be stored in memory [12] ([12] also presents practical experiments and benchmarks on searchable encryption on relational databases). However, relying on an index is not always possible. Building and maintaining indices is costly, especially if the dataset is very dynamic. Indices also require some sort of appropriate keyword assignment.

8   Conclusion and Future Work

We put three algorithms for searchable encryption into practice, namely the index-per-keyword based CGK scheme, the index-per-document based HK scheme the and the sequential scan based SWP scheme. We implemented them in Java and used Apache Cassandra as underlying database. We pointed out strengths and weaknesses in practical environments and quantified their performance in a distributed environment. Furthermore we discussed optimization strategies.

The CGK scheme is not as fast as the others when encrypting with roughly 23,000 words per second. With HK encrypting up to 95,000 and SWP encrypting even up to 130,000 words per second, it is 4–5 times slower. Still the results indicate that a practical usage of all schemes in real world applications seems feasible. The same applies for searching, where the SWP scheme processes up to 530,000 and the HK scheme up to 660,000. The expensive encryption procedure of the CGK Scheme pays off in the search process, in which it is 8–10 times faster than the others.

Future work can extend these results in various ways. On the one hand there is the need to support other functionality required by database queries. There are approaches for the search of multiple keywords at the same time, but with the effort of additional data structures [13,14]. Schemes for order preserving encryption like [15,16] can be used for range scans as well as for database internals like managing timestamps and sorting row keys. Thereby as much cryptographic functionality as possible should be done using Cassandras user defined functions to make sure encryption can be used in environments with no other components (e.g. like front ends), too. However for some tasks (e.g. query rewriting) a proxy client between the application and the database is inevitable. On the other hand tests with larger datasets in much larger clusters are required. Therefore we intend to run tests on popular cloud computing platforms like Google Cloud Platform or Amazon EC2, which provide the functionality for deploying Apache Cassandra and other NoSQL databases.

Acknowledgement. This work was partially funded by the DFG under grant number WI 4086/2-1.

References

1. Brewer, E.: A certain freedom: thoughts on the CAP theorem. In: Proceedings of the 29th ACM SIGACT-SIGOPS Symposium on Principles of Distributed Computing, p. 335. ACM (2010)

2. Bösch, C., Hartel, P., Jonker, W., Peter, A.: A survey of provably secure searchable encryption. ACM Comput. Surv. (CSUR) **47**(2), 18 (2014)
3. Song, D.X., Wagner, D., Perrig, A.: Practical techniques for searches on encrypted data. In: Proceedings of the 2000 IEEE Symposium on Security and Privacy, S&P 2000, pp. 44–55. IEEE (2000)
4. Curtmola, R., Garay, J., Kamara, S., Ostrovsky, R.: Searchable symmetric encryption: improved definitions and efficient constructions. In: Proceedings of the 13th ACM Conference on Computer and Communications Security, pp. 79–88. ACM (2006)
5. Hahn, F., Kerschbaum, F.: Searchable encryption with secure and efficient updates. In: Proceedings of the 2014 ACM SIGSAC Conference on Computer and Communications Security, pp. 310–320. ACM (2014)
6. Lakshman, A., Malik, P.: Cassandra: a decentralized structured storage system. ACM SIGOPS Operating Syst. Rev. **44**(2), 35–40 (2010)
7. Brewer, E.A.: Towards robust distributed systems. In: PODC, vol. 7 (2000)
8. Popa, R.A., Redfield, C., Zeldovich, N., Balakrishnan, H.: CryptDB: processing queries on an encrypted database. Commun. of the ACM **55**(9), 103–111 (2012)
9. Cash, D., Jarecki, S., Jutla, C., Krawczyk, H., Roşu, M.-C., Steiner, M.: Highly-scalable searchable symmetric encryption with support for boolean queries. In: Canetti, R., Garay, J.A. (eds.) CRYPTO 2013, Part I. LNCS, vol. 8042, pp. 353–373. Springer, Heidelberg (2013)
10. Chase, M., Kamara, S.: Structured encryption and controlled disclosure. In: Abe, M. (ed.) ASIACRYPT 2010. LNCS, vol. 6477, pp. 577–594. Springer, Heidelberg (2010)
11. Kamara, S., Papamanthou, C., Roeder, T.: Dynamic searchable symmetric encryption. In: Proceedings of the 2012 ACM Conference on Computer and Communications Security, pp. 965–976. ACM (2012)
12. Cash, D., Jaeger, J., Jarecki, S., Jutla, C., Krawczyk, H., Rosu, M.C., Steiner, M.: Dynamic searchable encryption in very large databases: data structures and implementation. In: Proceedings of the Network and Distributed System Security Symposium (NDSS), vol. 14 (2014)
13. Cao, N., Wang, C., Li, M., Ren, K., Lou, W.: Privacy-preserving multi-keyword ranked search over encrypted cloud data. IEEE Trans. Parallel Distrib. Syst. **25**(1), 222–233 (2014)
14. Wang, B., Yu, S., Lou, W., Hou, Y.T.: Privacy-preserving multi-keyword fuzzy search over encrypted data in the cloud. In: 2014 Proceedings of the IEEE INFO-COM, pp. 2112–2120. IEEE (2014)
15. Boldyreva, A., Chenette, N., O'Neill, A.: Order-preserving encryption revisited: improved security analysis and alternative solutions. In: Rogaway, P. (ed.) CRYPTO 2011. LNCS, vol. 6841, pp. 578–595. Springer, Heidelberg (2011)
16. Kerschbaum, F., Schröpfer, A.: Optimal average-complexity ideal-security order-preserving encryption. In: Proceedings of the 2014 ACM SIGSAC Conference on Computer and Communications Security, pp. 275–286. ACM (2014)

AndroSSL: A Platform to Test Android Applications Connection Security

François Gagnon[(✉)], Marc-Antoine Ferland, Marc-Antoine Fortier,
Simon Desloges, Jonathan Ouellet, and Catherine Boileau

Cybersecurity Research Lab, Cégep de Sainte-Foy, Québec, Canada
frgagnon@cegep-ste-foy.qc.ca
http://www.cegep-ste-foy.qc.ca/cybersecurity

Abstract. Developing secure mobile applications is not an easy task;
especially when dealing with SSL/TLS since very few developers possess
experience with those protocols. This paper presents AndroSSL, an automated platform to assess the security of (SSL/TLS) connections established by Android applications. AndroSSL assists mobile application
developers by testing their applications for man-in-the-middle attacks,
and, successful, pinpoints the reason why the application is vulnerable.

Keywords: Privacy · SSL · MitM · Android · Test-Bed · Automated
experiment

1 Introduction

Mobile application developers are facing a new and difficult security challenge.
While traditional web applications, common in the desktop world, rely on web
browsers to manage secure communications, each mobile application must deal
with this element on its own. Establishing a secure channel using the SSL/TLS
protocol [3] requires the client to check the validity of the SSL[1] certificate
received from the server. An application accepting an invalid certificate would
allow an attacker to impersonate the real server through a man-in-the-middle
(MitM) attack.

The last decade has shown that validating an SSL certificate is a difficult
and error-prone task. Even big players (e.g., web browser developers) have a
hard time getting it right (see[2] CVE-2008-4989, CVE-2009-1358, CVE-2009-
2510, CVE-2009-3046, CVE-2010-1378, CVE-2014-1266). It would be unrealistic
to believe all (even most) mobile application developers will rise to the task
easily; especially since a lot of mobile applications are developed by non-expert
programmers (much less security specialists).

AndroSSL is a framework aiming to help mobile developers test their applications against connection security flaws. It relies on virtualization to provide a

---

[1] The terms SSL and TLS are used interchangeably throughout this paper.

[2] http://www.cve.mitre.org/.

© Springer International Publishing Switzerland 2016
J. Garcia-Alfaro et al. (Eds.): FPS 2015, LNCS 9482, pp. 294–302, 2016.
DOI: 10.1007/978-3-319-30303-1_20

low cost and highly automated platform. Moreover, by offering a wide range of tests (in several different contexts), it is meant to provide detailed information regarding vulnerabilities in the certificate validation process.

The paper is structured as follows: Sect. 2 provides an overview of AndroSSL, while Sect. 3 details the methodology used to mount MitM attacks. Section 4 discusses related work. Finally, Sect. 5 concludes with a summary of our findings and an opening on upcoming future work.

2   Experiment Test-Bed

The objective of AndroSSL is to perform automated SSL MitM attacks against Android applications. When a MitM attack succeeds, it stands as proof that the application is vulnerable. Automation makes AndroSSL interesting for non-security experts (e.g., mobile app developers), since AndroSSL users do not have to worry about the inner working of security protocols.

To automated its process, AndroSSL uses the AVP test-bed which relies heavily on virtualization to accomplish its mission. Android virtual devices (AVD) running on the Google QEMU emulator are used to host the applications to be tested, while standard virtual machines running in VMWare Workstation are used to host the required custom servers (e.g., DNS, Gateway, Fake SSL server). AndroSSL will run on any machine capable of running the Android Development Kit.

When testing the security of an application, AndroSSL will go through eight steps:

1. Load a scenario describing the experiment.
2. Configure the network services needed (e.g., DNS, Fake SSL server).
3. Start an AVD.
4. Install the targeted Android application and launch it.
5. Start recording different aspects of the experiment (e.g., network traffic, Android internal log (logcat), screenshots of the AVD).
6. Interact with the application to trigger a legitimate login attempt.
7. Serve a fake[3] SSL certificate to the application.
8. Analyze experiment logs to determine if a security flaw was successfully exploited.

The experiment specifications (*scenario*) is given to the system through an XML file. The scenario indicates which AVDs to use for the experiment, what information is to be recorded (e.g., network traffic, Logcat) and what actions are to be performed by the AVDs.

During the execution phase, AVP manipulates AVDs through the instrumentation of various Android virtualization technologies. It executes the AVDs with their applications and then collects experiment data. AVP supports a wide range

---

[3] Meaning a certificate that should be considered invalid from the application's point of view.

of actions and data collection capabilities. Regarding AndroSSL, the most important actions are: start/stop AVDs[4] and install/start applications. AVP supports several data gathering capabilities; those leveraged by AndroSSL are: network traffic recording and Android logcat recording.

Once the experiment is over, post-analysis of the log files can be performed, see Sect. 3.2.

2.1   User Simulation

The most challenging requirement of AndroSSL towards its test-bed is the need for proper user-simulation to lead an application to a specific state in order to trigger remote (possibly secure) connections. Our approach has been to manually pre-record (only once for each app) the sequence of actions leading the application to initiate a secure connection, then replay this action sequence automatically (as many times as needed) in AndroSSL experiments. Although this introduces manual intervention, it does not deviate from the objective of AndroSSL to help developers test their apps automatically. Indeed, not every developer has the knowledge to mount a MitM attack or to analyze and interpret the network traffic and logs, but, it will be easy for them to record their intended action sequence.

3   Methodology

The methodology behind AndroSSL has two components: the various scenarios used to attack the tested applications and the analysis of collected data to determine whether the attack was successful or not. Since some results will be discussed, a description of the experiment dataset comes first.

3.1   Dataset

AndroSSL has been used to test 90 Android applications against 6 different attack scenarios. All these applications required Internet access and were downloaded from the top 500 most popular of each categories on the Google Play Store.

3.2   Analysis

Three components are considered during the automated analysis of a run (that is, one application tested against one attack scenario): SSL server logs, network traffic and Logcat.

When the SSL handshake is completed with a fake server, the success for the MitM is confirmed. Hence, the server logs are a good source of information.

Network traffic is analyzed to find the plain password or a standard unsalted hash. This method allows to applications not using SSL to exchange credentials.

---

[4] With the possibility to use snapshots.

Custom or salted hashes are more difficult to handle. In these cases, a heuristic search for keywords could be used, but manual confirmation would be required.

Initially, logcat was not intended to be part of our result analysis. During the development phase, a search query was run by mistake on the logcat output file and returned surprising results. The password we used was broadcasted inside the AVD for a number of apps (10 out of 90). It turns out that those apps were relying on an API to query the server. The API will (or won't) use SSL properly to send the credentials to the server; this is also tested by AndroSSL. The broadcast of credentials inside an Android device is problematic as another installed application could manage to receive those broadcasts[5] (e.g., the CatLog Logcat Reader App[6]).

3.3   Attack Scenarios

The chosen apps have been tested against 6 attack scenarios. These scenarios, as well as the results, are presented below.

3.3.1   Actual Server

The first scenario consists of letting the application connect to its actual server without any attempts to attack the app. No particular network configuration is required here. No meaningful results were expected. However, analysis of the network traffic turned out to be quite rich:

- 9 apps send the user's password in clear to the server. Anyone capturing the network traffic would catch the credentials.
- 1 app hashes (SHA-256 unsalted) the user's password before sending it to the server un-encrypted.

3.3.2   Static URL

Two attack scenarios build the certificate using a static hostname. That is, the hostname is not related to the URL requested by the application. The network configuration schema of Fig. 1 is used for these scenarios. The app queries a fake DNS (step 1) which will redirect the traffic to our fake SSL server (step 2). Every SSL connection will be served using the same static certificate (step 3). Two test cases rely on a static certificate.

Self-Signed. This scenario is the easiest MitM involving SSL to perform for an attacker: create a self-signed certificate for a random hostname and use that certificate for a MitM attack. Figure 1 shows the network configuration underlying this attack scenario. Applications vulnerable to this attack are broken at two levels: chain validation (the certificate is self-signed) and source validation (the certificate is not for the expected hostname). 8 apps were vulnerable to this attack: 2 hash the password with MD5 (unsalted), the other 6 do not hash.

---

[5] Since Android 4.3, root privileges are required to access logcat.
[6] https://play.google.com/store/apps/details?id=com.nolanlawson.logcat.

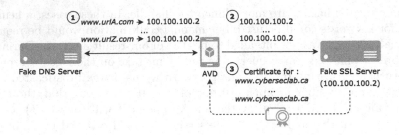

Fig. 1. Static URL network configuration

Valid. This scenario is also easy to perform for an attacker: obtain a valid certificate for a domain you really own (15 min and 15 dollars) and use that certificate for a MitM attack. Being a static case, the network configuration of Fig. 1 is used again here. Applications vulnerable to this attack are broken at source validation (the certificate chain is legitimate, but it is not for the expected hostname). The same 8 apps as in the previous case fell for this attack.

3.3.3 Dynamic URL

Three attack scenarios build the certificate using a dynamic hostname. That is, the hostname is related to the URL requested by the application. For the test cases requiring a dynamic certificate (i.e., where the certificate's hostname matches the one requested by the application), a more complex network configuration is deployed, see Fig. 2. The DNS server attributes sequential IP addresses by incrementing the last byte by one at every request (step 1 in Fig. 2). The first request receives IP 100.100.100.1, the second gets 100.100.100.2, and so on. Then, a Gateway (IPTables[7]) will redirect SSL traffic towards the fake SSL server, but to a specific port (steps 2 and 3). For instance, IP 100.100.100.1 would get port 11001, while IP 100.100.100.255 would get 11255; the last three digits of the port match the last byte of the IP. When the SSL server receives a request on port $11xyz$, it can associate this request with the URL originally requested to the DNS server (port $11xyz$ implies IP $100.100.100.xyz$, which can then be matched to a URL in the DNS memory). Hence, the server is able to dynamically construct an SSL certificate with the expected hostname (step 4).

Self-Signed. This scenario requires generating a self-signed certificate at runtime for the specific hostname requested by the app. Applications vulnerable to this attack are broken at chain validation (the certificate is self-signed). 12 applications fell for the attack, including the 8 discussed in the previous (static url) attacks. The 4 new vulnerable applications validate the hostname properly but not the chain (none of them hashes the password). The others were already known to be broken both for hostname and chain validation.

---

[7] http://ipset.netfilter.org/iptables.man.html.

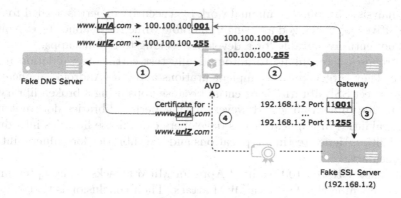

Fig. 2. Dynamic URL network configuration

Signed by Self-Signed. A self-signed certificate is generated once. Then, for each request a certificate is generated for the corresponding hostname and signed by the self-signed. Applications vulnerable to this attack are broken at chain validation. The same 12 apps as in the previous case fell for this attack.

Signed by Real. A real certificate is first obtained for a controlled URL (Like in the *Valid* test case of Sect. 3.3.2). Then, for each request a certificate is generated for the corresponding hostname and signed by the real certificate. Applications vulnerable to this attack are broken at chain validation for a specific check: a real end-user certificate should not have the authority to sign other certificates (it is neither a root nor an intermediate certificate; it is a leaf). 12 applications fell for the attack, the same 12 as in the previous scenario.

3.3.4 Other Scenarios
Since there are so many subtleties when validating SSL certificates, other scenarios will be created to test different flaws (e.g., expired certificates).

4 Related Work

[6] performed a manual analysis of popular security libraries and concluded that SSL certificate validation is completely broken in non-browser software. Their analysis is not targeted towards Android applications and is fully manual. Hence, this method is not appropriate to average developers testing their apps.

[4] proposed an automated approach relying on static analysis of Android application source code to find potential SSL certificate validation problems. An automated static analysis of 13 500 Android applications by their Mallodroid tool flagged 1 074 of them as being potentially vulnerable to MitM attacks. Furthermore, manual MitM attacks were performed on a subset of 100 potentially vulnerably apps. This analysis confirmed 41 vulnerable to MitM. Although the

static analysis is automatic, manual work by a security expert is needed to avoid false positives (apps flagged as being vulnerable while they cannot be exploited). Again, not entirely suitable for a developer seeking to test his apps.

[1] proposes a technique to automatically test certificate validation in SSL libraries. They target libraries implementations and not (Android) applications. Having correct SSL libraries is essential because apps using a broken library risk inheriting its vulnerabilities. However, having perfect libraries does not mean no vulnerabilities in applications as developers can misuse libraries introducing vulnerabilities. Hence testing applications and SSL libraries for vulnerabilities is complementary.

[7] manually tested 100 Android Apps for MitM attacks. 32 accepted invalid certificate opening the door to a MitM attack. Their conclusion is that "...[there is a] need to give developers more effective tools that can help them detect and fix issues before the app is in production...".

[5] proposes a way to improve the security of mobile applications by changing development practices related to SSL connections handling. Although this major step would certainly have a positive outcome, exhaustive testing will always play an important role (especially in security sensitive areas where new flaws are to be discovered).

Google released the *nogotofail* [2] tool to test client side SSL certificate validation. A few difference with AndroSSL are worth mentioning. *nogotofail* provides no automation for user interaction on the client side. The user interaction has to be done (and repeated) entirely manually. Having no automation for user interaction means *nogotofail* is not limited to Android applications; it can be used to test any client. *nogotofail* is not limited to client-side validation as it includes bugs like Heartbleed, POODLE and gotofail. It seems that two scenarios are built in *nogotofail* to test for client-side certificate validation: one static (Invalid Hostname Certificate [2]) and one dynamic (hinted in [8]). It is not clear how easily *nogotofail* can be extended with other scenarios.

[9] proposed an approach similar to AndroSSL where the experiment is fully automated and no security experts are required. However, the methodology of SMV-Hunter differs from AndroSSL making the two approaches complementary. SMV-Hunter's fully automated support is a great advantage, especially for large scale analysis. However, when SMV-Hunter fails (complex UI controls, invalid heuristic path), AndroSSL could take over to provide a more precise control of the user interaction. AndroSSL provides a more exhaustive set of test scenarios; using a variety of certificates and different network configurations (while SMV-Hunter tests for a single attack scenario). Having multiple scenarios allows AndroSSL to provide precise information regarding the certificate validation vulnerabilities in an application. For instance, a few applications tested were successfully attacked in the dynamic URL setup while the attempts failed in the static URL setup. This leads to the conclusion that those applications validate the certificate's hostname, but do not properly validate the signature chain.

5   Conclusion

The main lesson we learned from our experimentation is that mobile application developers are not aware of the security challenges they face. Some applications, not even relying on SSL, are just too easy to attack. Tools such as AndroSSL should facilitate security testing for mobile app developers.

Table 1. Result summary

Network configurations	Test cases	Vulnerable apps	Nb
Actual Server	Logcat	3, **4**, 34, 35, 36, 37, 54, **72**, **73**	9
	Network	3, 34, 35, 36, 37, 54, **63**, **67**, **70**, **71**	10
Static URL	Self-Signed	14, 16, 46_H, 53_H, 64, 68, 87, 89	8
	Valid		
Dynamic URL	Self-Signed	**9**, 14, 16, **25**, **26**, 46_H, 53_H, 64,	12
	Signed by Self-Signed	68, 87, 89, **90**	
	Signed by Real		
Total		**25**	

5.1   Summary Results

Table 1 provides a summary of the problems found automatically by AndroSSL when testing 90 popular Android applications. For each test case, the list of vulnerable apps is given (each app being represented by a numeric ID). Apps in bold were vulnerable to a single experiment (this illustrates the need for a multi test-cases approach), and subscript H indicates apps hashing the password client side (no salt). The apps appearing more than once (e.g., 14 and 34) have multiple weaknesses (14 does not validate the certificate hostname nor the chain while 34 sends the clear password into the Android log and also on the network). Overall, AndroSSL determined that 25 apps have a vulnerability. If we remove the apps that are just sending the password into the Android log[8], we are still left with 22. 10 apps sent the user credential through the network over a non-encrypted channel. Another 12 apps have a broken SSL certificate validation procedure (8 accepting certificate with an invalid hostname and an invalid chain while the other 4 accept certificates with an invalid chain as long as they have the proper hostname).

---

[8] Although this is problematic and should be addressed, we could consider this flaw as more difficult to exploit.

5.2 Future Work

Several tasks are planned to continue the development of AndroSSL:

– Adding new network configurations is a definitive priority, particularly to have the possibility to hijack SSL connections only (and target only 1 URL) while letting non-SSL connections flow towards the legitimate server. This will provide a better understanding regarding the conditions required for a successful MitM attack. This should allow for more successful attacks.
– Adding new test cases (i.e., new "fake" certificates) is an ongoing task as there are many subtle cases worth testing.

References

1. Brubaker, C., Jana, S., Ray, B., Khurshid, S., Shmatikov, V.: Using frankencerts for automated adversarial testing of certificate validation in SSL/TLS implementations. In: Proceedings of the 2014 IEEE Symposium on Security and Privacy (SP) (2014)
2. Brubaker, C., Klyubin, A., Condra, G.: nogotofail (2014). https://github.com/google/nogotofail
3. Dierks, T., Rescorla, E.: Rfc5246 tls v1.2 (2008). https://tools.ietf.org/html/rfc5246
4. Fahl, S., Harbach, M., Muders, T., Smith, M., Baumgartner, L., Freisleben, B.: Why eve and mallory love android: an analysis of android SSL (in)security. In: Proceedings of the 2012 ACM Conference on Computer and Communications Security (CSS 2012), pp. 50–61 (2012)
5. Fahl, S., Harbach, M., Perl, H., Koetter, M., Smith, M.: Rethinking SSL development in an appified world. In: Proceedings of the 2013 ACM Conference on Computer and Communications Security (CSS 2013), pp. 49–60 (2013)
6. Georgiev, M., Iyengar, S., Jana, S., Anubhai, R., Boneh, D., Shmatikov, V.: The most dangerous code in the world: validating SSL certificate in non-browser software. In: Proceedings of the 2012 ACM Conference on Computer and Communications Security (CSS 2012), pp. 38–49 (2012)
7. Onwuzurike, L., Cristofaro, E.D.: Danger is my middle name: experimenting with SSL vulnerabilities in android apps. In: Proceedings of the 2015 ACM WiSec (2015)
8. Sillars, D.: Using nogotofail to find issues with your https connections (2015). http://developerboards.att.lithium.com/t5/AT-T-Developer-Program-Blogs/Using-nogotofail-to-Find-Issues-with-Your-HTTPS-Connections/ba-p/39891
9. Sounthiraraj, D., Sahs, J., Lin, Z., Khan, L., Greenwood, G.: SMV-Hunter: large scale, automated detection of SSL/TLS man-in-the-middle vulnerabilities in android apps. In: Proceedings of the 2014 Network and Distributed System Security Symposium (NDSS 2014) (2014)

Onion Routing in Deterministic Delay Tolerant Networks

Adrian Antunez-Veas[1] and Guillermo Navarro-Arribas[1(✉)]

Department of Information and Communications Engineering,
Universitat Autònoma de Barcelona (UAB), 08193 Cerdanyola, Spain
aantunez@deic.uab.cat, guillermo.navarro@uab.cat

Abstract. Deterministic DTNs are networks where the behavior is
known in advance or where a repetitive action occurs over time like in
public transportation networks. This work proposes the application of
an onion routing approach to deterministic DTNs to achieve anonymous
communications. We show how the prior stage of path selection in onion
routing can be achieved using the information provided by deterministic
networks.

1 Introduction

In this paper we consider how to provide anonymity in Delay Tolerant Networks
(DTN). DTNs [6] provide end-to-end communication in environments lacking
continuous connectivity or presenting long delays. We focus our work in a class
of DTNs called deterministic DTNs, which are such networks where the behavior
is known in advance or where a repetitive action occurs over time. We will
show that in such scenarios anonymous communications can be established using
an onion routing [8] approach which takes into account the particularities of
deterministic DTNs.

Deterministic DTNs [2,9] fit perfectly with the concept of oracle schemes.
Oracle schemes are a subset of DTN routing protocols. In this schemes there is
a set of nodes that have nearly full knowledge of the network and its planned
evolution [6]. There are oracles that can answer any question regarding contacts
between nodes at any point in time, this oracles are called contacts oracle [11].
Contacts oracle schemes are used in deterministic scenarios where the oracle
node can have full details of occurred contacts as well as the future ones.

We consider public transportation networks as deterministic because every
node performs the same route periodically so this route can be known in advance.
This information can be shared among all nodes in the network in order to let
them be an *oracle*, i.e.: let them have full knowledge of the whole network. It is
important to note that, despite these networks are nearly deterministic, an error
needs to be assumed for exceptional situations.

Providing anonymous communications in DTNs is not easy and has not been
deeply considered. It is said that onion routing is not applicable to DTNs because
it needs to know the route in advance to construct the onion structure of cryptographic layers for each node [1]. Nevertheless, this protocol can be applicable

© Springer International Publishing Switzerland 2016
J. Garcia-Alfaro et al. (Eds.): FPS 2015, LNCS 9482, pp. 303–310, 2016.
DOI: 10.1007/978-3-319-30303-1_21

in deterministic DTNs, where source routing can be possible. Previous research work on the use of onion routing in DTNs is very scarce. One of the most relevant is [16], which uses attribute based encryption to per perform the layering process between groups of nodes. Our approach is simpler since we apply the onion routing directly as in conventional networks and does not require the formation of groups.

In Sect. 2 we introduce our proposal, simulations and provided in Sects. 3 and 4 discusses the proposal. Finally, Sect. 5 concludes the paper.

2 Onion Routing for Deterministic DTN

We describe our approach to provide anonymous communication in deterministic DTNs by using an onion routing approach. We first need to obtain a model of the network, and then provide means for the sender to establish the onion routing circuit (the path to the destination).

2.1 Deterministic DTN Model from a Public Transportation Network

We model the network as a dynamic graph $G = (V, E)$. The set of vertices V is the set of DTN nodes, and the edges E are the contacts between nodes. Dynamic graphs provide a good way to store dynamic information about the network. In our case we associate two attributes to each edge, the instant of time when the connection opportunity occurs and how long this contact has been.

As an example of deterministic DTN we use a urban public transportation network. More precisely for illustration purposes we will focus in a small public bus network from a university campus. The public transportation network that operates inside the Autonomous University of Barcelona (UAB) campus is composed by 5 buses that make different routes around the campus. It is important to note that every single bus makes the same route daily. This scenario can be seen as a good example of deterministic networks, where each bus can be equipped with a DTN node with wireless connectivity.

To obtain the mobility model, first, we export the campus road map from OpenStreetMap into SUMO (Simulation of Urban MObility) [4], filtering some unnecessary items like buildings and railways with the JOSM (Java OpenStreetMap) editor tool [12].

Once the campus roads were imported in SUMO, we recreate the buses movements taking into consideration the official bus schedule of the UAB public transportation network. In addition, we can tune some bus characteristics like acceleration and deceleration parameters in order to get coherent travel times.

Finally, we convert the bus model to a NS-2 mobility trace [14], which can be used in NS-3. We used the NS-3 simulator to obtain the contact related data of the campus network, i.e.: information about the duration of the contacts as well as the instant of time when they occurred. This contact information is used to build the dynamic graph that serves as the base model of the deterministic DTN.

2.2 Path Selection

We have a source node s willing to send a message to a destination d at time t using onion routing. In onion routing we need to choose the number of nodes n where the message will pass through. Node s obtains a path to perform the layering process and send the message. The time required to exchange the message between nodes is defined as tt. To make even harder the path guessing from third parties, as the network knowledge is shared among all nodes, the node s obtains a set of k paths in order to choose one of them randomly.

To sum up, we define a method $get\_paths(s, d, t, n, k, tt)$ that will retrieve a set of up to k paths given the t, n, and tt parameters.

The procedures shown in Algorithms 1 and 2 are an example of deterministic selection of paths. Both of them inherit values to filter out unneeded paths. Specifically, in Algorithm 1, from a given $node$ at time $currentTime$ we return a set of neighbors that are available or will be available to forward the message. In Algorithm 2 we perform a recursive search to get up to k paths of length n from $source$ to $destination$.

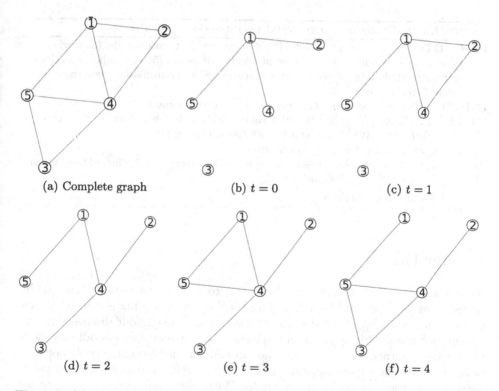

Fig. 1. In (a) the accumulative graph $(t = [0, +\infty))$ can be seen. In $(b) - (f)$ different snapshots in given instants of time showing the evolution of the dynamic graph are depicted.

Figure 1 shows an example of contact data representation using a dynamic graph. Applying our path selection method with the following parameters: source node $s=1$, destination node $d=5$, starting time $t=0$, number of paths $k=4$, number of nodes of each path $n=5$ and transmission time $tt=1$, we get the following paths:

— *Path: 0* — $(1:0) \rightarrow (2:0) \rightarrow (4:1) \rightarrow (1:2) \rightarrow (5:3)$. Arrival time: 4
— *Path: 1* — $(1:0) \rightarrow (2:0) \rightarrow (4:1) \rightarrow (3:2) \rightarrow (5:4)$. Arrival time: 5
— *Path: 2* — $(1:0) \rightarrow (4:0) \rightarrow (1:1) \rightarrow (4:2) \rightarrow (5:3)$. Arrival time: 4
— *Path: 3* — $(1:0) \rightarrow (4:0) \rightarrow (2:1) \rightarrow (4:2) \rightarrow (5:3)$. Arrival time: 4

(node: t): Means forward the message to node at time t.

So, we get 4 different paths composed by 5 nodes each, i.e.: origin and destination plus 3 onion routers, so 4 layers will be performed. From the given set of paths, the source node s will need to choose one in order to perform the onion routing itself. To make guessing the source node more difficult, the path to send the message will be chosen randomly from the given set.

Algorithm 1. Procedure to get valid neighbors of a given node

---

INHERIT: (1) *source*, source node. (2) *destination*, destination node. (3) t, when the message will be sent. (4) k, maximum number of paths. (5) n, number of nodes for each path (including source and destination). (6) tt, transmission time required to forward the message.

INPUT: (1) *host*, host node. (2) *currentTime*, current time.

OUTPUT: (1) *validNeighbors*, a set of valid neighbors to whom forward the message.

1: **procedure** GETAVAILABLENEIGHBORS (host, currentTime)
2:     **for each** $nbr \in host.neighbors()$ **do**
3:         **if** $(nbr.activationTime + nbr.contactDuration - tt) \geq currentTime$ **then**
4:             $validNeighbors.add(nbr)$
5:     **return** $validNeighbors$

---

3   Simulations

As explained in Sect. 2.1, we use NS-3 [13] to model and simulate the public transportation deterministic DTN. The DTN modules are under current development in NS-3 [19], so we decided to implement a neighbour discovery in the application layer. This application broadcasts beacon messages periodically looking for new contact opportunities. The interval time is the time to wait between beacons while the expiration time is the time a neighbour is considered valid, these parameters can be set up manually. With this simulation environment we are able to test our proposed method (cf. Sect. 2) on the small campus transportation network.

As an example, in Fig. 2, after fixing $s=1$; $d=5$; $t=0$ and $k=10$, we consider the time required to route a message with the n value from $n=5$ to $n=40$. We

---

Algorithm 2. Procedure to get paths that follows the inherited requirements

INHERIT: (1) *source*, source node. (2) *destination*, destination node. (3) *t*, when the message will be sent. (4) *k*, maximum number of paths. (5) *n*, number of nodes for each path (including source and destination). (6) *tt*, transmission time required to forward the message.

INPUT: (1) *currentPath*, current path. (2) *currentTime*, current time.

OUTPUT: (1) *paths*, a set of paths that follows the inherited requirements.

```
 1: procedure GETPATHS(currentPath, currentTime)
 2:     if currentPath.size() ≠ n and paths.size() < k then
 3:         node ← currentPath.last()
 4:         validNeighbors ← GetAvailableNeighbors(node, currentTime)
 5:         for each nbr ∈ validNeighbors do
 6:             oldPath ← currentPath
 7:             nbr.sendingTime ← max(nbr.activationTime, currentTime) + tt
 8:             currentPath ← nbr
 9:             if nbr = destination and currentPath.size() = n and currentPath ⊈ paths
    then
10:                 validNeighbors.add(nbr)
11:             else
12:                 GETPATHS(currentPath, nbr.sendingTime)              ▷ Recursive part
13:                 currentPath ← oldPath
14:     return paths
```

---

computed the average delivery time of the *k=10* given paths. The minimum number of nodes allowed in onion routing is 5, i.e.: at least 3 routers plus source and destination nodes. Unlike it is the common case in traditional networks, in DTNs not always the shortest paths are the quickest ones, but even so we can see in the figure an increasing tendency.

4 Discussion

Unlike traditional onion routing, our approach could suffer from the predictability of the routing path. This is why the proposed method in Sect. 2.2 returns a set of *k* paths, and the final path is selected at random from the set. This lowers the probability for an attacker to guess the source of a communication by predicting the path. The exact probability will depend in the concrete scenario and setup. Besides this point, our approach presents the same security problems and benefits of traditional onion routing.

We can then consider threats imposed by passive adversaries (observe traffic patterns) and active adversaries (perform actions against other nodes or modify information in transit).

We assume that there is a prior secure key distribution procedure. The required network information as well as the cryptographic keys are distributed to the nodes at a previous stage, i.e.: before starting the periodical routing. The public keys of the nodes are known to each other and used to establish each onion

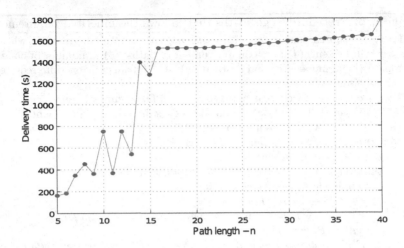

Fig. 2. Average delivery time considering the variation of the path length.

layer. Unlike current popular implementations of onion routing such as Tor [3] we cannot use Diffie-Hellman or similar interactive approaches to derive session keys in a DTN scenario. Symmetric session keys can be directly established or generated from a seed provided by each node to the successor node as in [8,15]. At the moment we use directly public key encryption since most applications over DTN only need to send small quantities of data in one direction.

4.1 Passive Adversaries

As explained in [10], if the attacker is the destination of the message, he can obtain information from the delay between messages. This kind of attack does not work when the sending start time, known as t in our path selection method, is not highly deterministic [18].

Another attacker model is a set of compromised nodes that work together to retrieve information breaking the users privacy. One possible situation is the multiple decryption. An attacker will be able to decrypt more layers, or messages if one of the nodes is the destination, because they have their corresponding keys. To overcome such attacks the n value can be increased, i.e.: the number of nodes that will have to pass through the message. A message will have as much layers as nodes are in the path. There is a trade-off between efficiency and security when deciding the value of n that needs to be studied in future research.

Another possible scenario where a set of compromised nodes work together is the source node periodicity analysis. There are scenarios where a node or a set of them rarely transmit information to others, discarding this nodes from the probable source set, a globally passive adversary can improve guessing the source of a message. To solve this issue the creation of dummy packets when ingress throughput drops below a certain threshold may help to prevent such attacks [16].

To decrease the probability of guessing the path when several nodes are compromised and one of them is the destination, different paths are retrieved using our path selection method and one of them is chosen randomly. By this way, we pretend to make harder to guess the sender of the message simply analysing the origin and the destination of every compromised node in the path as well as the sending time.

4.2 Active Adversaries

As is the previous case, an attacker controlling a single node will be unable to extract the source of a message due to the use of multiple layers of encryption [16]. There are several possible attacks against onion routing by malicious nodes in the network like congestion attacks [5], location based attacks [7], and attacks based on latency analysis [10].

An attacker who has control of a node of the network can attack other nodes to shut them down leading to undelivered messages. This Denial of Service attacks can be addressed improving the robustness of the nodes.

Message modifications by attackers are easily detected using cryptographic hash methods. Other attacks like masquerading (nodes pretending to be different nodes) are solved as layers of encryption check the node identity.

5 Conclusions

We have presented an onion routing based approach for deterministic DTNs. We also provide the means to easily model the concrete case of DTN networks deployed on urban public transportation systems. This enables to some extent establishing anonymous communications in these class of networks using a well known approach.

The presented idea is an initial step and will require further development. We will search and analyze efficient path selection mechanisms, as currently our method is non efficient because it explores every possible path. The efficiency comes crucial when resource-constrained computers are involved like tiny computers used in IoT, that could fit perfectly in each bus in our scenario, involving a very low deployment cost. Another future research branch can be to decrease the impact of active attacks like black holes using a reputation system. Path selection take this value into consideration. This is not an easy approach, since it can lead to security vulnerabilities by easing the path selection predictability. The more reputation a node has, the most probable it is for the node to be chosen nodes in the path.

We also note that contrary to more common mobile adhoc networks, deterministic DTNs are specially suited to support big delays and disruptions. This is interesting in our approach since it helps in providing a more stochastic path selection (a note can force a big delay to avoid path prediction through best path selection).

Acknowledgments. Support by Spanish MINECO project TIN2014–55243-P, and Catalan AGAUR project 2014-SGR-691, is acknowledged.

References

1. Bhutta, N., Ansa, G., Johnson, E., Ahmad, N., Alsiyabi, M., Cruickshank, H.: Security analysis for delay/disruption tolerant satellite and sensor networks. In: International Workshop on Satellite and Space Communications, IWSSC 2009, pp. 385–389 (2009)
2. Cardei, I., Liu, C., Wu, J., Yuan, Q.: DTN routing with probabilistic trajectory prediction. In: Li, Y., Huynh, D.T., Das, S.K., Du, D.-Z. (eds.) WASA 2008. LNCS, vol. 5258, pp. 40–51. Springer, Heidelberg (2008)
3. Dingledine, R., Mathewson, N., Syverson, P.: Tor: The Second-Generation Onion Router. In: USENIX Security Symposium. USENIX Association (2004)
4. DLR: SUMO - Simulation of Urban MObility, Insitute if Transportation Systems, Deutsches Zentrum für Luft- und Raumfahrt (DLR)
5. Evans, N.S., Dingledine, R., Grothoff, C.: A practical congestion attack on tor using long paths. In: USENIX Security Symposium, pp. 33–50 (2009)
6. Farrell, S., Cahill, V.: Delay- and Disruption-Tolerant Networking. Artech House, Norwood (2006)
7. Feamster, N., Dingledine, R.: Location diversity in anonymity networks. In: Proceedings of the 2004 ACM Workshop on Privacy in the Electronic Society, pp. 66–76. ACM (2004)
8. Goldschlag, D., Reed, M., Syverson, P.: Hiding routing information. In: Anderson, R. (ed.) IH 1996. LNCS, vol. 1174, pp. 137–150. Springer, Heidelberg (1996)
9. Hay, D., Giaccone, P.: Optimal routing and scheduling for deterministic delay tolerant networks. In: Sixth International Conference on Wireless On-Demand Network Systems and Services, WONS 2009, pp. 27–34. IEEE (2009)
10. Hopper, N., Vasserman, E.Y., Chan-Tin, E.: How much anonymity does network latency leak? ACM Trans. Inf. Syst. Secur. **13**(2), 13:1–13:28 (2010)
11. Jain, S., Fall, K., Patra, R.: Routing in a delay tolerant network, vol. 34. ACM (2004)
12. OSM: JOSM, OpenStreetMap (OSM). https://josm.openstreetmap.de
13. Nsnam: NS-3 webpage. https://www.nsnam.org
14. Raj, C., Upadhayaya, U., Makwana, T., Mahida, P.: Simulation of vanet using NS-3 and SUMO. Int. J. Adv. Res. Comput. Sci. Softw. Eng. **4**, 563–569 (2014)
15. Reed, M.G., Syverson, P.F., Goldschlag, D.M.: Anonymous connections and onion routing. IEEE J. Select. Areas Commun. **16**(4), 482–494 (1998)
16. Shi, C., Luo, X., Traynor, P., Ammar, M.H., Zegura, E.W.: Arden: anonymous networking in delay tolerant networks. Ad Hoc Netw. **10**(6), 918–930 (2012)
17. Tor Project. https://www.torproject.org/
18. Vakde, G., Bibikar, R., Le, Z., Wright, M.: Enpassant: anonymous routing for disruption-tolerant networks with applications in assistive environments. Secur. Commun. Netw. **4**(11), 1243–1256 (2011)
19. Zhou, D.: DTN Bundle Protocol. https://www.nsnam.org/wiki/Current_Development

Security Enforcement by Rewriting:
An Algebraic Approach

Guangye Sui[✉] and Mohamed Mejri

Departement of Computer Science, Laval University, Quebec, Canada
suiguangye@hotmail.com

Abstract. This paper introduces a formal program-rewriting approach that can automatically enforce security policies on non trusted programs. For a program P and a security policy Φ, we generate another program P' that respects the security policy and behaves like P except that it stops any execution path whenever the enforced security policy is about to be violated. The presented approach uses the $\mathcal{E}BPA^*_{0,1}$ algebra which is a variant of BPA (Basic Process Algebra) extended with variables, environments and conditions. The problem of computing the expected enforced program P' will turn to resolve a linear system which we already know how to extract the solution by a polynomial algorithm.

Keywords: Program rewriting · Process algebra · Security policy · Security enforcement

1 Introduction

1.1 Motivation and Background

Security in information systems is one of the most important preoccupations of today's systems. This paper aims to automatically and formally enforce security policies in some systems. Fortunately, there are already some fundamental results that allow understanding which security policies can be enforced and by which mechanism [2–4]. Execution Monitoring belongs to the class of dynamic analysis techniques that includes many other interesting works like [5,6]. Static analysis [7,8] approaches, on the other hand, can be used to significantly decrease the overhead involved by dynamic approaches.

Recently, program rewriting [9,10] techniques show their promising future since they gather advantages of previous techniques. The basic idea is to rewrite an untrusted program statically so that the new generated version respects some security requirements. They don't require the execution of the target program, they just introduce some modifications in some critical points. In [11,12], authors present a program rewriting approach based on $BPA^*_{0,1}$. In this paper, we want to extend the expressiveness of the algebra language by handling variables, conditions and environments. This new algebra is called $BPA^*_{0,1}$ with environment and denoted by $\mathcal{E}BPA^*_{0,1}$.

© Springer International Publishing Switzerland 2016
J. Garcia-Alfaro et al. (Eds.): FPS 2015, LNCS 9482, pp. 311–321, 2016.
DOI: 10.1007/978-3-319-30303-1_22

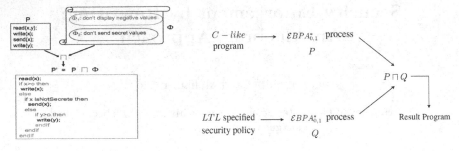

Fig. 1. Idea   **Fig. 2.** Security policy enforcement process

1.2 Problem

To clarify the idea, let us consider the academic example shown by Fig.1. Given a security policy Φ and a process P, we want to define an operator $\sqcap$ that generates a process P' containing the enforcement of Φ on P. P' respects Φ, preserves all the good behaviors of P and it does not introduce any new ones. Generally P' is computed by inserting some tests in P at some critical points so that the security policy will always be respected. The red text in P' of Fig.1 is the test inserted to enforce Φ_2 and the green one is the test added to enforce the policy Φ_1.

1.3 Methodology

The methodology that we adopt is the following :

- We introduce a new algebra $\mathcal{E}BPA_{0,1}^*$, which takes variables, conditions and environment into consideration. We suppose that the program P is a given as a process or it can be transformed to a process in $\mathcal{E}BPA_{0,1}^*$. This process algebra is expressive enough to handle an expressive simplified version of C-like programs (we will not take into consideration pointer for example).
- We suppose that the security policy Φ is given as a formula in the LTL (Linear Temporal Logic) [1]. We know how to translate it into a term in $\mathcal{E}BPA_{0,1}^*$.
- We define an operator $\sqcap$ that enforces Φ on P as shown in Fig. 2. Basically, the operator $\sqcap$ transforms the problem of enforcing Φ on P to a problem of generating a set of equations in $\mathcal{E}BPA_{0,1}^*$ and resolving them.
- We prove that the secure version of program generated by $\sqcap$ is sound and complete with respect to the inputs. The soundness states that all the traces of the new generated process respect the security policy and they belong to the set of traces of the original insecure one. The completeness property, or transparency, on the other hand, states that any trace of the original program that respects the security policy should be kept in the secure version.

1.4 Organization

This paper is structured as follows: Section 2 introduces the specification language $\mathcal{E}BPA_{0,1}^*$ (syntax + semantics), trace-based equivalence and some of its interesting properties. Section 3 formalizes the problem by transferring it into the computation of the intersection of two algebra processes. Section 4 introduces an algorithm that allows resolving the previous problem. Section 5 introduces a prototype that implements our approach. Finally, Sect. 6 shows some concluding remarks and future directions.

2 $\mathcal{E}BPA^*_{0,1}$: Specification Language

$BPA^*_{0,1}$ [12,14] is a basic process algebra to specify a sequential programs that may contains sequences, choices and loops. However, to be able to specify more interesting systems, it is important to endow the algebra with conditions, variables and environments. This section gives syntax and semantics of $\mathcal{E}BPA^*_{0,1}$. We first give the definitions of some necessary ingredients.

2.1 Ordered Sorted Algebras and Environment

To be able to specify variables with different types (boolean, integer, etc.), we define an ordered sorted algebra in [15], which is a special case of Many-Sorted Algebras [13]. We also denote by LSA any many-ordered sorted algebra where its sorts form a lattice.

We define an environment as a mapping from a set of variables to the set of domains. If for instance $S = \{bool, int, float\}$, then $e = \{x_1 \mapsto bool, x_2 \mapsto bool, x_3 \mapsto int, x_4 \mapsto float\}$ is an example of environment. Since $\langle S, \subseteq \rangle$ forms a lattice, we consider that a variable is a free variable in an environment, if its domain is equal to the lowest upper bound of S. The formal definition of an environment and a free variable are available in [15]. We are also interested by a following particular case of substitutions.

Definition 1 (Free Substitution). *Let e be an environment. A substitution σ is considered as free in e (or e-free) if for all $x \mapsto t$ in σ, we have $x \in F_v(e)$.*

We denote by $mgu(t_1, t_2, e)$, the mgu of t_1 and t_2 that respects the sorts of variables given within e. In [15], we give an algorithm allowing computing $mgu(t_1, t_2, e)$ when it exists. In the remaining part of this paper, we adopt the following notations:

- $\mathcal{E}$: We use $\mathcal{E}$ to denote the set of all valid environments.
- $\mathcal{V}(e)$: If $e \in \mathcal{E}$, $\mathcal{V}(e)$ denotes the set of variables in environment e.
- $\mathcal{V}(t)$: If t is a term, $\mathcal{V}(t)$ denotes the set of variables in t.
- $F_v(e)$: If $e \in \mathcal{E}$, $F_v(e)$ denotes the set of free variables in e.
- $N_v(e)$: If $e \in \mathcal{E}$, $N_v(e)$ denotes the set of non-free variables in e (i.e. $N_v(e) = \mathcal{V}(e) - F_v(e)$).

2.2 Syntax of $\mathcal{E}BPA^*_{0,1}$

In the sequel, we define $\mathcal{E}BPA^*_{0,1}$ that allows having conditions, variables and environment. More precisely:

- Let $\mathcal{A}$ be a Lattice Sorted Algebra (LSA). a, a_1 and a_2 range over $\mathcal{A}$.
- Let $\mathcal{B}$ be defined by the following BNF-grammar. $b, b_1, b_2 :: = 0 \mid 1 \mid a_1 == a_2 \mid a_1 < a_2 \mid \bar{b} \mid b_1.b_2 \mid \quad b_1 + b_2$ such that $(\mathcal{B}, +, ., \bar{\ }, 0, 1)$ is a boolean algebra
- Let c range over $\mathcal{B}$ and e range over $\mathcal{E}$.

The syntax of $\mathcal{E}BPA^*_{0,1}$ ($BPA^*_{0,1}$ with boolean algebra and variable) is given by the following BNF-grammar: $P, Q ::= a \mid c \mid P + Q \mid P.Q \mid P^*Q \mid \lambda x P \mid [P]_e$

Informally, the semantics of $\mathcal{E}BPA^*_{0,1}$ is as follows:

- a is a process that executes the atomic action a.
- c is a boolean process that is in a deadlock state if it is evaluated to 0 and finishes normally if it is evaluated to 1.
- $P + Q$ and $P.Q$ are a choice and a sequential composition of P and Q respectively.
- P^*Q is the process that behaves like $P.(P^*Q) + Q$.
- $\lambda x P$ behaves like P except that we limit the scope of the variable x to P.
- $[P]_e$ defines the process P running in the environment e.

We use the following priorities between operators (from high to low): "$[]$", "λ", "$*$", "$.$", "$+$". Also, the set of processes in $\mathcal{E}BPA^*_{0,1}$ will be denoted by $\mathcal{P}$ in this paper.

2.3 Semantics of $\mathcal{E}BPA^*_{0,1}$

The operational semantics of $\mathcal{E}BPA^*_{0,1}$ is defined by the transition relation $\rightarrow \in \mathcal{P} \times \mathcal{A} \times \mathcal{P}$ given by Table 2, where:

- $[\![-]\!]_\mathcal{B}$ is an evaluation function from $\mathcal{B}$ to $\{0, 1\}$.
- "$\downarrow$" is the unary relation on $\mathcal{P}$ and it allows knowing whether a process P can immediately terminate with success, defined by the inference rules in Table 1.
- $eff : \mathcal{A} \times \mathcal{E} \longrightarrow \mathcal{E}$ updates an environment based on the effect of a given action.

Table 1. Definition of the operator $\downarrow$

$(R^1) \dfrac{\square}{1\downarrow}$	$(R^{[]e}) \dfrac{P\downarrow}{[P]_e\downarrow}$	$(R^*_r) \dfrac{Q\downarrow}{(P^*Q)\downarrow}$	$(R_{\downarrow}) \dfrac{P\downarrow \quad Q\downarrow}{(P.Q)\downarrow}$	
$(R^+_{l\downarrow}) \dfrac{P\downarrow}{(P+Q)\downarrow}$	$(R^+_{r\downarrow}) \dfrac{Q\downarrow}{(P+Q)\downarrow}$	$(R^c) \dfrac{[\![c(v_1...v_n)]\!]_\mathcal{B}=1}{[c(x_1...x_n)]_e\downarrow}$	$(v_1...v_n) \in (s_e(x_1)...s_e(x_n))$	

Table 2. Operational semantics of $\mathcal{EBPA}_{0,1}^*$.

$(R^a) \dfrac{\square}{a \xrightarrow{a} 1}$	$(R^c) \dfrac{\square}{c(x_1,...,x_n) \xrightarrow{c(x_1,...,x_n)} 1}$	$(R_i) \dfrac{P\downarrow \quad Q \xrightarrow{b} Q'}{P.Q \xrightarrow{b} Q'}$	$(R_r) \dfrac{P \xrightarrow{b} P'}{P.Q \xrightarrow{b} P'Q}$
$(R_l^+) \dfrac{P \xrightarrow{b} P'}{P+Q \xrightarrow{b} P'}$	$(R_r^+) \dfrac{Q \xrightarrow{b} Q'}{P+Q \xrightarrow{b} Q'}$	$(R_l^*) \dfrac{P \xrightarrow{b} P'}{P*Q \xrightarrow{b} P'.P*Q}$	$(R_r^*) \dfrac{Q \xrightarrow{b} Q'}{P*Q \xrightarrow{b} Q'}$

$$(R_a^{[]e}) \dfrac{P \xrightarrow{a(x_1...x_n)} P'}{[P]_e \xrightarrow{a(v_1...v_n)} [P']_{eff(a,e)}} \quad (v_1...v_n) \in (s_e(x_1)...s_e(x_n))$$

$$(R_c^{[]e}) \dfrac{P \xrightarrow{c(x_1...x_n)} P',\ [c(x_1...x_n)]_e\downarrow,\ [P']_e \xrightarrow{b} [Q]_{e'}}{[P]_e \xrightarrow{b} [Q]_{e'}} \qquad (R^\lambda) \dfrac{P[x\mapsto y] \xrightarrow{\alpha} P'}{\lambda x P \xrightarrow{\alpha} P'} : y\ is\ a\ fresh\ variable.$$

2.4 Trace Based Equivalence

In this section, we introduce variants of trace-based equivalence that will be used to compare processes. We denote by Σ the closure of $\mathcal{A} \cup \{\epsilon\}$ using the operator ".". such that $(\Sigma, ., \epsilon)$ is a monoid. If τ and τ' are in Σ and they are equivalent with respect to the monoid properties ($x = \epsilon.x$, $x = x.\epsilon$, $(x.y).z = x.(y.z)$), we write $\tau \simeq \tau'$.

Definition 2 (Traces of a process). *Let x, x' and x'' be processes, α be an action or a condition. An element $\tau \in \Sigma$ is a trace for x if there exists a process y such that $x \xrightarrow{\tau} y$, where $\twoheadrightarrow$ is a relation in $\mathcal{P} \times \Sigma \times \mathcal{P}$ defined as following:*

$$\frac{\square}{x \xrightarrow{\epsilon} x} \qquad \frac{x \xrightarrow{\tau} x' \quad x' \xrightarrow{\alpha} x''}{x \xrightarrow{\tau.\alpha} x''}$$

The following ordering relation will be used to compare two traces.

Definition 3 (Trace Ordering ($\preceq$)). *Let τ, τ', τ_1 and τ_2 be traces, a be an action, c be a condition, $x, x_1, ..., x_n$ be variables and β be a variable or a constant. We define $\preceq$ as the smallest ordering relation (transitivity, reflexivity and anti-symmetry) respecting the following properties: 1. If $\tau \simeq \tau'$, then $\tau \preceq \tau'$ 2. $\tau.c.\tau' \preceq \tau.\tau'$.*

3. $\tau.(x == \beta).a(x_1...x...x_n).\tau' \preceq \tau.a(x_1...\beta...x_n).\tau'$.

We are also interested in comparing traces in a specified environment.

Definition 4 (Trace ordering in an environment $e.(\preceq_e)$). *Let τ, τ' be traces and $e \in \mathcal{E}$. We define $\preceq_e$ as the smallest ordering relation (transitivity, reflexivity and anti-symmetry) respecting the following properties:*

1. If $\tau \preceq \tau'$, then $\tau \preceq_e \tau'$;   2. $\tau\sigma \preceq_e \tau$ for any e-free substitution σ.

Now, we extend the definitions of $\preceq$ and $\preceq_e$ to processes as follows.

Definition 5 (Process ordering($\preceq$) and Process ordering in an environment e ($\preceq_e$)). *Let $P, Q \in \mathcal{P}$. We say that $P \preceq Q$ (respectively $P \preceq_e Q$), if $\forall \tau \in \Sigma$, we have:*

1. $P{\downarrow}\tau$ then $\exists\tau' \in \Sigma$, such that $:Q{\downarrow}\tau'$ and $\tau \preceq \tau'$ (respectively $\tau \preceq_e \tau'$) .

2. $P \xrightarrow{\tau} 1$ then $\exists\tau' \in \Sigma$, such that $:Q \xrightarrow{\tau'} 1$ and $\tau \preceq \tau'$ (respectively $\tau \preceq_e \tau'$).

When a process runs in its environment, it produces closed traces. We use the following definition to compare processes running in environments.

Definition 6 (Ordering processes running in environments($\sqsubseteq$)). *Let* $[P]_{ep}$ *and* $[Q]_{eq}$ *be two processes,* $ep, eq \in \mathcal{E}$ *and* $\tau \in \Sigma$. *We say that* $[P]_{ep} \sqsubseteq [Q]_{eq}$, *if:*
  $[P]_{ep}{\downarrow}\tau$ *then* $\exists\tau' \subset \Sigma$ *such that* $[Q]_{eq}{\downarrow}\tau'$ *and* $\tau \simeq \tau'$.

Based on the previous ordering, we define the following equivalence relations:

Definition 7 ($\approx$, $\sim_e$ and $\sim$). *Let* P *and* Q *be two processes. We say that* $P \approx Q$ *(respectively* $P \sim_e Q$ *;* $P \sim Q$ *) , if* $P \preceq Q$ *and* $Q \preceq P$ *(respectively* $P \preceq_e Q$ *and* $Q \preceq_e P$ *;* $P \sqsubseteq Q$ *and* $Q \sqsubseteq P$ *) .*

3   Problem Formalization

Given a program P and a security policy Φ, the goal of this work is to generate another program P' that respects the security policy Φ and preserves the good behaviors of P without introducing new ones. More precisely, the intersection of P and Φ should respect two conditions (Correctness and Completeness) as already formally stated in [12]. To simplify the presentation, we integrate the two conditions in one operator called greatest common factor with respect to an ordering relation $\sqsubseteq$ (denoted $gcf(\sqsubseteq)$) or shortly gcf if $\sqsubseteq$ is clear from the context) defined as follows:

Definition 8 (Greatest Common Factor ($gcf(\sqsubseteq)$)). *Let* P *and* Q *be two processes. The gcf of* P *and* Q *with respect to* $\sqsubseteq$, *denoted by* $P \sqcap Q$, *is a process* R *that respects the following three conditions: 1:* $R \sqsubseteq P$. *2:* $R \sqsubseteq Q$. *3: For all* R' *such that* $R' \sqsubseteq P$ *and* $R' \sqsubseteq Q$, *we have* $R' \sqsubseteq R$.

Now, the problem of enforcing a security property Q on a program P in an environment e turns to a problem of finding $[P]_e \sqcap [Q]_e$. To simplify the resolution of the problem, we extend the definition of a gcf to two ordering relations $\sqsubseteq_1$ and $\sqsubseteq_2$:

Definition 9 ($gcf(\sqsubseteq_1, \sqsubseteq_2)$). *The* $gcf(\sqsubseteq_1, \sqsubseteq_2)$ *of two processes* P *and* Q *is a process* R *respecting the following conditions: 1:* $R \sqsubseteq_1 P$. *2:* $R \sqsubseteq_2 Q$. *3: For all* R' *such that* $R' \sqsubseteq_1 P$ *and* $R' \sqsubseteq_2 Q$, *we have* $R' \sqsubseteq_1 R$.

Definition 10 ($\sqcap_e$). *Let* $e \in \mathcal{E}$. *We introduce* $\sqcap_e$ *as a shortcut for* $gcf(\preceq, \sqsubseteq_e)$.

A gcf is not unique, but they form an equivalence class. The following theorem gives a main result showing the relationship between $([P]_e \sqcap [Q]_e)$ and $[P \sqcap_e Q]_e$.

Theorem 1. *Let P and Q be two processes and $e \in \mathcal{E}$, then we have :*

$$[P]_e \sqcap [Q]_e \sim [P \sqcap_e Q]_e$$

Proof. See Appendix in [15].

This theorem reduce the problem of finding $[P]_e \sqcap [Q]_e$ to computing $P \sqcap_e Q$. In the next section, we propose an algorithm allowing to compute $P \sqcap_e Q$.

4 Problem Solving

In this section, we first give the main proposition on which our algorithm is based. Finally, we give the algorithm that implement the operator $\sqcap_e$.

4.1 Main Theorem

Hereafter, we give the main theorem for our algorithm. First, we give some useful definitions and intermediary results. The following definition separates a substitution.

Definition 11 ($\sigma_{\prec}$ and $\sigma_{\approx}$). *Let σ be a substitution, e be an environment. We divide σ into two parts $\sigma_{\prec}^e$ and $\sigma_{\approx}^e$ (or shortly $\sigma_{\prec}$ and $\sigma_{\approx}$, when e is clear for environment):*

Here, we define a function that transforms a substitution to a condition.

Definition 12 ($\ulcorner - \urcorner$). *Let $\sigma \in \Gamma$, we define $\ulcorner \quad \urcorner : \Gamma \rightarrow \mathcal{B}$ as following:*
$\ulcorner \emptyset \urcorner = 1$ and $\ulcorner \{x \mapsto t\} \cup \sigma \urcorner = (x == t).\ulcorner \sigma \urcorner$

The following operator is used to compute the intersection of two actions.

Definition 13 (∇_e). *Let $a_1, a_2 \in \mathcal{A}, e \in \mathcal{E}$. We define $\nabla_e : \mathcal{A} \times \mathcal{A} \rightarrow \Sigma \times \Gamma$ as following:*

$$a_1 \nabla_e a_2 = \begin{cases} \{(\ulcorner \sigma_{\prec} \urcorner .a_1 \sigma_{\approx}, \sigma_{\approx})\}, & \text{if } \sigma = mgu(a_1, a_2) \text{ exists} \\ \{(0, \emptyset)\}, & \text{else} \end{cases}$$

Before computing the intersection between two processes, we need to transform them to their guarded form. The notion of guarded process is defined as following.

Definition 14 (Guarded Process and Guarded Intersection). *Let α be an action or a condition, and $P, Q \in \mathcal{P}$ and R and S be processes or intersections. We define a guarded process and a guarded intersection as following:*

- α and $\alpha.P$ are guarded.
- $P \sqcap_e Q$ is guarded if P is guarded and Q is guarded
- $R + S$ is guarded if R is guarded and S is guarded

Here, we give rules that transform any intersection to an equivalent guarded one.

Definition 15 (Normalization Rules). *We denote by* $\mathcal{NR}$, *following rewriting system.*

- $0.P \to 0, 1.P \to P \ \ P + 0 \to P, 0 + P \to P$
- $P \sqcap_e 0 \to 0, 0 \sqcap_e P \to 0 \ \ P \sqcap_e 1 \to 1, 1 \sqcap_e P \to 1$
- $R \sqcap_e P + Q \to R \sqcap_e P + R \sqcap_e Q$; $\quad P + Q \sqcap_e R \to P \sqcap_e R + Q \sqcap_e R$
- $R \sqcap_e (P + Q).T \to R \sqcap_e P.T + R \sqcap_e Q.T$
- $(P + Q).T \sqcap_e R \to P.T \sqcap_e R + Q.T \sqcap_e R$
- $R \sqcap_e P^*Q \to R \sqcap_e P.(P^*Q) + R \sqcap_e Q$
- $P^*Q \sqcap_e R \to P.(P^*Q) \sqcap_e R + Q \sqcap_e R$
- $R \sqcap_e P^*Q.T \to R \sqcap_e P.(P^*Q).T + R \sqcap_e Q.T$
- $P^*Q.T \sqcap_e R \to P.(P^*Q).T \sqcap_e R + Q.T \sqcap_e R$
- If R is guarded, then $R \sqcap_e (\lambda x P) \to R \sqcap_e P[x \mapsto y]$, y is a fresh variable.
- If R is guarded, then $(\lambda x P) \sqcap_e R \to P[x \mapsto y] \sqcap_e R$, y is a fresh variable.
- If R is guarded, then $R \sqcap_e (\lambda x P).Q \to R \sqcap_e P[x \mapsto y].Q$, y is a fresh variable.
- If R is guarded, then $(\lambda x P).Q \sqcap_e R \to P[x \mapsto y].Q \sqcap_e R$, y is a fresh variable.

If R is a process or an intersection, we denote by $R{\Downarrow}$ its normal form using the rewriting system $\mathcal{NR}$. Once, we transform a process to its guarded form, we need to know how to compute $\alpha.P \sqcap_e \beta.Q$, to generate intersection. To that end, we need first to compute the intersection between α and β and then compute the intersection between P and Q. However, we need to carefully take care of the following fact: the intersection between α and β can succeed only under a substitution that needs to be propagated forward to the intersection of P and Q, and, on the other side, the intersection of P and Q can succeed only under a substitution that needs to be propagated backward to the intersection of α and β. Hereafter, we give some definitions that help us to better formalize the issue of forward and backward propagation of substitutions.

Definition 16. – *Suppose that* Γ_1 *and* Γ_2 *are sets of substitutions, we define their composition* $(\circ)$ *as following:* $\Gamma_1 \circ \Gamma_2 = \bigcup_{\sigma \in \Gamma_1} \bigcup_{\sigma' \in \Gamma_2} \{\sigma \circ \sigma'\}$

– *Let* Υ *be the set of substitutions form* $\mathcal{X} \to \mathcal{A}$. *We extend the definition of* Υ *to* $\Upsilon(X)$ *to include also unknown or partially known substitutions. More precisely,* $\Upsilon(X)$ *is the smallest set respecting the following conditions: 1:* $\Upsilon \subset \Upsilon(X)$. *2:* $z \in \Upsilon(X)$ *for any variable* z *that range over substitutions. 3: if* σ_x *and* σ_y *are in* $\Upsilon(X)$ *then* $\sigma_x \circ \sigma_y$ *is in* $\Upsilon(X)$.

Definition 17 (T). *Let* $e \in \mathcal{E}$, $a_1, a_2 \in \mathcal{A}$, $c \in \mathcal{B}$, $P, Q \in \mathcal{P}$ *and* R *and* S *be processes or intersections. We inductively define the function* $T : \mathcal{P} \longrightarrow 2^{\Upsilon(X)}$ *as follows:*

$$T(0) = \emptyset \quad T(1) = \emptyset \quad T(R + S) = T(R) \cup T(S)$$
$$T(a_1.P \sqcap_e a_2.Q) = \{\sigma\} \circ \Gamma_{P \sqcap_e Q} \quad if \ a_1 \nabla_e a_2 = \{(a, \sigma)\}$$
$$T(c.P \sqcap_e Q) = \Gamma_{P \sqcap_e Q} \quad T(P \sqcap_e c.Q) = \Gamma_{P \sqcap_e Q}$$

To simplify the presentation of the algorithm, we introduce following definitions.

Definition 18 (First Order Intersection). *Let* $P, Q \in \mathcal{P}$, $a_1, a_2 \in \mathcal{A}, c_1, c_2 \in \mathcal{B}$ *and* $e \in \mathcal{E}$, *we define function* $\mathcal{I} : \mathcal{P} \to \mathcal{P}$ *as following:*

$$\mathcal{I}(P + Q) = \mathcal{I}(P) + \mathcal{I}(Q) \qquad \mathcal{I}(c_1.P \sqcap_e c_2.Q) = \sum_{\sigma_\partial \in \Gamma_{(P \sqcap_e Q)}} (c_1.c_2)\sigma_\partial.\left(P\sigma_\partial \sqcap_e Q\sigma_\partial\right)$$

$$\mathcal{I}(a_1.P \sqcap_e a_2.Q) = \sum_{\sigma_\partial \in \Gamma_{(P\sigma_\delta \sqcap_e Q\sigma_\delta)}} a\sigma_\partial.\left(P\sigma_\partial\sigma_\delta \sqcap_e Q\sigma_\partial\sigma_\delta\right) \text{ where } (a, \sigma_\delta) \in a_1 \nabla_e a_2$$

$$\mathcal{I}(c_1.P \sqcap_e a_2.Q) = \sum_{\sigma_\partial \in \Gamma_{(P \sqcap_e a_2.Q)}} c_1\sigma_\partial.\left(P\sigma_\partial \sqcap_e (a_2.Q)\sigma_\partial\right)$$

$$\mathcal{I}(a_1.P \sqcap_e c_2.Q) = \sum_{\sigma_\partial \in \Gamma_{(a_1.P \sqcap_e Q)}} c_2\sigma_\partial.\left((a_1.P)\sigma_\partial \sqcap_e Q\sigma_\partial\right)$$

Definition 19 $((P \sqcap_e Q)\downharpoonleft)$. *We denote by* $(P \sqcap_e Q)\downharpoonleft$ *the normal form of* $P \sqcap_e Q$ *and define it as follows:* $(P \sqcap_e Q)\downharpoonleft = \mathcal{I}((P \sqcap_e Q) \Downarrow)$

Now we introduce our main theorem for generating the set of equations as follows:

Theorem 2. *Let* P *and* Q *be two processes and* $e \in \mathcal{E}$, *if* $\mathcal{V}(P) \subseteq N_v(e)$, *then we have:*

$$1. \ P \sqcap_e Q \approx (P \sqcap_e Q)\downharpoonleft \qquad 2. \ \Gamma_{P \sqcap_e Q} = T((P \sqcap_e Q)\Downarrow)$$

Proof. Due to the lack of space, the proof is in [15].

4.2 Algorithm

Based on Theorem 2, we write an algorithm allowing generating a linear system where $P \sqcap_e Q$ could be extracted from its solutions. This algorithm is as follows:

Algorithm 1. Calculate $X \sqcap Y$ in $\mathcal{E}BPA^*_{0,1}$, where $e \in \mathcal{E}$, $\mathcal{V}(X) \subseteq N_v(e)$, $G = \phi$, $E = \phi$, $S = \{(X, Y)\}$

1:**DO**   Get one element $s = (P, Q)$ from S and remove s from S.
    $E \longleftarrow E \cup \{e \longleftarrow \left(P \sqcap_e Q \approx (P \sqcap_e Q)\downharpoonleft\right)\}$
    $G \longleftarrow G \cup \{g \longleftarrow \left(\Gamma_{P \sqcap_e Q} = T((P \sqcap_e Q)\Downarrow)\right)\}$
    For each $P_i \sqcap_e Q_i\sigma_\partial$ in the right side of e,
    If $P_i \sqcap_e Q_i$ does not appear (modulo commutativity of $\sqcap_e$
        and ACIT properties of $+$ in [11]) in the left side of any equation in E
    Do $S = S \cup (P_i, Q_i)$;   **End If**   **End For each**
    WHILE $(S \neq \phi)$
2: Solve equations in G to get all the value of Γ.   3: Substitute all Γ in E.
4: **While** there exists $P_i \sqcap_e Q_i$ in the right side of any equation in E' that does not appear (modulo commutativity of $\sqcap_e$) in the left side on any equation **do**
    $E \longleftarrow E \cup \{e \longleftarrow P_i \sqcap Q_i \approx (P_i \sqcap_e Q_i)\downharpoonleft\}$ **End While**
5: Return the solution of the linear system E.

- The complexity and the termination of the algorithm is discussed in [15].
- The system E and G generated by the algorithm are linear systems. They can be solved by using the method we discussed in [15].

The examples that show how our approach works is available in [15].

5   Prototype

We developed, using JAVA and JSP, a prototype that implement our approach. It is a web application and available online at [16]. It allows end users to input their process either in $BPA_{0,1}^*$, $\mathcal{E}BPA_{0,1}^*$ or C-Like language, their security policies in either $BPA_{0,1}^*$, $\mathcal{E}BPA_{0,1}^*$ or the LTL logic and shows the results together with the details of the intermediary steps in a text format or in a latex format.

6   Conclusion

This paper presents a formal and automatic approach to enforce security policies on untrusted programs. To specify both policies and programs, this paper firstly introduces $\mathcal{E}BPA_{0,1}^*$, a process algebra with variables. Then, we explain why our main problem is equivalent to computing the intersection of two algebra processes. Therefore, based on the notion of derivatives, we give an algorithm to compute this intersection. Since we increased the expressiveness by including variables into process algebra $CBPA_{0,1}^*$, the main propositions and the algorithm have bean upgraded to take into consideration these enhancements. As future works, we are interested about applying the approach to web application security problems, such as access control problem, sql injection, etc.

References

1. Pnueli, A.: The temporal logic of programs. In: Proceedings of the 18th IEEE Symposium on FOCS, pp. 46–57 (1977)
2. Schneider, F.B.: Enforceable security policies. ACM Trans. Inf. Syst. Secur. **3**(1), 30–50 (2000)
3. Alpern, B., Schneider, F.: Recognizing saftey, and liveness. Distrib. Comput. **2**(3), 117–126 (1987)
4. Clarkson, M.R., Schneider, F.: Hyperproperties. In: J. Comput. Secur. 7thInternational Workshop on Issues in the Theory of Security (WITS 2007) **18**(6). IOS Press, Amsterdam (2010)
5. Walker, D.: A type system for expressive security policies. In: POPL 2000: Proceedings of the 27th ACM SIGPLAN-SIGACT Symposium on Principles of Programming Languages, pp. 254–267. ACM (2000)
6. Khoury, R., Tawbi, N.: Corrective enforcement of security policies. In: Degano, P., Etalle, S., Guttman, J. (eds.) Formal Aspects in Security and Trust. LNCS, vol. 6561, pp. 176–190. Springer, Heidelberg (2010)
7. Clarke, E.M., Schlingloff, B.H.: Model checking. In: Handbook of Automated Reasoning, pp. 1635–1790 (2001)

8. Necula, G.: Proof-carring code. In: Proceedings of the POPL 1997, pp. 106–119. ACM Press (1997)
9. Deutsch, P., Grant, C.: A flexible measurement tool for software systems. In: 71 Proceedings of the IFIP Congress Information Processing, pp. 320–326. Yugoslavia (1971)
10. Langar, M., Mejri, M., Adi, K.: Formal enforcement of security policies on concurrent systems. J. Symb. Comput. **46**(9), 997–1016 (2011)
11. Sui, G., Mejri, M., Ben Sta, H.: FASER (formal, automatic security enforcement by rewriting): an algebraic approach. In: Computational Intelligence for Security and Defence Applications (CISDA) (2012)
12. Mejri, M., Fujita, H.: Enforcing security policies using algebraic approach. SoMeT **182**, 84–98 (2008)
13. Pardo, A.: Many-sorted algebras. grupo de métodos formales instituto de computación facultad de ingenierá
14. Bergstra, J.A., Klop, J.W.: The algebra of recursively defined processes and the algebra of regular processes. In: Paredaens, J. (ed.) Automata, Languages and Programming. LNCS, vol. 172, pp. 82–94. Springer, Heidelberg (1984)
15. https://drive.google.com/file/d/0B8V7WaS6PT37U29XLThkLXhVWlk/view?usp=sharing
16. FASER   website.   http://web_security.fsg.ulaval.ca:8080/enf/enforce-cbpa-program.jsp

Author Index

Printed in the United States
By Bookmasters